THE
ENCYCLOPEDIA
OF HANDHELD
WEAPONS

First published in 2002 by Brassey's

An imprint of **Chrysalis** Books Group

www.chrysalisbooks.co.uk

This edition published in North America in 2004 for Borders Press
100 Phoenix Drive
Ann Arbor, MI 48108
USA

ISBN 1 85753 388 7

Printed and bound in Thailand

THE
ENCYCLOPEDIA
OF HANDHELD
WEAPONS

EDITED BY JAMES MARCHINGTON

**CHRYSALIS
BOOKS**

CONTENTS

CONTENTS

CONTENTS

'The supreme act of war is to subdue the enemy without fighting.'

Sun Tzu, The Art of War (approx 490BC).

The Changing Face of War

Warfare has changed beyond all recognition since the early twentieth century. And yet the changes we have seen in the last 50-100 years are just the beginning. Over the next few decades warfare will continue to change and develop at a phenomenal pace.

At the end of the twentieth century, the world caught a glimpse of future warfare. In conflicts such as the Gulf War and Kosovo, Western powers, led by the United States, conducted a distant, push-button campaign in which few soldiers even got mud on their boots, still less saw the enemy or came close enough to engage the enemy with small arms.

Modern warfare is a high-tech affair more like a video game than the old, crude business of mud, blood, bullets and cold steel. Perhaps – hopefully – we will never again see trench warfare conducted in the manner of the First World War, a bloody stalemate fought in atrocious conditions by a generation for whom living and dying, even during peacetime, was a harsher affair than the public of today care to contemplate.

Today's wars are about media soundbites, air supremacy, the 'surgical strike', minimising 'collateral damage', and avoiding at almost any cost the politically unacceptable sight of body bags returning from some foreign land. In our society, the public simply will not tolerate the idea of their sons (and daughters) dying to uphold freedom and democracy in some former colony, or to protect supplies of cheap oil to keep the nation's trucks and cars on the move.

If the United States had begun to forget the lesson of Vietnam, it was brought firmly home in Mogadishu, where the sight of American dead being dragged through the streets by a screaming mob became a political disaster for the government of the day.

Billions of dollars have gone into producing 'stand off' weapons launched, unmanned, from deep within safe territory. Once, life was cheap – so cheap that a commander would weigh up his men's lives in their hundreds as if they were so many bullets or shells. Today a single life is too high a price to pay if a billion-dollar missile could do the same job.

Seeing 'The Other Side of the Hill'

Since the dawn of civilisation, commanders have struggled to know about the disposition of their own and the enemy's troops, in order to make sound decisions. In the past, the generals would occupy a piece of high ground – a hilltop or ridge that gave a panoramic view of the battlefield. But even the highest vantage point could not show whether reinforcements were coming up from behind, just out of view. As the battle raged, smoke would linger and begin to obscure the view, adding to the confusion that became known as 'the fog of war'.

The first Duke of Wellington summed it up well when, towards the end of his life, he said: 'All the business of war, and indeed all the business of life, is to endeavour to find out what you don't know from what you do; that's what I called "guessing what was at the other side of the hill".'

With today's hi-tech spy satellites, reconnaissance UAVs (Unmanned Aerial Vehicles), thermal imaging and image intensifiers, there is no longer any need to guess what is over the hill. When everything is working as it should, one need only glance at the computer screen to see not only who is the other side of the hill, but also how many tanks they have, how fast they are moving, and which one fired the last round.

Today the 'high ground' is tens of thousands of metres above the battlefield, and is occupied by the side with the biggest budget for satellites and spy planes – invariably the United States. The same technology provides a powerful means of command and control, with communications systems that enable a general in his Pentagon office to talk to individual commanders on the ground, or a field commander to call up air support just as easily as if he was ordering a pizza.

Thermal imaging, satellite imaging, GPS (Global Positioning System), and IFF (Identification Friend or Foe) all contribute to lift the veil of uncertainty and confusion that was once the commander's greatest problem. UAVs flit about over the battlefield, locating enemy positions and relaying pictures back to the 'pilot' safely ensconced in his bunker. Out in space, way beyond the range of vision, satellites watch every movement, while AWACS aircraft monitor, or jam, enemy communications.

If an enemy position needs to be taken out, there is no need to send in troops to risk their lives. It becomes a simple matter to program the target's longitude, latitude and altitude into the GPS guidance system of a missile, and send 1000lb or 2000lb of high explosive unerringly on its way.

If it does become necessary to put troops on the ground, modern communications make it possible to issue orders instantly and unambiguously to gun and tank crews, aircraft and field commanders – a major leap from the not-so-distant days of semaphore, flags and field telephones. For those nations that can afford the technology, the 'fog of war' that plagued commanders since thousands of years BC has finally been lifted.

Whatever would Wellington and Napoleon have made of it?

There is greater sophistication to come. Technology moves on apace, and the capabilities of satellites and unmanned vehicles leap ahead with every passing year. Already CCTV, sensors and UAVs are replacing humans in areas such as sentry duty and patrolling. Why risk highly-trained troops when a clever piece of hardware is more alert, more observant, and politically more expendable.

Modern Hand-held Weapons

With this dramatic change in warfare, you would expect to see a corresponding leap in the personal weapons carried by the soldier. And yet, at the dawn of the twenty-first century there is little sign of such change. The hand-held weapons of today rely on the same basic technology that they did at the beginning of the twentieth century.

Suppose you could, by some trick of magic or technology, take yourself back to a trench in the First World War, and show the soldiers there the modern squaddie's kit. They would marvel at his boots and clothing, gasp in awe at his CD Walkman, his radio, and even his rations. But his weapon? Ah yes, here are the bullets in the magazine, here's the bolt, the trigger, the muzzle. The sight looks good – our snipers have something like that. But the bullets seem a bit small. Do they really kill an enemy if you hit him? Not that often? No, I thought not.

True, in the days of the First World War the infantryman's rifle was a single-shot, bolt-action weapon. But semi- and fully-automatic weapons were not far off, and by the Second World War there were a good many hand-held autos in use, the US Garand, German MP38 and MP40 and British Bren and Sten being just a few of the more obvious examples.

Pistols, too, have changed little since John Moses Browning developed his recoil-operated semi-automatic in the early years of the twentieth century. Indeed, his Colt 1911 and Browning Hi-Power are still in widespread use today. Even the modern-looking, hi-tech designs like the SIG and Glock draw heavily on Browning's original ideas, despite the use of modern materials and computer-controlled machinery in their manufacture.

Back in the 1950s and 60s, it would have seemed unthinkable that these relatively crude designs would linger on. Surely by the twenty-first century we would all be flying around in anti-gravity suits, and shooting up our enemies with hand-held laser blasters? It hasn't happened yet, although this vision of the future may yet prove accurate.

Knives have changed even less. Again we see the conservative introduction of modern materials and manufacturing methods. A modern combat knife may have a blade of specially produced stainless steel, hardened by electrical induction rather than heating in a furnace. Its handle may be moulded into a futuristic-looking, ergonomic piece of rubbery Kraton, rather than formed from a stack of leather washers. But take two paces back and it would be hard to tell it from its predecessors.

The designers of today's wide range of blade

shapes have drawn from various cultures around the world, so perhaps we have more variety available to us today from the commercial Western makers, but essentially the modern combat knife is the same tool it was 100 years or even 200 years ago.

Reasons for Inertia

Perhaps this apparent inertia should not surprise us, at least in the area of knives. A knife is a basic tool used for a thousand and one different tasks; specialisation would only make it less versatile – and therefore less useful. There is little scope for improvement in the design of a spoon, a hammer or a spade. These are simple tools developed over thousands of years by those who use them daily. Tested and developed by generations of users, they are as nearly perfect as it is possible to make them. Better materials may come along, but no amount of clever design can improve on their simple elegance of form and function. So it is with knives.

How many times has a man sat by a campfire and contemplated his knife, turning it over in his hand, feeling its weight and balance, wondering if it could do with a little bit extra here or less there? If there is an improvement to be made to the basic design of a knife, someone, somewhere, has already tried it.

Rifles and pistols are much newer technology than the knife, but they too have been developed and improved over many years. From the days of the first muzzle-loading arquebus, countless highly intelligent, practical minds have applied themselves to the challenge of making a firearm that is easier to carry and use, is faster to shoot, and delivers a more lethal projectile more accurately at a greater range.

As in so many areas, there is no such thing as the perfect rifle or pistol. Any design is a compromise, in which the design team have made a number of decisions about the best trade-off between mutually exclusive but desirable characteristics: more firepower versus lighter weight, greater range versus less recoil, greater efficiency versus a less complicated (and hence both cheaper and more reliable) mechanism, and so on.

Throughout the history of firearms, great kudos and riches awaited the man who could deliver significant improvements – Colt, Browning and Kalashnikov, for example, became wealthy men and household names thanks to their particular contributions to the development of the firearm.

It would be rash to suggest that there is no further scope for improvement in the design and function of the firearm, but it is difficult to see how one could produce any great leap forward in rifle and pistol performance with the range of technologies known to us today.

The weapons that currently command the most widespread admiration and respect from soldiers are by no means the most modern or sophisticated. Assault rifles such as the M16 and the AK47/74, and the HK MP5 series of sub-machine guns, are still prized more highly than their more modern, hi-tech alternatives.

This is not through any Luddite tendency on the soldiers' part. Soldiers, especially special forces such as the British Special Air Service (SAS) and Special Boat Service (SBS), are always quick to adopt new technology when it brings them significant benefits – less weight to carry, improved communications, or greater destructive power that can be brought to bear more quickly on the enemy. For example, before GPS units were regularly issued, special forces troopers were buying their own hand-held civilian units because they recognised the enormous benefits that the new technology could bring to their work.

Yet the same soldiers stubbornly refuse to adopt more 'modern' assault rifles and insist on carrying the Vietnam-era M16 rifle which, for all its faults, is light to carry, reliable if correctly maintained, fast and accurate. Many of them would cheerfully use the even older technology of the Soviet AK or Kalashnikov – a weapon that has proved its ability to be used, misused, dunked in water and even buried in sand, and still come out shooting.

In close quarter battle this is the kind of weapon a soldier wants in his hands – one that he can rely on to be working at the vital moment when, in a kill-or-be-killed confrontation, the latest bit of clever technology becomes a complete irrelevance, and what really matters is total 100 per cent reliability, together with that combination of weight, shape and balance which goes to provide intuitive handling.

There is a parallel here in sport shooting with shotguns. A fine English shotgun is light and responsive, and 'fits' the user so that he can raise it and shoot at a rocketing partridge in the blink of an eye, This is true snap shooting with a weapon that, through a combination of good design and familiarity, becomes an extension of the body, so that pointing it is like pointing your finger. Military weapons tend to be clunky and agricultural and, despite the lip service paid to 'ergonomics', few come anywhere near achieving this. Anyone used to shooting with a good quality shotgun would find even the best military weapon handles like a plank of wood in comparison. This can be overcome to a large extent by training and plenty of practice, but the same amount of practice with a truly responsive weapon would yield still better results.

Those who design military small-arms might learn some home truths if they spent a few hundred hours walking-up grouse in the Highlands of Scotland. Nothing could be better for teaching the value of ergonomics in producing a weapon that can be carried ready for instant use for hours on end without fatigue, and that, when the action explodes around you without warning, comes instinctively to the shoulder and swings on to the target without conscious effort. The traditional English side-by-side shotgun passes this test with flying colours; few other weapons even come close.

So rifles, pistols and knives have changed little in recent years. The great steps forward have been at the opposite end of the scale – the hi-tech weapons such as cruise missiles, 'smart' bombs, directed energy weapons, and the ships and aircraft used to deliver them.

It is worth noting that, if hand-held weapons have not changed greatly since the mid-twentieth century, the same cannot be said of the rest of the soldier's personal kit. From his Kevlar helmet to his Gore-Tex boots, the modern soldier is equipped far better than his counterpart a generation or two ago could ever have dreamed. This trend will certainly continue, with modern materials and technology providing ever lighter and more effective clothing, rations, communications and so on. We will also see the individual soldier becoming increasingly integrated into the battlefield electronics system.

Changes on the Horizon

We have seen that one reason why hand-held weapons have changed so little in recent years is that they are relatively simple items that, unlike hi-tech battlefield electronics, have already been subject to several generations of development. The law of diminishing returns applies here: as hand-held weapons become better, it requires proportionally more time and effort to improve them further.

Another reason for the slow-down in progress with hand-held weapons is that there is not the same pressure of necessity driving them forward. Centuries ago a nation could gain a massive advantage in battle if they developed a bigger, stronger longbow with a range 50yd greater than the enemy's.

Today, when the battlefield is dominated by high-tech aircraft, armoured vehicles and missiles, there is no great advantage in having a slightly better pistol or rifle – and so no great pressure to devote money and technical resources to achieve relatively minor improvements in firearms technology. Such efforts will be more productive if devoted to stealth technology, smart bombs and UAVs.

And yet change is coming in hand-held weapons too.

The US Army's Land Warrior programme provides a vision of tomorrow's soldier and his equipment. This programme is based on the principle that the battlefield of the future will belong to the side that not only has the most lethal firepower, but can bring it to bear precisely when and where it will have the greatest effect.

To quote from a Land Warrior contractor's brochure: 'Tomorrow's soldier must no longer be an isolated fighting man operating with limited support in a remote location. His life, and the course of the battle, will rely on fast decisions and informed actions. The dismounted soldier needs increased lethality, extended command and control, greater mobility, and enhanced sustainment. Improve these capabilities and you improve the most important requirement – his survivability. This program is developing the Integrated Soldier-System, making him an integral part of the Digitized Battlefield – the Land Warrior!'

The integrated parts, or 'components', of this system will include special lightweight protective clothing and body armour; modular load-carrying equipment; a helmet with sophisticated electronic aids such as video cameras, night vision and laser sensors; and a computer/radio system providing data and voice communication with other members of the squad. Advanced software will provide the soldier with a map of the battlefield, visible through a flip-down eyepiece, which is updated in real-time to show not only his own location and that of his comrades, but also identify and prioritise enemy targets.

A cynic would find it amusing that this same brochure shows the digitized 'warrior of the future' posing Action Man style with a Vietnam-era M16A2 assault rifle — hardly the cutting edge of weapons technology! However plans are well advanced for an updated weapon to be put in the hands of tomorrow's US infantryman. The weapon is called the OICW, or Objective Individual Combat Weapon (no doubt it will have gained a more catchy title by the time it reaches general issue).

This weapon is discussed in more detail within the body of this book, but essentially it consists of two weapons in one: a 5.56mm 'Kinetic Energy' weapon (a rather grand-sounding term meaning it fires bullets – the same bullets as the M16); and a 20mm HE (High Explosive) weapon, firing a bursting grenade-type shell. The clever part is the fire control system, which consists of a day/night sight and laser range-finding device. This not only tells the soldier where to aim in order to hit the target, it also sets the fuse on the 20mm shell so that it bursts directly over the heads of the enemy, with devastating results.

The net result will be greatly increased effective range – up to 1000 metres – and a much greater probability of killing or incapacitating the enemy. If the United States could only bring itself to reconsider the use of the outdated 5.56mm round – perhaps replacing it with the 5.7 ¥ 28mm round used in FN's P90 – the weapon could be better still. But regardless of this the OICW, when it finally comes into service towards the end of the first decade of this century, will represent a true leap forward in hand-held military weaponry. Some might say it is long overdue.

A Word of Warning

So the next few decades will see some dramatic developments in hand-held weapons, particularly in the infantryman's standard weapon, his assault rifle. Yet it is wise to remember that all this technology is fallible. History has shown us time and time again that relying too heavily on sophisticated equipment can prove fatal.

There are places in the world where, due to adverse climate and terrain, technology fails to provide the promised advantages. The Gulf War was fought in ideal conditions for hi-tech warfare: great expanses of open desert, with little or no cover where the enemy could hide from spy satellites and aircraft, and few 'dead spots' for radio communications. By contrast, the conflict in Kosovo showed all too clearly how an unsophisticated but cunning enemy can use climate, terrain and political shenanigans to his advantage. Time after time the United State's theoretical technical advantage, and vastly superior air power, was negated by the Serbs' clever use of age-old tricks such as decoys, troops masquerading as civilians, civilian convoys made to look like troop movements, or simply hiding in caves.

Manufacturers of hi-tech surveillance equipment are fond of using phrases like 'No place to hide' in their marketing. We should be wary of taking this too literally. A wily and dedicated enemy can still hide very effectively in dense jungle, rugged mountains and even in the midst of a civilian population – especially if they have the sympathy of the local population. Che Guevara's 'war of the flea' has a good few centuries left in it yet – and a First World War revolver is just as capable of killing as it ever was.

Special forces soldiers are fond of quoting 'Murphy's Laws of Combat', a collection of humorous 'laws' which contain more than a grain of truth. These include such gems as: 'The only thing more accurate than incoming enemy fire is incoming friendly fire'; 'Remember your weapon was made by the lowest bidder'; and 'If your attack is going really well, it's an ambush.' Experience with high-tech kit at the sharp end has led to various additions to Murphy's Laws, such as: 'Fail-safe devices never fail until you need them'; 'Radios will fail as soon as you need fire support'; and 'If it's stupid and it works, it ain't stupid.'

The important point to remember here is that the combat zone is another world – a world where people and objects do not behave as they do on paper or even on exercises. This is recognised in the British Army's *Design for Military Operations – The British Military Doctrine*, which is worth quoting at length:

'The tempo and extent of operations will be exhausting to those engaged in the battle and in sustaining it. Battle stress will be compounded by surprise and its consequent shock effect, by unfamiliar threats and weapons, by setbacks and the intensity of the conflict. Fatigue and stress will tend to deaden the reactions of commanders and soldiers operating even relatively simple weapons systems: the more complex the system the more errors may be compounded. Moral support, rest and the rapid treatment of psychological casualties will assume great significance. The opportunities for the "friction" of war. . . will be far greater on the modern battlefield: as STA [Surveillance and Target Acquisition], CIS [Command Information Systems] and communication systems are degraded "friction" will become progressively worse.'

This is why soldiers with combat experience tend to prefer the simpler, less technically advanced types of weapons. Most people struggle to programme a video recorder in the comfort of their own living room. When bullets are flying around your head, you are scared, exhausted and slipping about in the mud, you do not want to be remembering complicated formulae or programming instructions. You want a weapon that you

simply point at the enemy and pull the trigger – and the more noise, flame and lead that it throws in the enemy's general direction, the more comfortable you feel. Weapons like the Kalashnikov fulfil this requirement perfectly, which partly explains their enduring popularity among terrorists, insurgents and conventional armed forces alike.

The other reason for this popularity is their availability – the result of decades of Cold War, when the major powers sponsored uprisings and conflicts around the world, supplying countless thousands of rifles, mines, grenades and other military hardware to their chosen groups to fight their proxy wars in places such as Angola, Afghanistan and Somalia. When the Cold War ended, all this weaponry was not simply thrown away. It was kept – and prized – by people whose only alternative form of defence (or attack) against a dictator or invader may be agricultural hoes and machetes. Whether you think this is a good thing or a bad thing depends on which side you are most likely to be fighting. In any case, it is a fact, and anyone living, working or fighting in such areas needs to take account of the widespread availability of such weapons.

This is the main reason why many of the weapons described and illustrated in this book seem outmoded, or even obsolete. Weapons have a knack of staying around for a very long time, and reappearing when the need arises. No-one knows how many 'souvenirs' were brought back by soldiers returning from the two World Wars of last century, or how many of these remain hidden in attics. What is certain is that such weapons have an uncomfortable habit of reappearing in the hands of criminals and terrorists. Likewise, antiquated weapons, perhaps provided by one of the superpowers during the Cold War, may be pressed into service by insurgents with no access to the latest military technology. The modern soldier with his modern assault rifle cannot afford to ignore even the humblest old bolt-action hunting rifle.

Fighting for Peace

'Fighting for peace is like screwing for virginity.'
Anon.

13

We have seen how the nature of warfare has changed in recent years. Let us not forget that the need and justification for waging war have changed too. The major Western nations no longer seek to conquer and occupy large sections of the world beyond their borders. Some might say they can, in any case, dominate other nations more effectively with the pervasive influence of their global brands and television culture. Today, US or British troops, for examole, are more likely to find themselves playing the role of the world policeman, 'peace keeping' in a troubled Balkan state or African dictatorship.

This too has important implications for the soldier's personal weapons. Nowadays, perhaps, more than ever before, soliers are likely to find themselves facing a mob of angry civilians, whether at home or abroad. Such a group can be as threatening and as deadly as a trained enemy force. But as the British found in Northern Ireland on what has come to be dubbed 'Bloody Sunday', shooting civilians is politically unacceptable, no matter what mood they are in at the time. You may feel perfectly justified in using live rounds to repel overwhelming numbers of attackers bent on smashing your head in with bricks and bottles. But when the dust settles, and the world's media count up the dead and wounded, there is only one conclusion: soldiers shot and killed 'unarmed' civilians.

This explains the thinking behind the many 'sub-lethal' weapons and munitions available and in development. Bird-shot, water-cannon, CS gas and rubber bullets have for many years been used to disperse rioters, but they are far from perfect. In recent years we have seen many new ideas, including guns that shoot nets or disperse sticky foam, electric shock batons (widely criticised as they are all too easily used for torture), and numerous ways of delivering a variety of irritant and incapacitating gases.

Most recently (at the time of writing) the United States has demonstrated a type of directed energy weapon using electromagnetic radiation in the 'microwave' sector of the spectrum. Directed at a rioter or other undesirable from a range of 100 metres or so, it produces an 'uncomfortable sensation similar to burning' (translation: it hurts like hell). The theory goes that, when you find yourself facing a group of stone-lobbing rioters who refuse to disperse, you whip out the 'scorcher', give 'em a quick toasting and they run off home.

Personally I find this hard to believe. For one thing, it suggests a complete lack of understanding of crowd dynamics. Successfully striking back at an angry mob does not make them break off and return home quietly. It makes them more angry. It escalates the situation. If you can hurt them at a distance, they try wrapping themselves in wet rags or Bacofoil, and look round for more effective weapons to hurt you at the same distance.

Plus a weapon of this type offers enormous scope for misuse. Put the average squaddie in an internal security environment and within a few weeks he has developed an intense hatred for his adversaries. This was all too apparent in Northern Ireland, where sub-lethal munitions like the infamous 'rubber bullets' were misused and even 'adapted' with coins and the like to make them more damaging.

It is all too easy to picture a scenario in which a group of squaddies, enraged by the recent death of one of their comrades, make a game of 'toasting' a troublemaker caught at the end of a blind alleyway. The political fall-out would be embarrassing, to say the least, and it would not be long before such weapons were banned.

The whole concept of 'sub-lethal' weaponry is fraught with such problems. Any weapon capable of causing sufficient discomfort or incapacitation to turn back an angry rioter without causing permanent damage or death must inevitably be wide open to misuse by soldiers who generally have little love or respect for their adversaries.

Nevertheless, the political imperative for crowd control without killing means that such weapons will continue to be developed and deployed, with varying degrees of success, in the future. Unfortunately for the soldier, it is he who will suffer when such weapons fail, and be berated for his 'over-reaction' when they prove too effective.

The time must come, however, when it becomes technologically possible to produce a true 'stun gun' which will reliably render unconscious everyone in a given area for a significant length of time without causing them any lasting damage. At that moment, the whole nature of internal security work, and indeed warfare itself, will change dramatically – perhaps for the better.

For the whole of recorded history, man has devoted his energies to making bigger and more destructive weapons. More than once during the Cold War, we came within minutes of obliterating life on Earth. Maybe at last we are beginning to concentrate our efforts on weapons that will allow us to resolve conflict with less, rather than more, death and destruction.

SEMI-AUTOMATIC PISTOLS

Looking at the latest crop of semi-automatic* military and police pistols, a number of trends are immediately apparent. Perhaps most obvious is the trend towards the use of synthetic materials – 'plastics' or polymers which are strong yet light, resist corrosion and can be formed into contoured shapes which would be prohibitively expensive to machine from steel or alloy.

Magazine capacity keeps going up, with a minimum of 13 or 14 rounds now the accepted norm. This sort of capacity, even in the ubiquitous 9mm Parabellum round, requires a double-stack magazine, with a correspondingly chunky butt. This is not a problem in military and overt police use, but is difficult to conceal for covert operations, with the result that slimmer compact models of many pistols are also produced. There remains a market for the even more compact 'pocket pistol', usually with a simple blowback mechanism, for this type of work.

The Colt/Browning short-recoil mechanism has proven remarkably resilient; around 100 years after it was developed by John Moses Browning, this mechanism is little altered in the vast majority of modern pistols. Some of the more radical attempts to improve on the dropping-barrel principle have taken root, but many more have fallen by the wayside.

Ammunition, too, has remained virtually unchanged. Today's NATO soldiers still use the 9mm Parabellum round first developed at the turn of the century, albeit with more technologically advanced powders and primers. This round has become almost a world-wide standard, with even the US armed forces abandoning the .45ACP round along with the legendary M1911 Colt.

The double-action mechanism is certainly here to stay, generally in conjunction with some form of de-cocking device which allows the user to drop the hammer onto a chambered round – this means the weapon can be carried loaded and ready to fire, but requires a deliberate pull of the trigger to draw back the hammer and release it, minimising the chance of an accident.

Double-action only (DAO) mechanisms keep rearing their head, but have failed to gain widespread acceptance. This type of mechanism never leaves the hammer in the full-cock position, requiring a double-action pull for each shot. This is said to have advantages in military and police work, but has yet to gain widespread acceptance in these fields and is considered unsuitable for civilian target shooting. Some manufacturers have hedged their bets, offering the option of double-action or DAO in a single pistol – the H&K USP and Browning BDM spring to mind.

Safety systems are increasingly becoming automatic – inertia firing pins, for example, which are too short to reach the cartridge primer if simply pressed in, relying on the inertia imparted by the hammer's blow to drive them forward and fire the round. Automatic firing pin locking mechanisms are becoming more common, too – these lock the firing pin in its rearward position, and only release when the trigger is pulled through to its full extent.

All these work towards the 'load and forget' ideal of a gun that is carried ready for instant action, but cannot discharge until the user deliberately operates the trigger – although no safety system has yet been designed which can determine whether the user's decision to fire is a wise one!

These trends all tend towards increasing mechanical complexity, something which may look fine in a manufacturer's brochure, or even on the range, but experienced soldiers know that in battle the crudest systems are usually the most reliable. The demanding trials used by modern armies to select their weapons, together with the inevitable cost restraints, act as a restraining influence on designers who might otherwise become carried away with ever more sophisticated mechanisms.

It is no coincidence that, despite a wealth of sophisticated offerings, the world's military and police forces continue to favour the more robust, simpler pistols that can be relied on to do the business even in the harshest conditions.

---

*Purists will argue that the correct term is 'self-loading pistol' and that there is no such thing as 'semi-automatic'. Strictly speaking this is correct, but the term 'semi-automatic' is so widely used and understood that it would be pedantic not to use it here.

BACKGROUND

Based on the Beretta 92 design, the Z-88 was produced to meet the South African police requirement for a new pistol. Due to the arms embargoes in force at the time, it was difficult for South Africa to acquire weapons from overseas, and the weapon was designed to police specifications by Armscor in Pretoria.

OPERATION

The Z-88 has a double-action locked-breech mechanism. A floating wedge between the barrel and frame provides the barrel lock-up, similar to the Beretta 92. Indeed, the weapon is very similar in appearance and function to the Beretta (*see* separate entry for Beretta 92).

CONTROLS

Safety catch/de-cocking lever at rear left of slide. Slide release catch on frame above trigger. Magazine release catch on left grip, just behind trigger guard.

SERVICE

South African police and security services, since 1989.

Manufacturer:	Armscor, Pretoria, South Africa
Model:	Z-88
Calibre:	9mm Parabellum
Action:	Double-action locked-breech semi-automatic
Feed:	15-round magazine
Sights:	Blade and notch open sights
Weight:	950g approx.
Length:	215mm approx.
Barrel:	125mm approx.

BACKGROUND

Available in 9mm Short or 7.65mm ACP, the A-60 is a compact design. Similar in appearance and dimensions to the Walther PP series, it is a compact pistol which is intended largely for police use and for self-defence. It is a development of the A-50, which was a very similar pistol but offered single-action with a lower capacity (7-round) magazine.

OPERATION

A double-action blowback type mechanism, with the barrel fixed to the frame. When the pistol is fired, the gas pressure generated simply blows the slide/breech block rearwards, away from the fixed barrel. The empty case is drawn from the chamber by the extractor attached to the slide. As the slide travels rearwards, the empty case strikes the ejector and is thrown out through the ejection port in the right hand side of the slide. The slide rides over the hammer, re-cocking the mechanism, before reaching the end of its travel, to be thrown forwards again by the slide spring, collecting the next round from the magazine and loading it into the breech.

CONTROLS

Ambidextrous safety catch on rear of slide – up (parallel with barrel) for 'Fire', exposing red dot. Magazine catch in grip, to rear of trigger guard, reversible for left or right-handed operation.

Manufacturer:	Astra, Spain
Model:	A-30
Calibres:	9mm Short, 7.65mm ACP
Action:	Fixed barrel blowback, double-action
Feed:	12-round magazine (7.75mm), 13 rounds 9mm
Sights:	Blade and notch open sights
Weight:	720g
Length:	168mm
Barrel:	89mm

Astra A-60.

BACKGROUND

Astra's A-70 is a single-action pistol designed for the military and police market, although it also has a following among civilian target shooters. It is a compact pistol, with a slim butt housing a single-stack magazine with a capacity of eight 9mm Parabellum rounds. However, its all-steel construction makes it relatively heavy for its size, and gives a chunky feel. Design features include a swept-up trigger guard to allow a high grip on the butt, and chequered grip straps and trigger guard. The trigger guard is shaped to facilitate a two-handed hold.

OPERATION

The A-70 is a single-action semi-automatic, operating on the Browning-type dropping barrel principle, but with the locking achieved in the SIG manner, with a squared-off breech area on the barrel locking into the ejection port.

CONTROLS

Controls are laid out in the Colt 1911 pattern, with a manual safety catch at the left rear of the frame, below the slide. There is also an automatic firing pin safety mechanism which locks the firing pin until the trigger is fully pulled. The hammer has a half-cock notch. The magazine catch is located on the left grip, behind the trigger guard.

Manufacturer:	Astra, Spain
Model:	A-70
Calibres:	9mm Parabellum, .40S&W
Action:	Single-action
Feed:	8-round magazine (9mm), 7-round magazine (.40)
Sights:	Blade and notch open sights, rearsight driftable for windage
Weight:	830g
Length:	166mm
Barrel:	89mm
Variants:	A-70 Inox – stainless steel finish

Astra A-70.

BACKGROUND
Very similar to the A-70, but with a double-action mechanism. Intended for military and police use, and has also proved popular with civilian shooters. Available in stainless steel (Inox), and lighter alloy framed (A-75L) versions.

OPERATION
Double-action semi-automatic with de-cocking system.

CONTROLS
Ambidextrous de-cocking lever at the rear of the frame, just below the slide, in place of the manual safety found on the A-70. The A-75 has the same automatic firing pin safety mechanism and half-cock position on the hammer. The magazine catch is on the grip, behind the trigger guard, and is reversible for left or right handed operation.

Manufacturer:	Astra, Spain
Model:	A-75
Calibres:	9mm Parabellum, .40S&W, .45ACP
Action:	Double-action semi-auto
Feed:	8-round magazine (9mm), 7-round magazine (.40)
Sights:	Blade and notch open sights
Weight:	880g
Length:	166mm
Barrel:	89mm
Variants:	A-75 Inox (stainless steel)
	A-75L (lightweight alloy frame)
	A-75 45 .45 auto calibre, 7+1 capacity

Astra A-75.

BACKGROUND

Manufactured by Astra of Spain, and claimed to be in service with 'several' (unspecified) countries. This pistol, like the A-70, is very reminiscent of the SIG series pistols. The front of the trigger guard is shaped to facilitate a two-handed grip. The pistol features a locked-breech double-action mechanism and a staggered-column magazine with a capacity of 15 rounds. This pistol has now been superseded by the A-90 (qv).

OPERATION

Like the A-70, the A-80 operates from a locked breech, using a Browning-type dropping-barrel locking mechanism. The trigger mechanism is double-action, with a de-cocker.

CONTROLS

The A-80 has a de-cocking lever on the left side of the frame which releases the hammer and lets it fall safely, catching it before it contacts the rearmost end of the firing pin. This allows the user to uncock the hammer mechanism on a loaded chamber and carry the gun ready for a quick double-action shot. The de-cocking lever can be replaced with a left-handed version which is located on the right side of the frame.

The firing pin has an additional safety device, which keeps it locked unless the trigger is fully pulled – so even allowing the hammer to fall accidentally will not fire the weapon if the trigger has not been pulled.

The weapon has no manual safety catch. The extractor gives an indication of a loaded chamber – it protrudes when there is a round in the chamber. This gives a visual indication (the red upper surface is visible), and can also be felt.

The magazine catch is located at heel of butt.

SERVICE

Said to be in service in 'several' countries; now superseded by A-90.

Manufacturer:	Astra, Spain
Model:	A-80
Calibres:	9mm Parabellum, 9x23mm, .39 Super Auto, .45ACP, 7.65mm Parabellum
Action:	Double-action with de-cocking lever
Feed:	15-round magazine
Sights:	Blade and notch open sights, rear adjustable for windage. White inlays for easier alignment in poor light
Weight:	985g
Length:	180mm
Barrel:	96.5mm

BACKGROUND

An updated version of the A-80, this is a full-size service pistol with styling and controls similar to the SIGs. The A-90 has a manual safety catch on the slide in addition to the de-cocking lever. The double-action mechanism has been improved and the sights are adjustable.

OPERATION

This weapon has a double-action mechanism, which can be fired in single-action mode or used (in conjunction with the de-cocking lever) to carry the pistol loaded and ready to fire, but with the hammer dropped.

CONTROLS

A variety of controls give the user several options in which condition to carry the pistol. There is a de-cocking lever which allows the hammer to be dropped safely with a round in the chamber. There is also an ambidextrous manual safety catch, located at the rear of the slide, which can be applied with the hammer in any position; it moves part of the firing pin out on the hammer's path,

making it impossible for a blow of the hammer to be transferred to the round in the chamber. As a further level of safety, the front portion of the firing pin is locked until the trigger is pulled fully back. Unlike the A-80, the A-90's magazine catch is located on the grip, behind the trigger guard, and is reversible for left or right handed operation.

Manufacturer:	Astra, Spain
Model:	A-90
Calibres:	9mm Parabellum
Action:	Double-action semi-automatic with de-cocking lever
Feed:	17-round magazine (9mm), 9-round magazine (.45)
Sights:	Blade and notch open sights, adjustable rearsight, fixed foresight
Weight:	1,000g
Length:	180mm
Barrel:	96.5mm

4

Astra A-90.

Astra A-100.

BACKGROUND
The A-100 is very similar to the A-90, but is aimed at markets that prefer no manual safety catch. It still offers a de-cocking lever and the automatic firing pin safety of the earlier models.

OPERATION
Double-action short-recoil semi-automatic (locked on the Browning-type dropping barrel principle) with de-cocker.

CONTROLS
As A-90 (ie de-cocking lever and automatic firing pin safety), but with no manual safety catch. Magazine release catch is located in the grip, behind the trigger guard, where it can be operated by the thumb of the firing hand, and is reversible for left or right handed operation.

Manufacturer:	Astra, Spain
Model:	A-100
Calibres:	9mm Parabellum, .40S&W, .45ACP
Action:	Double-action with de-cocking lever
Feed:	17-round magazine (9mm), 13-round magazine (.40), 9-round magazine (.45)
Sights:	Blade and notch open sights, rearsight adjustable for windage, interchangeable for elevation
Weight:	985g
Length:	180mm
Barrel:	96.5mm
Variants:	A-100L – lightweight alloy frame
	A-100 Inox – stainless steel finish

BACKGROUND

The Beretta Model 1951 (or M951) was the first locked-breech military pistol produced by the company. Used by the Italian army from 1953 to 1982, it was adopted by the Egyptian army (and was produced in Egypt in the 1960s as the Helwan), as well as the Israeli Defence Forces, Nigerian police force and other police and military users. Now superseded by weapons such as the Beretta 92 models, it was widely issued and can still be encountered in conflict zones and civilian ownership worldwide.

OPERATION

This pistol uses a short-recoil single-action mechanism. The slide must be drawn back to load a round and cock the hammer. On firing, the barrel and slide remain locked together as they begin their rearward travel. An unlocking plunger then releases the barrel from the slide, and halts the barrel's rearward movement, as the slide continues rearwards to cock the mechanism again and load a fresh round as it returns under spring pressure.

CONTROLS

The magazine catch is in a somewhat unusual position, at the lower left of the butt. This is typically operated by the thumb of the free hand. The safety is a push-through button at the top rear of the butt. For safe, it is pushed to the left; for fire, it is pushed to the right.

SERVICE

Italian forces 1953–1982. Egyptian and Israeli armies, Nigerian police, and other police and military users.

Manufacturer:	P Beretta, Italy
Model:	M1951
Calibres:	9mm Parabellum
Action:	Locked-breech single-action semi-automatic
Feed:	8-round magazine
Sights:	Blade and notch open sights
Weight:	870g
Length:	203mm
Barrel:	114mm
Variants:	A selective fully automatic version with a forward pistol grip is available

Beretta Model 1951.

. **Beretta Model 1951, selective fully automatic version.**

BACKGROUND

The Bobcat is a tiny pistol designed as a last-resort back-up weapon for personal protection. Although a very small pistol, it includes a number of features that one might expect to find in a more conventionally-sized weapon – it is a double-action semi-automatic, with a thumb-operated safety catch. The pistol is available in either .22LR or .25ACP – rounds that are at the lower end of the scale for stopping power, but a good deal better than nothing!

A more recent model, the Tomcat, has a recurve trigger guard for two-handed operation and will fire the more powerful .32ACP round.

OPERATION

The Bobcat is a straight blowback pistol; the barrel is fixed in position and the slide is literally blown back by the gas pressure and recoil generated when a round is fired. Being a double-action mechanism, the weapon can be carried with the hammer down and fired without manually cocking – pulling the trigger first cocks the hammer, then drops it to fire the round. On firing, the slide action extracts and ejects the empty case, cocks the mechanism, and loads the next round. Alternatively, the hammer may be cocked manually for a single-action first shot.

The Bobcat has an unusual tip-up barrel which is hinged at the muzzle end. This allows the user to unlatch the barrel to load or unload a round from the chamber without operating the slide.

CONTROLS

Thumb-operated safety catch at rear of frame, at top of grip. Magazine catch in side of grip, two-thirds of the way towards the heel. Tip-up barrel release latch located in frame, above and slightly behind trigger.

Manufacturer:	P Beretta, Italy
Model:	Model 21 Bobcat
Calibres:	.22LR, .25ACP
Action:	Double-action blow-back semi-automatic
Feed:	8-round magazine in .25, 7 in .22LR
Sights:	Blade and notch open sights
Weight:	325g
Length:	125mm
Barrel:	61mm

Beretta Model 21 Bobcat.

BACKGROUND

The Beretta Models 81, 84 and 92 all went into production at the same time, in the mid-1970s. The Models 81 and 84 are very similar, both being blowback designs. The 92 has certain similarities, but is fundamentally different, being a short-recoil operated weapon (*see* separate entry for this weapon). The Model 81 and its derivatives are still in use with a good many police and security forces, and have also proved popular with civilian shooters.

The family are nowadays marketed under the name 'Cheetah', and include models 83, 84, 85, 86 and 87. The Cheetah is a double-action pistol, designed with the firing pin shorter than the breech block for increased safety. The firing pin needs a sharp blow from the hammer to overcome the resistance of its spring and fire the round by the inertia of the firing pin. The idea is that the firer can safely lower the hammer with his thumb onto a loaded chamber (instead of a de-cocking lever). The Model 84 is virtually identical to the Model 81, except that it is in 9mm Short calibre instead of the 81's 7.65mm.

There are a great many derivatives and variants of the basic Models 81 and 84. The various model numbers generally indicate a change of calibre: the 87 is .22LR rimfire, the 85 a 9mm Short and the 82 a 7.65mm. Capacities vary according to calibre.

Most models in the range are available in BB and F variants. The BB models have a single stack box magazine in place of the staggered high capacity magazines of the 81 and 84. This makes them lighter and easier to conceal. BB models also have a loaded chamber indicator in the shape of a pin which projects from the slide, showing red, when a round is in the chamber. BB versions also have a redesigned safety system, incorporating a safety catch which breaks the connection between the trigger and the sear; in addition, the firing pin is locked until the trigger is pulled back.

F models offer all the features of the BBs, as well as a de-cocking mechanism built into the safety catch. By applying the safety catch, the hammer is dropped safely against an interceptor. When the safety catch is applied, the slide is also locked.

Beretta Model 84.

OPERATION

The 81/84 and derivatives use a semi-automatic blowback double-action. With a round chambered, the weapon can be fired single-action from a cocked hammer, or double-action from a dropped hammer. Certain models (see above) offer a de-cocking facility to facilitate carrying with the hammer lowered onto a loaded chamber. The firing pin being shorter than the breech block and the additional safety mechanisms built into the later models all help to reduce the chance of the gun being accidentally fired when carried loaded.

CONTROLS

The magazine release on the 81/84 is located at the front of the left grip, behind the trigger guard. It can, however, be reversed for left-handed operation. See above for description of safety catch and de-cocking lever options of various models.

SERVICE

The 81/84 and derivatives are used by a number of police and security services around the world. The guns are also used by civilian shooters.

Manufacturer:	P Beretta, Italy
Model:	84
Calibres:	9mm Short
Action:	Double-action blowback
Feed:	13-round magazine (Mod 84), 8-round magazine (Mod 85)
Sights:	Blade and notch open sights
Weight:	660g
Length:	172mm
Barrel:	97mm
Variants:	Models 81/82 7.65mm ACP
	Model 83 9mm Short, 4-inch barrel, 7-round magazine
	84/85 Models 9mm Short
	87 and 89 Models are .22LR calibre, single action only
	Model 87LB has an extra long barrel (150mm)
	'BB' models have an improved safety system and a single-stack magazine which has a reduced capacity and allows a slimmer butt
	'F' models also have a de-cocking mechanism

Beretta Model 84.

BACKGROUND

The Beretta Model 86 Cheetah looks a lot like the other Cheetah models, but is a more recent design which was introduced in the mid-1980s. Even so, it employs a tip-up barrel which harks back to earlier designs. The barrel is pivoted at the muzzle end and is released by a catch at the breech end. By releasing the barrel and tipping it up, it can be cleaned without stripping the weapon.

OPERATION

Aside from the unusual tip-up barrel (see above), the Beretta Model 86 is operated much like any regular double-action blowback semi-automatic. The tip-up barrel facilitates loading a round into the chamber in addition to a full magazine (although this is straightforward enough in weapons without this feature – you simply load a full magazine, rack the slide, then remove the magazine and insert another round to top it up).

CONTROLS

The weapon has an ambidextrous safety catch and de-cocking lever. A loaded chamber indicator shows red with a round in the chamber. The barrel latch, which releases the barrel so it can be tipped up, is located on the right side of the frame, below the breech end of the barrel and directly above the trigger.

Manufacturer:	P Beretta, Italy
Model:	86
Calibres:	9mm Short
Action:	Double-action blowback semi-automatic
Feed:	8-round magazine
Sights:	Conventional blade and notch open sights
Weight:	660g
Length:	186mm
Barrel:	111mm

Beretta Model 86.

BACKGROUND

Developed at the same time as the Models 81 and 84, the Model 92 is altogether a bigger and more powerful weapon, firing the 9mm Parabellum round favoured by many military and police users. It offers a double-action mechanism, and a double-stack magazine with a capacity of 15 rounds. It has the characteristic Beretta cut-away slide design, which gives it a distinctive

Beretta Model 92FS.

silhouette as well as helping to avoid certain types of stoppage.

The Model 92 has been developed to provide a number of variations, perhaps the most successful being the 92FS, which was adopted by the US armed forces. This version is basically the same pistol as the original Model 92, but with minor variations – the trigger guard is shaped to facilitate a two-handed grip; there is a lanyard ring; the barrel is internally chromed; and the external finish is in 'Bruniton', a Teflon-type material.

Other 92 models are in service with the Italian armed forces and police, the French police and police and armed forces of a number of other countries.

OPERATION

The Model 92 uses the short-recoil principle, with a wedge-shaped locking block to lock the barrel in place when the action is closed. When the gun is fired, the block is driven downwards to unlock the barrel from the slide and stop the barrel's rearward movement. The

Beretta Model 92FS.

weapon has a double-action mechanism, which can be fired either as single or double-action.

CONTROLS

The controls on the 92 series have been developed over the years and vary depending on the model. The original 92 had the safety catch on the frame (located rear left); in the S model this moved to the slide and served a dual function as a de-cocking lever. It also moves the trigger bar away from the sear and locks the firing pin so that even if the hammer is drawn back and released, or the weapon dropped on the ground, it will not fire.

In the SB and F models, the safety catch is ambidextrous (levers on either side of the slide, for left- and right-handed operation) and the magazine release button can be mounted on the left or right of the grip. In the original models the magazine release button was in the bottom rear of the grip; in SB and F models it has been moved to the more convenient position at the rear of the trigger guard, where it can be operated by the thumb of the firing hand without releasing the grip.

SERVICE

92FS adopted by the US Army as the Pistol M9 in 1985. Current model in service with Italian armed forces and police, French Gendarmerie Nationale and numerous other military and police forces worldwide.

Manufacturer:	P Beretta, Italy
Model:	92FS
Calibres:	9mm Parabellum
Action:	Short-recoil double-action semi-automatic
Feed:	15-round magazine
Sights:	Blade and notch open sights, rearsight dovetailed to frame
Weight:	960g
Length:	217mm
Barrel:	125mm
Variants:	92S with de-cocking lever
	92B with ambidextrous de-cocking lever
	92C compact version (197mm long)
	92F with modified trigger guard suitable for two-handed grip
	92G with no manual safety
	92D double-action only
	92M stainless steel version with single-stack magazine
	96 Series in .40S&W calibre
	98 Series in 9mm x 21
	Centurion Series with standard frame but reduced barrel length
	Brigadier series with specially strengthened and recontoured slide and frame

Beretta Model 92FS.

BACKGROUND

This weapon is perhaps better described as a machine pistol, since it will fire a three-round burst at each pull of the trigger. The basic design is the same as the Model 92, but the barrel is extended and has a muzzle brake to counter the tendency of the muzzle to climb during three-round burst fire. To aid control of the weapon, there is a fold-down grip in front of the trigger guard, and an optional shoulder stock which can be fitted to the rear of the butt. The optional 20-round magazine extends below the bottom of the butt.

OPERATION

The 93R is loaded and fired in the same way as the Model 92 pistol, except that the firer selects single shots or three-round burst fire by means of a selector switch located at the rear left of the frame. Even with the shoulder stock fitted, and a firm hold on the foregrip, it takes some practice to keep all the bullets of a three-round burst in a reasonably sized group.

CONTROLS

The safety catch is located above and to the rear of the trigger, with the fire selector switch above the left grip, close to the rear of the frame. The selector switch has two positions, marked with a single white dot for single shots, three dots for three-round burst fire. The magazine release catch is found in the conventional position, on the left side of the butt just behind the trigger guard.

Manufacturer:	P Beretta, Italy
Model:	93R
Calibres:	9mm Parabellum
Action:	Double-action selective fire (single-shot semi-auto or three-round bursts)
Feed:	15- or 20-round magazine
Sights:	Blade and notch open sights
Weight:	1,129g
Length:	240mm
Barrel:	156mm

Beretta Model 93R.

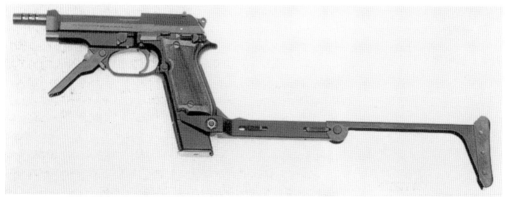

Beretta Model 93R.

The Jetfire is very similar to the Bobcat (qv), but offers single-action only. It is slightly more compact, lighter, and has a different trigger guard and blade design. It features the same tip-up barrel system, and has a capacity of 8+1 rounds of .25ACP.

Manufacturer:	P Beretta, Italy
Model:	Model 950 Jetfire
Calibres:	.25ACP
Action:	Blow-back single-action semi-automatic
Feed:	8-round magazine
Sights:	Fixed blade and notch open sights
Weight:	280g
Length:	120mm
Barrel:	60mm

Beretta Model 950 Jetfire.

BACKGROUND

The Beretta 8000 series or 'Cougar' pistols are compact frame weapons designed for undercover work and for use as 'off duty sidearms'. The design of the Beretta 92 does not lend itself to being adapted to compact dimensions – the return spring assembly lies in the front part of the frame/slide and can only be shortened by a relatively small amount.

The Cougar series was developed to provide a more compact design. The basic controls and layout are much the same as the 92, but the gun has a chubbier and deeper shape, with a closed-top slide in place of the 92's open-top design. The locking system is totally different to the 92 (see below), and the internal layout allows the barrel to be made considerably shorter - giving the Cougar its 'compact' dimensions.

The pistol is designed with rounded edges to help avoid it snagging in a holster or clothing, and has a number of ergonomic features to facilitiate quick and effective operation.

OPERATION

The Cougar employs a rotary locking system which is claimed to improve accuracy as well as providing the strength to cope with modern high-powered ammunition in a relatively small pistol. When the weapon is fired, the recoil pushes the slide and barrel back, locked together by a series of lugs. As they move back, a tooth

on the central block rotates the barrel by a cam action. After the barrel has rotated approximately 30 degrees, the locking lugs on the barrel clear the locking recesses, freeing the slide to continue rearward and compressing the recoil spring. The slide extracts and ejects the spent shell, cocks the hammer and then reverses direction to chamber the next round from the magazine. The rotation of the barrel and the action of the barrel and slide against the central block help to absorb the recoil shock with the result that the Cougar has an unusually low felt recoil. Positive lock-up of barrel and slide also ensures good alignment of the barrel with the sights, contributing to accuracy.

CONTROLS

The magazine release button is located in grip, at the rear of trigger guard, and can be swapped to left or right to suit the individual user. The safety catch is ambidextrous and is located at the rear of the slide. All Cougar models have an automatic firing pin blocking device. F models have a manual safety catch/de-cocking lever, while D models have no manual safety. G models have a de-cocking lever, but no manual safety.

Manufacturer:	P Beretta, Italy
Model:	8000 series (Cougar)
Calibres:	9mm Parabellum, .41AE, .40S&W
Action:	Rotary locking double-action semi-automatic
Feed:	15-round magazine (10 in .41, 11 in .40)
Sights:	Blade and notch open sights
Weight:	925g
Length:	180mm
Barrel:	92mm
Variants:	F models – with safety/de-cocking lever
	D models – no manual safety, no hammer spur
	G models – de-cocking lever without manual safety
	Inox models – sand-blasted stainless finish and walnut grips

Beretta 8000 Cougar.

BACKGROUND
Originally designed for military and police applications, the Bernadelli P-018 has proved more successful with civilian users.

OPERATION
The P-018 is a locked-breech double-action semi-automatic pistol, with a block locking system which helps to reduce felt recoil.

CONTROLS
The magazine catch is located at heel of butt. There is a manual safety catch at the left rear of the frame.

SERVICE
Designed for police and military use, but has sold well on the commercial market.

Manufacturer:	V Bernadelli, Italy
Model:	P-018
Calibres:	9mm Parabellum
Action:	Double-action locked-breech semi-automatic
Feed:	15-round magazine
Sights:	Blade and notch open sights
Weight:	998g
Length:	213mm
Barrel:	122mm
Variants:	Compact version 109mm long with 14-round magazine

BACKGROUND

The Browning High-Power 9mm is a classic design, created by John Moses Browning, which has been adopted by armies and police forces worldwide. Although now somewhat dated, it is still in military service today, more than 60 years after it was first produced, having seen service in just about every conflict from the Second World War onwards, including the Falklands, the Gulf War, Northern Ireland and the former Yugoslavia.

The High-Power was first designed in 1925, but it was ten years before it was introduced in 1935, using the same 9mm Parabellum ammunition that had been developed for the Luger Pistole '08. Its greatly increased magazine capacity of 13 rounds (compared to the Luger's eight) immediately appealed to soldiers on both sides in the Second World War. The Fabrique Nationale (FN) factory at Liège in Belgium fell to the Germans in 1940, and was used to produce weapons for Germany and her allies for the next four years. At this point, production for Britain and Allied forces was switched to the John Inglis factory in Toronto, Canada.

The High-Power's design followed the swinging link mechanism developed by John M Browning and used in the Colt 1911 – a principle that has laid the foundations for a great many of the pistols that have followed (witness the number of guns in this book whose operation is described as 'Browning type'). Weapons such as the CZ75/85, which have become classics in their own right, owe much of their design to the Colt 1911 and the Browning High-Power. The gun itself has been widely copied and produced under licence, in countries as far apart as Argentina and Indonesia.

Even today, the High-Power is still officially in service with many police, security and military forces and can be encountered among paramilitary forces, as well as retaining a loyal following among civilian shooters.

OPERATION

The Browning High Power's mechanism is the classic single-action automatic. It is highly regarded as a good, solid, workmanlike design – thoroughly reliable and well suited to police and military use. It is relatively accurate and recoil is no more severe than one would expect with a standard 9mm. It is worth taking a look at the mechanism in detail, since it provides the basis of so many pistols which have followed.

To load the pistol, you insert a loaded magazine into the magazine well in the butt, and push it home so the magazine catch engages. At this stage the chamber is empty, and the hammer is not cocked.

To cock the mechanism and load a round into the chamber, grasp the slide and pull it backwards against spring pressure – the slotted surfaces on either side of the slide provide extra grip for thumb and forefinger of the 'weak' hand. As the slide comes back, it pulls the hammer back and pushes it downwards, compressing the mainspring, until the sear engages in the bent of the trigger mechanism, holding the hammer in the cocked position. When the slide reaches its rearmost position, you release it to fly forward under spring pressure. As it travels forwards, the breech face collects the first round in the magazine, pushing it into the chamber. The weapon is now ready to fire. The safety catch may be applied at this stage, leaving the pistol in the 'cocked and locked' mode.

On firing, pressure on the trigger releases the hammer sear from the bent, allowing the pressure of the mainspring to drive the hammer forward against the rearmost end of the firing pin. This drives the forward end of the firing pin into the percussion cap in the chambered round, causing it to fire.

As the bullet travels up the barrel, the force of recoil drives the barrel rearwards. A series of lugs on the barrel are engaged in corresponding slots in the slide, so the slide is driven rearwards also. After the barrel and slide have travelled rearwards for approximately 5mm, a cam draws the barrel downwards, disengaging the lugs. The slide continues to travel rearwards, while the barrel halts. The extractor on the breech block draws the empty case out of the chamber. As the slide continues rearwards, the empty case hits the ejector and is thrown out of the ejection port on the right side of the slide. The slide rides over the hammer, cocking it again, before reaching the end of its travel and being driven forwards again by spring pressure.

As the slide returns, collecting a fresh round from

the magazine on the way, it pushes the barrel forward again, and the cam forces the barrel up to engage the lugs once again. When there are no more rounds in the magazine, the magazine follower pushes up the slide stop, and the slide is held to the rear. When you insert a fresh magazine, you then press down the slide stop to allow the slide to fly forward and load the first round.

The Browning has a magazine safety mechanism, which has been criticised as being unnecessary and results in an increased trigger pull. This safety mechanism disengages the trigger sear lever when there is no magazine in the gun. It prevents the gun being fired when the magazine is removed, but there is still a round in the chamber. The mechanism can be over-ridden by placing a finger up the magazine well, and depressing the spring-loaded safety lever. Some shooters have the mechanism removed by a gunsmith – a relatively easy job – to improve the trigger pull and allow magazines to drop away cleanly when the magazine release button (located on the left side of the grip, level with the bottom of the trigger guard) is pressed.

CONTROLS

Controls on the Browning High-Power are unsophisticated by today's standards, but they are robust and effective. The safety catch is located on the left rear of the frame above the grip, and can be operated with the thumb of the firing hand. It is a basic safe fire switch design – up (red dot covered) for 'safe', down (red dot visible) for 'fire'. It can be applied when the gun is cocked and ready to fire, to place it in the 'cocked and locked' condition.

The slide stop is located on the left of the frame above the trigger. It is applied automatically by the magazine follower when the last round in the magazine is fired, locking the slide open. To release the slide once a fresh magazine has been inserted, the stop is pushed down with the thumb.

The magazine release catch is a spring-loaded press button on the left side of the grip, immediately behind the trigger. It can be operated with the thumb of the firing hand, while the free hand catches the released magazine or reaches for a fresh one.

SERVICE

Widely used by military and police forces from the Second World War onwards. Nowadays steadily being replaced, but still in service with British armed forces, and many others worldwide, at time of writing

Manufacturer:	Fabrique Nationale, Belgium. Widely copied and produced under licence
Model:	Model 1935 'High-Power'
Calibre:	9mm Parabellum
Action:	Single-action short-recoil semi-auto
Feed:	13-round magazine
Sights:	Simple open sights in military models, but adjustable sights often fitted to civilian and target shooting versions
Weight:	882g
Length:	200mm
Barrel:	118mm
Variants:	Mk 2 and Mk 3 versions produced in 1980s

A modern version of the Browning GP35 9mm High-Power.

An early Browning GP35 9mm High-Power.

BACKGROUND

The Browning BDA is essentially an updated High-Power GP35, offering double-action and an ambidextrous safety catch/de-cocker. It incorporates a number of improvements and extra features over the High-Power, such as an improved extraction/ejection/feed mechanism, an automatic firing pin safety, contoured grip and reversible magazine release catch. Key component parts have also been strengthened, and the weapon has been reduced in weight and made more compact.

A variant of the BDA is the BDAO, designed specifically for law enforcement use. This gun has no manual safety/decocker, and operates on double-action only (DAO). It is designed to be very simple to use and maintain, and can be field stripped in under one minute.

OPERATION

The BDA uses the same dropping-barrel system as the GP35 High-Power, but with a double-action trigger/hammer mechanism. This means that the first shot can be fired double-action, after which the pistol re-cocks itself at each shot and is fired in single-action mode.

The BDAO has a double-action only (DAO) mechanism, so the hammer is not cocked by the slide; each shot is fired double-action, with the pull of the trigger first raising the hammer and then dropping it onto the firing pin to fire the next round.

CONTROLS

The BDA has an ambidextrous safety catch/de-cocker located at rear of the frame beneath the slide. There is also an automatic firing pin safety mechanism. The magazine release catch is on the grip at the junction with the trigger guard, and can be set for left- or right-handed operation.

The BDAO has no manual safety, but does incorporate passive safety systems which lock the firing pin until the trigger is pulled through. The magazine release catch is as for BDA.

Manufacturer:	Fabrique Nationale, Belgium.
Model:	BDA
Calibre:	9mm Parabellum
Action:	Double-action short-recoil semi-auto
Feed:	14-round magazine
Sights:	Blade and notch open sights fitted in dovetails – driftable for windage. Luminous spot sights available
Weight:	875g
Length:	200mm
Barrel:	118.5mm
Variants:	Browning BDAO – double-action only model with no manual safety/de-cocker

Browning BDA.

BACKGROUND

The Browning BDM takes the basic design of the legendary High-Power and brings it up to date with a selectable double-action mechanism and various other refinements. The grips are recessed into the frame, rather than the more familiar method of screwing grip plates or 'scales' onto the outside of the frame. The safety catch has not just a double function but a triple one; it also acts as both de-cocking lever and slide release.

OPERATION

A switch on the left of the slide offers the choice of 'P' (pistol) or 'R' (revolver) mode. 'Pistol' mode gives a double-action first shot, followed by single-action shots until the 15-round magazine is empty – in other words, a conventional double-action mechanism. Changing to 'Revolver' mode switches the weapon to double-action only (DAO), so that the hammer is dropped after each shot, and pulling the trigger first raises the hammer before dropping it to fire the next round. The mode switch is flush with the slide to prevent it being snagged on clothing etc, and is slotted so it can be operated with the edge of a coin or cartridge rim.

CONTROLS

The triple-function safety catch/de-cocking lever/slide release is located on left rear of frame. Pushing the lever down releases the slide (if it is back) and lowers the hammer safely. The lever must be up to fire. The mode switch is on the left of the slide – 'P' for pistol or double-action, 'R' for revolver or double-action only (DAO). The magazine release is on the left grip, behind trigger guard, for operation with thumb of firing hand.

Manufacturer:	Fabrique Nationale, Belgium
Model:	BDM (Browning Dual Mode)
Calibre:	9mm Parabellum
Action:	Selectable double-action/double-action only (DAO) semi-automatic
Feed:	15-round magazine
Sights:	Blade and notch open sights, rear adjustable for windage
Weight:	850g
Length:	200mm
Barrel:	120mm

Browning BDM.

BACKGROUND

For sheer firepower, as well as space-age looks, you would have to go a long way to match the Calico M950. This weapon is a shortened, semi-auto version of the Calico sub-machine gun. Instead of the 14 or 15 rounds offered by conventional modern pistols, the Calico's massive tubular magazine, mounted on top of the weapon, holds 50 – and there is even a 100-round version for anyone who feels that 50 may not be enough!

The weapon has an extended fore-end section, allowing it to be fired two-handed using the same grip as a rifle, although without the shoulder stock. The helical magazine is mounted on the top rear of the frame, raising the sighting plane; indeed, the rearsight is built into the magazine. Frame and receiver are constructed of aluminium.

OPERATION

The M950 action is a modified version of the Calico sub-machine gun. It operates a roller-delayed blowback system similar to that seen in Heckler & Koch weapons such as the MP5. The bolt is in two sections, which on firing are locked by rollers which engage into recesses in the frame. The recoil pushes the forward bolt section against the rear bolt section, forcing the rollers inwards until they release and allow both sections to recoil against a return spring. The movement of the bolt ejects the spent case downwards (through an ejection port in the floor of the receiver), re-cocks the hammer mechanism and loads a fresh round from the magazine on the return stroke. As the rear part of the bolt closes up against the forward part, it pushes the rollers back into engagement ready for the next cycle.

CONTROLS

Manual safety catch located on left side of frame, in recess in front of trigger. Magazine release catch located on the left side of the magazine. Cocking lever travels in slot on left of frame, above and in front of trigger, with projecting spur.

Manufacturer:	Calico, USA
Model:	M950
Calibre:	9mm Parabellum
Action:	Single shot semi-automatic version of Calico SMG
Feed:	50- or 100-round helical magazine attached to top rear of frame
Sights:	Open sights, with rearsight incorporated into top of magazine
Weight:	1,000g
Length:	356mm
Barrel:	152mm
Variants:	Sub-machine gun version available (see separate entry in that section)

Calico M950.

BACKGROUND

The Colt .45, or Model 1911, needs no introduction. A legend in its own time, the weapon served the US armed forces for more than 70 years – several generations of soldiers developed a great affection for this gun as they fought through two World Wars, the Philippines, Korea, Vietnam and many smaller actions. Even today, though the design looks somewhat dated alongside the modern SIGs and Glocks, it is highly regarded by civilian shooters, police and military alike, both for its robust simplicity and for the awesome man-stopping power of its relatively slow-moving (253m/sec) .45 calibre round.

The Colt traces its history back to the previous century – it was in the late 1890s that John Moses Browning first began developing automatic sporting and military pistols. His Colt .38 military pistol appeared in 1898 and a .45 calibre version followed in 1905. This was one of several pistols which were trialled by the US Army Ordnance Board and was provisionally accepted in 1907. A number of modifications were made, resulting in the definitive 1911 Model. Further modifications were developed from 1921–1926, which led to the 1911A1 model. This had a slightly shorter hammer spur, a more arched shape at the top of the rear of the grip and cutaway sections behind the trigger to accommodate the firer's finger.

A number of variations on the basic model have been produced over the years. For example, a 'silenced' version was produced by La France and an officers' version was made in the 1970s. The weapon has been widely copied and produced under licence, for example by sub-contractors in the USA, and in Argentina, Canada and Norway. The pistol has also won a devoted following among civilian shooters, and a huge range of different variants and customised versions have been produced.

OPERATION

The Colt 1911 uses the swinging link mechanism that has become known as the Browning action (since it was designed by John M Browning; the Browning High-Power pistol that also uses this mechanism was designed several years later, in 1925, and was not produced for another 10 years after that).

The barrel has a series of lugs on the upper surface of its breech end, which engage into corresponding slots in the inside top surface of the slide. The barrel is

Colt 1911A1.

attached to the frame by a swinging link. This link is vertical when the barrel is in the forward position. On firing, the slide recoils and, via the lugs, draws the barrel back with it. As the barrel moves rearwards, the link pivots about the slide stop pin through the frame, drawing the barrel downwards and disengaging the lugs from the slide. The barrel then stops moving, while the slide continues rearwards, compressing the slide spring housed under the barrel. The extractor claw fitted to the breech face draws the fired case from the breech and ejects it, while the slide rides over the hammer to re-cock the mechanism.

When the slide reaches the full extent of its travel, the slide spring throws it forwards again. As it travels forwards, it collects the next round from the magazine and pushes it into the chamber. When the breech face meets the barrel, it pushes the barrel forwards. The swinging link forces the barrel upwards, engaging the lugs once again so that the pistol is ready to fire the next round.

CONTROLS

The Colt's controls are basic by modern standards, but well placed and easy to operate, even in the heat of battle. The Colt is a single-action design, requiring the hammer to be cocked before it can be fired. It has a simple manual safety catch, located at the rear left of the frame above the grip. This can be applied with the hammer cocked to carry the pistol in the 'cocked and locked' condition. There is an additional safety device: a grip safety which locks the firing mechanism unless it is pressed in by the firer's hand around the grip. This reduces the chance of the gun firing accidentally – if dropped, for instance, or if the trigger snags in clothing, undergrowth or equipment.

The slide stop catch is located on the left side of the frame, above the trigger. The magazine catch is a press-button just behind the trigger, in front of the left grip.

SERVICE

The 1911/1911A1 was the US Armed Forces' service pistol from 1911 until the Beretta 92F was adopted in 1985. It is still in widespread service with military and police forces worldwide, and is also one of the world's most popular civilian pistols, both for target shooting and, where local laws permit, for self-defence.

Manufacturer:	Colt and other US manufacturers. Numerous copies produced worldwide, including Spain, Argentina, Mexico and Norway
Model:	M1911A1 (Earlier model 1911 produced until 1926)
Calibre:	.45ACP
Action:	Single-action Browning type semi-automatic
Feed:	8-round magazine
Sights:	Basic combat sights (numerous variations and custom-fitted sights available for civilian target shooting etc)
Weight:	1,130g
Length:	219mm
Barrel:	127mm
Variants:	Numerous variations of the basic service pistol have been produced, offering for instance alternative calibres, a shorter barrel and slide, or more ergonomic controls. Additionally, many customised and 'special' versions of the pistol have been made, with special grips and finishes, target sights, etc.

BACKGROUND

The Colt 2000 marked a significant change of direction for Colt, since the design (by Reed Knight and Eugene Stoner) abandoned the dropping barrel associated with Colt and Browning in favour of a rotating barrel locking system. The trigger mechanism is double-action only (DAO), a sure sign that this was intended as a police and military pistol rather than being aimed at civilian target shooters. One of the perceived drawbacks of the DAO system is that the necessarily heavier and longer trigger pull undermines accuracy, and the 2000 design addressed this by employing roller bearings in the mechanism to smooth and lighten the pull. Following the modern trend, the weapon had a polymer frame and steel slide. The pistol failed to achieve the success that Colt had envisaged, and it was taken out of production in 1994.

OPERATION

The barrel and slide are locked together by a series of lugs around the chamber end of the barrel. These engage into corresponding slots in the breech block part of the slide, and are locked in place by rotation of the barrel (the principle is similar to the bayonet fitting on a light bulb). On firing, the barrel and slide recoil together for a short distance, the bottom barrel lug moving in a curved slot which rotates the barrel through approximately 30 degrees, until the other lugs release the slide. The barrel then stops, and the slide continues its rearward movement, ejecting the spent case, and loading a fresh one from the magazine on its return stroke. As the slide pushes the barrel back into its forward position, the curved slot rotates the barrel again to re-lock the action. The hammer is internal, and is not cocked by the slide, since this is a double-action only mechanism; the hammer is raised and then dropped by the action of pulling the trigger. The cam block, which is an integral part of the mechanism, absorbs much of the initial recoil, and considerably reduces the recoil felt by the user.

CONTROLS

The Colt 2000 is a double-action only (DAO) pistol, and as such has no mechanical safety catch – the trigger must be pulled to raise the hammer and fire the weapon. The hammer is internal, and not visible without stripping the pistol. The magazine release catch is ambidextrous, and located in the grips behind the trigger guard. The slide release catch is located on the frame above the left grip.

SERVICE

The Colt 2000 failed to appeal to military and police users, and production ended in 1994.

Manufacturer:	Colt, USA
Model:	2000
Calibre:	9mm Parabellum
Action:	Double-action only (DAO) semi-automatic with rotating barrel lock-up
Feed:	15-round magazine
Sights:	Blade and notch open sights
Weight:	822g
Length:	190mm
Barrel:	114mm

Colt 2000.

BACKGROUND

The CZ75 was born during the 1970s, at the height of the Cold War. It leaned heavily on the Browning locking lug design, but offered greater accuracy than the Browning High-Power at the time due to the tight manufacturing tolerances of the locking lugs. This also improved the gun's reliability and prolonged its effective life.

Intended purely for export (the 9mm Parabellum is not a standard Warsaw Pact calibre), the CZ75 quickly earned an excellent reputation for dependability, and has become one of the world's best selling pistols of all time.

The CZ85 was developed as an ambidextrous version of the same pistol – the operating controls are duplicated on the right side of the frame. Some other small modifications were made at the same time, either to simplify manufacture or to improve the weapon's operation.

OPERATION

The CZ75's operating system is based on the Colt/Browning dropping barrel method. The barrel has a cam-shaped extension beneath the chamber and locking lugs on its top surface about one-third of its length from the breech. The lugs lock into recesses in the inside surface of the slide and are held in the locked position by the cam when the breech is closed. On firing, the barrel and slide recoil together for a short distance until the cam acts to lower the barrel and unlock the slide, which then continues rearwards to eject the spent case, cock the hammer, and load the next round before closing again and re-locking.

The mechanism is double-action, so the pistol can be fired from an uncocked hammer, but there is no de-cocking device to help the user put the gun into this condition, although on most examples the hammer does have a half-cock position.

CONTROLS

The CZ75 has a manual safety catch the left of the frame, above the left grip, in a position where it can be readily operated by the thumb of the firing hand, so long as the user is right-handed. There is no de-cocking lever, but on most examples the hammer does have a half-cock position. The magazine release catch is a press-button located on the left grip, behind the trigger guard. The

CZ 75.

CZ 85.

slide release catch is on the left of the frame, above the trigger.

The CZ85 has ambidextrous controls: the safety catch and slide release catch are duplicated on the right side of the frame to facilitate left-handed use.

SERVICE

The CZ75 and 85 were developed for export, and were never intended as a Czech service weapon. Both pistols have proved popular worldwide with users such as bodyguards, who appreciate their accuracy, simplicity and reliability. The pistols have been widely copied and produced under licence by makers such as Tanfoglio and Springfield Armoury.

Manufacturer:	CZ, Czechoslovakia
Model:	CZ75
Calibre:	9mm Parabellum
Action:	Double-action short-recoil semi-automatic
Feed:	15-round magazine
Sights:	Blade and notch open sights
Weight:	980g
Length:	203mm
Barrel:	120mm
Variants:	CZ75B has an automatic firing pin safety system CZ75BD also has a de-cocking lever in place of the manual safety catch. CZ85 is basically the same weapon, but with controls duplicated on either side of the frame to suit left- or right-handed shooters. The rearsight in the CZ85 is adjustable for windage by means of a small screw, and some small changes have been made to the firing mechanism.

The diminutive CZ92 is an easily concealed weapon designed for last-resort personal protection. Measuring just 128mm long, it fires the .25 Auto round and has a capacity of 8+1. It has a DAO (double-action only) mechanism, and there is no manual safety catch. Operation is by simple blowback.

The magazine release catch is located in the heel of the butt, and there is a magazine safety which blocks the firing mechanism when the magazine is removed.

Manufacturer:	CZ, Czechoslovakia
Model:	92
Calibre:	.25 Auto
Action:	Double-action only (DAO) blowback semi-automatic
Feed:	8-round magazine
Sights:	Channel cut in top of slide
Weight:	430g
Length:	128mm
Barrel:	63.5mm

CZ 92.

BACKGROUND

The CZ100 is a true new generation CZ pistol which marks a complete departure from its hugely successful predecessors, the CZ75 and 85. It has a frame of synthetic polymer, with a steel slide which moves outside the frame. It is a double-action only (DAO) design, and cannot be fired in single-action mode. The lock-up mechanism is completely different to the Browning-style lug design of the CZ75/85, using a squared-off section at the rear of the barrel which fits into the ejection port, similar to the SIG design.

In addition to the usual U and post open sights, the CZ100 also offers the option of a dedicated laser sight, which clips onto the front of the trigger guard. The laser pointer is activated by pressure on the trigger.

OPERATION

The CZ100 is a short-recoil semi-automatic, with the breech locked on firing and released only when the barrel and slide have recoiled back a short distance. The locking mechanism is different to the earlier CZ models, however, using a squared-off chamber section of the barrel which locks into the ejection port in the slide. As the slide and barrel travel rearwards, the barrel is cammed down (as in a Browning-type action) to unlock the slide and allow it to complete its cycle. The hammer is not cocked by the slide, however; this is a double-action only (DAO) mechanism, and requires a double-action pull at each shot to raise the hammer before dropping it onto the firing pin.

CONTROLS

No manual safety catch. Slide release catch at top of left grip. Magazine release catch on grip, behind trigger guard. No external hammer.

SERVICE

Designed for law enforcement and personal defence, the CZ100 has yet to be adopted as a service pistol by any military or police forces at time of writing

Manufacturer:	CZ, Czechoslovakia
Model:	100
Calibres:	9mm Parabellum, .40S&W
Action:	Double-action only (DAO) semi-automatic
Feed:	13-round magazine (10 rounds in .40)
Sights:	Blade and notch open sights, with white dot/U to facilitate shooting in poor light; dedicated laser pointer also available
Weight:	680g
Length:	177mm
Barrel:	95mm
Variants:	CZ101 offers a slimmer grip, with a single-stack magazine that reduces capacity to 7 in 9mm and 6 in .40.

CZ 100.

Background

The most significant innovation of the Five-Seven is its ammunition, which promises to give the user the ability to engage and defeat an enemy wearing light body armour at the limit of accurate range – something that conventional military pistol ammunition cannot do.

Developed by FN Herstal of Belgium, the Five-Seven (spelt Five-seveN in FN's literature) fires the same 5.7 ¥ 28mm ammunition as the P90 sub-machine gun (qv), forming a key part of what FN call the 5.7 ¥ 28mm Weapons System.

The SS190 ammunition weighs around half the weight of a conventional NATO standard 9mm round yet gives much improved performance. The SS190 bullet consists of a two-part steel and aluminium core inside a steel jacket, and can penetrate modern fragmentation vests and helmets at ranges up to 200 metres. Its trajectory is almost flat up to 200 metres, and the recoil is 30 per cent less than a 9mm round. All the bullet's energy is transferred to the target on impact, increasing its effectiveness and reducing the risk to friendlies or civilians.

A variety of ammunition natures are available, including the standard ball, tracer, subsonic and training.

Operation

A DAO (double-action only) pistol, the Five-Seven has no hammer, and no decocking lever, reducing the number of controls and making it simple to operate. It can be carried safely with a round in the chamber. The makers claim it has particularly low recoil, with minimal muzzle jump, allowing quick, accurate follow-up shots.

A number of dedicated accessories are available, including a laser assembly and tactical light for target illumination. There is also a 'Tactical' model of the pistol which offers single-action operation. This gives a lighter trigger pull for greater accuracy.

Controls

The Five-Seven pistol is designed with no protruding parts, and can be field stripped quickly without tools. The conventional appearance of the pistol belies the innovative approach that has gone into its design. The controls are arranged in the normal way, but are set into the lines of the pistol's body so that it does not catch in clothing and webbing. One noteworthy feature is the oversized trigger guard, which allows the pistol to be used easily when wearing gloves.

Manufacturer:	FN Herstal, Belgium
Model:	Five-SeveN
Calibres:	5.7 ¥ 28mm
Action:	Semi-automatic
Feed:	20-round box magazine
Sights:	Blade foresight and notch rearsight. Laser sighting system available.
Weight:	618g empty, 744g loaded with 20 rounds.
Length:	208mm
Variants:	DAO, 'Tactical' single-action version available.

BACKGROUND

The Glock 17, developed in the early 1980s, was something of a mould-breaker in pistol design – perhaps not surprisingly from a company which previously had concentrated on knives and other edged tools, and could approach the business of designing a pistol from a uniquely objective angle. The weapon's use of polymers (although not the first gun to do so) and modern-looking design, with squared off slide and uncluttered lines, did not appeal to everyone, but it has since proved itself to be a robust and dependable weapon and has been widely adopted by military, police forces and civilian shooters, as well as inspiring numerous look-alikes.

The basic operating principle is nothing revolutionary – the Browning-type short-recoil dropping barrel system – although using the elegant SIG-type development of this principle, where a squared-off breech locks into the ejection port.

The firing mechanism is a little more radical, however, with no hammer *per se* but instead a self-cocking striker mechanism which is cocked and released as the trigger is pulled. This is virtually a double-action only (DAO) mechanism without the external hammer, but neatly sidesteps the objections of those who do not like the DAO system.

The trigger system also incorporates two safety mechanisms: a safety spur which blocks the trigger until released by the pressure of the user's finger on the trigger blade, and a firing pin locking mechanism which is released by the movement of the trigger.

A number of variants have been produced. The original Model 17 is produced in a long, target version. The Model 18 is a selective-fire version which can fire on semi- or full-auto (certain crucial parts are not interchangeable with the Model 17). The Model 19 is a compact version of the 17. Models 20, 21 and 22 are basically the 17 in the heavier calibres of 10mm Auto, .45ACP and .40S&W. The Model 23 is the .40 equivalent of the compact Model 19.

OPERATION

The Glock 17 and derivatives use the short-recoil dropping barrel system, with the squared-off breech end of the barrel locking into the ejection port. On firing, the barrel and slide recoil together for a short distance, until a cam under the breech of the barrel engages into a spur on the frame. This draws the barrel down and out of engagement before arresting its rearward travel. The

Glock 17 Pistol.

slide continues rearwards to eject the spent case and load a fresh round into the chamber.

The firing mechanism is cocked by the pulling of the trigger, and uses an internal striker rather than an external hammer.

CONTROLS

Controls on the Glock series are minimal, and deliberately kept as simple as possible. There is no manual safety catch. A safety spur on the trigger blade locks the trigger and prevents it being pulled except by a finger-sized object pressing against the blade in the normal way. A firing pin safety mechanism locks the firing pin until the trigger is pulled to fire.

There is no external hammer, the weapon being fired by an internal striker which is first cocked and then released by the action of pulling the trigger.

The push-button magazine catch is located on the left grip, behind the trigger guard. The slide release catch is located above the left grip. A small switch-type catch which releases the slide for stripping is set into a recess in the frame above the trigger.

The Model 18 has a fire selector on the left side of the slide, just below the rearsight, to select semi-auto or full-auto fire.

SERVICE

The Glock 17 was selected by the Austrian army in the early 1980s. It was later adopted by the armies of India, Jordan, Norway, Thailand and a number of other military and police forces worldwide. It has also proved popular with civilian users.

Manufacturer:	Glock, Austria
Model:	17
Calibre:	9mm Parabellum
Action:	Double-action only (DAO) semi-automatic
Feed:	17-round magazine
Sights:	Blade and notch open sights with white U and dot to facilitate aiming in poor light
Weight:	650g
Length:	188mm
Barrel:	114mm
Variants:	Glock 17L – long-barrelled version for target shooting
	Glock 18 – selective full-automatic version with extended 33-round magazine
	Glock 19 – compact model measuring 177mm long
	Glock 20 – 10mm Auto calibre version
	Glock 21 – .45ACP
	Glock 22 – .40S&W
	Glock 23 – .40S&W compact version

Twin-stack magazines.

BACKGROUND

The H&K P7 was produced in response to a German police requirement for a new pistol, with a demanding set of specifications. The new pistol had to be capable of being fired without the need to release any form of locking or safety mechanism, but must be safe against accidental discharge – a tall order.

H&K's answer was to design an innovative grip cocking/safety mechanism. The front portion of the butt consists of a large sprung lever which cocks the mechanism when the butt is gripped in the hand. Firing the pistol then requires a relatively light single-action pull of the trigger. If the butt is released, the mechanism is de-cocked again, ensuring that the weapon cannot fire unless it is held properly in the hand.

The action is a radical departure from the norm, too. It is essentially a delayed blowback system, using the gas pressure from the fired round to hold the breech closed until the bullet has left the muzzle. A port in the barrel vents off a portion of the gas into a cylinder, where it acts on a piston which is connected to the slide. The gas pressure resists the movement of the piston, holding the slide in the closed position until the bullet has left the barrel and the gas pressure has fallen sufficiently to allow the piston to move.

The original model, now designated P7M8, has an 8-round magazine; the P7M13 has a double-stack magazine holding 13 rounds.

OPERATION

The pistol has an unusual gas piston delay system to slow down the opening of the breech after firing – see description above. A simple blowback version, the P7K3, is also available.

CONTROLS

The H&K P7 has a unique grip cocking/safety action, which ensures that the pistol cannot fire unless the grip is held firmly in the user's hand. This prevents the weapon being discharged accidentally if dropped. There is no additional manual safety catch. The magazine catch is ambidextrous – press-down levers located on both grips, behind the trigger.

SERVICE

Adopted by the German police and security forces in the 1970s.

Manufacturer:	Heckler & Koch, Germany
Model:	P7
Calibres:	9mm Parabellum, .40S&W
Action:	Delayed blowback semi-automatic
Feed:	13-round magazine
Sights:	Blade and notch open sights, rearsight adjustable for windage, foresight elements interchangeable for elevation. White marks on sights for shooting in poor light, with luminous versions available
Weight:	800g
Length:	171mm
Barrel:	105mm
Variants:	P7M8 – slimmer butt with reduced capacity 8-round magazine
	P7K3 – simple blowback version available in .22LR, 7.65mmACP and 9mm Short

Heckler & Koch P7.

BACKGROUND

The H&K USP (Universal Self-loading Pistol) looks much like other new generation pistols, such as the modern SIGs and Glocks. Like these weapons, the USP uses modern fibre reinforced polymers as well as steel in the design, reducing its weight considerably. Inside, it has an ingenious recoil damping system, which reduces the recoil felt by the user. This makes it possible to fire a series of aimed shots much more quickly – the recoil produces little more than a flick of the wrist, and the pistol is quickly brought back onto the aim.

The USP was conceived as a 'system' rather than just a pistol, and there are laser sights and a silencer designed specifically for the weapon. The silencer minimises the muzzle flash as well as reducing the sound of the pistol firing. The laser sight fits onto slots in the frame, just ahead of the trigger guard, and is switched on by the firer taking up the pressure on the trigger. It projects a red dot onto the target, making it possible to fire aimed shots without bringing the weapon up to the eye.

OPERATION

The H&K USP is a very easy weapon to shoot, thanks to its light weight (770g in 9mm calibre) and the low recoil which results from its unique recoil damping system. Combined with the laser sight, it can be fired accurately even when shooting quickly and instinctively at fleeting targets. For these reasons, it was adopted by the US Special Operations Command (SOCOM) as the Offensive Handgun Weapon System (OHWS) for US Navy Seals, US Army Special Forces, and Delta Force. This is a departure from the normal approach to handguns, which are generally seen as a 'last resort' defensive weapon rather than an 'offensive' weapon to be used in hostage rescue actions and the like, where poorly aimed shots may result in collateral damage or casualties among innocent civilians and hostages.

The USP's mechanism is based on the Browning system, but has been cleverly redesigned to incorporate the recoil damping system which buffers both the barrel and the slide in their rearward movement, preventing the recoil forces being transmitted to the frame and so

to the firer's hand. On firing, the barrel and slide are initially locked together, and are forced back as one by the recoil. As they travel rearwards, the barrel tilts down and unlocks from the slide. At the same time, the barrel catches in a sprung buffer, which arrests its rearward movement. The slide continues rearwards, while the buffer spring pushes the barrel back into its forward position. At the end of its stroke, the slide hits the buffer, compressing the buffer spring which then pushes it forward again to its initial position, collecting the next round from the magazine and feeding it into the breech ready for the next shot. In addition to saving the user from the effects of recoil, making it easier to fire aimed shots in quick succession, the recoil damping mechanism and light weight of parts such as the slide also reduce the wear on the pistol's working parts, helping to ensure a long life and reducing the need for maintenance.

CONTROLS

The USP has a modular trigger and safety system, so the user can specify the mechanism required, or adapt an existing weapon to operate with a different mechanism, simply by exchanging a few parts. The standard weapon (Variant 1 or V1) has a single/double-action trigger mechanism, and a manual safety catch/de-cocking lever on the left side. This can be switched across to the right side (V2) for a left-handed user. Variants 3 and 4 offer manual de-cocking only (no manual safety) in left-and right-handed versions.

The single/double-action trigger mechanism can be adapted to a double-action only (DAO) design, as in Variants 5–8, which provide automatic de-cocking after every shot. Variants 9 and 10 have the single/double-action trigger, but with no de-cocking facility. Thus just about every possible combination of controls can be provided, to suit the needs of very different types of user.

All the variants are equipped with automatic firing pin and hammer safeties, which disengage when the trigger is being pulled, to prevent accidental firing if the pistol is dropped. The basic open sights on the weapon consist of a square profile foresight, which aligns with a square U-shaped notch rearsight. The foresight has a

Heckler & Koch USP.

single white dot, with two white dots on the rearsight, permitting quick sight alignment in poor light. The open sights can still be used, of course, when the laser sight is fitted and in use.

For cleaning and regular maintenance, the USP is designed to be field stripped quickly and easily without the need for tools.

SERVICE

The .45 calibre USP was selected as the Offensive Handgun Weapon System of the US Special Operations Command (SOCOM), and is therefore in use by US Navy Seals, US Army special forces, and Delta Force. It has also been adopted (as the P8) by the *Bundeswehr* as a replacement for the Walther P5.

Manufacturer:	Heckler & Koch, Germany
Model:	Universal Self-loading Pistol (USP)
Calibres:	9mm x 19, .40 S&W, .45 ACP
Action:	Recoil-operated semi-automatic with re-designed Browning action
Feed:	15-round magazine (9mm), 13 rounds in .40, 12 rounds in .45
Sights:	Square foresight and square-U notch rearsight, both set in dovetails and with white dots for quick alignment in poor light
Weight:	720g (9mm), 780g (.40), 783g (.45)
Length:	194mm (9mm & .40), 200mm (.45)
Barrel:	136mm (9mm & .40), 141mm (.45)
Variants:	Ten variants are available, designated V1–V10, offering single/double-action or double-action only (DAO), controls on left or right side, manual safety catch, and manual or automatic de-cocking; all these are available in all three calibres

BACKGROUND

Developed in the 1950s, the Makarov appears to be based firmly on the Walther PP pistol, and became the standard handgun of Soviet forces and many of their allies. It is considerably smaller and lighter than the Tokarev which it largely superseded, and fires a less powerful cartridge – a 9mm round designed specially for the pistol and designated 9mm Makarov, which falls between the 9mm Parabellum and the 9mm Short in power.

Like the Walther PP, the Makarov is a simple blowback design, but it has a simpler trigger mechanism which, although easier to manufacture, results in a rather heavy double-action trigger pull. Although similar in many ways to the Walther, the Makarov's grip is chubbier and more upright than the Walther's, making it rather more awkward to shoot.

OPERATION

The Makarov is a simple blowback design, with the breech block forming part of the slide. On firing, the fixed barrel remains in position, and the slide/breech is 'blown' back by the pressure generated in the barrel. The rearwards movement of the slide extracts the empty case, cocks the hammer, and chambers the next round from the magazine on the return stroke.

The pistol has an unusual double-action trigger mechanism, and a de-cocking/safety lever. This means that it can be loaded and the hammer safely dropped on the loaded chamber. Then to fire the gun, all that is needed is to release the safety catch and pull the trigger. Subsequent shots can be fired in single-action mode, since the slide re-cocks the mechanism at each shot.

CONTROLS

Manual safety catch/de-cocking lever located at left rear of slide— up is 'safe', which moves a block into position between the hammer and firing pin, locks the slide, and releases the hammer to de-cock the mechanism. Magazine release catch is located at heel of butt. Slide release below slide on left side of frame, above trigger.

SERVICE

Widely used by armed forces of former Soviet Union and her allies.

Manufacturer:	State factories, former Soviet Union
Model:	Makarov PM
Calibre:	9mm x 18 Makarov (will not fire the almost identical 9x18mm Police round)
Action:	Blow-back double-action semi-automatic
Feed:	8-round magazine
Sights:	Blade and notch open sights
Weight:	663g
Length:	160mm
Barrel:	91mm
Variants:	There are numerous copies and derivatives of the Makarov, for instance the East German 'Pistole M'

Markarov PM.

BACKGROUND

By all normal criteria the Luger '08 should be long obsolete. And yet it has earned such a following that no book on handguns would be complete without mentioning it. Even today, it is still shot by a loyal band of enthusiasts, and collectors' editions are still produced – even though production ceased in 1945 and by modern standards it is over-engineered, over-complicated and entirely unsuitable as a military pistol. Enthusiasts point to the weapon's strength and high quality of engineering and to its innate 'pointability', giving a good natural aim as the weapon feels like an extension of the user's hand and arm.

Adopted by the German army in 1908, the Luger '08 has an elaborate 'toggle' breech mechanism. The weapon has a distinctive shape, with the magazine housed in a sharply-angled butt, an almost circular trigger guard, and an unshrouded barrel protruding from the action.

The weapon was produced in a number of variations, notably the long-barrelled 'Artillery' Luger which was issued to support troops as an alternative to a carbine. This could be fitted with a wooden shoulder stock and a helical drum or 'snail' magazine with a 32-round capacity.

OPERATION

The Luger '08's toggle breech mechanism was an ingenious design which combines strength and elegance, but has not endured and been copied in the same way as the Colt/Browning dropping barrel system. Part of the reason for this must be that the mechanism is basically an 'open' one, which does not resist the entry of dirt and water as effectively as the relatively 'closed' slide design – a vital consideration for a battle pistol.

The mechanism basically consists of an articulated breech block, hinged in the middle, which operates in a similar way to an over-centre locking catch. On firing, the two pieces of the block are in a straight line, and locked firmly against the breech end of the barrel. The block and barrel recoil together for a short distance until the toggle strikes the angled top surface of the frame, driving it upwards to unlock the mechanism. The block hinges in its centre, drawing back from the barrel to extract the fired round, while the hammer mechanism is re-cocked. At the end of the stroke the block is driven forwards again by a powerful spring, chambering the next round. As the action closes, the toggle piece moves downwards to lock up the mechanism again ready for the next shot.

Mauser Luger '08 (Parabellum).

CONTROLS

Cocking/loading is achieved by grasping the milled surfaces of the toggles and pulling them up and back against spring pressure before releasing. There is a safety catch on the left of the frame near the rear of the gun. The magazine catch is located on the left grip, just behind the trigger guard.

SERVICE

Widely used by German armed forces during both World Wars, this pistol is now considered obsolete, but has attracted a loyal following especially among collectors, and 'special editions' are still produced by Mauser.

Manufacturer:	Various German manufacturers, including Mauser-Werke AG, Germany
Model:	Parabellum M1908
Calibres:	9mm Parabellum, 7.65mm Parabellum
Action:	Toggle-locking recoil-operated semi-automatic
Feed:	8-round magazine (helical 32-round 'snail' magazine was produced for 'Artillery' variant)
Sights:	Blade and notch open sights; some models may have adjustable tangent-type rearsight mounted at breech end of barrel
Weight:	850g
Length:	223mm
Barrel:	102mm
Variants:	Long or 'Artillery' version with 200mm barrel was issued to support troops and German Navy

BACKGROUND

Produced in the early 1990s, the Mauser 80SA is basically a copy of the Browning High-Power. Its operation, controls and general appearance are identical. In fact, the weapon is such a close copy that most parts are reckoned to be interchangeable with those of a Browning GP35. Although sold under the Mauser name, the weapon is actually produced in Hungary as the FEG FP9, which is finished to a high standard in the Mauser factory.

The Model 90DA has a similar background – manufactured in Hungary as the FEG P9R, and finished by Mauser in Germany. It is basically a double-action version of the 80SA, with an oversize safety catch at the rear of the slide which also doubles as a de-cocking lever.

Manufacturer:	Mauser-Werke, Germany (produced in Hungary as FEG FP9 and finished in Mauser factory)
Model:	80SA
Calibre:	9mm Parabellum
Action:	Single-action semi-automatic
Feed:	14-round magazine
Sights:	Blade and notch open sights
Weight:	900g
Length:	203mm
Barrel:	118mm
Variants:	Model 90DA is almost identical, but has a double-action mechanism, with larger trigger guard and safety/de-cocking lever: compact version of 90DA also available

OPERATION

The Mauser 80SA's operation is identical to that of the Browning GP35 'High Power' - the archetypal lug-locking cam-dropped barrel short recoil semi-automatic (*see* the entry for that pistol for a description of the operating system).

The 90DA is little more than the 80SA with a double-action trigger and a de-cocking lever on the slide. This adds 4oz to the gun's weight, and the magazine has the capacity for 14 rounds instead of 13; in all other respects the weapons are essentially identical.

CONTROLS

Both models are cocked and loaded by inserting a full magazine, grasping the slide at the rear, drawing it back to its full extent and releasing it. Both have a magazine release catch on the left grip, just behind the trigger guard. The slide release catch is located on the left side of the frame, above the trigger.

The 80SA has a manual safety catch on the left rear of the frame, above the left grip. The 90DA has a de-cocking lever/safety on the left rear of the slide; pressing down on the lever locks the firing pin, disconnects the trigger and drops the hammer safely onto a loaded chamber.

The Enforcer is manufactured by Olympic Arms in the USA. It is a .45ACP weapon with a six-round magazine, and is based on the Colt 1911 design. It has an unusual contoured grip, with a protrusion to fit between the second and third fingers of the firing hand. The slide release and safety catch are extended for ease of operation; there is a grip safety, and the weapon has a distinctive black widow spider logo etched into the walnut grips.

Manufacturer:	Olympic Arms, USA
Model:	Enforcer
Calibre:	.45ACP
Action:	Single-action short-recoil semi-automatic
Feed:	6-round magazine
Sights:	Blade and adjustable notch open sights
Weight:	36oz
Length:	7.3ins
Barrel:	3.8ins

Olympic Arms Enforcer.

BACKGROUND

Introduced in the late 1980s, the P-85 was a distinctive-looking pistol which came relatively late into the 9mm high-capacity service pistol field. The P Series has never really achieved the success that experts feel it deserves. The weapon has, however, earned a reputation for strength and reliability. The original P-85 was superseded by a Mk II version, and then by the P-89. The range now includes Models 90, 93 and 94. In the process, the internal mechanism was revamped somewhat. The outward appearance changed, too, with the rather angular lines and stepped slide of the earlier models replaced by a smoother look. The muzzle end of the slide/barrel is rounded off to give a convex shape in the 93 and 94 models.

OPERATION

The P-85 and its successors have a short-recoil double-action semi-automatic mechanism, locked by a Browning-type dropping barrel. However, instead of the Browning's lug-locking system, the squared-off breech end of the barrel locks into the ejection port in the slide, in the same manner as the modern SIG pistols.

CONTROLS

There is an ambidextrous safety catch located at rear of slide; pressing down locks the firing pin, moves a block in-between the hammer and the firing pin, and disconnects the trigger. The slide release catch is on left of frame, above trigger.

The magazine release catch is ambidextrous and is located in the grip where it meets the trigger guard; it will release the magazine if pressed in at either side.

SERVICE

Largely civilian use.

Ruger P series KP93DAO.

Ruger P series KP94.

Manufacturer:	Sturm, Ruger & Co, USA
Model:	P-85
Calibre:	9mm Parabellum
Action:	Short-recoil double-action semi-automatic
Feed:	15-round magazine
Sights:	Blade and notch open sights, adjustable for windage, with white dot inserts for shooting at night
Weight:	907g
Length:	200mm
Barrel:	114mm
Variants:	KP89 – 9mm
	KP90 – .45ACP
	KP93 – 9mm, 'REM' finish
	KP94 – 9mm, 'REM' finish
	KP944 – .40 Auto, 'REM' finish
	Above available in manual safety version (no suffix), de-cock only (DC suffix), or double-action only (DAO suffix)

BACKGROUND

The SIG P210 was developed during the Second World War and proved to be an excellent pistol, although its cost prevented it being more widely adopted. This was one of the first pistols to use a design in which the slide runs in rails inside the frame – a system which is conducive to reliability and accuracy, and which has been adopted in a number of more recent pistol designs.

OPERATION

On firing, the slide and barrel recoil together, locked together by lugs. As they move rearwards, a cam pulls the lugs out of engagement and the barrel stops. The slide continues its rearwards movement, ejecting the spent case, re-cocking the hammer, and collecting the next round from the magazine on the return stroke, loading it into the chamber and pushing the barrel forward again to the firing position. As the barrel moves forward, the cam pushes it back into engagement with the slide, locking the two together ready for the next shot.

CONTROLS

Manual safety catch on left frame, above firer's thumb - up for 'safe', down for 'fire'. Magazine release catch located at heel of butt.

SERVICE

Adopted by the Swiss Army in 1949; also Dutch Army, and was popular with civilian shooters.

Manufacturer:	SIG, Switzerland
Model:	P210
Calibre:	9mm Parabellum
Action:	Lug-locked short-recoil single-action semi-automatic
Feed:	8-round magazine
Sights:	Blade and notch open sights, some (target) models with rearsight adjustable for windage and elevation
Weight:	900g
Length:	215mm
Barrel:	120mm
Variants:	Several variants produced, including P210-2 (sand-blasted finish and plastic grips), P210-4 (special model for West German Border Police), P210-6 (target model), P210-5 (target model with long barrel); model 49 was developed from the P210, and became the Swiss Army issue pistol

SIG P210.

BACKGROUND

The P220 was developed in the early 1970s in conjunction with Sauer of Germany, enabling the pistol to be sold outside Switzerland despite stringent firearms export restrictions in that country. The gun was based on the P210 but substantially re-designed – both updating its operation and making it easier and cheaper to manufacture. The design made use of investment castings instead of being machined from solid steel.

OPERATION

The P220 has a conventional double-action mechanism with a de-cocking lever, allowing it to be fired either single-action or double-action. When used in the double-action mode, the hammer can be safely dropped onto a loaded chamber by means of the de-cocking lever, so that the pistol can be carried in a safe condition but ready to fire by simply pulling the trigger. A firing pin safety mechanism locks the firing pin so that an accidental blow to the hammer/pin will not fire the gun – the pin is only released when the trigger is fully pulled.

The mechanism operates on the Colt/Browning-type short-recoil principle, but with a modified locking mechanism. On firing, the slide and barrel are locked by the squared-off chamber part of the barrel, which engages into the rectangular ejection port on the top of the frame. The slide and barrel recoil a short distance together before a cam beneath the barrel engages in the frame, dropping the barrel out of engagement and arresting its travel. The slide continues rearwards to eject the spent case, re-cock the hammer mechanism, and load the next round on the return stroke, before pushing the barrel back into its locked position ready to fire again.

CONTROLS

De-cocking lever located on left of frame, just behind and above the trigger. Just behind the de-cocking lever is the slide lock, which is used to release the slide when stripping the weapon. Slide lock catch located on left of frame, above trigger. Magazine release catch on heel of butt in 9mm, 7.65 and .38 versions; on left grip behind trigger on .45.

SERVICE

In service with the Swiss Army as Pistole 75, and adopted by the Japanese Army, and by numerous special forces and police around the world.

Manufacturer:	SIG-Sauer, Switzerland/Germany
Model:	P220
Calibres:	9mm Parabellum, 7.65mm Parabellum, .45ACP, .38 Super
Action:	Short-recoil double-action semi-automatic
Feed:	9-round magazine (7 in .45)
Sights:	Blade and square notch with white dot system for shooting in poor light. Rearsight can be drifted in dovetail for windage; interchangeable rearsights available for elevation adjustment
Weight:	750g
Length:	198mm
Barrel:	112mm
Variants:	P225, P226, P228 and P229 were developed from the P220 - see separate entries

SIG P220 9mm.

SIG P220 .45.

61

BACKGROUND

The P225 was developed from the P220 as a more compact version for police work where a smaller, concealable weapon was required. The P220's dimensions were reduced, and some improvements made to the firing pin safety mechanism. It proved successful, and was adopted by Swiss and German police, the US Secret Service and various special forces.

OPERATION

Although of smaller overall dimensions, the operating system of the P225 is identical to the P220. As in that weapon, the slide and barrel are locked by the squared-off chamber part of the barrel, which engages into the rectangular ejection port on the top of the frame. See P220 for description of operating system.

CONTROLS

The de-cocking lever is located on the left of the frame, at the top of the grip, where it falls just above the user's thumb. Pushing this lever down will drop the hammer safely onto a loaded chamber. An automatic firing pin safety mechanism locks the firing pin except when the trigger is pulled fully back to fire. The slide lock catch is located on the left of the frame, above the trigger.

SERVICE

Swiss and German police forces, US Secret Service, and various special forces etc.

Manufacturer:	SIG-Sauer, Switzerland/Germany
Model:	P225
Calibre:	9mm Parabellum
Action:	Short-recoil double-action semi-automatic
Feed:	8-round magazine
Sights:	Blade and notch open sights
Weight:	740g
Length:	180mm
Barrel:	98mm
Variants:	P226 is development of P225 (see separate entry)

BACKGROUND

The P226 was developed from the P225 as a contender in the US Army's trials for a new combat pistol. To meet the US Army criteria, the magazine capacity was increased from 8 rounds to 15 (by using a double stack magazine, which in turn means a fatter grip). The magazine release was also moved to fall close to the thumb of the firing hand, behind the trigger guard, and was made ambidextrous. The P226 was highly rated in the trials, but was beaten on price by the Beretta 92F. However, it has been adopted by a number of police and military forces worldwide.

OPERATION

The operating system of the P226 is identical to the P220/P225. As in those weapons, the slide and barrel are locked by the squared-off chamber part of the barrel, which engages into the rectangular ejection port on the top of the frame. See P220 for description of operating system.

CONTROLS

De-cocking lever at top of left grip, behind and above trigger. Note that the catch behind this is the slide release, used when stripping the weapon. As in P220/P225, there is an automatic firing pin safety, which locks the firing pin until the trigger is pulled to fire the weapon.

The ambidextrous magazine release catch is located in grips behind the trigger guard, where it can be operated by the thumb of the firing hand, whether the pistol is fired from the left or right hand. The slide lock catch is located on the left of the frame, above the trigger.

SERVICE

Adopted by several military and police forces around the world.

Manufacturer:	SIG-Sauer, Switzerland/Germany
Model:	P226
Calibre:	9mm Parabellum
Action:	Short-recoil double-action semi-automatic
Feed:	15-round magazine
Sights:	Blade and notch open sights
Weight:	750g
Length:	196mm
Barrel:	112mm

SIG P226.

BACKGROUND

Based firmly on the highly successful P220 and its derivatives, the P228 and P229 combine a compact design with a large magazine capacity, making it particularly suitable for work such as close protection where concealability is an issue, but a high level of firepower may be called for. The P228 is in the ubiquitous 9mm Parabellum calibre, while the P229 also offers the .40S&W favoured by some users, particularly in the United States.

OPERATION

The operating system of the P228 and P229 is identical to the P220/P225/P226. As in those weapons, the slide and barrel are locked by the squared-off chamber part of the barrel, which engages into the rectangular ejection port on the top of the frame. See P220 for description of operating system.

CONTROLS

Controls on the P228/P229 are broadly the same as on the other P220 series pistols. De-cocking lever at top of left grip, behind and above trigger. Slide release catch located behind de-cocking lever. Automatic firing pin safety, which locks the firing pin until the trigger is pulled to fire the weapon. Slide lock catch located on left of frame, above trigger.

The magazine release catch is located in the grip behind the trigger guard. It is not ambidextrous in the true sense, since it is only on one side, but it can be swapped easily from one side to the other to suit left-or right-handed users.

SERVICE

Widely used by security forces and for close protection worldwide.

SIG P228 9mm.

SIG P229 9mm US version.

SIG P229 .40.

Manufacturer:	SIG-Sauer, Switzerland/Germany
Model:	P228/P229
Calibres:	9mm Parabellum (P228), .40S&W (P229)
Action:	Short-recoil double-action semi-automatic
Feed:	13-round magazine in 9mm, 12 rounds in .40
Sights:	Blade and notch open sights, both foresight and rearsight set in dovetails
Weight:	830g (P228), 865g (.40)
Length:	180mm
Barrel:	98mm
Variants:	P228SL and P229SL have stainless steel slide

BACKGROUND

The SIG P230 is a totally different weapon to the P220 series. Like the Walther PP, which it resembles in size and outline, it is a blowback pocket pistol firing the smaller 9mm Short or 7.65mm ACP calibres. It offers single or double-action, with a de-cocking lever so that the hammer can be dropped safely onto a loaded chamber. The magazine has a shelf at the foot which effectively extends the rather small butt of the pistol, making it easier to control in use.

The P230 has found favour with several Swiss police units, as well as a good many police forces in the United States.

OPERATION

The P230 uses the blowback principle rather than the mechanically more complex short-recoil mechanism found in the P220 series weapons. When the pistol is fired, the gas pressure generated simply blows the slide/breech block rearwards away from the fixed barrel. The empty case is drawn from the chamber by the extractor attached to the slide. As the slide travels rearwards, the empty case strikes the ejector and is thrown out through the ejection port in the right hand side of the slide. The slide rides over the hammer, re-cocking the mechanism, before reaching the end of its travel, to be thrown forwards again by the slide spring, collecting the next round from the magazine and loading it into the breech.

CONTROLS

Controls are similar to the P220 series. There is a de-cocking lever on the left side of the frame, near the top of the grip, where it can be operated by the thumb of the firing hand. This lever drops the hammer safely onto a loaded chamber. There is no manual safety; an automatic firing pin safety device, similar to that in the P220 series, locks the firing pin until the trigger is pulled to fire the weapon.

SERVICE

Numerous Swiss and US police forces.

Manufacturer:	SIG-Sauer, Switzerland/Germany
Model:	P230
Calibre:	9mm Short, 7.65mm ACP
Action:	Blowback double-action semi-automatic
Feed:	7-round magazine (8 in 7.65mm)
Sights:	Blade and notch open sights
Weight:	460g
Length:	168mm
Barrel:	92mm

SIG P230.

BACKGROUND

The Sigma was S&W's answer to the Glock – indeed, it could easily be mistaken for a Glock at first sight, as it shares many features as well as an overall 'look' and the widespread use of polymer materials in the gun's construction. S&W have added a few extra features of their own, such as an unusual hinged trigger blade. The pistol is generally regarded as reliable and accurate, although the trigger pull can take some getting used to.

OPERATION

Operation of the S&W Sigma is very similar to the Glock 17 – see entry for that weapon for description of operating system.

CONTROLS

Automatic safety mechanism. Ambidextrous magazine release catch on grip, at rear of trigger guard.

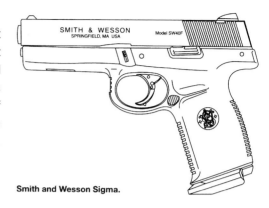

Smith and Wesson Sigma.

Manufacturer:	Smith & Wesson, USA
Model:	Sigma
Calibre:	9mm
Action:	Short-recoil double-action semi-automatic
Feed:	17-round magazine
Sights:	Blade and notch open sights with 3-dot system for rapid alignment
Weight:	26.36oz
Length:	190mm
Barrel:	114mm

BACKGROUND

These pistols are known collectively as Smith & Wesson's 'Third Generation' pistols. Designed in conjunction with US law enforcement agencies, they all feature the Browning-type dropping-barrel recoil-operated semi-automatic system, and fixed barrel bushings for improved accuracy. Other features include a bevelled magazine housing for speedier reloading, three-dot sights, and a triple safety mechanism with an ambidextrous manual safety catch, automatic firing pin safety mechanism and a magazine safety. Trigger guards are contoured to facilitate a two-handed grip, and are over-sized to accommodate a gloved hand.

The system of model numbers appears complicated at first, but follows a logical pattern. The first two digits indicate the version and calibre – the 4043 is a .40 calibre weapon, for instance, while a 6904 is a 9mm Parabellum, the 6 indicating that it is a compact version. The last two digits indicate the materials and finish – 04 meaning that the pistol has a alloy frame, carbon steel slide and stainless steel barrel, for instance.

OPERATION

The S&W 'Third Generation' pistols all operate on the Browning-type short-recoil dropping-barrel principle, in which the barrel is locked to the slide at the moment of firing, and the two travel rearwards together for a short distance before the barrel is cammed downwards to release the slide, allowing it to continue rearwards to eject the spent case, cock the action again, and load a fresh round on the return stroke.

The various models offer slightly different mechanisms, with some models featuring a de-cocking lever so the weapon may be carried with the hammer down on a loaded chamber, while others are double-action only (DAO).

CONTROLS

Ambidextrous safety catch/de-cocking lever (depending on model) located at rear of slide. Slide release catch on left of frame, above trigger. Magazine catch on left grip, at junction with trigger guard.

SERVICE

Used by some US law enforcement agencies and by some civilian target shooters, but has yet to be taken into military service.

Manufacturer:	Smith & Wesson, USA
Model:	'Third Generation' pistols – 4-digit model numbers eg 3904, 5906, 4043, etc
Calibres:	9mm Parabellum, 10mm Auto, .40S&W, .45ACP
Action:	Browning-type dropping-barrel short-recoil double-action (or DAO) semi-automatic
Feed:	Box magazine, capacity 8–14 rounds depending on model/calibre
Sights:	Blade and notch open sights with three-dot system for rapid alignment in all lighting conditions
Weight:	666g–1,020g, depending on model/calibre
Length:	175mm (6900 series)–216mm (4500 series)
Barrel:	89mm (6900 series)–127mm (4500 series)
Variants:	3900 series – 9mm first model, with 8-round magazine (incl 3913 - special ladies' version designated 'Ladysmith')
	5900 series – 9mm later model, with high-capacity 14-round magazine
	6900 series – 9mm compact version, with 12-round magazine
	4000 series – .40 calibre
	4500 series – .45 calibre
	1076 – 10mm calibre model developed for the FBI

Smith and Wesson Model 4910.

BACKGROUND

The Firestar is one of the smallest 9mm Parabellum pistols and is manufactured by Star of Spain, a long-established gunmaker with a history of supplying the Spanish armed forces. An all-steel pistol, it follows the Browning short-recoil dropping-barrel system and has controls laid out in the same way as the Colt 1911.

OPERATION

Operating on the Colt/Browning dropping barrel system, the Firestar has three locking lugs on the upper surface of the barrel which lock into the slide. A shaped cam in the breech lump drops the barrel after a short rearwards movement on firing, unlocking the lugs and freeing the slide to complete its stroke. The barrel is tapered at the muzzle so that it locks in position when closed, doing away with the need for a barrel bushing. The slide runs on rails inside the frame. Operation is single-action only.

CONTROLS

The Firestar has an ambidextrous manual safety catch located in the rear of the frame at the top of the grips. There is also an automatic firing pin safety mechanism. The magazine release button is located in the left grip, at the rear of the trigger guard. A magazine safety mechanism (which prevents the pistol being fired without a magazine in position) tends to make the magazine 'hang up', so it does not drop away freely when the release catch is pressed.

Manufacturer:	Star, Spain
Model:	Firestar
Calibre:	9mm Parabellum
Action:	Single-action Browning-type short-recoil semi-automatic
Feed:	7-round magazine
Sights:	Fixed blade and notch open sights with three-dot system
Weight:	798g
Length:	163mm
Barrel:	86mm
Variants:	Firestar Plus – high-capacity version with 13-round magazine

BACKGROUND

The Star Model 30 was introduced in 1988 as an updated version of the Model 28. It is a double-action 9mm semi-automatic, operating on the Browning dropping-barrel principle. Unusually, the slide runs on rails on the inside of the frame – something normally associated with SIG pistols. This keeps the slide and barrel more firmly in alignment through its travel, and is generally thought to lead to improved accuracy. The Model 30 has been adopted by the Spanish police force. There is a smaller version with a light alloy frame, the Model 30PK.

OPERATION

The Model 30 follows the Browning dropping-barrel system, with two ribs on the upper surface of the barrel which mate into corresponding notches in the inner surface of the slide. On firing, the slide and barrel are locked together as they travel rearwards for a short distance, until a cam forces the barrel down, disengaging the ribs so that the slide can continue rearwards to extract and eject the fired case, before returning under spring pressure to chamber the next round and close the breech ready for the next shot.

CONTROLS

The Model 30 has an unusual safety mechanism which locks the firing pin and retracts it into the slide, where it cannot be struck by the hammer. The safety does not, however, affect the trigger and hammer mechanism, so the trigger can be pulled and the weapon 'dry fired' with the safety catch applied. There is also a magazine safety, which prevents the weapon firing when there is no magazine in place. The magazine safety tends to make magazines 'hang up' when released, so the manufacturers have designed the mechanism so it can be removed if required.

SERVICE

Spanish police and armed forces; also Peru.

Manufacturer:	Star, Spain
Model:	Model 30M
Calibre:	9mm Parabellum
Action:	Browning-type short-recoil semi-automatic
Feed:	15-round magazine
Sights:	Blade and notch open sights, adjustable for windage, with luminous three-dot system
Weight:	1,140g
Length:	205mm
Barrel:	120mm
Variants:	Model 30PK - compact version with light alloy frame: length 193mm, weight 860g

BACKGROUND

The Israeli Desert Eagle was developed as a long-range sporting pistol – primarily for long-range target shooting and the sport of silhouette target shooting which is popular in the United States. The original Desert Eagle fired the powerful .357 Magnum revolver cartridge, but later models have been developed for even more powerful ammunition – .44 Magnum, .41 Action Express, and now even the massive .50 Action Express.

Although its weight and bulk limit the Desert Eagle's usefulness as a military pistol, it has been adopted by some special forces who perceive a need for a high-powered, long-range handgun for certain types of operation. In the larger calibres especially, the Desert Eagle is quite a handful, both in its physical size and its recoil, and requires considerable skill and training to shoot accurately at the long ranges which it is theoretically capable of.

OPERATION

The Desert Eagle uses a rotating bolt to lock the breech. At the moment of firing, the bolt is locked against the barrel. Some of the gas produced by the cartridge is vented from the barrel into a cylinder in the frame below the barrel. To achieve the necessary delay, this gas passes forwards through a channel beneath the barrel. The gas acts on a piston which pushes the slide rearwards. A cam rotates the bolt to unlock it before it is drawn back to extract and eject the spent case. The slide continues rearwards, re-cocking the hammer, before returning to load the next round and lock up the breech again ready for the next shot.

CONTROLS

Ambidextrous safety catch at rear of slide locks firing pin and breaks the connection between trigger and hammer mechanism. Magazine catch on grip, behind trigger guard. Slide release catch at top of left grip.

SERVICE

Originally intended for civilian target shooting, the Desert Eagle has been adopted by a small number of security forces for its long range capabilities and high stopping power.

Manufacturer:	Ta'as Israel Industries, Israel
Model:	Desert Eagle
Calibres:	.357 Magnum, .44 Magnum, .41AE, .50AE
Action:	Delayed gas piston operated semi-automatic
Feed:	9-round magazine
Sights:	Blade and notch open sights, adjustable target sights available. Upper surface of barrel grooved to accept telescopic sights
Weight:	1,760g
Length:	260mm
Barrel:	152mm
Variants:	355mm long target barrel also available

Desert Eagle.

BACKGROUND

Based firmly on the CZ75, the Jericho is produced by what used to be Israel Military Industries and now goes by the name of Ta'as Israel Industries. The Jericho is styled on the company's massive Desert Eagle, but is of more conventional dimensions and intended for regular military and security use. It makes use of the Browning-type dropping barrel system, but has the slide running on rails inside the frame: a design which gives good support to the slide and contributes to accuracy.

The Jericho was originally offered as a 'convertible' pistol, with interchangeable parts enabling it to fire either the 9mm Parabellum or the .41 Action Express (the two cartridges have the same rim dimensions). Later models are convertible from 9mm to .40 Smith & Wesson.

OPERATION

The Jericho is a recoil-operated semi-automatic, operating on the Browning principle with a lug-locked barrel that is dropped by a cam arrangement to release it from the slide on firing. The working parts bear a close resemblance to the CZ75, on which the Jericho was based.

CONTROLS

Two full-size models are available, the F with an ambidextrous safety on the frame, and the R with a slide mounted safety/de-cocking lever. The safety also locks the firing pin and disconnects the trigger from the hammer mechanism. Magazine release is a push button on the left grip, at the rear of the trigger guard. The slide release catch is located on the left side of the frame, above the trigger.

Manufacturer:	Ta'as Israel Industries, Israel
Model:	Jericho 941
Calibres:	9mm Parabellum, .41AE, .40S&W
Action:	Recoil-operated semi-automatic
Feed:	16-round magazine in 9mm, 12 rounds in .40, 11 rounds in .41
Sights:	Blade and notch open sights, adjustable for windage, with Tritium inserts for night use
Weight:	1,100g
Length:	207mm
Barrel:	110mm
Variants:	F model has safety catch on the frame, R model has de-cocking lever on the slide. FS is 'short' model; FB is 'compact'

Jericho.

BACKGROUND

The Tanfoglio TA90 started as a straightforward copy of the CZ75 (qv) built under licence, but the manufacturers have made various alterations over the years and now offer a range of guns that are distinct from the CZ75. The basic model, the TA90, is of similar dimensions to the CZ75. It uses the same Browning-type short-recoil dropping-barrel system, with a double-action mechanism.

Variations include weapons chambered for 7.65mm Parabellum, 9mm x18 and 9mm x21, and there is a compact 9mm Parabellum version. The company also produce variants for civilian target shooting.

OPERATION

The TA90 is a double-action semi-automatic, firing from a locked breech using the Browning dropping-barrel system – as in the CZ75. On firing, the barrel and slide recoil together for a short distance before a cam arrangement forces the barrel down and out of engagement with the slide.

The variants are mechanically the same as the TA90.

CONTROLS

The standard model has a manual safety catch/de-cocker on the left of the slide. This locks the firing pin and drops the hammer safely on a loaded chamber. 'Combat' models have a manual safety on the left side of the frame which locks the trigger but does not de-cock the mechanism. An automatic firing pin safety mechanism also locks the firing pin until the trigger is fully pulled. The magazine catch is located on the left grip behind the trigger guard. The slide release catch is located on the left the of frame above the trigger.

Manufacturer:	Tanfoglio, Italy
Model:	TA90
Calibres:	9mm Parabellum (variants in other calibres)
Action:	Double-action Browning-type short-recoil semi-automatic
Feed:	15-round magazine
Sights:	Blade and notch open sights, adjustable for windage. Fully adjustable sights on target models
Weight:	1,015g
Length:	202mm
Barrel:	120mm
Variants:	TA90 available in 'Combat' version and in various finishes
	GT30 – 7.65mm Parabellum
	TA18 – 9mm x18
	GT21 – 9mm x21
	'Baby' 9mm – 9mm Parabellum compact version: length 175mm, weight 850g

Tanfoglio TA90.

BACKGROUND

The PT92 AF is basically Taurus' copy of the Beretta 92, in 9mm Parabellum. It is also available as the PT99 AF version with adjustable sights. Although basically the same as the Beretta, the PT92/99 offers the additional feature of a frame-mounted safety catch/de-cocking lever which makes it possible to fire the first shot in the conventional double-action mode, or in the cocked-and-locked mode.

The guns are available in a choice of finishes, with blued barrel/slide or stainless steel on an alloy frame. There are also compact versions, such as the PT92 C, and the PT908 with a slim butt and a reduced capacity of eight rounds. Models 100 and 101 are essentially the same gun in .40S&W calibre.

OPERATION

The operating system is the same as in the Beretta 92: the short-recoil principle, with a wedge-shaped locking block to lock the barrel in place when the action is closed. Refer to the entry for the Beretta 92 for more details.

CONTROLS

The ambidextrous safety catch/de-cocking lever is at the rear of the frame below the slide. In the 'safe' position (up), this locks the hammer in either position - cocked or uncocked. Pressing the lever down past the 'fire' position drops the hammer safely onto a loaded chamber. There is also an automatic firing pin safety, which locks the firing pin until the trigger is correctly pulled through. The magazine release catch is located on the left grip behind the trigger guard. The slide release lever is on the left side of the frame, above the trigger.

SERVICE

Its relatively low price makes the Taurus range a popular alternative to the Beretta with civilian shooters.

Manufacturer:	Taurus, Brazil
Model:	PT92 and PT99
Calibres:	9mm Parabellum (Model PT100 and PT101 in .40S&W)
Action:	Double-action wedge-locked short-recoil semi-automatic
Feed:	15-round magazine
Sights:	Fixed blade and notch open sights; adjustable version on PT99
Weight:	949g
Length:	215mm
Barrel:	124mm
Variants:	A number of versions of the basic pistol are available, including compact and target variants. The PT908 is a slimmer version with 9-round magazine.

Taurus PT92/PT99AF.

BACKGROUND

The Tokarev became the standard Warsaw Pact pistol after the Second World War, and was produced in large numbers in the former Soviet Union as well as in countries such as China and Yugoslavia. It appears to have been based on the M1911 Colt, and uses a Browning-type dropping-barrel short-recoil operating system. However, various aspects of the Colt design were changed, including the safety system. It also has the hammer/mainspring in the form of a removable assembly in the rear of the butt. This pistol is now considered obsolete; production is thought to have ceased in the Soviet Union in the mid-1950s. However, production continued for longer in other parts of the world, and the sheer number of weapons produced means that the pistol is still encountered from time to time, particularly in the hands of terrorist/guerrilla groups which at one time received Communist support.

OPERATION

Although the locking system is redesigned, the Tokarev still uses the Colt/Browning-type locking mechanism to achieve a short-recoil semi-automatic action. The barrel is locked to the slide at the time of firing, and the two travel together rearwards for a short distance before they are unlocked and the barrel halts, the slide continuing its cycle before returning to chamber the next round and push the barrel back into the firing position.

CONTROLS

The Tokarev has no manual safety catch, although there is a half-cock position on the hammer. The slide catch is located on the left of the frame, above the trigger. The magazine release catch is at the heel of the butt.

SERVICE

Former Soviet Union/Warsaw Pact armed forces; may still appear today in the hands of guerrilla/terrorist forces.

Manufacturer:	State factories of former Soviet Union and Warsaw Pact countries
Model:	Tokarev TT-33
Calibre:	7.62mm x 25 Pistol
Action:	Browning-type short-recoil single-action semi-automatic
Feed:	8-round magazine
Sights:	Blade and notch open sights
Weight:	840g
Length:	196mm
Barrel:	116mm
Variants:	Much copied in Warsaw Pact countries

Tokarev TT-33.

BACKGROUND

The Uzi is totally different to the conventional pistols which predominate in this section. Its square shape and reliance on sheet steel construction mark it out as a pistol developed from a purely functional military sub-machine gun. In fact it is a semi-automatic version of the well-known Uzi SMG, shortened and lightened, and with a mechanism that will not fire on fully automatic. Although it lacks the cosmetic appeal of many other pistols, it does offer certain advantages, not least that of familiarity to those who have trained on the SMG version. Its relatively heavy weight and large size help to control the recoil, making it easier to fire a number of aimed shots in quick succession. In certain circumstances, its intimidating appearance could also be an advantage.

Manufacturer:	Ta'as Israel Industries, Israel
Model:	Uzi pistol
Calibres:	9mm Parabellum (Model 45 in .45ACP)
Action:	Closed-breech blowback semi-automatic
Feed:	20-round magazine (will also accept 25-round and 32-round SMG magazines)
Sights:	Blade and notch open sights protected by folded steel channels. Fully adjustable, with white marks to aid alignment in poor light
Weight:	1,650g
Length:	240mm
Barrel:	115mm
Variants:	Fully automatic SMG version (see appropriate section of this book)

OPERATION

The Uzi pistol operates on a closed-breech blowback system, similar to the Uzi sub-machine gun: there is no lock-up mechanism to hold the breech closed, simply the inertia of the bolt. The pistol's mechanism is altered so that it will fire on semi-automatic only, and cannot be readily converted back to fully automatic. The firing pin in the SMG is simply a protrusion in the breech block, which fires the round as the breech closes. In the pistol, the firing pin is a separate part. The breech is closed onto a chambered round to make the weapon ready to fire, but it will not fire until the trigger is pulled and the firing pin falls onto the cartridge primer.

CONTROLS

Cocking handle runs in channel on upper surface of receiver; pull back to open the breech/cock the mechanism, release to allow bolt to close under spring pressure. Safety catch at top of left grip – forward for 'fire', back for 'safe'. Magazine release catch at foot of left grip.

SERVICE

Developed largely for civilian use, but with some military applications.

BACKGROUND

The first locked-breech pistol to use a double-action mechanism, the P38 replaced the Luger 08 as the German Army's official pistol in 1938. It was re-adopted when the *Bundeswehr* re-formed in the 1950s. The P38 has a protruding barrel reminiscent of the Luger and a cut-away slide which leaves a section of the top of the barrel exposed.

OPERATION

The barrel and slide are locked together by a wedge. As the slide and barrel recoil, this wedge is cammed downwards to release the slide, which then continues rearwards to eject the spent case, cock the hammer and load the next round on the return stroke – pushing the barrel forward so that the wedge raises it and locks it in position again ready to fire the next shot.

Walter P38.

CONTROLS

Safety catch on left rear of slide, which doubles as de-cocking lever. Magazine catch at heel of butt.

SERVICE

German Army from 1938; also armed forces of Norway, Chile, Portugal, *et al.*

Cutaway drawing showing operation of Walther P38.

Manufacturer:	Carl Walther, Germany
Model:	P38
Calibre:	9mm Parabellum
Action:	Short-recoil double-action semi-automatic
Feed:	8-round magazine
Sights:	Blade and notch open sights
Weight:	960g
Length:	213mm
Barrel:	127mm
Variants:	P38K shortened version developed in mid-1970s. Current version is designated Walther P1

BACKGROUND

In the 1970s the German police were looking for a new pistol, and a re-design of the P38 provided the answer in the shape of the P5. The requirement was for a double-action design with enhanced safety features, and the minimum of preparation before the weapon could be brought to bear on a target.

OPERATION

The P5 uses the same breech locking and trigger mechanism as the P38, but has a short barrel encased within the slide (as opposed to the P38's protruding barrel and cut-away slide). Its operation is basically that of a short-recoil semi-automatic. As in the P38, the barrel and slide are locked together by a wedge. As the slide and barrel recoil, this wedge is cammed downwards to release the slide, which then continues rearwards to eject the spent case, cock the hammer and load the next round on the return stroke, pushing the barrel forward so that the wedge raises it and locks it in position again ready to fire the next shot.

CONTROLS

To address the safety requirements of the German police at the time, the P5 has an ingenious firing pin safety mechanism to prevent it firing unless the trigger is fully pulled. The firing pin normally lies in a dropped position, with its rearmost end aligned with a recess in the hammer. Even if the hammer is pulled back and released, or receives a sharp blow to the spur, the hammer does not strike the end of the firing pin. When the trigger is pulled, however, a lever raises the firing pin to line up with the striking surface of the hammer, and the pistol can fire.

SERVICE

German police, Netherlands police, Portuguese and other armed forces.

Manufacturer:	Carl Walther, Germany
Model:	P5
Calibre:	9mm Parabellum
Action:	Short-recoil double-action semi-automatic
Feed:	8-round magazine
Sights:	Blade and notch open sights, with rearsight adjustable for windage
Weight:	795g
Length:	180mm
Barrel:	90mm
Variants:	P5 Compact introduced in 1988. P1A1 has additional cross-bolt safety catch

Walther P5.

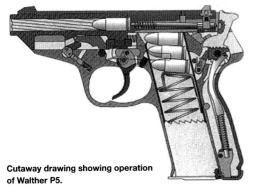

Cutaway drawing showing operation of Walther P5.

BACKGROUND

With the P88 Walther moved away from the P38 design which had also formed the basis of their P5. Launched in 1988, the P88 uses the Browning-type tilt-barrel system to lock the action, which is simpler and cheaper to manufacture. This was not a complete re-design, however. The P88 retains the P38/P5 double-action trigger mechanism, and the firing pin safety system is the same as that used in the P5, with the pin held out of alignment with the hammer until the trigger is fully pulled.

This pistol also has a much greater capacity than its predecessors, using a double-stack magazine to provide a capacity of 15 rounds. The breech end of the barrel is squared-off in cross-section, and is visible through the rectangular ejection port in the top of the slide when the action is closed.

OPERATION

The P88 uses the Colt/Browning-type dropping barrel system to lock the mechanism, rather than the wedge-lock method employed in its predecessors, the P38 and P5. However, instead of a series of lugs and grooves (as used in the Colt and Browning mechanisms), the locking of slide to action is achieved by the squared-off breech end of the barrel locking into the rectangular ejection port in the top of the slide. The likely reason for this is that it is a cheaper system to manufacture, and does not require such close tolerances to achieve accuracy and reliability.

CONTROLS

The P88 has completely ambidextrous controls: the de-cocking/slide release lever and magazine release catch are duplicated on the right side of the frame.

Manufacturer:	Carl Walther, Germany
Model:	P88
Calibre:	9mm Parabellum
Action:	Short-recoil double-action Browning-type semi-automatic
Feed:	15-round magazine
Sights:	Blade and notch open sights, with rearsight adjustable for windage
Weight:	900g
Length:	187mm
Barrel:	102mm
Variants:	Compact version with 14-round capacity

Walther P88.

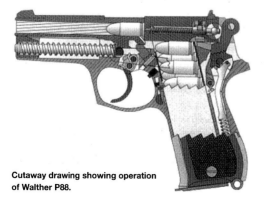

Cutaway drawing showing operation of Walther P88.

BACKGROUND

Introduced in 1929 as a police pistol, the Walther PP was one of the first designs to offer a true double-action mechanism in a semi-automatic pistol. It has a simple blowback mechanism and first appeared in 7.65mm calibre. Other calibres were offered later, including .22LR, 6.35mm and 9mm Short.

Another innovative feature at the time was the PP's loaded chamber indicator. This takes the form of a spring-loaded pin which is pushed back by the rim of the case in the chamber so that the end protrudes from the rear of the slide above the hammer. This gives an instant visual check that the weapon is loaded, and can also be felt in the dark.

The PP was intended mainly to be carried in a holster by police officers, and was widely adopted by police forces in the 1930s. However, it also became popular with civilians and was used extensively by the German military during The Second World War. The weapon was produced by Manurhin of France for a number of years, and has been widely copied by manufacturers worldwide, especially after the expiry of Walther's various patents on the design.

The Walther PPK, which appeared in 1931, is basically a scaled-down version of the PP, intended for undercover use by plain-clothes police. Although the mechanical operation is basically the same, the frame and mechanism were completely re-designed. Its small size makes it relatively easy to conceal, but the butt is rather too small for a firm hold, so the magazine was fitted with an extension to improve the grip. In addition to being widely adopted by uniformed and plain clothes police, the PPK proved popular with off-duty police in the USA, where a special version, the PPK/S, was sold to circumvent the size restrictions laid down in the Gun Control Act of 1968. The PPK achieved some notoriety as the chosen weapon of the fictional spy 'James Bond' in the books by Ian Fleming.

Operation

The Walther PP operates on the straight blowback principle – the breech/slide is thrown back by the force of gas pressure generated when the pistol is fired. The

Walther PP

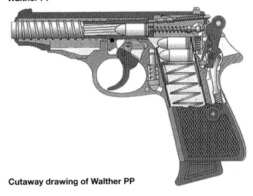

Cutaway drawing of Walther PP

Walther PPK.

Cutaway drawing of Walther PPK.

only delay comes from the inertia of the slide/breech assembly. The barrel remains fixed in position as the slide moves rearwards. An extractor claw on the slide draws the fired case from the chamber, and the case is ejected out through the ejection port in the slide when it hits the ejector spur. The slide continues rearwards to ride over the hammer and re-cock the mechanism before reaching the end of its stroke and being driven forwards again by spring pressure. As it moves forwards, it collects the next round from the magazine, and loads it into the now empty chamber.

The pistol was one of the first semi-automatics to offer a double-action mechanism. This has the advantage for police work that it can be carried with a round loaded in the chamber, but with the hammer down; the pistol can then be fired by simply releasing the safety catch and pulling the trigger, without the need to cock the hammer manually as you would with a single-action mechanism. The safety catch locks the firing pin so that dropping or knocking the pistol will not fire the round in the chamber.

To load the pistol, insert a full magazine, pull back the slide and release to cock the mechanism and load a round into the chamber. Then move the safety catch/de-cocker down to lock the firing pin and drop the hammer safely onto the live round. The pistol can then be carried loaded and with the safety 'on'. To fire, all that is required is to push the safety 'off' (up) and pull the trigger. The mechanism re-cocks on firing, so subsequent shots can be fired in single-action mode.

In comparison with other pistols available in the 1930s, this made the PP faster to bring into action when required; this, combined with its convenient size and streamlined shape, goes a long way to explaining its popularity with police and other users.

The PPK, although substantially re-designed, offers the same mechanical operation in an even smaller and more concealable package.

CONTROLS

Safety catch located on left rear of slide. Up is 'fire', down is 'safe' and locks the firing pin and de-cocks the mechanism by dropping the hammer safely onto a loaded chamber. Loaded chamber indicator protrudes from rear of slide when a round is loaded in the chamber – this can be seen and felt. Magazine release catch

located at top of butt, in front of left grip where it can be operated by the thumb of the firing hand.

Controls are in the same positions on the PPK, and serve the same functions, but are correspondingly smaller.

SERVICE

Both widely adopted by police forces, and still in service today with some undercover police and close protection teams.

Manufacturer:	Carl Walther, Germany
Model:	PP
Calibres:	.22LR, 6.35mm, 7.65mm, 9mm Short
Action:	Double-action blowback semi-automatic
Feed:	8-round magazine
Sights:	Fixed blade and notch open sights
Weight:	710g
Length:	162mm
Barrel:	85mm
Variants:	Also manufactured by Manurhin of France for a period after WW2, and has been widely copied

Model:	PPK
Calibres:	6.35mm, 7.65mm, 9mm Short
Action:	Double-action blowback semi-automatic
Feed:	7-round magazine
Sights:	Fixed blade and notch open sights
Weight:	580g
Length:	148mm
Barrel:	80mm
Variants:	Also manufactured by Manurhin of France in the 1940s/1950s. PPK S variant designed to circumvent US gun control laws of the late 1960s

REVOLVERS

The trend in military weapons has been away from revolvers towards the high-capacity 9mm semi-automatics, but there is still a demand for the revolver among police forces, civilian target shooters and, where local laws permit, for self-protection. The revolver is often portrayed as more robust and reliable than a semi-automatic, and less prone to malfunction – although modern semi-automatic designs are narrowing the gap in this area.

Capacities for revolvers are considerably lower than for most semi-automatics, with a six-round cylinder being the norm, but on the other side of the coin many revolvers are chambered for powerful 'man-stopping' rounds which can be relied on to stop an assailant with a single well-placed shot – something that cannot be said of the 9mm Parabellum round most common in semi-automatics. Certainly a compact double-action revolver firing a powerful cartridge provides an awesome level of firepower in a readily concealable package that can be brought quickly into action when required.

Revolvers generally have changed little over the past 100 years or so. Grips may have evolved to fill the shooter's hand better and modern production methods may make use of computer-controlled machinery, but essentially the double-action revolver is little changed since the latter part of the 19th Century.

Even cosmetically, things change very slowly in the world of revolvers: Colt's Python, launched in 1955, is still typical of the modern revolver both in its looks and its operation, with its double-action mechanism and automatic safety device. What significant developments there have been have tended to be in ancillary areas – speed-loaders, sighting systems, holsters and the like. In the guns themselves, the use of modern materials such as polymers has been restricted to the grip; frames, barrels and cylinders are still made of steel.

It is difficult to imagine any major changes in revolver design over the next few decades. Developments in areas such as caseless ammunition and polymer technology will no doubt open up new possibilities – such as the use of polymers in cylinder and frame, or even interchangeable pre-loaded cylinders made of polymer material. Whether manufacturers and users would consider such developments worth the trouble, however, is another matter. With the big military contracts being in the field of semi-automatics, it seems likely that most manufacturers' design and development effort will be concentrated in that area.

One interesting new development in this field, however, is the Medusa revolver from Phillips & Rodgers in the USA. This weapon is specifically designed to chamber, fire and extract more than 25 different cartridges in the 9mm to .38 range. For the civilian shooter this is probably of little more than passing interest, but for the military user the implications are wide-ranging. Ammunition resupply can be a serious problem in some of the world's far-flung battle zones, and a weapon that will digest just about any handgun round found locally is an enormous advantage. Significantly, P&R also supply conversion kits for other popular revolvers. This is a theme that is likely to prove popular with military users, and seems destined to provide an important line of development for some years to come.

BACKGROUND

The Astra Models 44 and 45 are solidly built military-style revolvers in .44 Magnum and .45 Colt calibres. Other than the calibre, they are basically the same gun. Each has a swing-out cylinder with an ejector rod which clears all six chambers with one stroke. The foresight is steeply ramped and the rearsight is fully adjustable. As with the Model 960 (qv), the 44 and 45 have an adjustable mainspring to regulate the power of the hammer's blow.

OPERATION

The Models 44 and 45 have a double-action mechanism which rotates the cylinder to the next position and raises and drops the hammer as the trigger is pulled. The gun can also be cocked manually and fired single-action.

CONTROLS

There is no manual safety catch, but as on the Model 960 there is an automatic safety mechanism which uses a transfer bar to prevent the hammer striking the firing pin unless the trigger is pulled through. A thumb catch on the left of the frame releases the cylinder to swing out to the left of the frame. Ejection is via an ejector rod which is pushed in to eject any cases in the chambers.

Manufacturer:	Astra, Spain
Model:	Models 44 & 45
Calibres:	.44 Magnum (Mod 44) and .45 Colt (Mod 45)
Action:	Double-action revolver
Feed:	6-shot cylinder
Sights:	Ramped foresight; adjustable notch rearsight
Weight:	1,280g (44), 1,240g (45)
Length:	293mm
Barrel:	152mm (216mm barrel also available)

BACKGROUND

The Astra Model 960 is a service pattern double-action revolver intended for police use, and was developed from Astra's earlier Cadix model. The weapon has a swing-out cylinder and an ejector rod which sits in a shrouded housing under the barrel. The mainspring pressure is adjustable to give a stronger or weaker hammer blow to the firing pin. The gun comes in a range of barrel lengths and finishes.

Manufacturer:	Astra, Spain
Model:	960
Calibre:	.38 Special
Action:	Double-action revolver
Feed:	6-shot cylinder
Sights:	Ramped foresight; adjustable notch rearsight
Weight:	1150g
Length:	241mm
Barrel:	102mm (152mm also available)

OPERATION

The 960 is a double-action weapon; pulling the trigger rotates the cylinder to align the next chamber with the barrel, at the same time pulling back the hammer and then releasing it to fire the round. The gun can also be cocked manually, and fired single-action.

CONTROLS

The thumb catch on the left of the frame, below the hammer, releases the cylinder to allow it to swing out to the left of the frame. Pushing in the ejector rod will eject any spent cases or live rounds in the cylinder. There is no manual safety catch, but the gun does have an automatic firing pin safety mechanism which prevents the hammer striking the firing pin unless the trigger is fully pulled through.

SERVICE

Used by police forces in various countries.

Astra Model 960.

BACKGROUND

The Astra Police is a short-barrelled double-action .357 Magnum revolver intended for law enforcement and security services use. It is solidly built, and designed for quick, instinctive use. The foresight is smoothed off to minimise the chance of it snagging in a holster or clothing and the rearsight is a simple groove in the top strap. There is no manual safety catch, and the swing-out six-shot cylinder is emptied by an ejector rod.

OPERATION

The Astra Police has a simple double-action mechanism – pulling the trigger rotates the cylinder to align the next round, raises the hammer and drops it again to fire. The gun can also be cocked manually and fired single-action.

CONTROLS

There is no manual safety device, the relatively long double-action pull providing good security against accidental firing. A thumb catch on the left of the frame releases the cylinder to swing out to the left, and the chambers are emptied by pushing the ejector rod which is normally protected in a shrouded housing under the barrel.

Manufacturer:	Astra, Spain
Model:	Police
Calibres:	.357 Magnum (.38 Special and 9mm Parabellum also available)
Action:	Double-action revolver
Feed:	6-shot cylinder
Sights:	Smoothed, ramped foresight; non-adjustable rearsight is a groove in the top strap
Weight:	1,040g
Length:	212mm
Barrel:	77mm

Astra Police.

BACKGROUND

The Colt Anaconda has achieved almost legendary status as Colt's largest double-action revolver, firing the fearsome .44 Magnum cartridge. Made from stainless steel, it is finished to a high standard and has a ventilated rib to dissipate barrel heat and reduce the effects of heat haze on the sighting plane. The ejector rod is protected in a housing which extends the full length of the barrel.

OPERATION

The Anaconda is a double-action weapon; pulling the trigger rotates the cylinder to align the next chamber with the barrel, at the same time pulling back the hammer and then releasing it to fire the round. The gun can also be cocked manually and fired single-action.

CONTROLS

There is no manual safety catch; a hammer block is retracted automatically as the trigger is pulled through. The cylinder latch is located on the left of the frame, behind the cylinder; pulling the latch rearwards releases the cylinder and allows it to swing leftwards out of the frame. Any rounds in the chambers are ejected by pushing the ejector rod to the rear.

Manufacturer:	Colt Firearms, USA
Model:	Anaconda
Calibres:	.44 Magnum (also available in .45 Colt)
Action:	Double-action revolver
Feed:	6-shot cylinder
Sights:	Ramped red insert foresight on ventilated rib; adjustable white outline rearsight
Weight:	1,672g (with 203mm barrel)
Length:	346mm (with 203mm barrel)
Barrel:	203mm (8"), 153mm (6"), 102mm (4")
Introduced:	1990

Colt Anaconda.

BACKGROUND

The Colt Detective Special first appeared in 1927 as a shortened version of the Police Positive Special. It fired the .38 Special round and was designed to be convenient to carry and conceal. It had a relatively slim, small butt with a rounded end and the rearsight was a simple groove in the top strap. It proved immensely popular, with around 1,500,000 of these guns being made between 1927 and 1986 when production ceased.

The Detective Special was re-introduced in 1993, with a more up-to-date look, although the frame and basic design was largely unchanged. The modern Detective Special has a chubbier barrel with ejector rod shroud, and a much deeper butt with a contoured black composite grip with a groove for the little finger. It still has a 2" barrel, and is chambered for the .38 Special round. The foresight is ramped at a very shallow angle, running the entire length of the barrel, to avoid snagging; the rearsight remains a simple groove in the top strap.

OPERATION

The Detective Special is a double-action revolver, with a mechanism which rotates the cylinder to the next position and raises and drops the hammer as the trigger is pulled. The gun can also be cocked manually and fired single-action.

CONTROLS

There is no manual safety. The cylinder latch is located on the left of the frame, behind the cylinder. Pulling the latch rearwards releases the cylinder and allows it to swing to the left out of the frame. Any rounds in the chambers are ejected by pushing the ejector rod to the rear.

Colt Detective Special.

Manufacturer:	Colt Firearms, USA
Model:	Detective Special
Calibre:	.38 Special
Action:	Double-action revolver
Feed:	6-shot cylinder
Sights:	Ramped foresight; rearsight is a groove in the top strap
Weight:	22oz
Length:	179mm (6⅞")
Barrel:	50mm (2")
Introduced:	1927–1986; re-introduced 1993

BACKGROUND

The King Cobra was introduced as a budget-priced alternative to the widely respected, but somewhat expensive, Colt Python. It shares many of the Python's design features, and has a similar look, but is a separate gun in its own right and a competitor to the Ruger GP100 and S&W's L frame series. The gun has an ejector rod shroud that extends the full length of the barrel. Grips are very similar to the other Colt 'snakes': contoured chequered rubber with medallion inserts and finger grooves. There is a choice of 6" or 4" barrel, and the finish is stainless steel only.

OPERATION

The King Cobra is a double-action revolver; pulling the trigger rotates the cylinder to bring the next chamber into alignment with the barrel, and raises and then drops the hammer, at the same time moving a transfer bar into position to transmit the hammer blow to the firing pin. The gun can also be cocked manually and fired single-action.

CONTROLS

No manual safety catch; pulling the trigger through raises a transfer bar to relay the hammer's blow to the firing pin. The cylinder latch is located on the left of the frame, behind the cylinder; pulling the latch rearwards releases the cylinder and allows it to swing leftwards out of the frame. Any rounds in the chambers are ejected by pushing the ejector rod to the rear.

Manufacturer:	Colt Firearms, USA
Model:	King Cobra
Calibre:	.357 Magnum
Action:	Double-action revolver
Feed:	6-shot cylinder
Sights:	Ramp foresight with red insert; adjustable rearsight with white outline
Weight:	42oz (4"barrel)
Length:	228mm (9") (4" barrel)
Barrel:	102mm (4") or 153mm (6")
Introduced:	1986

Colt King Cobra.

BACKGROUND

The Python is perhaps the most famous of Colt's modern revolvers and has a good reputation for reliability and accuracy. In production since 1955, it has set the style for the various Colt revolvers that have followed: the ejector rod shroud extends the full length of the barrel, and it has a chunky black rubber wraparound grip with finger grooves and inset medallions. There is a ventilated rib which runs the length of the barrel and the trigger blade is grooved. The gun comes in a choice of stainless steel or blued finish, and is chambered for the powerful .357 Magnum cartridge.

Manufacturer:	Colt Firearms, USA
Model:	Python
Calibres:	357 Magnum (and will fire .38 Special)
Action:	Double-action revolver
Feed:	6-shot cylinder
Sights:	Ramp foresight, adjustable notch rearsight
Weight:	1,360g (8" barrel)
Length:	343mm (8" barrel)
Barrel:	203mm (8"), 153mm (6"), 102mm (4")
Introduced:	1955

OPERATION

A double-action revolver, the Python can also be cocked manually and fired single-action. In double-action mode, pulling the trigger rotates the cylinder to the next position, and raises and drops the hammer.

CONTROLS

There is no manual safety catch. There is an automatic safety mechanism which blocks the hammer until the trigger is pulled through. The cylinder latch is located on the left of the frame, behind the cylinder. Pulling the latch rearwards releases the cylinder and allows it to swing to the left, out of the frame. Any rounds in the chambers are ejected by pushing the ejector rod to the rear.

Colt Python.

BACKGROUND

A compact double-action revolver chambered for the .357 Magnum cartridge, the MR73 was developed in the early 1970s by Manurhin, a company which had produced Walther semi-automatic pistols under licence after the Second World War. It is widely used by French and other police forces, and is also used for civilian shooting (target versions are available).

Based on the Smith & Wesson design, the MR73 also has a number of unique features, such as a roller-bearing trigger mechanism which has a very smooth action. Various models are made, offering 'combat' or target sights and a choice of barrel lengths.

Manufacturer:	Manurhin, France
Model:	MR73
Calibre:	.357 Magnum
Action:	Double-action revolver
Feed:	6-shot cylinder
Sights:	Ramped foresight and rearsight groove in top strap (combat models); adjustable target sight models also available
Weight:	880g
Length:	195mm
Barrel:	63mm (2 1/2"). 3", 4", 5 1/4", 6" and 8" also available

OPERATION

The MR73 is a double-action revolver; pulling the trigger rotates the cylinder to align the next chamber with the barrel, at the same time pulling back the hammer and then releasing it to fire the round. The gun can also be cocked manually and fired single-action.

CONTROLS

There is no manual safety catch. The cylinder release catch is located on the left of the frame behind the cylinder, and is pushed forward with the thumb of the firing hand to release the cylinder so this can swing out to the left of the frame. The ejector rod, which is normally housed in the shroud under the barrel, can then be pushed rearwards to eject any cases from the chambers.

SERVICE

In service with French police and others.

BACKGROUND

The Ruger GP 100 replaced the company's highly successful police revolver, the Security Six, in 1987. Although broadly the same design, the GP 100 included a number of improvements on the Security Six. The frame was strengthened and cylinder notches offset from the chambers to increase strength. In the firing position, the cylinder is locked firmly in place by Ruger's patented system. The trigger guard and mechanism are designed as a sub-assembly that can be removed complete for cleaning and maintenance. The ejector rod shroud extends the full length of the barrel, altering the balance and handling of the weapon.

The pistol is chambered for either .357 Magnum or .38 Special. There are various models available, with either fixed or adjustable sights and with barrels of 76mm, 102mm or 152mm. In the long barrelled version, a short ejector shroud is also available.

OPERATION

The GP 100 is a double-action revolver, with a cylinder chambered for six rounds. Due to its transfer bar safety system, the GP 100 can be carried fully loaded and with the hammer down, ready to be drawn and fired double-action at a moment's notice. As normal for a double-action revolver, when required the GP 100 can also be cocked manually and fired single-action.

CONTROLS

The GP 100 has no manual safety catch, but there is an automatic safety device in the form of a transfer bar which moves into position between the hammer and firing pin as the trigger is pulled through; if the hammer falls without the trigger being pulled, it will not strike the firing pin and so the gun will not fire. The cylinder catch is located on the left of the frame, behind the cylinder – push it forward to unlock the cylinder and allow it to swing out to the left for unloading/loading. Pushing in the ejector rod will eject any live rounds or empty cases in the chambers.

Manufacturer:	Sturm, Ruger & Co, USA
Model:	GP 100
Calibres:	.357 Magnum, .38 Special
Action:	Double-action revolver
Feed:	6-shot cylinder
Sights:	Blade foresight and adjustable notch rearsight with white outline; fixed rearsight models also available
Weight:	1,247g (with 102mm barrel)
Length:	238mm
Barrel:	76mm, 102mm, 152mm
Introduced:	1987

Ruger GP 100.

BACKGROUND

Introduced in 1979, the Redhawk marked a major step in Ruger's revolver design. The frame is designed to be immensely strong, with extra thickness in important areas – the barrel threads, the top strap and the side walls (the design does away with a sideplate). The trigger and hammer mechanism were completely new, and utilise a clever design which uses a single spring, one end of which drives the hammer while the other powers the trigger. This weapon also uses Ruger's patented system for locking the cylinder firmly in position at the moment of firing, bolting the swinging crane into the frame.

The Super Redhawk appeared in 1987, and is similar to the standard Redhawk. However, it incorporates the mechanical design features and improvements of the GP 100, and has a heavy extended frame with Ruger's scope mounting system on the top strap. The gun has Ruger's 'Cushioned Grip' scales of Santoprene with wood panels. It comes in .44 Magnum calibre only, and is made of stainless steel with a brushed satin finish. Barrel length options are 190mm (7 1/2") and 241mm (9 1/2").

OPERATION

Although the Redhawk introduced a number of improvements, its operation is the same as any double-action revolver: the gun may be carried with the chambers loaded and the hammer down, and fired double-action by simply pulling the trigger through; alternatively it may be cocked manually and fired single-action.

CONTROLS

The Redhawk incorporates Ruger's floating firing pin and transfer bar safety mechanism: on pulling the trigger through, the transfer rises so that the hammer's blow is transferred to the firing pin to fire the round in the chamber. There is no manual safety catch. The cylinder catch is located on the left of the frame, behind the cylinder; it is pressed forward to release the cylinder and allow it to swing out to the left for loading/unloading. To empty the chambers, the cylinder is opened and the ejector rod is pressed rearwards.

Manufacturer:	Sturm, Ruger & Co, USA
Model:	Redhawk
Calibre:	.44 Magnum
Action:	Double-action revolver
Feed:	6-shot cylinder
Sights:	Fixed ramp foresight, adjustable notch rearsight with white outline. Super Redhawk accepts Ruger scope mount
Weight:	1,474g (Redhawk, 140mm barrel)
Length:	280mm
Barrel:	140mm, 190mm (Super Redhawk 190mm, 241mm)
Introduced:	Redhawk 1979, Super Redhawk 1987

Ruger Super Redhawk.

BACKGROUND

The Ruger 101 is a small framed five-shot revolver, incorporating various features and improvements which had been built into the acclaimed GP100 introduced in the same year. It complements the GP100 and Redhawk models, providing a comprehensive range of revolvers for police and security use.

The lock mechanism is assembled on the trigger guard, which can be removed as a complete unit, simplifying maintenance work on the gun and allowing a 'meatier' frame around this area. Cylinder notches are offset, so they are cut into the strongest part of the cylinder between the chambers. On firing, the chamber is locked in place by a spring-loaded latch mechanism invented by Ruger, which gives added strength and ensures correct alignment of chamber and bore.

The gun is made of stainless steel and has a full length ejector rod shroud. Sights are of the 'combat' type, with a ramped foresight and the rearsight being a groove cut in the top strap. A range of barrel lengths are offered, and calibres include .38 Special, .22LR and .357 Magnum

OPERATION

A double-action revolver, the SP101 can also be fired in single-action mode by cocking the hammer manually. In double-action mode, pulling the trigger rotates the cylinder to align the next round, raises and then drops the hammer to strike the firing pin. A double-action only (DAO) version is also available, with a spur-free hammer to prevent snagging.

CONTROLS

There is no manual safety catch. The cylinder is released by pushing in the catch on the left of the frame with the thumb. The cylinder then swings out to the left, and any empty cases or unfired rounds in the chambers are ejected by pushing in the ejector rod, which normally sits in the full-length shroud under the barrel.

Manufacturer:	Sturm, Ruger & Co, USA
Model:	SP101
Calibres:	.38 Special, .22LR, .32H&R, 9mm Parabellum, .357 Magnum
Action:	Double-action revolver
Feed:	5-shot cylinder (.38 Special, .357 Magnum and 9mm Parabellum); 6-shot cylinder (.22LR, .32H&R)
Sights:	Ramped foresight; combat-style rearsight is a simple groove in top strap
Weight:	709g (57mm barrel)
Length:	Depends on barrel length
Barrel:	57mm (2 1/4"), 63mm (2 1/2)", 78mm (3 1/16"), 101mm (4")
Variants:	Double-action only (DAO) version also available with no spur to hammer
Introduced:	1988

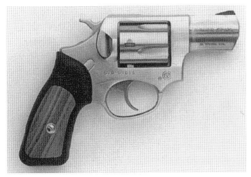

Ruger SP101.

BACKGROUND

Smith & Wesson manufacture a huge range of revolvers, with over 30 models and numerous variations, plus many 'specials' produced by the Smith & Wesson Performance Center. The range has evolved over many years, and at first sight it can be difficult to make sense of all the different models. However, the simplest way to understand the range is to break it down into frame sizes.

The smallest S&W frame size is known as the J frame. These revolvers typically measure under 200mm overall, even with a 76mm (3") barrel, and weigh under 700g. They have a cylinder capacity of five rounds in .38 Spl, or six in .32 S&W Long. These guns are generally carried concealed for personal protection, perhaps by civilians, or off-duty or undercover police officers.

J frame revolvers may be chambered for .22LR, .22WMR, .38 Special, or even 9mm Luger – a rimless round intended for semi-automatic pistols, but catered for in the Model 940. S&W now also make a range of guns intended specifically for ladies, and the Model 36 is available as the Model 36LS or 'LadySmith', with grip dimensions designed to fit a lady's hand.

OPERATION

The S&W J frame range includes a variety of models, but all operate in basically the same way, with a double-action revolver mechanism. The chambers (usually 5) in the cylinder are loaded, and the gun carried with the hammer down. Pulling the trigger through operates the automatic safety mechanism and fires the gun. This can be repeated until all the loaded rounds have been fired.

Most J frame revolvers can also be cocked manually, by pulling the hammer back with the thumb, and then fired in single-action mode. However, some models have a concealed hammer and are effectively double-action only. The J frame hammer is powered by a coil spring, unlike the larger framed S&Ws which have a leaf mainspring.

CONTROLS

The layout of controls on the J frame weapons is largely the same throughout the range. There is no manual safety, but a hammer block prevents the hammer striking the firing pin and firing a round until the trigger is fully pulled through. The cylinder catch is located on the left of the frame, behind the cylinder. It is pushed forward with the thumb to release the cylinder, which can then swing out to the left of the frame for unloading/loading.

Manufacturer:	Smith & Wesson, USA
Model:	J frame models (details below refer to Model 36 'Chief's Special)
Calibre:	.38 Special
Action:	Double-action revolver
Feed:	5-shot cylinder
Sights:	Fixed blade & notch open sights
Weight:	694g
Length:	191mm
Barrel:	76mm (3"); 63.5mm (2 1/2") also available
Introduced:	1950

Smith & Wesson Model 649 – a hammerless variant.

Smith & Wesson Model 37.

BACKGROUND

Smith & Wesson's medium-sized frame is called the K frame; the L frame is essentially the same, and has the same size grip, but is marginally heavier and bulkier in crucial areas to give extra strength for shooting magnum ammunition.

As with other S&W frame sizes, there is a host of models based upon the K/L frame, chambered in a wide range of ammunition from .22 rimfire to .357 Magnum. Perhaps the most familiar to law enforcement officers worldwide is the Model 19, chambered for .357 Magnum/ .38 Special, which was standard issue in many police forces.

OPERATION

As with the previously described J frame S&Ws, the K and L frame revolvers have a double-action mechanism. The larger frame size makes it possible to have an extra chamber in the cylinder, so K/L frames have a six-shot capacity. Other than this, their operation is the same as the J frames.

CONTROLS

There is no manual safety catch. A hammer block provides a safety mechanism against accidental firing, and is retracted automatically when the trigger is pulled through. The cylinder catch is located on the left of the frame, behind the cylinder. It is pushed forward with the thumb to release the cylinder, which can then swing out to the left of the frame for unloading/loading.

Manufacturer:	Smith & Wesson, USA
Model:	L frame models. Details below refer to Model 586 'Distinguished Combat Magnum' in blued carbon steel finish; also available in stainless steel finish as Model 686
Calibre:	.357 Magnum
Action:	Double-action revolver
Feed:	6-round cylinder
Sights:	Blade foresight; adjustable notch rearsight
Weight:	1,502g (with 8" barrel)
Length:	351mm (with 8" barrel)
Barrel:	219mm (8"), 153mm (6"), 102mm (4"), 63.5mm (2 1/2")
Introduced:	1981

Smith & Wesson Model 10.

BACKGROUND

Smith & Wesson's N frame is the largest and heaviest series of revolvers, designed to handle the most powerful Magnum ammunition. The range includes models such as the 27 and 657, chambered for Magnum rounds like the .357 Magnum, .41 Magnum and .44 Magnum. The Model 29, in .44 Magnum, was popularised by films such as the Clint Eastwood *Dirty Harry* series as 'the most powerful handgun in the world'. One N frame revolver, the 625, is chambered for the .45ACP – a rimless round intended for the M1911 Colt semi-automatic. To fire the semi-automatic round it is necessary to use half-moon clips to hold the rounds in place in the cylinder, although it is possible to use a rimmed .45 case.

As with the other S&W frame sizes, there are many different models in the N frame range, offering different barrel lengths, grips, finishes, etc.

OPERATION

The operation of the S&W N frames is the same as the J, K and L frames described previously. They have a double-action mechanism, with a six-shot cylinder. With a full cylinder, they may be carried with the hammer down and fired double-action by pulling the trigger through; alternatively they may be cocked manually and fired single-action.

CONTROLS

As with other frame sizes of S&W revolver, the N frames have a hammer block which prevents the hammer from striking the firing pin unless the trigger is pulled through. There is no manual safety catch. The cylinder latch is located on the left of the frame, and is pressed forward with the thumb to release the cylinder and allow it to swing out to the left of the frame for loading/unloading. Chambers are emptied by pressing in the ejector rod which, when the cylinder is closed, is protected in a shroud beneath the barrel.

Manufacturer:	Smith & Wesson, USA
Model:	N frame models. Details below refer to Model 29
Calibres:	.44 Magnum (other N frame models in .357 Magnum, .41 Magnum and .45 ACP)
Action:	Double-action revolver
Feed:	6-shot cylinder
Sights:	Fixed blade foresight; adjustable notch rearsight
Weight:	1,459g (with 219mm barrel)
Length:	353mm
Barrel:	219mm (8 5/8"); also available in 153mm (6") and 102mm (4")
Introduced:	1955

Smith & Wesson N Frame Model 29.

SUB-MACHINE GUNS

The rise of the modern assault rifle has made the sub-machine gun (SMG) largely irrelevant in conventional military operations. Armed with a relatively light, short and easily pointable fully automatic weapon such as the Steyr AUG, FAMAS, M16, AK or SA80, the modern infantryman has little need for an SMG; his weapon already fills that role for clearing trenches and bunkers, as well as offering greater range and accuracy when required.

SMGs have therefore become something of a specialist weapon, used for specific roles: for example in hostage rescue operations by special forces, where the ballistics of a pistol round are more appropriate; but the SMG offers advantages over the pistol in accuracy, capacity and rate of fire. Compared to an assault rifle, an SMG is also more easily carried and, where necessary, concealed, making it suitable for certain types of bodyguard or 'close protection' work. And, of course, the SMG is still favoured by terrorists, organised criminals and drug gangs for much the same reasons.

The SMG is sometimes portrayed as an inaccurate, indiscriminate weapon, spraying automatic fire uncontrollably across a wide arc. While this is, to an extent, true of certain weapons in this category, there are a good many modern SMGs that are capable of accurate and precise firing, either in single-shot mode or in 'burst fire'. The Heckler & Koch MP5, for instance, would never have achieved its widespread popularity among police and anti-terrorist forces if it could only spray a hail of bullets in the general direction of the target. Hostage rescue operations and the like require almost surgical precision. The MP5, with its roller-locked bolt mechanism, is favoured by the UK's SAS and armed police units because it offers selectable, accurate fire to ranges of up to 100 yards, with the ability to mount a wide range of modern target illumination and sighting devices – quite the reverse of the SMG's popular image.

With the assault rifle now firmly established as the infantryman's standard personal weapon, and becoming ever lighter and more controllable, it seems unlikely that we will see a resurgence of the traditional SMG, although assault rifles will continue to become more like SMGs. Already we have shortened versions of assault rifles which sit comfortably in the SMG category – the AKSU version of the AK and the 9mm Parabellum versions of the Steyr AUG and Colt Commando, for instance. Then there are 'new generation' SMGs like the FN P90, which is almost a modern 'bullpup' assault rifle in its own right, and firing a specially developed round which is similar in many ways to an assault rifle round. As the years go by, the line between the two categories of weapon is likely to become increasingly blurred.

BACKGROUND

The AKSU is basically a shortened version of the familiar AK-74 5.45mm assault rifle, and fires the same round. It first saw action with Soviet forces in Afghanistan in the early 1980s, where it was used by troops needing a more compact weapon than the standard AK-74: armoured vehicle crews and some special forces, for instance.

The AKSU has a folding skeleton buttstock, and a shorter barrel and gas tube than that of the AK-74. There is a large compensator fitted to the muzzle to counter the effects of firing a rifle round in such a short barrel. Another interesting characteristic of the AKSU is that the receiver cover is hinged at the front end, rather than simply lifting off as in the AK-74 and AK-47.

Versions of the AKSU have been produced chambered for the 5.56mm NATO cartridge, as used in the US M16 and the UK's SA80.

OPERATION

The AKSU's operation is essentially the same as that of the AK-74 that it is derived from. It is a gas-operated automatic. On firing, gas is vented from the barrel into a tube which runs parallel to and above the barrel. The gas acts on a piston attached to the bolt, forcing it rearwards to eject the spent cartridge and ride over the hammer to cock the mechanism. As the bolt travels rearwards, it compresses a coil spring. When the bolt reaches the limit of its travel, the spring forces it forwards again, collecting the next round from the magazine and chambering it. If the selector switch is set to full automatic, and the trigger is still depressed, then the hammer is released to fire the next shot; otherwise the gun is ready to fire again when the trigger is next pulled.

CONTROLS

The controls on the AKSU will be immediately familiar to anyone who has fired an AK-74 or AK-47. The safety catch/selector switch is located on the right side of the receiver; in the 'safe' (up) position it covers the cocking handle slot to prevent the ingress of dirt and debris. It is moved down to its middle position for automatic fire, and fully down for single shots. The magazine catch is located in front of the trigger guard: grasp the magazine and pull the catch forward with thumb to release. The bolt cocking handle protrudes from the right side of the receiver: pull fully back and release to cock mechanism and load a round from the magazine.

SERVICE

Soviet forces since the early 1980s.

Manufacturer:	State factories of former Soviet Union
Model:	AKSU-74
Calibre:	5.45 x 39.5mm Soviet
Action:	Gas-operated selective fully automatic
Feed:	30-round magazine
Rate of fire:	700rpm
Sights:	Blade and notch open sights, tangent rearsight adjustable for windage and elevation
Weight:	2,700g
Length:	490mm
Barrel:	206mm

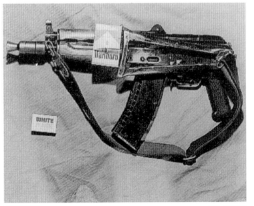

AKSU-74.   (Ian Hogg)

BACKGROUND

The BXP was produced by Armscor for the South African Defence Force and South African police. A compact conventional blowback sub-machine gun, it fires the ubiquitous 9mm Parabellum round and has a folding skeleton buttstock.

OPERATION

The BXP fires from an open bolt and is operated by simple blowback: the gas pressure generated in the barrel on firing literally blows the bolt back to eject the spent case and load the next round. The weapon has what is known as a telescoping or wrap-around bolt. That is to say, the bolt has a projecting section which extends forward of the breech and shrouds the barrel. This keeps the overall length of the gun relatively short and moves the centre of gravity forward, making the weapon easier to control during automatic fire.

CONTROLS

The cocking handle is located in a slot on the top of the receiver: it is pulled fully back and released to cock the weapon and load a round from the magazine, or to clear the chamber with the magazine removed. There is an ambidextrous safety catch, located at the top of the grip behind the trigger guard. Up is 'safe'; push down for 'fire'. Fire selection is via the trigger: the first pull gives single shots, while a second pull gives automatic fire.

SERVICE

South African Defence Force and police.

Manufacturer:	Armscor, South Africa
Model:	BXP
Calibre:	9mm Parabellum
Action:	Blowback fully automatic, selective via trigger pressure
Feed:	22- or 32-round magazine
Rate of fire:	1,000rpm
Sights:	Blade and notch open sights, adjustable. Provision for fitting collimating sight
Weight:	2,500g
Length:	387mm
Barrel:	208mm

Armscor BXP.

(Ian Hogg)

BACKGROUND

The FMK has been the standard issue SMG of the Argentine army since the mid-1970s, and was in service at the time of the Falklands War. Its appearance suggests its design was influenced by the US M3 'grease gun' and the Israeli Uzi. It has a simple tubular receiver mounted on a box-shaped frame/grip; the magazine passes through the grip. There is a ribbed fore-grip, and a telescopic wire buttstock. The weapon fires the 9mm Parabellum round. It offers selective fire and is simple, solid and reliable.

OPERATION

The FMK is a blowback sub-machine gun with a wrap-around bolt; the bolt extends forward of the breech to enclose the breech end of the barrel. The bolt is unlocked and is blown back by the gas pressure generated on firing, ejecting the spent case and re-cocking the mechanism before collecting the next round from the magazine and loading it into the chamber.

CONTROLS

The cocking handle is located on the left side of the receiver and incorporates a guard to protect its slot against ingress of dirt and debris. To cock and load the weapon, insert a full magazine, pull the cocking handle fully back, and release. The safety catch/selector is located on left side of grip/frame: up for 'safe', middle position for single shots, fully down for automatic fire. There is also a grip safety to prevent the weapon firing unless it is held properly around the grip.

SERVICE

Argentine armed forces since 1974.

Manufacturer:	Fabrica Militar de Armas Portatiles, Argentina
Model:	FMK Model 2
Calibre:	9mm Parabellum
Action:	Blowback selective fully automatic
Feed:	25-round magazine
Rate of fire:	650rpm
Sights:	Blade and aperture open sights, flip rearsight pre-set for 50 and 100 yards
Weight:	3,400g
Length:	523mm
Barrel:	290mm

BACKGROUND

Beretta's Model 12 sub-machine gun is immediately recognisable by its distinctive shape, with its tubular receiver, fore-grip, and forward-raked magazine. Designed in the 1950s, it has been refined and developed over the years and is still in production as the Model 12S, which has a more conventional safety catch/selector arrangement than the original Model 12. Model 12s may have a folding stock or a detachable wooden type; the 12S has a folding metal skeleton stock.

The Model 12 was adopted by the Italian armed forces as well as various other countries including Saudi Arabia, Nigeria, Libya and Brazil; the Model 12S superceded the 12 as the standard SMG of Italy's armed forces and has also been sold to various other countries.

OPERATION

The Models 12 and 12S operate on the blowback principle, with the gas pressure in the barrel blowing the bolt back on firing. The bolt travels rearwards to eject the empty case and cock the mechanism, and loads the next round on its return stroke. The bolt is the 'telescoping' or wrap-around type, with much of its bulk forward of the breech at the moment of firing. This improves the balance of the weapon, and reduces vibrations and the tendency of the muzzle to climb when fired on full automatic.

CONTROLS

The cocking handle is located on the left side of the receiver and travels in a longitudinal slot. To cock and load the weapon, insert a full magazine, pull the cocking lever fully back, and release. The magazine catch is on the underside of the trigger guard.

On the earlier Model 12 there is a grip safety which must be pushed in (by the hand holding the grip) to cock or fire the weapon. A push button safety catch above the left grip locks the grip safety in the 'safe' position. On the later Model 12S this button was replaced with a more conventional safety catch/selector switch. Up is 'safe', the middle position gives single shots and down is full auto. The grip safety is retained and operates independently of the safety/selector.

SERVICE

Italian armed forces and various other countries.

Manufacturer:	P Beretta, Italy
Model:	Model 12S
Calibre:	9mm Parabellum
Action:	Blowback selective fully automatic
Feed:	20-, 32- or 40-round magazine
Rate of fire:	550rpm
Sights:	Blade and aperture open sights, with flip-type aperture rearsight
Weight:	3,200g
Length:	418mm
Barrel:	200mm

Beretta Model 12S.

Beretta Model 12S with buttstock folded.

BACKGROUND

The Calico M-960A is a futuristic-looking sub-machine gun with an enormous magazine capacity of either 50 or 100 rounds of 9mm Parabellum which it fires at a rate of 750rpm. First produced in 1990, it makes extensive use of modern plastic materials, with steel used where necessary – for the barrel and bolt etc. The weapon weighs just 2.17kg and measures 647mm long with the buttstock retracted. The basic design is very similar to the Calico M950 pistol (qv), with the addition of the extending buttstock and forward grip.

OPERATION

The M-960A uses an unusual helical feed magazine which is available in two sizes, offering a capacity of 50 or 100 rounds. The magazine is located above the rear portion of the receiver and rounds are fed through a slot in the floor of the magazine into the receiver, to be collected by the bolt on its return stroke and fed into the chamber.

The trade-off for this high capacity is the rather large bulk on the top of the weapon. The weight of loaded rounds (which is considerable) is centred above the firing hand, so the effect on the weapon's balance is not as bad as might be imagined, but if the weapon is fired from the shoulder the magazine does rather obstruct the firer's vision of the area around the target.

A compensator is fitted to the muzzle to direct some of the gases forwards and upwards, to counter the tendency for the muzzle to climb on firing.

CONTROLS

A combined safety catch/selector switch is located in the front of the trigger guard. This is ambidextrous, and can be operated from either side, either with the free hand or with the trigger finger. With the lever to the rear, the catch is on 'safe'. Pushing it forward one stop allows single shots; pushing it fully forward gives fully automatic fire.

The magazine catch is located on top of the receiver, and is squeezed in to release. The cocking lever is on the left side of the receiver, forward of the trigger guard. This has a large crescent-shaped extension which is pulled back and released to load a round from the magazine and cock the mechanism ready to fire.

Manufacturer:	Calico, USA
Model:	M-960A
Calibre:	9mm Parabellum
Action:	Selective fully automatic
Feed:	50- or 100-round helical magazine
Rate of fire:	750rpm
Sights:	Open 'battle sights', with rearsight moulded into magazine casing. Foresight screw adjustable for windage
Weight:	2,170g
Length:	647mm (buttstock retracted), 835mm (buttstock extended)
Barrel:	330mm
Introduced:	1990

Calico M-960A.

(Ian Hogg)

BACKGROUND

The SAF is the current Chilean Army issue weapon at the time of writing. Its design is based on the SIG550 rifle, which is manufactured under licence in Chile, and has a number of common parts.

The SAF fires the 9mm Parabellum round, with a 20- or 30-round magazine. There are a number of versions: the standard model has a folding buttstock, but there is also a fixed butt model, a version with an integral silencer and a shortened model with no butt and a fixed 'broomhandle' type forward grip.

SERVICE

Chilean armed forces and police; also export sales.

Manufacturer:	FAMAE, Chile
Model:	SAF
Calibre:	9mm Parabellum
Action:	Selective single shots, three-round burst or fully automatic
Feed:	20-or 30-round box magazine
Rate of fire:	1,200rpm
Sights:	Open post and aperture sights, with rotating turret rearsight similar to MP5 offering a choice of apertures
Weight:	2,900g
Length:	410mm (640mm with folding buttstock extended)
Barrel:	200mm

SAF.

(Ian Hogg)

BACKGROUND

The Chinese Type 79 sub-machine gun is a lightweight weapon, weighing just 1.9kg, with a folding buttstock. Cheaply produced from steel stampings, it has many similarities with the AK series of assault rifles: the rectangular receiver and safety catch in particular look and operate very much like those of an AK-47 or AK-74. This simplifies training of soldiers who are already familiar with AK series weapons. The Type 79 fires the Soviet 7.62 x 25mm pistol round at a rate of fire of 650rpm and uses a 20-round box magazine.

The Type 85 is a modified version of the Type 79, using a cylindrical receiver and a larger capacity (30-round) box magazine.

OPERATION

Full details of these weapons are not known, but they are believed to operate on a rotating bolt principle, allowing the bolt to be made lighter than is necessary in a simple blowback mechanism. It is thought that gas is bled off from the barrel to operate a piston which drives an operating rod, which in turn rotates the bolt and releases it.

CONTROLS

The Type 79 has a manual safety catch/selector switch on the right side of the receiver. This looks and operates very much like the safety/selector on AK rifles – in the 'safe' position (up), it shuts off the cocking slot, preventing ingress of grit and debris. Moving the lever down one click gives single shots; down again to the second click allows fully automatic fire.

The cocking lever is on the right side of the receiver (as in the AK series) and the magazine release catch is located at the front of the magazine housing.

Manufacturer:	China North Industries, Beijing
Model:	Type 79
Calibre:	Soviet 7.62 x 25mm pistol
Action:	Selective fully automatic, thought to be rotating bolt mechanism
Feed:	20-round box magazine
Rate of fire:	650rpm
Sights:	Open blade and aperture sights
Weight:	1,900g
Length:	470mm (buttstock folded), 740mm (buttstock extended)
Barrel:	225mm
Introduced:	1980

Chinese type 85, silenced version. *(Ian Hogg)*

Chinese type 79. *(Ian Hogg)*

BACKGROUND

The concept behind the P90 was to provide a sort of scaled-down assault rifle for support troops: a weapon that would be compact enough to be carried by signals troops, drivers, engineers, medics and the like without getting in the way, yet provide sufficient firepower to be effective when the occasion demands. As such it is on the borderline between the sub-machine gun and the assault rifle, and has been categorised as a Personal Defence Weapon (PDW) rather a than sub-machine gun.

This is indicative of the direction that infantry weapons have been taking in recent years. With modern armies relying more and more heavily on high-tech, large-scale weapons and equipment, there is less call for the traditional infantry rifle. Modern battles are more likely to be either long-range affairs, beyond the reach of a rifle, or very short range house-clearing/bunker-busting operations where a full-length rifle would be cumbersome and slow to bring to bear. More and more troops are carried right onto the battlefield in armoured vehicles of one sort or another, and a full-length rifle is unnecessarily cumbersome in an IFV, hence the rise of carbine and bullpup infantry weapons such as the SA80.

The P90 was intended to supersede the sub-machine gun and its ubiquitous 9mm Parabellum round. It was to be easier to shoot and more accurate than an SMG while offering better range and stopping power. The first step was to produce the ammunition, since no existing round fulfilled the requirements. This was the SS90, a bottlenecked rimless round which looks a lot like a scaled-down version of the standard NATO 5.56mm round, but with a more sharply pointed projectile – a boat-tailed 'spire point' to give it its official description. The projectile itself weighs 25 grains, and achieves an extremely fast muzzle velocity of 850m/sec. It has an effective range of 150m and offers outstanding penetration, passing through 48 layers of Kevlar at 150m. The bullet has a full metal jacket and is filled not with lead but with a hard plastic material. Its centre of gravity is well to the rear so that it tumbles violently on hitting the human body, causing a massive wound channel which far exceeds the performance of the standard 9mm Parabellum round.

A more recent development has seen the round shortened by 2.7mm, achieved by shortening the bullet, while the case retains the same dimensions. This bullet weighs 2.02g, slightly heavier than the original SS90 due to a change of core material, and has a slightly lower muzzle velocity of 715m/sec compared to the original 850m/sec. Performance is almost identical to the original round, the higher weight making up for the lower velocity.

The P90 itself looks and handles quite unlike any other weapon with its moulded plastic curves and squat shape. It measures just 500mm long and weighs 3kg with a full magazine of 50 rounds. Its combat sling allows it to be carried in various positions so it can be slung over the user's body and forgotten about while he gets on with his tasks, yet it is quickly ready for action if needed.

The body casing of the P90 is a one-piece polymer shell which houses all the main parts, offering good protection from the knocks of military life as well as from ingress of dust and debris. The design incorporates a thumbhole-type pistol grip, forward grip and hand protector to keep the forward hand away from the muzzle. The sights are mounted on a raised platform at the muzzle end of the weapon. The buttstock doubles as a container for a cleaning kit, which is accessed by a slide-off butt-plate.

The P90's magazine is just as unusual as the rest of the weapon. This sits on top of the receiver, parallel to the barrel, with the 50 rounds stacked at 90 degrees to the bore. As these feed through towards the action under spring pressure, they follow a curved track which turns them through 90 degrees and presents them to the action in the correct alignment. The magazine is made of semi-transparent polymer, allowing the firer to see the remaining rounds with a quick glance at the top of the weapon.

OPERATION

To load the P90, offer up a full magazine to the slot in the rear of the sight mounting, locate it in position and snap it down to engage the magazine catch. Grasp the cocking handle on the left of the receiver, pull fully back and release. Select single shot or fully automatic fire by moving the safety catch to the '1' or 'A' position. Take aim and squeeze the trigger. On automatic, the first pull of the trigger will give a single shot; pulling the trigger fully back gives automatic fire – users find this more convenient than using the single-shot setting on the safety/selector switch.

The action is a straight blowback from an unlocked breech. This is very much like a standard SMG, but the P90 employs a separate firing pin – unlike a typical SMG which has a protrusion on the breech block that fires the round as it is chambered. Fired cases are ejected downwards through an ejection port just behind the grip.

The P90 is designed to be fully ambidextrous; it can be fired equally well from right or left shoulder, with no alteration. As well as being advantageous to left-handed shooters, this is significant in battle, where a soldier may need to fire left-handed round an obstruction to remain behind cover.

CONTROLS

Manual safety/selector catch located within trigger guard below trigger – rearwards is 'safe', push forward one click for single shots, two clicks for full automatic fire. Ambidextrous cocking lever is located on sides of receiver, towards muzzle end. Pull back and release to clear the chamber and/or load a round from the magazine. Magazine catch (ambidextrous) located on sides of buttstock, just behind magazine.

Latest models are fitted with British-made 1x magnification Ring Sight collimating sight, with day/night graticule, allowing use with one or both eyes open. A laser pointer may be fitted to the hand protecting spur beneath the muzzle, with a switch in the hand grip. This allows the weapon to be fired with precision, even from the hip.

SERVICE

Believed in service with Saudi armed forces, and some Far Eastern countries.

Manufacturer:	Fabrique Nationale, Belgium
Model:	P90
Calibre:	5.7 x 28mm
Action:	Blowback, selective fully automatic
Feed:	50-round box magazine
Rate of fire:	900rpm
Sights:	Integral open sights and British-made Ring Sight 1:1 collimating optical sight with day/night graticules. Laser target pointer can be built in to hand protector below muzzle
Weight:	2,680g (3,000g loaded)
Length:	500mm
Barrel:	250mm
Introduced:	1990

FN P60.

BACKGROUND

First produced in 1957, the Franchi LF57 made extensive use of pressed steel – one of the earlier examples of this type of construction, which has since proved popular as a means of manufacturing military weapons quickly and relatively cheaply. In fact the entire gun is made from steel stampings, except for the barrel and bolt. The manufacturer, Luigi Franchi, has gone on to produce a number of successful military and civilian weapons, including the infamous SPAS 12 and SPAS 15 assault shotguns. The LF57 sub-machine gun, however, had a relatively short life. It was used by the Italian armed forces in the 1960s, and a number were exported to the United States, but the weapon was discontinued in the early 1980s.

OPERATION

The LF57 operates on the blowback principle, with the bolt being thrown back by the pressure generated in the chamber when a round is fired – only the inertia of the bolt and the relatively light pressure of the return spring counteracts this force. As the bolt travels rearwards in the receiver, it extracts the fired case, ejects it through the ejection port in the right side of the receiver, and then returns under spring pressure, collecting another round from the magazine to load into the chamber and fire.

The LF57 is designed with an overhung bolt; this has a large part of its bulk above and forward of the breech face. This has two useful functions. First, it raises the centre of gravity, which reduces the tendency of the muzzle to climb during a burst of automatic fire. Second, it allows a longer barrel, which makes better use of the propellant powder in the cartridge since there is more time for the burning powder to act on the bullet.

CONTROLS

The LF57's cocking handle travels in a slot on the left side of the receiver. To load, insert a charged magazine, then pull the cocking handle back to its fullest extent and release. The safety catch is a simple grip safety in the forward edge of the grip; this is released automatically when the grip is held in the hand.

SERVICE

In production 1957–1980; was used by Italian armed forces and exported.

Manufacturer:	Luigi Franchi, Italy
Model:	LF57
Calibre:	9mm Parabellum
Action:	Blowback, non-selective, fully automatic
Feed:	30-round box magazine
Rate of fire:	450rpm
Sights:	Blade and notch open sights, rearsight adjustable for windage
Weight:	3,300g
Length:	420mm (680mm with folding buttstock extended)
Barrel:	205mm

Franchi LF57. *(Ian Hogg)*

BACKGROUND

Widely copied and made under licence, the Carl Gustav Model 45 sub-machine gun is one of the oldest SMGs still in service. It first appeared, as its model number implies, in 1945. Some three years later, in 1948, it was improved by the addition of a well-designed double-stack magazine holding 36 rounds; other small improvements were also made at this time, and the weapon re-designated the M45B. Other variants include the M45C, which has a bayonet lug, and the M45E which offers the option of selective fire.

A simple and robust design, the M45B has stood the test of time and is in service with the armies of Sweden, Ireland and Indonesia. It has also been made under licence in Egypt as the 'Port Said', and has been copied in various countries such as Czechoslovakia. A modified version of the M45B, incorporating a sound moderator, was used by US Special Forces in Vietnam.

OPERATION

The Gustav M45B is a simple design, based around a tubular receiver which houses a bolt and return spring. With a charged magazine in position, the weapon is cocked by pulling back the cocking handle on the right side of the receiver until it engages in the trigger mechanism. The bolt can be locked in this position by lifting the cocking handle to rotate the mechanism anti-clockwise and engage the cocking handle in a slot. There is no separate safety catch.

On firing, the bolt flies forward to collect a round from the magazine, load it into the chamber, and fire it. The bolt is then driven rearwards by gas pressure, ejecting the fired case and returning under pressure of the return spring to continue the cycle until the trigger is released or the magazine is empty.

CONTROLS

The controls on the M45B are simple and effective, in keeping with its functional design. The cocking handle travels in a slot on the right side of the receiver, and can be rotated into a slot to lock it in its rear position. It can also be locked in the closed position, by pushing the handle inwards so that its other end engages in a hole in the left of the receiver. There is no separate safety mechanism, and the trigger is a simple stop-go mechanism – pull to fire, release to stop. The magazine catch is located at the rear of the magazine housing, beneath the receiver.

SERVICE

In service with the Swedish, Irish and Indonesian armed forces, licence-built in Egypt and copied elsewhere.

Manufacturer:	FFV Ordnance, Sweden
Model:	Carl Gustav M45B
Calibre:	9mm Parabellum
Action:	Blowback, non-selective, fully automatic
Feed:	Double-stack 36-round box magazine
Rate of fire:	600rpm
Sights:	Blade and notch open sights
Weight:	3,900g
Length:	552mm (808mm with folding buttstock extended)
Barrel:	213mm
Introduced:	1945; M45B 1948.

Carl Gustav Model 45B.

BACKGROUND

The Heckler & Koch MP5 series of sub-machine guns stands apart; it is really in a class of its own. These German-made weapons are correctly described as sub-machine guns – firing what is basically a pistol round on fully automatic in a weapon designed to be held two-handed. But it is hard to conceive something so different from the crude, inaccurate weapons that typify the class. The MP5 is a sophisticated weapons system which employs advanced design and manufacturing to produce what is really a high quality selective-fire carbine which happens to fire the 9mm Parabellum round.

Based on Heckler & Koch's G3 assault rifle, the MP5 was developed in the mid-1960s. It was quickly adopted by West Germany's police forces and has since been widely adopted by numerous police and military forces worldwide. It is particularly favoured for internal security and anti-terrorist operations, and is used by many special counter-terrorist units including Britain's Special Air Service.

The MP5 achieved fame when it was used by the SAS to break the Iranian Embassy siege in 1980. The weapon is particularly suited to the hostage rescue role, for a number of reasons. Its 9mm Parabellum round is sufficiently lethal to produce an effective 'knock-down' of a terrorist, especially with multiple hits from burst or fully automatic fire, without the problems of over-penetration that would occur with rifle calibres, such as passing through a wall or aircraft skin and injuring civilians many hundreds of metres away. The weapon is outstandingly accurate for a sub-machine gun, and can be fitted with various sighting devices and target illuminators to allow accurate shooting at ranges of 100 metres or more. It has proved robust and reliable; despite some suggestions that it is susceptible to jamming due to ingress of dirt and debris, Britain's SAS have found that with normal routine maintenance, a jam is virtually unheard of when using good quality metal jacketed ammunition. The weapon is also compact and handles well, making it suitable for insertion and entry techniques such as abseiling, keyholing etc which are often required in hostage rescue work. Furthermore, the level of after-sales service and back-up provided by Heckler & Koch (now part of Britain's Royal Ordnance) is very good, with tactical training and armourers' courses available in addition to the essential spare parts and so on.

The MP5 is so far ahead of its competition in this area that it looks set to continue as the standard weapon of counter-terrorism and internal security forces for a good many years to come. In its semi-automatic carbine form it is favoured by Britain's armed police units such as SO19, and is used for armed response to security incidents, royalty and diplomatic protection, and for airport security operations.

VARIANTS

The MP5 comes in a number of variants – it is really a family of weapons rather than a single weapon. Essentially it is available with a fixed buttstock, a folding buttstock or with no buttstock. These may or may not have a three-round burst option, and may or may not be silenced. The various combinations of these options produce a long list of variants, designated with a suffix of letters and numerals. There is also a 'K' (*Kurz* = 'short') variant, which has a short 115mm barrel, a vertical broomhandle-type fore-grip, and no buttstock. This too may have a three-round burst option, and may be had with low-profile sights which are less likely to snag when the weapon is carried concealed.

OPERATION

The MP5 is unusual for a sub-machine gun in that it fires from a closed, locked bolt. The locking is achieved by a roller mechanism. The bolt is in two parts: the bolt head, which lies against the cartridge head, and the larger mass of the main bolt body. When the bolt is closed, inclined planes on the bolt body press against rollers, pushing them outwards into recesses and locking the bolt head in place against the breech. On firing, the gas pressure is resisted by the bolt head locked in place. After a delay, the bolt body begins to withdraw, allowing the rollers to unlock. At this point the two parts of the bolt travel rearwards together, extracting and ejecting the fired case. When the bolt reaches the extent of its travel, it is returned by spring pressure, collecting a fresh round from the magazine and chambering it before the roller lock deploys again as the bolt body moves up against the bolt head. This delayed-action blowback system makes the MP5 considerably more accurate than a simple blowback mechanism

CONTROLS

Controls on the MP5 series are ergonomically designed and add to the weapon's overall balance and ease of handling. The cocking lever travels in a slot in the upper left quarter of the receiver tube and has a large, three-quarter moon knob that is easily operated even with gloved hands. The safety catch/selector switch is located above and behind the trigger; it takes the form of a large flip switch which is easily operated with the thumb of the firing hand. Upper position is 'safe', down one or two clicks provides single shot and fully automatic or three-round burst fire, depending on the model. The magazine catch is located at the rear of the magazine well, where it is easily operated by the thumb of the hand grasping the magazine.

The basic sights are similar to those on the G3 rifle: a blade foresight contained within a protective ring and a rotating turret rearsight offering a series of apertures of different sizes to suit different conditions and users. The MP5 system allows a variety of target illumination

and sighting systems to be mounted and a number of companies have developed their own 'bolt on' systems for the MP5 series. Laser systems which project a red dot onto the target have become popular for counter-terrorist and police work; in certain circumstances simply shining the dot onto a target may be enough to convince him that resistance is futile, and help to resolve the situation without the need to fire.

Target illumination systems have come a long way since the Iranian Embassy siege, when the SAS troops

The storming of the Iranian Embassy in 1980.

Heckler & Koch MP5K.

111

storming the building had D-cell Maglite torches mounted on the top of their MP5s like telescopic sights. Nowadays the preferred torch is smaller, like the Sure-Light, and can be fitted within a replacement fore-end with an integral switch. Nevertheless it serves the same function: to illuminate a target so it can be rapidly identified and eliminated when other light sources have been deliberately removed by the assaulting force (by cutting power to the building or aircraft) for tactical advantage.

SERVICE

Widely adopted by police and counter-terrorist units worldwide, including Germany, US, Switzerland, and UK armed police units and SAS. Also manufactured in Greece as EMP5, used by Greek security forces and police.

Heckler & Koch MP5 A5.

Heckler & Koch MP5 A4.

Heckler & Koch MP5 SD5.

Manufacturer:	Heckler & Koch, Oberndorf-Neckar, West Germany (now owned by Royal Ordnance, UK)
Model:	MP5 (Specifications refer to MP5A2 unless indicated)
Calibre:	9mm Parabellum
Action:	Roller-locked delayed blowback, selective fully automatic
Feed:	15- or 30-round box magazine
Rate of fire:	800rpm
Sights:	Blade and aperture open sights, rearsight with revolving turret to provide range of aperture sizes. Various target illumination and laser pointer systems available
Weight:	2,550g
Length:	680mm (telescoping butt variants 490mm with butt retracted, K variants 325mm)
Barrel:	225mm (115mm on MP5K variants)
Variants:	MP5 A2 – Fixed stock, 225mm barrel
	MP5 A3 – Telescoping stock, 225mm barrel
	MP5 A4 – No buttstock, 225mm barrel
	MP5 A5 – As A3 with three-round burst option
	MP5 SD1 – No buttstock, silenced
	MP5 SD2 – A2 type buttstock, silenced
	MP5 SD3 – A3 type buttstock, silenced
	MP5 SD4 – As SD1 with three-round burst option
	MP5K – Short variant with 115mm barrel and no buttstock
	MP5K A1 – As MP5K but with low-profile sights
	MP5K A4 – As MP5K but with three-round burst option
	MP5K A5 – As MP5K A1 but with three-round burst option
Introduced:	1965

BACKGROUND

First produced in 1992, the Lusa A2 by Indep of Portugal has a number of features that look suspiciously similar to the H&K MP5 – the superposed cylinder receiver, for instance, the safety catch/selector lever and the angle and shape of the grip. No big surprise here, as Indep also manufacture the MP5 under license from Heckler & Koch.

Notwithstanding this, the Lusa is an entirely separate design in its own right and has proved to be robust and reliable. The bolt travels in the lower part of the receiver but has a large overhung section which travels in the upper section, where the return spring is also located.

OPERATION

The Lusa is a blowback type SMG, offering selective single shots or fully automatic fire. There is a telescoping buttstock and the magazine and housing form a vertical fore-grip.

CONTROLS

The cocking handle travels in a slot on the left side of the receiver (upper portion). The safety/selector switch is similar to that of the H&K MP5, offering four positions: 'safe', single shots, three-round burst and fully automatic.

SERVICE

The Lusa is in use with the Portugese armed forces, and has been offered for export, although sales outside its home country are not thought to be particularly high.

Manufacturer:	Indep, Lisbon, Portugal
Model:	Lusa A2
Calibre:	9mm Parabellum
Action:	Blowback, selective fully automatic
Feed:	30-round magazine
Rate of fire:	900rpm
Sights:	Blade and aperture open sights. Laser pointer systems available
Weight:	2,850g
Length:	458mm (585mm with telescoping buttstock extended)
Barrel:	160mm
Introduced:	1992

Indep Lusa. *(Ian Hogg)*

BACKGROUND

Designed in the mid-1960s by Gordon B Ingram, the Model 10 is also known as MAC-10, MAC being the initials of Military Armament Corp of the US which manufactured the weapon in the early 1970s. It was conceived as a relatively cheap 'use it and lose it' weapon for use by special forces in conflicts such as Vietnam. It is a simple blowback design, manufactured with a high proportion of pressed steel components,. The earliest models even had a pressed steel bolt, filled with lead to provide the necessary weight. The weapon was intended to be used with a screw-on moderator which cut down the otherwise deafening muzzle noise that is inevitable with a barrel less than six inches long.

The MAC-10 achieved a certain popularity, as well as some notoriety (partly due to being favoured by film and TV producers as the bad guys' weapon). However, the company was fraught with commercial problems, partly resulting from its involvement with various US government agencies during the Vietnam war, and ultimately went into liquidation.

Years later, the design was picked up by SF Firearms in the UK. This company has addressed the various drawbacks of Ingram's original design, and has introduced a number of improvements: improving the ergonomics of the grips, adding a detachable rigid polymer stock, and using an Uzi-style magazine. SF Firearms has retained the overhung bolt design, however, which allows most of the barrel to remain within the receiver and keeps the centre of gravity high and forward to reduce the tendency for the muzzle to climb during bursts of automatic fire. The bolt has also been modified to provide more reliable feeding and a camming hook replaces the less reliable extractor claw.

OPERATION

The original MAC-10, and its more recent derivatives, are simple blowback weapons. The barrel is approximately six inches long, of which only the last inch or so protrudes beyond the pressed steel box-shaped receiver. An overhung bolt allows most of the barrel to be inside the receiver. The original weapon was designed to fire the .45ACP round (as used in the Colt M1911 pistol used by US forces at the time). Modern versions are generally chambered for the 9mm Parabellum.

With its small size and high rate of fire (over 1,000rpm), the MAC-10 can be difficult to control on full automatic (it was rejected by the SAS for hostage rescue work on these grounds), although the SF Firearms fixed stock improves this aspect of its handling considerably.

CONTROLS

The cocking handle travels in a slot on the upper surface of the box-section receiver and sits directly in the line of sight; for this reason it has a cut-out notch. The handle can be rotated to lock the bolt in the closed position, in which case the notch is at 90 degrees to the line of sight,

Ingram/SF MAC-10 with silencer.

(Ian Hogg)

providing a visual reminder if the weapon is brought to the aim.

The safety catch is located inside the trigger guard, just in front of the trigger, and is slid forward for 'fire'. A separate selector switch is located on the left side of the receiver to select single shot or full automatic fire. The magazine catch is located in the heel of the butt.

SERVICE
Originally in production 1970–75; currently produced in modified form. Much beloved of film and TV producers, but rarely used by security and armed forces.

Ingram/SF MAC-10 without silencer. *(Ian Hogg)*

Manufacturer:	Originally Military Armament Corp, USA. Now manufactured by SF Firearms, UK
Model:	Ingram MAC-10
Calibres:	Originally .45ACP, now 9mm Parabellum
Action:	Blowback, selective fully automatic
Feed:	30-round box magazine
Rate of fire:	1,050–1,150rpm
Sights:	Blade and notch fixed open sights
Weight:	2,840g
Length:	270mm (600mm with detachable stock)
Barrel:	146mm

BACKGROUND

Produced at the end of the 1940s, the French MAT49 was the standard SMG of French armed forces for many years. It was not so much replaced, as the need for any type of SMG was negated by the changing face of modern warfare and because of the introduction of the FAMAS assault rifle, which itself has many characteristics normally associated with an SMG. However, even today the MAT49 may be encountered among French reservists and in former French colonies.

A compact and solidly built weapon, it makes good use of pressed sheet steel for parts such as the receiver and magazine housing. An unusual feature of this weapon is the hinged magazine housing, which allows the magazine to be folded forward so that it lies underneath the barrel. In this position the weapon is completely safe, since even if the bolt is operated it cannot feed a round into the chamber - yet the magazine can be swung into the 'ready' position at a moment's notice.

OPERATION

The MAT49 is a simple blowback weapon: the bolt is driven back by the gas pressure in the barrel as soon as this builds up sufficiently to overcome the inertia of the bolt. The bolt itself has a protrusion which passes some distance into the enlarged chamber of the barrel – an unusual design which has much the same effect as an overhung bolt.

The tilting magazine housing allows a wider range of tatical options than normal – a soldier may carry his weapon cocked and with the magazine in the locked forward position, for instance, in which condition it is totally safe from accidental discharge but can rapidly be deployed when needed.

CONTROLS

The MAT49 has a grip safety lever in the rear of the grip; this is held in the 'off' position by the firer's hand on the grip but instantly switches to 'safe' if the weapon is dropped or released. In the 'safe' position the bolt is locked in place so it cannot move. There is no additional manual safety device.

The cocking handle is located on the left side of the receiver, and operates in the normal way.

The hinged magazine housing has already been mentioned above. When the magazine is folded forward, the feed opening in the receiver is covered, preventing ingress of dirt and debris. A sprung cover serves the same purpose on the ejection port. The weapon has a telescoping wire stock.

SERVICE

Was the issue SMG of French armed forces. Now largely obsolete, but still used by French reserve forces and in former French colonies.

Manufacturer:	M.A.T., France
Model:	MAT49
Calibre:	9mm Parabellum
Action:	Blowback, non-selective fully automatic
Feed:	32-round box magazine
Rate of fire:	600rpm
Sights:	Blade and aperture open sights
Weight:	3,500g
Length:	404mm
Barrel:	230mm

MAT 49. *(Ian Hogg)*

BACKGROUND

The Madsen series of sub-machine guns began with the Model 1946, with later models designated 1950, 1953 and Mark II. These all share the same basic design, with the receiver formed from two pressed steel halves hinged together. When the weapon is assembled, the halves are held together by the barrel retaining collar. There is a folding rectangular skeleton stock, which is hinged at the back of the receiver and the bottom of the grip. The weapon is chambered for the 9mm Parabellum round and uses a 32-round box type magazine.

OPERATION

The Madsen has a simple blowback mechanism, with a fixed firing pin attached to the front face of the bolt. To cock the weapon, insert a loaded magazine and pull back the cocking handle on top of the receiver. In order to move the cocking handle, it is necessary to depress the grip safety located behind the magazine well. The mechanism holds the bolt in the rearmost position until the trigger is pulled (and the grip safety released), whereupon the bolt is released to fly forward under spring pressure, collect a round from the magazine and feed it into the chamber. The fixed firing pin fires the round as the bolt closes and the gas pressure immediately throws the bolt back to eject the fired case and begin the cycle again. When the trigger is released, the bolt is caught in its rear position.

CONTROLS

The cocking handle travels in a slot on the upper surface of the receiver; the Model 1946 has a U-section piece which partially wraps around the receiver, while later models have a cylindrical knob. The grip safety is a small lever located behind the magazine housing, and must be pressed forward to release the bolt or to pull the trigger. The magazine catch is on the rear surface of the housing itself. The Model 1953 Mark II has a selective fire switch – all others are non-selective.

SERVICE

Used by Danish police forces, plus some countries in South America and South-East Asia.

Manufacturer:	Dansk Industri Syndicat, Madsen, Denmark
Model:	Madsen Models 1946, 1951, 1953 and 1953 Mark II
Calibre:	9mm Parabellum
Action:	Blowback, fully automatic (selective on Mark II only)
Feed:	32-round box magazine
Rate of fire:	550rpm
Sights:	Fixed blade and notch open sights
Weight:	3,200g
Length:	528mm (794mm with stock extended)
Barrel:	198mm

Madsen.

BACKGROUND

The HM-3 is manufactured in Mexico and is in service with Mexican armed forces. Firing the 9mm Parabellum round, it is a simple blowback weapon. It has a wrap-around bolt which extends forward of the barrel; this helps to reduce the weight of the weapon, and improves its balance. The magazine is housed in the grip. The weapon has a clever folding buttstock which, in the folded position, provides a vertical foregrip.

OPERATION

The operating system of the HM-3 is the blowback type and there is a selector switch to provide either single shots or automatic fire. The weapon is designed to be used without taking either hand off the grips to release the safety or operate the selector switch, and the buttstock can be folded or extended with the weapon firmly held in both hands.

CONTROLS

A grip safety is built into the upper rear surface of the grip. The selector lever is located on the right side of the receiver above the trigger guard, where it can be operated without the firer releasing his grip on the weapon. The magazine catch is on the heel of the butt.

SERVICE

Mexican armed forces.

Manufacturer:	Productos Mendoza, Mexico
Model:	HM-3
Calibre:	9mm Parabellum
Action:	Blowback, selective fully automatic
Feed:	32-round box magazine
Rate of fire:	600rpm
Sights:	Protected blade and notch open sights
Weight:	2,980g
Length:	395mm (635mm with folding stock extended)
Barrel:	255mm

Mexico HM-3.

(Ian Hogg)

BACKGROUND

Peru's armed forces use the MGP-79A and MGP-87 sub-machine gun, a locally designed and manufactured weapon which fires the 9mm Parabellum round. It is a simple and robust weapon with a folding buttstock and offering selective fire. The MGP-79A was introduced in 1979 and has now been superseded by the MGP-87, which is mechanically very similar but has a slightly shorter barrel and butt, and omits the perforated barrel jacket seen on the earlier model.

OPERATION

The mechanism is housed in a tubular receiver and is a simple blowback design. To fire, insert a loaded magazine, draw back the cocking handle and release, then release the safety catch and pull the trigger. The magazine is compatible with Uzi magazines, which are interchangeable with the MGP's.

CONTROLS

The cocking handle travels in a slot in the left side of the receiver. In the earlier model the cocking handle stuck out sideways; in the MGP-87 the handle has a 90 degree bend so that it protrudes upwards. The safety catch is located on the left side of the receiver above the grip. The selector is on the left of the receiver behind the magazine housing, where it can be operated by the thumb of the hand grasping the magazine and housing.

SERVICE

Peruvian armed forces.

Manufacturer:	Sima-Cefar, Peru
Model:	MGP-79A and MGP-87 (Specifications below refer to MGP-87)
Calibre:	9mm Parabellum
Action:	Blowback, selective fully automatic or single shots
Feed:	20- or 32-round magazine (interchangeable with Uzi type)
Rate of fire:	800rpm
Sights:	Protected blade and notch open sights
Weight:	2,900g
Length:	MGP-87: 500mm (766mm with stock extended)
Barrel:	194mm

Peru MGP-87.

(Ian Hogg)

BACKGROUND

Peru's Sima-Cefar, who make the Peruvian armed forces' standard sub-machine gun, the MGP-87, also make a 'mini' sub-machine gun intended for special forces and close protection work. This is the MGP-84, a shortened version of the MGP-87; it has no exposed barrel, and the magazine housing is incorporated into the pistol grip. The folding buttstock is arranged so that it provides a foregrip when folded.

OPERATION

The operation of the MGP-84 is of the simple blowback type, as in the MGP-87. The weapon is laid out like a pistol and can be fired one-handed if required, although this is not conducive to accuracy, and bursts of more than two or three rounds become widely spread.

CONTROLS

The safety catch and fire selector are combined in a single switch, located on the left side of the receiver above the forward edge of the trigger guard. The cocking handle travels in a slot in the upper left quarter of the tubular receiver

SERVICE

Peruvian armed forces.

Manufacturer:	Sima-Cefar, Peru
Model:	MGP-84 'Mini'
Calibre:	9mm Parabellum
Action:	Blowback, selective fully automatic
Feed:	20- or 32-round box magazine (interchangeable with Uzi type)
Rate of fire:	700rpm
Sights:	Protected blade and notch open sights
Weight:	2,310g
Length:	284mm (503mm with butt extended)
Barrel:	166mm

Peru MGP-87.

(Ian Hogg)

BACKGROUND

The Czech Skorpion is more accurately described as a machine pistol. It is laid out like a pistol, with no foregrip. It has a folding wire skeleton buttstock, which when folded wraps around the barrel giving the weapon a characteristic silhouette. Intended for use by armoured vehicle crews, the Skorpion offers selective single shots or automatic fire. It has a simple blowback operation, incorporating a rate reducer to slow down the rate of fire which would otherwise be excessive due to the relatively light weight of the bolt.

The weapon was originally designed to fire the rather feeble but widely available .32ACP pistol round, although versions have been chambered for various other rounds, including .380ACP, 9mm Makarov and 9mm Parabellum.

OPERATION

The basic operation of the Skorpion is much the same as a conventional sub-machine gun. A loaded magazine is inserted in the magazine housing and the cocking handle drawn back and released, whereupon the bolt is held by the trigger mechanism against spring pressure. The safety/selector catch is released, and the trigger pulled to allow the bolt to fly forward, chambering a round and firing it as the bolt closes. Gas pressure drives the bolt back again, and the cycle repeats as long as the trigger is pressed and rounds remain in the magazine.

The rate reducer is a hook which catches the bolt at its rearmost position and holds it there. The hook mechanism drives a plunger down into the pistol grip against spring pressure. The plunger reaches the end of its travel, and returns to release the hook and allow the bolt to fly forward again.

CONTROLS

The combined safety catch and selector switch is located on the left of the frame, above the grip. The vertical position is 'safe'; the catch is rotated back for single shots or forward for automatic fire. The cocking knobs travel in slots on each side of the receiver, and are grasped with the finger and thumb of the non-firing hand. The magazine catch is a button on the left side of the frame just behind the magazine housing.

SERVICE

Was issued to some Czech units and widely distributed to Soviet supported regimes during the Cold War.

Manufacturer:	State ordnance factories, Czechoslovakia
Model:	Skorpion Model 61
Calibres:	.32ACP; also produced in .380ACP, 9mm Makarov and 9mm Parabellum
Action:	Blowback, selective fully automatic
Feed:	10- or 20-round magazine
Rate of fire:	840rpm
Sights:	Blade and notch open sights
Weight:	1,590g
Length:	269mm (513mm with butt extended)
Barrel:	112mm

Skorpion Model 61 (stock folded).　　　　　*(Ian Hogg)*

Skorpion Model 61 (stock extended).　　　　　*(Ian Hogg)*

BACKGROUND

Introduced in 1984, the Socimi employed precision castings for the receiver rather than pressed steel. It was light and compact and earned a reputation for simplicity and reliability. The balance of the weapon is good and it can be fired successfully one-handed.

The manufacturer went into liquidation in 1989, and the design was taken over by Luigi Franchi, who marketed the weapon as the LF821.

OPERATION

The Socimi 821 offers selective single shots or fully automatic fire, operating on the blowback principle. Operation is standard for a straightforward blowback SMG: insert a loaded magazine into the magazine housing/grip, operate the cocking handle, select single shots or fully automatic, and pull the trigger. The bolt is held back against spring pressure until the trigger is pulled, and on full auto continues to cycle until either the trigger is released or the magazine is emptied.

CONTROLS

The cocking handle travels in a slot in the upper surface of the box-section receiver. The combined safety catch/ fire selector is located on the left of the frame, at the top of the grip: the rearmost position is 'safe', one click forward for single shots, two clicks forward for automatic. There is also a grip safety located in the upper rear surface of the grip. The magazine catch is located at the bottom of the left grip.

Manufacturer:	Socimi, Italy (Design later taken over by Luigi Franchi)
Model:	Socimi Type 821
Calibre:	9mm Parabellum
Action:	Blowback, selective fully automatic
Feed:	32-round box magazine
Rate of fire:	600rpm
Sights:	Blade and aperture open sights, with flip rearsight for 100m and 200m
Weight:	2,450g
Length:	400mm (600mm with folding buttstock extended)
Barrel:	200mm
Introduced:	1984

Socimi Type 821.

(Ian Hogg)

BACKGROUND

Launched in 1983, the Spectre is an unusual sub-machine gun in a number of ways. It fires from a closed bolt and has a double-action mechanism similar to a double-action pistol: pulling the trigger cocks the hammer, then releases it as the trigger is pulled through to fire the chambered round. A de-cocking mechanism allows the weapon to be carried with a round in the chamber, but with the hammer down – relatively safe to carry, but ready for immediate action. An automatic safety mechanism prevents the hammer striking the firing pin unless the trigger is pulled.

Another unusual feature of the Spectre is a four-stack magazine, which has a capacity of 50 rounds in a manageabley sized box magazine.

The weapon is made with extensive use of pressed steel in parts such as the receiver and folding buttstock, and is available in a number of variants, including a carbine (C model), and pistol (P model).

OPERATION

The Spectre's operation is unusual for a sub-machine gun. Most SMGs use an open bolt system, with a fixed firing pin in the form of a stud on the breech face; the round is fired by the forward movement of the bolt, the stud hitting the primer as the bolt closes, and the bolt is immediately thrown back by the gas pressure generated in the barrel. In the Spectre, there is a separate firing pin which is struck by a hammer after the bolt has closed on a live round. This permits the use of a double-action mechanism similar to that found in modern semi-automatic pistols. A loaded magazine is inserted and the cocking handle drawn back and released. The bolt flies forward under spring pressure, loading a live round into the chamber. The hammer remains in the cocked position, held by the trigger mechanism. Operating the de-cocking lever will now release the hammer without firing the round, so that the weapon can be carried with the hammer down on a loaded chamber. Pulling the trigger will draw back the hammer, then release it to fire;

Spectre M-4 (showing lhs). *(Ian Hogg)*

Spectre M-4 (showing rhs). *(Ian Hogg)*

123

firing will continue until either the trigger is released or the magazine is empty.

The bolt mechanism incorporates a forced draught device to ventilate the barrel for cooling. This counters the tendency for the barrel of a closed-bolt SMG to overheat during automatic fire.

CONTROLS

The de-cocking lever is ambidextrous, and is located in the receiver above the grip. Pressing the lever down releases the hammer without firing the chambered round. The selector switch is forward of the de-cocking lever, above the trigger guard; this is also ambidextrous and can be operated by the trigger finger, permitting the selection of single shots or fully automatic fire. The magazine catch is located in the rear of the magazine housing. Safety is provided by the de-cocking mechanism and automatic firing pin locking; there is no separate safety catch.

Manufacturer:	Sites, Italy
Model:	Spectre M-4
Calibre:	9mm Parabellum
Action:	Double-action, de-cockable, closed bolt, blowback, selective fully automatic
Feed:	Four-stack 50-round box magazine
Rate of fire:	850rpm
Sights:	Protected adjustable blade and notch open sights
Weight:	2,900g
Length:	350mm (580mm with butt extended)
Barrel:	130mm
Variants:	Spectre C – semi-automatic carbine with 420mm unshrouded barrel
	Spectre P – semi-automatic pistol with no foregrip or folding buttstock
Introduced:	1984

BACKGROUND

The Star Model Z-84 replaced earlier Star models in 1985 as the standard SMG of the Spanish armed forces. It marked a complete departure from earlier designs, which had been based around a tubular receiver; the Z-84 has a box-section receiver made from pressed sheet steel, and makes use of investment castings for internal parts. With its boxy receiver and magazine housed in the grip, and protruding below it, the weapon looks a lot like the Israeli Uzi. It is a simple and effective design, which has proved robust and reliable in use. Some thought has gone into ensuring that the action is protected against the ingress of dirt and debris: the cocking handle is mounted on a separate plate which closes under spring pressure once the handle is released, so covering the cocking handle slot; the ejection port is normally sealed by the bolt and opens only momentarily when a spent case is being ejected, at which time any debris in the opening will be blown clear by the blast of gases.

OPERATION

The Star Z-84 is a simple blowback design, despite the various features added to keep dirt and debris out of the mechanism. The bolt is the wrap-around type, with a recessed breech face which overhangs the chamber end of the barrel at firing. This improves the weapon's balance, making it easier to control during automatic fire, and making it possible to fire the weapon effectively one-handed. There is a folding buttstock, which folds up over the top of the receiver when not in use.

CONTROLS

The cocking handle is located on the right side of the receiver, in a slot which is closed by a spring-loaded dust cover. The safety catch is a push-through button inside the trigger guard: push left to right for 'fire'. The fire selector is a sliding switch on left side of the receiver, just above the trigger guard: forward for single shots, rearward for fully automatic. The magazine catch is in the heel of the butt.

SERVICE

Adopted by the Spanish armed forces in 1985.

Manufacturer:	Star, Spain
Model:	Z-84
Calibre:	9mm Parabellum
Action:	Blowback, selective fully automatic
Feed:	25 or 30 round box magazine
Rate of fire:	600rpm
Sights:	Adjustable blade and aperture open sights, with flip rearsight for 100m and 200m
Weight:	3,000g
Length:	410mm (615mm with folding stock extended)
Barrel:	215mm

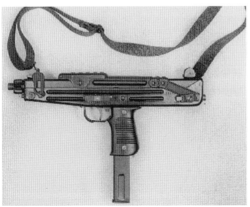

Star Model Z-84. *(Ian Hogg)*

125

BACKGROUND

By rights the Sterling should be long obsolete. In production since 1953, it replaced the Second World War Sten as the standard SMG of the British Army in the 1960s and bears the design hallmarks of having evolved from the Sten. It is a simple design, with a tubular receiver housing a bolt and return spring. The trigger assembly is attached on the underside of the receiver tube and the magazine housing is in the left side so that the magazine extends horizontally. The standard model has a ventilated barrel shroud and a folding skeleton stock which, in the folded position, lies under the barrel.

Sterling Armament Co folded in 1988 and was purchased by Royal Ordnance, who took over the tooling and production of spare parts. The weapon has not been produced since then. During its heyday, however, the Sterling was widely produced and sold, and was used in more than 50 countries around the globe. It is no longer British Army issue, but a number of Sterlings are still held by reserve forces, and the weapon may be encountered in the hands of criminal and terrorist groups virtually anywhere.

OPERATION

The operating principle of the Sterling is about as simple as an SMG can get. A heavy bolt travels in the tubular receiver, with a return spring pressing it towards the breech of the barrel. To operate, a loaded magazine is inserted in the magazine housing and the cocking lever pulled rearwards and then released. This leaves the bolt in its rearmost position, held by the trigger mechanism. The safety catch is released and the trigger pulled, releasing the bolt to fly forwards and collect a round from the magazine, then load it into the chamber and fire it by means of a fixed firing pin which aligns with the cartridge primer as the round is pushed home into the chamber. In fact the cartridge fires as the bolt is still moving forward. The gas pressure generated on firing pushes the bolt back again against the return spring. The extractor claw on the bolt extracts the fired case, which is ejected out through the ejection port when it strikes the fixed ejector on the inside wall of the receiver. The cycle continues as long as the trigger is pulled and there are rounds in the magazine.

CONTROLS

The cocking handle travels in a slot in the upper surface of the tubular receiver. The magazine catch is at the rear of the magazine housing. The combined safety catch and fire selector switch is on the upper left of the grip, where it can be operated with the thumb of the trigger hand. It is marked '1' for single shots and '34' (the number of rounds in a full magazine) for full automatic.

SERVICE

Adopted by the British Army in the 1960s, the Sterling in it various forms has been sold worldwide to military, police and security forces. Although now considered obsolete, it is still in use around the globe.

Sterling L2A3/Canadian C1. *(Ian Hogg)*

Manufacturer:	Sterling Armament Co, UK (Taken over by Royal Ordnance in 1988)
Model:	Sterling L2A3 (Mark 4 Sterling SMG)
Calibre:	9mm Parabellum
Action:	Blowback, selective fully automatic
Feed:	34-round box magazine (other sizes were also produced)
Rate of fire:	550rpm
Sights:	Protected blade and aperture open sights
Weight:	2,720g
Length:	483mm (690mm with folding buttstock extended)
Barrel:	198mm
Variants:	Mark 5 Patchett/Sterling L34A1 – silenced version
	Mark 6 Sterling carbine – single shot only version for civilian US market
	Mark 7 Para Pistol – shortened version, in both single shot and selective fully automatic variants, for use in confined spaces
	Mark 8 – single shot version produced for police and security forces, firing from closed bolt

BACKGROUND

The futuristic looking bullpup design Steyr AUG assault rifle was developed to fire the NATO 5.56mm x 45 round, and in this form has been adopted by the armies of various countries, including Australia, New Zealand, Ireland, Saudi Arabia and Oman.

The manufacturers produce a conversion kit to allow the standard AUG rifle to be converted into a 9mm sub-machine gun. The conversion kit consists of a replacement barrel in 9mm calibre, a replacement bolt group, a magazine adapter and a magazine. The magazine used is the same as that used in the Steyr Mpi69 sub-machine gun (qv).

OPERATION

The conversion turns the AUG into a blowback weapon, with a one-piece bolt assembly. This has a separate firing pin, and fires from a closed bolt.

CONTROLS

The controls are the same as those on the standard Steyr AUG assault rifle. There is a cross-bolt safety catch above the trigger (press right to left for 'fire'). Fire selection is via trigger pressure: first pressure gives single shots; further pressure gives automatic fire. The magazine catch is at the rear of the magazine adapter/housing. The cocking handle is on the left side of the receiver.

SERVICE

The 5.56mm assault rifle version is in service with various armed forces around the globe, including Australia, New Zealand, Ireland, Saudi Arabia and Oman.

Manufacturer:	Steyr-Mannlicher, Austria
Model:	Steyr AUG Para
Calibre:	9mm Parabellum
Action:	Blowback, closed bolt, selective fully automatic
Feed:	32-round magazine
Rate of fire:	700rpm
Sights:	1.5x optical sight (standard on assault rifle)
Weight:	3,300g
Length:	665mm
Barrel:	420mm

Steyr AUG 9mm Para.

BACKGROUND

Produced from the end of the 1960s, the Steyr MPi69 is unusual in that it has a sling attached to the cocking lever and is cocked by pulling on the sling itself. Other than this it is a relatively straightforward 9mm sub-machine gun design, albeit a robust and effective one. The receiver is a rectangular box of sheet steel and is covered on three sides by a nylon housing which also forms the grip and contains the trigger mechanism. The bolt is the overhung variety, with a significant part of its mass forward of the breech on firing. This leads to improved balance and handling characteristics, as well as helping to reduce the overall length of the weapon.

The MPi81 is basically the same weapon, but the sling is attached to a conventional sling swivel and there is a cocking handle for cocking in the normal way.

OPERATION

Operation is straightforward blowback, with the weapon firing from an open bolt.

CONTROLS

Cocking on the MPi69 is done with the sling, which must be held out at right angles to the receiver before the mechanism can be cocked. The MPi81 has a standard cocking handle on the upper left surface of the receiver. The safety catch is a cross-bolt passing through the upper rear surface of the trigger guard: push through fully from right to left for full automatic fire; in its mid position the catch gives single shots only. In the full automatic position, the trigger provides fire selection: first pressure gives single shots, further pressure gives automatic fire.

There is a further safety device incorporated into the bolt, which has three sear positions. These engage in turn as the bolt travels rearwards, preventing the bolt flying forward and firing a shot if the main sear fails to engage (eg if the cocking handle slips during cocking, or if a low pressure round is fired which fails to drive the bolt fully back).

Manufacturer:	Steyr-Mannlicher, Austria
Model:	MPi69 and MPi81
Calibre:	9mm Parabellum
Action:	Blowback, selective fully automatic
Feed:	32-round box magazine
Rate of fire:	550rpm
Sights:	Blade and aperture open sights, flip rearsight graduated for 100m and 200m
Weight:	3,130g
Length:	465mm (670mm with telescopic butt extended)
Barrel:	260mm
Introduced:	1969

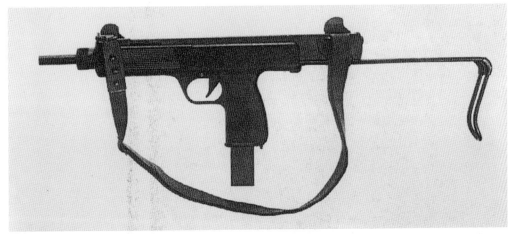

Steyr MPi 81.

The Steyr TMP or 'Tactical Machine Pistol' superseded the MPi69 and MPi81 in 1993. It is intended to provide the firepower of a sub-machine gun in a package the size and weight of a pistol. It offers true fully automatic fire, with a 15- or 30-round magazine, and is chambered for the ubiquitous 9mm x 19 Parabellum round. The outer casing is of black polymer and there is a distinctive broom-handle type extension on the foregrip to allow two-handed operation.

Manufacturer:	Steyr-Mannlicher, Austria
Model:	TMP
Calibre:	9mm Parabellum
Action:	Locked bolt recoil-operated selective fully automatic
Feed:	15- or 30-round box magazine
Rate of fire:	900rpm
Sights:	Post and notch adjustable open sights
Weight:	1,300g
Length:	282mm
Barrel:	130mm

BACKGROUND
The Uru was adopted by the Brazilian army in 1977. It is a blowback design and makes extensive use of stampings, pressings and tube steel. The weapon has only 17 parts and uses no pins or screws; the weapon can be totally disassembled in around 30 seconds. It fires the 9mm Parabellum round and may have a fixed or folding stock. A silenced version is also available.

OPERATION
The Uru works on the blowback principle and offers selective single shot or fully automatic fire.

CONTROLS
The cocking handle travels in a slot on the upper right side of the tubular receiver. The safety catch/fire selector is on the left side of the frame, above the grip. 'Safe' is forward, single shot vertical, and fully automatic pointing to the rear. The magazine catch is in the rear of the magazine housing.

SERVICE
Brazilian armed forces.

Manufacturer:	Mekanika Industriae, Brazil
Model:	Uru
Calibre:	9mm Parabellum
Action:	Blowback, selective fully automatic
Feed:	30-round box magazine
Rate of fire:	750rpm
Sights:	Fixed blade and aperture open sights
Weight:	2,580g
Length:	425mm with stock folded
Barrel:	175mm

Uru Mekanika *(Ian Hogg)*

131

BACKGROUND

Developed in 1949 by Lieutenant Uziel Gal of the Israeli Army, the Uzi sub-machine gun has become one of the best-known weapons of its type throughout the world. A robust and reliable weapon, it is still in widespread use today.

The Uzi is recognisable by its pressed steel box-section receiver, the vertical grip through which the magazine passes,= and its ribbed plastic foregrip which partially shrouds the forward section of the receiver.

The Uzi has seen service with numerous armies around the world, including those of Israel, Belgium, Ireland, Thailand, West Germany and Iran. It is used by various police and security forces, as well as close protection operators. It is also prized by criminal and terrorist organisations.

OPERATION

The Uzi makes use of a principle known as advanced primer ignition. This means that the round is fired while the bolt is still travelling forward, allowing the bolt to be made lighter than would be necessary if it fired from a static bolt. The bolt is also overhung, which improves the balance and handling characteristics of the weapon, and allows a longer barrel than would otherwise be possible.

The weapon fires from an open bolt, ie the bolt is cocked and remains in the rear position until the trigger is pulled. On firing, the bolt flies forward, collecting a round from the magazine and engaging it in the extractor claw. As the bolt continues forward, the round is guided into the chamber, and the primer aligns with the fixed firing pin on the breech face. The friction of the case in the chamber is sufficient to drive the round back onto the firing pin, igniting the primer before the bolt is fully closed. As the bolt reaches its closed position and the gas pressure builds up, it is driven back again, drawing the empty case with it by means of the extractor claw. As the bolt moves back, the case is knocked out through the ejection port by a fixed ejector lug. The bolt continues rearwards against spring pressure, until it reaches the end of its travel. If the weapon is set to automatic fire, the trigger is still pressed, and there is still a round in the magazine, the bolt will come forward again to repeat the cycle.

CONTROLS

The cocking handle is on the top surface of the box-section receiver. There is a grip safety which prevents the bolt moving forward unless the weapon is held firmly in the hand. A combined safety catch/fire selector is located at the top of the left grip; this is a sliding catch which can be operated with the thumb of the trigger hand – back for 'safe', forward one click for single shots and two clicks for full automatic fire. The magazine catch is at the bottom of the left grip

SERVICE

Israeli armed forces, and widely exported to other countries worldwide.

Manufacturer:	Ta'as Israel Industries (formerly Israel Military Industries), Israel
Model:	Uzi
Calibre:	9mm Parabellum
Action:	Blowback, selective fully automatic
Feed:	32-round box magazine (25 round version also available)
Rate of fire:	950rpm
Sights:	Post and aperture open sights, with flip rearsight graduated for 100 and 200m
Weight:	3,700g
Length:	470mm (650mm with folding buttstock extended)
Barrel:	260mm

The Mini-Uzi is very much like the standard Uzi (qv) in all respects except its overall dimensions. Designed to be more easily concealed, it is favoured by security operators and undercover police. For details of operation and controls, see Uzi.

Manufacturer:	Ta'as Israel Industries (formerly Israel Military Industries), Israel
Model:	Mini-Uzi
Calibre:	9mm Parabellum
Action:	Blowback, selective fully automatic
Feed:	20-, 25- and 32-round box magazines
Rate of fire:	950rpm
Sights:	Protected post and aperture open sights
Weight:	2,700g
Length:	360mm (600mm with folding buttstock extended)
Barrel:	197mm

Mini Uzi.

(Ian Hogg)

The Micro-Uzi is the latest in the Uzi family, and like the Mini-Uzi is very similar to the standard Uzi (qv) in all respects except its overall dimensions, which are smaller again than those of the Mini-Uzi. It is designed to offer fearsome firepower in the smallest possible package. This it certainly achieves, although accuracy at medium to long range suffers as a result. For details of operation and controls, see Uzi.

Manufacturer:	Ta'as Israel Industries (formerly Israel Military Industries), Israel
Model:	Micro-Uzi
Calibres:	9mm Parabellum (also available in .45ACP)
Action:	Blowback, selective fully automatic
Feed:	20-round box magazine
Rate of fire:	1,250rpm
Sights:	Protected post and aperture open sights
Weight:	1,950g
Length:	250mm (460mm with folding stock extended)
Barrel:	117mm

Micro Uzi. *(Ian Hogg)*

Micro Uzi. *(Ian Hogg)*

135

BACKGROUND

The Ultralite was conceived, as its name suggests, as a lightweight sub-machine gun. Manufactured by Weaver in the USA, it makes considerable use of aluminium in the form of investment castings; key components are made of stainless steel for strength.

OPERATION

The Ultralite is a blowback weapon, firing from an open bolt. The bolt is overhung, surrounding the barrel when closed. This improves balance and handling, as well as providing a degree of protection for the firer in the event of a malfunction.

The weapon is designed to be easy to maintain: a permanent lubricant removes the need for oiling, and it can be field stripped quickly and easily without the need for tools.

CONTROLS

Cocking handle on top of receiver. Safety/selector switch above trigger. Magazine release catch on bottom left of magazine housing.

Manufacturer:	Weaver Arms, USA
Model:	PKS-9 Ultralite
Calibre:	9mm Parabellum
Action:	Blowback, selective fully automatic
Feed:	25-, 30- or 42-round box magazines
Rate of fire:	1,000rpm
Sights:	Protected blade and notch open sights; optical sighting devices can be fitted
Weight:	2,770g
Length:	416mm (without detachable stock)
Barrel:	181mm
Variants:	AP-9 Assault pistol – pistol version Nighthawk carbine – semi-automatic carbine firing from closed bolt

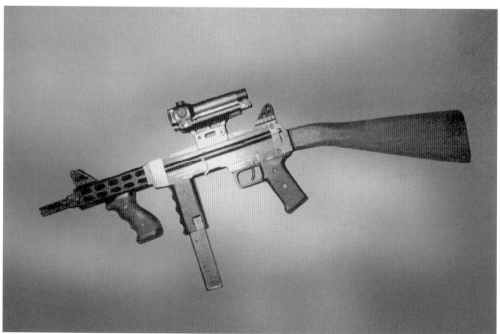

Weaver PKS-9 Ultralite.

(Ian Hogg)

ASSAULT RIFLES

The rifle is the infantryman's personal weapon, his own tool for use on the battlefield. At the beginning of gunpowder age warfare, crude hand-held weapons were wielded by specially trained infantrymen. By the time industrialisation allowed mass-produced firearms to be made available to large numbers of infantrymen, the character of the battlefield had already altered beyond all recognition – and was still changing at a remarkable pace.

Looking at firearm developments of the nineteenth century, one can see at a glance how rapidly changes were occurring. For example, in 1838 the British Army adopted the percussion system and only two years later the Prussian Army began to re-equip with the Dreyse breech-loading 'needle gun'. By 1851 the British Army had adopted the Minié rifle and in 1866 the French Army was taking the Chassepot rifle into service. In 1884 the German Army was introducing the Mauser bolt-action rifle into service and at the same time smokeless propellants were being developed, such as the French 'Poudre B' and the British 'Cordite' in 1890, only two years after the introduction of the Lee-Metford rifle which went on to be developed into the legendary .303 inch calibre Lee-Enfield bolt-action rifle which served for many years.

The lineage charting the development of the modern assault rifle can actually be traced directly back to events in the Second World War. Studies conducted by tacticians in Germany during the inter-war years revealed that infantrymen rarely identified targets at ranges of more than 400m, while basic weapon training meant that they had only a better-than-average chance of hitting a target of 300m range. Therefore, they concluded, why produce a round which was designed to carry out to ranges in excess of 1000m? With Adolf Hitler in power and Germany undergoing rearmament the study group attempted to 'sell' their theories to the Ordnance Supply Office. Unfortunately their idea of a short 7mm round came at a time when the German Army had billions of 7.92mm rounds of ammunition. Furthermore, it is understood that Hitler was deliberating over future infantry weapon designs.

Some sources claim that Hitler did not accept the concept of new rifle designs and was actively encouraging new sub-machine gun designs to augment the MP38 and MP40 designs. Other sources claim that he was seeking weapons with increased hitting distance. Whatever the reason, the weapon firing the new 'Short' 7.92mm round was brought in by back-door methods, obviously in an effort to circumvent political bickering, and was termed the MP43. Once sold on the idea, it was Hitler himself who coined the term 'Sturmgewehr' or assault rifle. By the end of the Second World War most armies had at least one semi-automatic rifle in service, with the most notable exceptions being Britain and Japan.

With many countries all but bankrupted by the effects of the war, funding for the development of small arms was severely limited. By the time of the Korean War most armies involved in the conflict were using rifles from the period of the Second World War. In the late 1940s Britain did flirt briefly with developing a semi-automatic rifle in the form of the EM2. This was a 'bullpup' design firing a cartridge of .280 calibre. At the time America was advocating the 7.62mm round as the way to go and so the programme to develop the EM2 was cancelled. By the early 1950s America was developing the Armalite Rifle Model AR-10 and the M14 rifle, both in the newly-accepted calibre of 7.62mm. In the event, the AR-10 was shelved in favour of the M14 rifle, which had a cyclic rate of 750 rounds per minute. This rifle served the US Army well into the 1960s, and gave sterling results during the Vietnam War.

The Belgian company of Fabrique Nationale in Herstal was the only European firearms manufacturer of note to make real advances in the design and development of semi-automatic rifles, and produced the FAL in the early 1950s. One of these early models was produced for trials by Britain in 1952/53, and from this arose the L1A1 Self-Loading Rifle, or SLR, which was only replaced in the 1980s, by the SA80 rifle, following some thirty years of service.

The new standard NATO round of 7.62mm was not readily accepted in all NATO countries, with France staying with 7.5mm as used in the MAS Modèle 49. Questions regarding the power of the new round were also raised following an incident in British Guiana (subsequently known as Guyana) in 1962. A detachment of 1st Battalion Coldstream Guards was deployed to disperse a rioting crowd which had ignored requests to clear the area. As an incentive to force the crowd to break up, a single shot was ordered to be fired at the crowd. At the time, this action was considered to be minimum force, but the single 7.62mm round fired from the SLR killed three people and wounded a fourth. If ever proof as to the efficacy of a high velocity round was needed, this was it. The FN FAL was adopted in various forms by a number of other countries, including Australia and Canada who knew it as the L2A1 and C1 respectively.

The continued involvement of US forces in the Vietnam War spurred on the American company of Colt to produce in large numbers the AR-15 rifle, more commonly known as the M16. This rifle fired a 5.56mm x 45 round and, like the FN FAL, has been taken into service in various forms by many armies around the world, including limited service with the British Army. In fact the 5.56mm (.223) round is now the standard NATO round, even being used by the French Army in their FAMAS.

At about the same time the Russians were developing the ubiquitous AK47, which by the late 1970s had exceeded a production run of over 35 million weapons. The design of this rifle was influenced by the wartime German MP43. It too fires a 7.62mm round, but of 39mm length as opposed to the NATO 7.62mm round which has a length of 51mm. The basic design of the AK47 has spawned a whole range of copies, such as the Chinese Model 56. During the Cold War the infantry of armies making up the Warsaw Pact were equipped with the AK47 rifle, and it is still built under licence in some former Warsaw Pact states. Variations on the original AK47 design included the Romanian version which has a forward pistol grip fitted, and versions with folding buttstocks. The Russian equivalent of NATO's now standard 5.56mm round is the 5.45mm for use with the AK74, which was first observed in 1979. Outwardly the AK74 is virtually identical to the AK47, with few modifications other than the change of calibre.

The most dramatic development to affect the design of assault rifles has been the rise of the 'bullpup' design. Even this has not resulted in a revolution in weapon design, with the SA80, FAMAS and AUG the only bullpup designs to have been produced in any significant numbers. The Austrian-designed AUG is the most versatile of all bullpup designs and is currently in widespread service, including the Army of the Republic of Ireland, Australia and New Zealand. The French FAMAS remains in sole use with the French Armed Forces and the British Army's SA80, really the resurrected EM2, has still not been sold overseas.

For the foreseeable future, it seems likely that the assault rifle will remain a box magazine-fed weapon of conventional layout. Experiments with new weapon designs and layouts are conducted from time to time, but by and large an army will stay with what it knows and trusts. For example, the Swiss are equipped with SIG-built weapons, the Americans have the M16 from Colt and Russia has its AK47 and AK74 designs from former state arsenals.

Most assault rifles are capable of firing rifle grenades, for anti-personnel, smoke and illuminating purposes. A large number of rifles can also be fitted with 40mm grenade-launcher systems under their barrels. These include the M16 with the M203 grenade launcher and the Austrian AUG. These grenades, fired from a separate barrel, act as a force multiplier to the infantryman and permit him to fire his rifle without being inhibited by a rifle grenade fitted to the end of the barrel.

This particular rifle from the Austrian company of Steyr is called a 'universal' gun, a claim borne out by the fact that it can be configured to a variety of roles and calibres, including 9mm and 5.56mm, and fitted with different barrels to suit the conversion. There is even a heavy-barrelled version equipped with a bipod which allows it to be used in the light support weapon role.

The weapon has a delicate appearance, but this is belied by the fact that it has been adopted by a large number of armies, including the Austrian Army and the Army of the Republic of Ireland. It can be used in all extremes of climates and terrains from desert to sub-zero conditions. The design of the AUG makes extensive use of plastic components more effectively than any other rifle of its type. In short, the AUG is the most successful bullpup design rifle in use anywhere in the world.

It can be field stripped without tools down into six main components: the barrel, receiver, trigger, bolt, magazine and stock. The basic 5.56mm version of the AUG can be converted into another configuration, such as the 9mm version or short-barrelled carbine version, by simply removing the receiver and barrel and replacing

them with the appropriate type. The AUG can also be converted into a sniping rifle, which features a low telescope mount instead of the usual optical sight with integral telescope. This allows the firer to mount a specialised sniping telescope or night-vision units.

The optical sight, which is fitted as standard to the assault rifle version of the AUG, has been optimised for battle ranges, with a black reticle ring in the centre of the field of vision. This allows the firer to place the sight onto a man-sized target and engage it at 300m ranges.

There are several aspects of this rifle which make it instantly recognisable: the high set optical sight in its standard form, the large buttstock, a forward hand grip which can be folded, and the distinctive handguard which forms part of the pistol grip. The magazine well is located behind the pistol grip in the traditional bullpup layout. The weapon can be quickly and easily converted to suit either left-handed or right-handed firers. This is done simply by changing the ejector from one side of the bolt to the other, and rotating the ejection port over to the

Troops of the Austrian Army carrying the Steyr AUG rifle in sub-zero mountain warfare conditions.

preferred side.

The receiver unit of the AUG is manufactured from aluminium die-casting which includes the seating for the barrel and the bearings for the two bolt guides. The bolt is of the rotating type with multi-lugs and this runs on the steel bolt guide rods which are held in the receiver.

(top) **An Austrian soldier mans a roadblock during a UN peacekeeping mission. He is carrying the Steyr AUG rifle.**

(bottom) **Members of the Austrian Army on exercise carrying the Steyr AUG rifle.**

(above) **Member of the Army of the Republic of Ireland in the doorway of an Alouette III helicopter. He is carrying the Steyr AUG rifle.**

(below) **The Steyr AUG fitted with the M203-type 40mm grenade launcher. Note separate trigger mechanism for firing the grenade.**

This eliminates contact between the receiver and the bolt. The return springs are concealed in the guide rods, the left-hand one of which, along with the cocking handle, serves to cock the weapon for firing by operating the bolt when loading, whilst the right-hand rod acts as the gas piston. The barrel unit of the AUG comprises the barrel itself, the gas port and cylinder, the gas regulator and a folding handle, which can be used to change barrels when converting the weapon from one role to another. The barrel locks into the receiver by a series of interrupted lugs, and, once aligned properly, the gas cylinder, which carries a short-stroke piston, is lined up with the right-hand bolt guide rod. The safety catch is located at the top of the pistol grip and is ambidextrous in action.

The weapon features no fire selector switch and instead relies on trigger pressure to achieve selective fire. For single shots the first pressure is taken up to the first sear action. After releasing the trigger and applying further pressure fully automatic fire is achieved. The automatic firing lever will prevent firing until the bolt is locked. This action, it must be said, does take a little getting used to. However, once it has been mastered it comes as second nature.

The weapon is supplied with ammunition from a 30-round capacity box magazine, and has a cyclic rate of 650 rounds per minute. However, to prevent the barrel from overheating too quickly the maximum number of rounds to be fired in full automatic is recommended as being no more than 150.

To field strip the AUG, the infantryman first checks that the weapon is in an unloaded and safe state. He then removes the barrel by pressing in the barrel locking stud with his thumb, and, using the handle, rotates it to the right until the lugs disengage and the barrel can be pulled forward. By turning the cocking handle to the left the bolt moves forward. The housing lock is pushed to the right until it engages and the housing group extracted through the butt, with the bolt assembly. The bolt assembly is removed from the housing group, the butt cap is depressed and the rear sling swivel, which acts as a securing pin, is removed from the left. The butt cap can then be removed and the removal of the trigger mechanism, by pulling it backwards from the butt, completes the stripping action. The infantryman need strip no further for normal field cleaning and servicing.

There are a number of other features and attachments which can be used with the AUG, such as rifle grenades, a knife-type bayonet and a blank firing attachment for training purposes. The rifle can also be fitted with a 40mm grenade launcher, which operates in a similar manner to the M203.

The AUG has been taken into service by various police forces around the world, as well as military units.

SPECIFICATIONS:

(Standard rifle version)

Calibre:	5.56mm x 45
Weight:	3.6kg
Length:	790mm
Barrel:	508mm
Rifling:	One turn in 228mm

(top) **The short-barrelled FN-FNC 5.56mm rifle as used by the Belgian Army.**

(middle) **The short-barrelled FN-FNC 5.56mm rifle as used by the Belgian Army.**

(bottom) **The standard FN-FNC 5.56mm rifle as used by the Belgian Army.**

The FNC assault rifle was introduced by the Belgian company, Fabrique Nationale of Herstal, and replaced the older Carabine Automatique Légère, or CAL, which had been produced by the same company. Fabrique Nationale, now a subsidiary of the French armaments company, GIAT, has produced many other weapons, including the FN-FAL which was taken into service by many countries. The Australians accepted the FN-FAL

The standard FN-FNC 5.56mm rifle as used by the Belgian Army.

into service as the L1A1, the Canadians knew it as the C1 and the British Army used a version known as the L1A1 self-loading rifle, all of which fired the 7.62mm x 51 cartridge.

The FNC assault rifle fires the smaller calibre 5.56mm x 45mm cartridge from a 30-round capacity magazine, with both military versions having a cyclic rate of fire of between 600 and 750 rounds per minute. The FNC can fire either the SS109 or M193 round, with only slight variation in muzzle velocity. The magazines used on the rifles are of the same type used by the M16, and can also be used on the Minimi light machine gun.

The two military versions are identical, except for the length of the barrel, and have folding butt stocks. There is the ability to fit reinforced polyamide butt stocks to the weapons as an optional feature, but the current trend appears to be for shorter rifles, which means designs with folding stocks are often adopted for service. There is a 'Law Enforcement' version of the FNC which differs from the two military versions only by having no three-round burst facility or the capability of firing fully automatic. Despite this, it can still fire at a cyclic rate of 60 rounds per minute, which should more than meet any law enforcement requirement.

The operation of the FNC is by gas, using the well-proven, almost standard, method of mounting the return piston and gas cylinder above the barrel. The breech is locked by a rotating bolt with a two-lug head, which locks into the barrel extension. This design reduces the stress on the bolt and bolt carrier, and so can be made much lighter. The overall weight of the weapon is kept to a minimum by manufacturing the body from pressed steel; the trigger frame is of light alloy and the forestock is plastic.

The rifles can be used either left or right handed and there is also the option of fitting a removable bipod to the standard, or long, version of the FNC. The sights on the weapons comprise an adjustable post-type for the front sight with a flip-type aperture rear sight, which has lateral adjustment for range settings. Most types of day and night sights can be fitted to the mounting bracket, provided they have NATO standard fittings. This may limit the range of optical devices capable of being used with the FNC, but it does eliminate the need to machine and fit special adapter brackets.

The fire selector switch is located on the left-hand side of the weapon, just above the trigger guard and features all the settings necessary, including fully automatic. The weapons are easy to field strip for cleaning and require no tools for this process. After unloading and making the weapon safe, the user pushes the body securing pin from the right-hand side, just above the pistol grip, and this releases the lower portion of the weapon to expose the working parts. Pulling the cocking handle back pulls the bolt assembly to the rear, where it can be withdrawn from the weapon.

The FNC rifles can be fitted with either the American-style M7 knife-type bayonet with an adapter bracket, or the tubular handled bayonet which was specially developed for the rifle and fits over the flash-hider. Unfortunately, this latter type of bayonet puts it in the same category as the British L85A1 bayonet and the bayonet fitted to the Swedish SG540 series of rifles, with its latent handling difficulties after firing. The FNC standard rifle can fire rifle grenades, for which purpose

145

the rifle is fitted with a gas-tap device that folds over the front sight and serves to prevent the flow of gas from the special ballistite cartridge from entering the cylinder. This device serves to give extra firing pressure to the rifle grenade and also acts as the sighting unit for the firer who aligns it along the upper surface of the grenade to gauge the best elevation for firing.

SPECIFICATIONS:

	Standard FNC	Short-barrelled FNC
Calibre:	5.56mm x 45 (SS109 or M193)	5.56mm x 45 (SS109 or M193)
Length:	997mm	911mm (Butt stock extended)
	766mm	666mm (Butt stock folded)
Weight:	3.8kg	3.7kg
Barrel:	449mm	363mm
Rifling:	Six grooves, right hand, one turn in 178mm	
Optional rifling:	Six grooves, right hand, one turn in 305mm	
Muzzle velocity:	965m/sec with M193 round	
	915m/sec with SS109 round	

The M76 assault rifle traces its origins back to the late 1950s, when Finland decided to produce a local copy of the Russian-built AK47. The first model to be developed was known as the M60 and featured plastic furniture in place of wooden; the muzzle brake was also slightly different from the Russian model.

The M60 was taken into service by the Finnish armed forces and became known as the M62. This remained the standard weapon of Finland's armed forces until 1976, when the M76 rifle appeared. This was actually a marketing move to take advantage of the different calibres and styles beginning to emerge at that time. So successful was this relaunch of the basic weapon that the Finnish armed forces also picked it up.

The M76 is available in either the Standard or the Law Enforcement M76 models. Each of these is also available in the 7.62mm x 39 (the calibre used by the former Warsaw Pact states) or 5.56mm x 45, which is the NATO standard. Each of the designs comes in three variants: one with a standard folding butt stock; one with all-plastic stocks; and a version which has a plastic forestock but wooden butt stock. These are known respectively as M76T (which has a tubular-shaped butt stock), the M76F with a folding plastic butt stock, and the M76W to indicate it has a wooden butt stock. There is a long-barrelled version, known as the M78, which is fitted with a bipod, but this is more commonly used as a Light Support Weapon rather than as an assault rifle.

The frame of the M76 series is manufactured entirely from milled chrome-alloy steel, as is the mechanism. This produces a very hard-wearing weapon able to withstand the rigours of the battlefield and extremes in terrain and climate. The rifle can be field stripped without the use of tools, and breaks down into six component parts: the frame, top cover, bolt assembly and return spring assembly, gas tube and guide.

Each version of the M76 uses box magazines, with capacities of 15, 20 or 30 rounds, and can achieve cyclic rates of 600 to 650 rounds per minute. The fire selector

(top) **The M76 rifle as used by the Finnish Army. This version has the tubular folding butt stock.**

(bottom) **M76 rifle with fixed wooden butt stock, as used by the Finnish Army.**

The Finnish M76 rifle stripped for cleaning. Note the cleaning kit, knife-type bayonet and the 20- and 30-round capacity magazines.

switch is located on the right-hand side of the weapon, along with the cocking handle, and has three settings. The top setting is 'safe', the middle setting allows a three-round burst, and the lower setting is for single shot. This configuration of cocking lever and fire selector might appear to be awkward, but they can be operated quite easily by right-or left-handed firers. However, the idea of a reciprocating cocking handle coming so close to the user's face could be unnerving for first-time firers of this weapon.

The M76T carries a cleaning kit – comprising a three-piece barrel rod, barrel brushes, screwdriver and oil bottle – inside the tubular frame of the butt stock. A knife-type bayonet can be fitted to each version of the M76. The foresight of the rifle is protected by a tunnel guard and is fully adjustable. The rear sight is of the folding-leaf type with peep-sight blade, and is graduated in 100m increments out to 600m range. For use in low light level conditions the sights can be turned inwards to expose illuminated surfaces to the firer who can use them to align on a target. This is not the most accurate means of engaging a target in darkening conditions, but is a good deal better than nothing at all.

SPECIFICATIONS:

Calibre:	5.56mm x 45 NATO
	7.62mm x 39 Russian/CIS
Weight empty:	3.9kg
Weight loaded:	4.520kg with 30-round magazine of 5.56mm
	4.910kg with 30-round magazine of 7.62mm
Length:	950mm (butt stock extended)
	710mm (butt stock folded)
Barrel:	420mm
Rifling:	Six grooves, right hand, one turn in 300mm (5.56mm)
	Four grooves, right hand, one turn in 250mm (7.62mm)
Muzzle velocity:	900m/sec (5.56mm)
	719m/sec (7.62mm)

The French Army's FAMAS, standing for Fusil Automatique, Manufacture d'Armes St Etienne, is known as the 'Bugle' because of its unusual profile. The distinctive long carrying handle, which also incorporates the sights, makes this bullpup weapon immediately recognisable. Since the end of 1979 the FAMAS has been used to arm the French armed forces, and to cope with the throughput of conscript servicemen the French armed forces have ordered some 700,000 units of this weapon. It is made all the more distinctive by the fact that it is entirely black in colour.

The FAMAS can fire in single or semi-automatic fire mode, three-round burst and fully automatic. It has two fire selector switches to allow these operations. First is the semi-automatic mode, and the switch for this setting is located at the trigger level. By setting this to position

'1' the other two modes of firing are rendered inoperative. Second is the three-round burst selector which is located on the underside of the mechanism unit. When the setting of '3' is selected the fully automatic mode is inoperative and conversely, when the 'R' for automatic mode is selected, the other firing functions are inoperative.

The FAMAS rifle fires standard 5.56mm x 45mm NATO rounds from box magazines with either a 20- or 30-round capacity, and has a cyclic rate between 1,000 and 1,100 rounds per minute. By pulling the trigger in the semi-automatic mode the connecting rod causes rotation of the sear drive, which in turn frees the hammer. Under the action of the hammer spring, the hammer rotates forward to strike the firing pin which hits the base of the round in the chamber and the weapon is fired. The hammer is recocked during the backward movement of the bolt and at the end of the stroke the hammer once more hooks onto the automatic sear. During the

(left) **The FAMAS 5.56mm rifle as used by the French Army. Note the cocking handle located under the carrying handle.**

(below) **Members of a French artillery unit equipped with the FAMAS. Note how the sling allows the crew to serve the gun with the need to put the weapon on the ground.**

(above) **Soldiers of the French Army crew a Milan anti-tank missile. The man standing is carrying the FAMAS rifle slung across his chest to allow him to perform other tasks.**

(below) **Two French mortar men with a FAMAS rifle.**

automatic mode the firing sequence is virtually the same, except that the hammer does not engage with the driven sear and fires as soon as the automatic sear is clear.

The three-round burst facility of the FAMAS is slightly more complicated. When the limiter is engaged and the trigger pulled, on each backward rotation of the hammer, the hammer rod in turn causes rotation of the limiter operating lever and the driving pawl. This causes the ratchet wheel to make one turn corresponding to the counting of the shot. The first round is counted when the hammer is released to strike the firing pin and its rod frees the operating lever, which returns to its original position supported on the hub of the ratchet wheel. On the third round being fired the limiter catch stops the hammer at the end of its backward movement, hooking it onto the lower catch of the hammer. This hooking is achieved by rotation of the ratchet wheel cam, which on the third shot causes the limiter catch to pivot. Firing is interrupted and when pressure is released from the trigger it releases the limiter catch in two stages.

The FAMAS was not in service in time to equip French troops going into Kolwezi in May 1978. However, it was much in evidence during the Gulf War of 1990–91

when it was used by the French contingent which made up part of the Coalition Forces facing Saddam Hussein's Iraqi troops during Operation DESERT STORM.

The FAMAS is one of only three proven bullpup rifle designs in current use. It can fire a wide choice of rifle grenades, including anti-personnel, illuminating and anti-tank. The firer can adopt any one of three firing positions when using rifle grenades from the FAMAS. Firstly he can adopt the prone position with the butt stock resting on the ground and the weapon either at the high angle, 75°, or low angle, 45°, to engage the target. These angles will allow the firer to engage targets between 140m to 360m and 70m to 180m respectively. The firing selector is always set in position '1' when firing rifle grenades. The firer can either stand or kneel to fire his weapon from the shoulder in the direct firing mode in which case he can quite easily engage moving targets out to ranges of 75m to 100m. The last method of firing rifle grenades from the FAMAS is to use the weapon's integral bipod for support and fire in the prone position.

The FAMAS will function in temperatures ranging from -40°C to +51.5°C, but when firing rifle grenades the lower end of operating temperatures fall off to -31.5°C. It is recommended that no more than four full magazines be fired through the FAMAS without allowing some time to cool down. Barrel life of the FAMAS is put at 10,000 rounds and 420 rifle grenade firings.

The FAMAS fires the SS109 5.56mm standard NATO round which will penetrate 3.5mm of mild steel plate at 625m range and 7mm of armour plate and 15mm of light alloy plate at 180m and 273m range respectively.

The magazine is inserted into the magazine well located behind the pistol grip and the cocking lever is mounted on the upper surface of the weapon's body and protected by the carrying handle. In fact, a warning instruction in the weapon handling manual warns against the firer putting his hand between the protective/carrying handle and the cocking lever slot during firing.

The FAMAS can be easily stripped for field cleaning without the use of tools. Firstly, the weapon is unloaded and cleared as being 'safe to handle' with the magazine removed. The locking for the butt stock assembly is removed, which allows this unit to be lifted. Removing the assembly pin on the protective handle allows this unit to be lifted clear and the butt assembly is stripped. The mechanism assembly stud is next removed, usually

pushed out of place with the tip of a bullet, and this permits the mechanism to be rotated and lifted clear of the body. By pulling back on the cocking lever the internal working parts of the rifle are removed.

The FAMAS has been evaluated by some overseas countries, but as far as this author is aware few if any sales have been made. That is not to say that potential customers are not happy with the weapon, merely that they are satisfied with the weapons they currently have in service.

The author has fired the FAMAS on a number of occasions, and found it to be a comfortable weapon, easy to control and with good handling.

There is a training system developed specially for the FAMAS which allows it to be fired on an indoor range, using compressed air to fire pellets on semi-automatic. This is a training aid which allows service personnel to become familiarised with the workings of the weapon before moving on to the outdoor range and 'live' ammunition.

The rifle is capable of having a knife-type bayonet mounted and a special 'universal' sling allows the weapon to be carried in several ways and still leave the user's hands free to complete other tasks. The FAMAS is currently in service with several French law enforcement agencies such as the Gendarmerie, as well as the French armed forces.

SPECIFICATIONS:	
Calibre:	5.56mm x 45mm
Weight:	3.610kg (without attachments)
Length:	757mm overall
Barrel:	488mm
Rifling:	Three grooves, right hand, one turn in 305mm
	Three grooves, right hand, one turn in 228mm
Muzzle velocity:	960m/sec

The German-designed Gewehr 3 rifle, or G3, is one of the most widely used weapons of its type in the world, being exported to five continents and built under licence in a number of countries. It is available in either 7.62mm or 5.56mm calibre. Among the many countries to use the G3 rifle are Turkey, Norway, Chad, Guyana and Pakistan; the latter also produces Heckler and Koch weapons under licence.

The basic G3 design is now quite old, but that is not to say that it has passed its usefulness as a frontline service weapon. Quite the contrary as many, even early examples, are still in use around the world. The standard model of the rifle is known as the G3A3, which was preceded by four models including the prototype, and this has a plastic forestock and butt stock. The G3A3 ZF is the version with a telescopic sight fitted and the G3A4 is the version fitted with a retractable butt stock. The Turkish defence company of Makina ve Kimya Endustrisi Kurumu manufactures the G3 rifle in 7.62mm calibre under licence in both the fixed and retractable butt stock versions.

The weapon uses the standard Heckler and Koch

delayed blowback design, using rollers as the method of delay. It has selective fire settings, including the usual safety setting, for either semi- or fully automatic fire with a cyclic rate of 600 rounds per minute, fed from a detachable 20-round box magazine. The weapon can be used to launch a whole range of rifle grenades either of the 'bullet trap' design or the type requiring ballistite cartridges. All types of rifle grenades can be fired from the G3, providing they have an internal tail diameter of 22mm.

When firing a grenade requiring a ballistite cartridge to launch it, the magazine is removed and a special blank cartridge is inserted. The firer can then engage targets out to 100m with some degree of accuracy. With the

The H&K G3 rifle fitted with an early small arms fire simulator, the SIMGUN. The small box fitted to the muzzle of the weapon emits a low-level, eye-safe, laser to simulate firing the weapon when blank rounds are used. Note the firer is wearing a receiver harness and has sensors on his helmet. These record a near miss or direct hit, activating an audible signal to warn the infantryman that he has been 'hit'.

(top) **Members of the newly-formed Franco-German brigade deploying from a helicopter. These are German troops and are carrying the G3 rifle.**

(bottom) **The H&K G3 rifle in its standard form seen from the left. Note the fire selector switch just above the pistol grip.**

'bullet trap' type rifle grenades the projectile is simply placed over the muzzle of the barrel and a standard ball round fired. Baffles inside the tail of the rifle grenade collapse as the round passes through them and the kinetic energy imparted propels the grenade. Rifle grenades are seen as allowing an infantryman to engage targets which are at ranges too far to be engaged with

hand grenades and too close for light mortars of 51mm and 60mm calibres.

The popularity of 40mm grenade launchers fitted under the weapon, in the manner of the M203 on the M16 rifle, has led to the development of a similar device for the G3. Although 40mm grenade launchers on weapons such as the G3 are becoming more popular, it is unlikely that they will ever replace the rifle grenade completely.

A sub-calibre training system using .22 inch rounds (5.6mm x 16mm) is available to familiarise troops with the handling and functioning details of the G3 at a fraction of the cost of normal rounds. To convert the rifle to .22 training roles, a sub-calibre insert is slid into the barrel 153 and fixed into position with pins; a special bolt and magazine are also used in place of the normal components. The magazine holds 20 rounds of .22 ammunition. This conversion allows troops to be trained on indoor ranges to acquire their battlefield skills in weapon handling and target engagement. The training system can be used before allowing troops to use full-bore calibres or as an all-weather aid.

For field training exercises the G3 can be fitted with a special 'blank firing adapter' which allows the weapon to be used in a realistic manner but only firing blank rounds. This allows troops to engage in large-scale training manoeuvres in complete safety.

To field strip the G3 the magazine is first removed and the cocking lever worked to ensure the chamber is empty. Two locking pins which secure the back plate are removed and the butt stock can be removed. By pushing out the single pin which holds the pistol grip, the trigger assembly is stripped out. Working the cocking handle once more allows the bolt assembly to be removed from the main body of the weapon, and this too can be stripped for cleaning.

The G3 is fitted with a post-type front sight and an adjustable rear sight which has a 'U' shaped battle setting and apertures with 100m increments out to 400m range. Trigger pull on the G3 can be set to between 3.6 and 4.1 kg. The G3A3 and G3A4 versions have components

which are interchangeable to increase commonality and reduce stock holding of spare parts.

Specifications of the G3 built under licence do not vary all that much from the original Heckler and Koch design, but for the purposes of this entry the specifications of the Turkish G3A3 and G3A4 are used.

SPECIFICATIONS:

Calibre:	7.62mm x 51mm
Weight:	4.40kg (G3A3 unloaded)
Weight:	4.70kg (G3A4 unloaded)
Length:	1,020mm (G3A3)
Length (G3A4):	1,020mm (butt stock extended
	840mm (butt stock retracted)
Barrel:	450mm
Rifling:	Four grooves, right hand, one turn in 305mm
Muzzle velocity:	800m/sec

German troops of the newly-formed Franco-German brigade deploy from an APC, carrying the H&K G3 rifle.

The German HK33E rifle designed by Heckler and Koch is unarguably one of the most versatile rifles to enter military service. There are five variants of the rifle, with the basic HK33E capable of being configured as a sniping rifle; it can also be fitted with an HK79 launcher to fire 40mm grenades, in the same manner as the M203 fitted to the M16A2.

The variants of the HK33E include models with fixed or retractable butt stocks, a rifle with bipod, the sniper version with telescopic sight, and the HK33EK, which is a shorter carbine version. The rifle fires the standard NATO 5.56mm x 45 round, with a cyclic rate of 750 rounds per minute. The rifle, which is basically a scaled-down version of the more powerful G3 rifle, uses the same delayed blowback system as the G3, firing from a closed breech.

The bolt comprises two main parts, with the bolt-head containing two rollers which are forced out into recesses in the barrel extension by angled faces on the bolt-body. When the weapon is fired, the gas pressure exerts force onto the bolt-face to drive it back, but the rollers have to move inwards before the bolt-head can move. The recesses are shaped to permit the slight rearward movement of the rollers to force them inwards. The mass of the bolt-body resists this movement, as does the force of the return spring, transmitted to the rollers by way of the angled faces lying between them. The bolt-body moves back four times the length of the bolt-face as the angled faces drive rearwards; at the same time the rollers move inwards. Once the rollers are clear of the recesses in the barrel extension the remaining gas pressure in the chamber forces the two parts of the block back together, but the two parts are

still displaced relatively by the rollers. The bolt-face holds the cartridge and after firing the spent case strikes the ejector and it is thrown out to the right-hand side of the weapon.

The barrel of the HK33E is chrome-plated to ensure long service life and is capable of accepting bayonets and of firing rifle grenades directly from the muzzle. The plastic stock of the rifle can be moulded in camouflage forms, including desert, jungle and standard drab green. The trigger assembly of the HK33E is virtually identical to the G3 and the ambidextrous fire selector switch allows the weapon to be fired in either single-shot, three-round burst or fully automatic modes.

The basic sights have a V-shaped rear sight for a battle setting, and other settings are marked at increments of 100m out to 400m range. The HK33E will accept various optical units including night-vision equipment. There is a separate unit, the HK79A1, which fires the 40mm x 46mm grenade. With this fitted the firer can engage targets out to 350m with no degradation in the overall performance of the rifle itself. The 40mm grenade-launcher unit can be fitted to the rifle, in place of the handguard, without the aid of tools. This device, which weighs only 1.4kg, can be fitted to all versions of the HK33E, including the carbine version.

An interesting novelty is the fact that the field cleaning kit for the HK33E, which includes barrel brushes and pull-through, is contained in the pistol grip.

The H&K 33E rifle seen from the left-hand side. Note the cocking handle on the forestock, just behind the front sight, the magazine release catch in front of the trigger guard, and the fire selector switch.

SPECIFICATIONS:

Calibre:	5.56mm x 45 NATO
Weight:	3.90kg·
Weight:	3.95kg (with retractable butt stock)
Length:	920mm (with fixed butt stock)
	740mm (with retractable butt stock collapsed)
	670mm (HK33EK with retractable butt stock collapsed)
Barrel length:	410mm (HK33E without flash suppressor)
	340mm (HK33EK without flash suppressor)
Rifling:	Six grooves, right hand, one turn in 178mm
Muzzle velocity:	900m/sec (HK33E)
	850m/sec (HK33EK)

The German-built Heckler and Koch HK53 was designed along the functional lines of the G3 assault rifle, which is also manufactured by Heckler and Koch. Although the HK53 has the appearance of a sub-machine gun, the fact that it fires a cartridge of 5.56mm x 45mm NATO standard puts it very firmly in the category of assault rifle. The company of Heckler and Koch cite that it is a sub-machine gun with the performance of an assault rifle, but all weapon encyclopaedias list the weapon in the category of rifles, including the eminent Jane's *Infantry Weapons*.

The HK53 features a recoil-operated roller-locked bolt system firing from the closed and locked position, which adds to the weapon's accuracy when firing the first round. The rollers delay the rearward motion of the breech-head until the pressure has dropped sufficiently to permit the breech-block to be blown back in safety. The weapon has a cyclic rate of 700 rounds per minute and settings, including 'safe', which permit the firer to operate the HK53 in semi-automatic, three-round burst or fully automatic roles. The fire selector switch is ambidextrous to allow for left-handed users or tactical requirements when firing from behind cover. The trigger mechanism of the HK53 is incorporated into the weapon's pistol grip and is identical to that fitted to the G3 rifle, a weapon of which it may be considered as a scaled-down version.

The barrel of the HK53 is cold-forged and free-floating, which means it does not come into contact with the receiver over its full length. Indeed, there is no change in point of impact when it has heated up even after prolonged firing.

The weapon can easily be stripped down into its sub-assemblies without tools for the purposes of cleaning and basic field maintenance. An extendable butt stock is featured to allow troops operating from APCs and helicopters to use it without snagging. The HK53 is capable of mounting a series of optical sights, including 4x24 telescopic sights and aiming-point projectors for accuracy when engaged in close-quarter actions, such as hostage situations. Unlike most standard assault rifle designs, the HK53 does not have the length to permit a 40mm grenade launcher to be mounted under the body, nor can standard rifle grenades be launched from the muzzle of the barrel. Despite that, it remains a functional weapon which has seen much service with police and some special military units. The foresight of the weapon is of the post-type and the rear sight has settings in 100m increments from 100m to 400m, and a 390mm sighting radius. The HK53 uses either 25- or 30-round capacity magazines.

The HK53 is classified as an assault rifle as it fires a 5.56mm rifle cartridge. However, due to its compact size it can serve in the role of an SMG. Note the position of the cocking handle, just behind the front sight, and the collapsible butt stock.

SPECIFICATIONS:

Calibre:	5.56mm x 45mm
Weight:	3.05kg (unloaded)
	3.65kg (with loaded 25-round magazine)
Length:	780mm (butt stock extended)
	590mm (butt stock retracted)
Barrel length:	211mm
Rifling:	Six grooves, right hand, one twist in 178mm
Muzzle velocity:	735m/sec

The origins of the Galil are well-documented, but to recap briefly it was designed by Israel Galil and Yaacov Lior, being heavily influenced by the rugged Kalashnikov AK47 design. The Israelis decided to rearm with 5.56mm calibre weapons after the Six Day War in 1967 a number of weapons using this calibre were brought in for trials, but these were unsuccessful. The design put forward by the team of Galil and Lior was chosen for adoption in 1972, because it was deemed to be the weapon which best suited the requirements of the Israeli armed forces.

The Galil rifle was first issued to Israeli troops in the 5.56mm calibre in 1973, but it is currently available in two calibres: 5.56mm x 45 and 7.62mm x 51. There are several variants on the basic Galil design, including the sniping version (qv), and these have in turn influenced the development of the South African R4 rifle.

Apart from the sniping version, all variants of the Galil feature a folding metal-framed butt stock, including the ARM which has an integral bipod, that doubles as a useful set of wirecutters, and allows the weapon to be used in the Light Support Weapon role. The Galil is of conventional layout, with the magazine in front of the

Israeli servicemen carrying the Short Assault Rifle (SAR) version of the Galil.

Israeli tank crew armed with the SAR version of the Galil.

pistol grip, and the cyclic rate for the ARM is 650 rounds per minute, whilst for the SAR, or Short Assault Rifle, the cyclic rate is 750 rounds per minute. The effective ranges for these weapons are 600m and 550m respectively.

There are three types of 5.56mm magazine available for use with the Galil. One has a 35-round capacity and another a 50-round capacity, which is particularly useful with the ARM version. The third type of magazine bears a white stripe to indicate that it is pre-loaded with ballistite cartridges for use when firing rifle grenades. In the 7.62 version the Galil uses a 25-round capacity magazine, with a 12-round capacity magazine also bearing the white stripe to indicate ballistite cartridges for rifle grenades. The Galil can be used to launch all types of rifle grenade, including anti-tank, anti-personnel, illuminating and smoke.

The Galil is gas-operated and functions on the rotating bolt locking system with selective fire, but no gas regulator. Instead, the gas block is pinned to the barrel and the gas track drilled back at 30 degrees into the gas cylinder. The piston rod and shank are both chrome-plated for durability and the bolt carrier forms an extension to the piston end. This is hollowed out over the bolt to accept the return spring.

The Galil fires from the closed bolt position and the cocking handle is attached to this to give a positive action for bolt closure. The cocking handle is angled upwards to allow the firer to cock the weapon with either hand.

The fire selector switch is located on the left hand side of the weapon by the trigger guard, and the magazine release catch is positioned just in front of the trigger guard, allowing the firer to change magazines with the minimum of lost time. The Galil is fitted with a post-type front sight protected by a short tube, as featured on the Finnish M76 and the German G3 rifles. The rear sight is of the flip-type with settings between 300m and 500m and a tritium night sight, which is separate from the daytime sight.

The Galil breaks down into six component parts for field cleaning. As with other rifles, the magazine is first removed and the weapon checked to ensure that there is no chambered round. Once it has been declared safe to handle, the guide rod of the return spring is pushed forward and the cover of the receiver is lifted off. The return rod and spring are removed. The cocking handle is withdrawn and the bolt is lifted clear of the receiver and rotated out of the carrier.

The ARM version also features a folding-type carrying handle, but the SAR version does not have this, nor does the standard AR (Assault Rifle) version.

The Galil is in use with the Israeli Defence Forces, and some numbers have been sold abroad. The Galil has been extensively used by Israeli forces in combat situations, where it has given good account of itself and has been proven to be a rugged design capable of absorbing punishing handling in even the harshest of conditions.

SPECIFICATIONS:

	5.56mm version	7.62mm version
Weight:	4.35kg (ARM with bipod and carrying handle)	4.0kg (ARM minus bipod and carrying handle)
	3.95kg (AR)	3.95kg (AR)
	3.75kg (SAR)	3.75kg (SAR)
Length:	979mm (ARM/AR with butt stock extended)	1,050mm (ARM/AR with butt stock extended)
	840mm (SAR with butt stock extended)	915mm (SAR with butt stock extended)
	742mm (ARM/AR with butt stock folded)	810mm (ARM/AR with butt stock folded)
	614mm (SAR with butt stock folded)	675mm (SAR with butt stock folded)
Barrel:	460mm (ARM/AR)	535mm (ARM/AR)
	332mm (SAR)	400mm (SAR)
Rifling:	Six grooves, right hand, one turn in 305mm	Four grooves, right hand, one turn in 305mm
Muzzle velocity:	950m/sec (ARM/AR)	850m/sec (ARM/AR)
	900m/sec (SAR)	800m/sec (SAR)

The Italian Army accepted the Beretta 70/90 assault rifle series into service in July 1990 to replace the older AR70/223 rifle, of which it is an improved version. The 70/90 series is made up of five weapons, all of which fire the 5.56mm x 45 cartridge. First is the standard AR70/90 which is for use by the ordinary infantryman. The SC70/90 is the carbine version of the weapon and is intended for use by special forces units. The SCS70/90 is the special carbine, short, for use by drivers and armoured troops. The SCP70/90 and AS70/90 are versions equipped with a grenade-launcher attachment and the light support weapon respectively.

The AR70/90 uses a 30-round capacity box magazine and the weapon has a cyclic rate of 680 rounds per minute. The magazine well has been designed to allow the weapon range to utilise the M16 type magazine. The magazine release catch can be operated by either hand and is located by the magazine housing. The SC version has a comparable cyclic rate to the AR, but the SCS version is set at 670 rounds per minute.

All the 70/90 series fire from the closed bolt position. The receiver of the weapon series is trapezoidal in section, with steel bolt guide rods welded in place, and uses a gas piston mounted over the barrel to actuate the bolt carrier and two-lug rotating bolt. All weapons in the series feature a detachable carrying handle which is removed when telescopic sights or night vision units are to be fitted. The carrying handle contains a luminescent light source as an aiming aid in low light conditions. The normal rear sight on the AR70/90 rifle is a two-position unit which is adjustable for windage and has apertures for 250m and 400m ranges. The front sight is of the normal blade-type.

The trigger mechanism can be altered to suit a

The 70/90 range of Italian weapons known as the AR, SC and SCS.

variety of functions. In the basic version the rifle can fire single rounds, three-round bursts or fully automatic. However, a system to restrict the action to single and three-round burst only is available. Likewise, the three-round bursts can be removed, leaving the weapon to function in either semi- or fully automatic fire only. The trigger guard can be rotated and placed alongside the pistol grip to allow the firer to use the weapon unrestricted when wearing gloves or mittens in subzero conditions. The gas cylinder has three settings, one for normal use, the second for use in adverse conditions and the last setting is closed for use when firing rifle grenades. The regulator is provided with an aiming device for use with rifle grenades and this impinges on the normal line of sight to give the firer a visual indication that it is set. In the normal, or lowered, setting this lever serves to prevent the firer from trying to load a rifle grenade with it in the wrong setting.

The 70/90 series can be fitted with a bayonet and the cleaning kit is carried in the base of the pistol grip. The AR70/90 rifle has a fixed butt stock but the SC and SCS versions both have folding butt stocks which collapse forward along the right-hand side of the weapon. The cocking handle is on the right-hand side of the weapon and can be operated by either hand.

SPECIFICATIONS:

	AR70/90	SC70/90	SCS70/90
Length:	998mm	986mm	876mm
	–	751mm (with	647mm (with
		butt stock folded)	butt stock folded)
Barrel length:	450mm	450mm	352mm
Weight:	3.990kg	3.990kg	3.790kg
Rifling:	Six grooves, right hand, one turn in 178mm		
	(all versions)		

The Type 64 rifle is used only by the Japanese Self-Defense Forces and was chosen for introduction into service following trials and field tests involving several weapon designs. The weapon fires the standard 7.62mm x 51mm NATO round, but with the propellant charge reduced by ten per cent, which produces a reduced muzzle impulse and recoil force to the firer. This limiting of the charge was due to the small physical stature of Japanese troops.

The Type 64 can fire the full charge NATO round, but it is necessary for the gas regulator to be adjusted so that the pressure of the gases reaching the piston head is reduced. The gas regulator, which controls the flow of gas to the gas cylinder and piston located above the barrel, has three port settings, and can be shut off completely to allow the Type 64 to fire rifle grenades.

The Type 64 is fed by a detachable box-type magazine which contains 20 rounds, and is conventional in appearance. The magazine is inserted into the magazine well under the body of the weapon and the release catch is located directly behind it.

The rifle, which was designed by General K Iwashita, uses the tilting block system as the method of locking. In action the block is lifted into engagement, after which it is lowered and carried back by the bolt carrier. The rifle has a cyclic rate of 500 rounds per minute, with a claimed effective range of 400m, and to assist in accuracy it is fitted with a bipod to the fore-end. The butt stock is fixed and of the straight-through design. The weapon has not been produced for the Japanese Self-Defense Force since 1990, but it is still in current use.

SPECIFICATIONS:

Calibre:	7.62 x 51 (reduced load)
Weight:	4.4kg (empty)
Length:	990mm
Length of barrel:	450mm
Rifling:	Four grooves, right hand, one turn in 250mm
Muzzle velocity:	700m/sec (reduced charge)
	800m/sec (full charge)

The Japanese Type 64 rifle which fires a cartridge with a reduced charge. This is being replaced in service by the lighter, more compact Type 89 rifle.

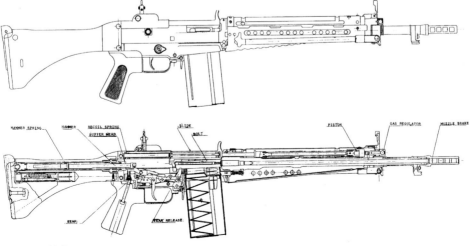

HAMMER SPRING HAMMER RECOIL SPRING BUFFER HEAD SLIDE BOLT PISTON GAS REGULATOR MUZZLE BRAKE

SEAR SEAR RELEASE

7·62 mm Type 64 rifle

Following the trend favoured by other armed forces, the Japanese Self-Defense Force has introduced the Type 89 rifle which fires the smaller 5.56mm x 45mm round. Manufactured by Howa Machinery Ltd, who also manufactured the Type 64 rifle, this new rifle was developed with the co-operation of the Technical Research and Development Institute of the Japanese Defense Agency.

This is a typical assault rifle design and is available in two forms: one with a folding butt stock; the other with a fixed butt stock. Both also feature an integral bipod fitted to the fore-end. The rifle is operated by the usual method of gas being ported off into the gas chamber mounted above the barrel.

The design is unusual in that the piston rod in the long gas expansion chamber is stepped – the front diameter of the rod is smaller than at the rear, and it is positioned some way back from the gas port. Gas is ported into the gas chamber, where it rapidly expands, and the piston moves the bolt carrier with a light flick. This increases the functional reliability and service life of the moving parts. The breech mechanism of the Type 89 is locked by a rotating bolt, which has a seven-lug head locking into the barrel extension.

The rifle uses either a 20- or 30-round detachable box magazine, and has a cyclic rate of between 650 RPM and 850 RPM. The rifle has a three-round burst facility in the form of a detachable device located at the rear of the trigger housing, which is separated from the trigger mechanism for semi- and fully automatic firing.

The rear sight is of the aperture-type, fully adjustable for elevation and windage, and is fitted with a ballistic cam. The front sight is of the square post-type and is also fully adjustable. In use the sight radius is 440mm.

SPECIFICATIONS:

Calibre:	5.56mm x 45mm
Weight:	3.5kg
Length:	916mm (butt stock extended)
	670mm (butt stock folded)
Barrel length:	420mm
Rifling:	Six grooves, right hand, one turn in 178mm
Muzzle velocity:	920m/sec

Japanese troops, armed with the Type 89 rifle, being transported by a UH-1B helicopter. The Japanese Type 89 rifle fires the 5.56mm x 45 round and is lighter and more compact than the older Type 64 rifle which it is replacing.

The South Korean K2 rifle fitted with the M203-type 40mm grenade launcher.

The industrial manufacturing base in South Korea continues to grow stronger. Developing an armaments industry to compete in an already crowded and highly competitive market is risky, but the Pusan-based company of Daewoo Precision Industries Ltd has successfully developed the K2 assault rifle for the South Korean Army.

The K2 fires the standard 5.56mm round. At first glance the K2 is similar to the Colt 'Commando' rifle, but closer inspection reveals that the design has taken the best features from the M16, the AK47 and even the FN-FNC to produce a reliable and robust weapon. There are two versions of the K2. The standard assault rifle has a solid butt stock that folds forward and lies alongside the right-hand side of the receiver, and is locked in place with a system similar to the FN-FNC weapon. The second version of the K2 is a carbine, which has a collapsible wire and plastic butt stock and has a much shortened barrel.

Both versions are gas-operated with selective fire, including a three-round burst capability. The K2 uses standard M16-type magazines containing 30 rounds, and

South Korean troops carrying the K2 assault rifle on an assault training course.

can fire either M193 or SS109 5.56mm calibre rounds. The K2 uses the long-stroke piston, associated with the AK47, to operate a rotating bolt. The upper and lower receivers, manufactured from aluminium alloy forgings, give the rifle the appearance of the M16, but despite this there is no commonality and parts are not interchangeable between the two weapons.

The three-round burst cycle does not reset when the trigger is released and, instead, continues to fire from the cycle setting when the trigger is pulled for a second time. In other words, if the firer has fired only two rounds previously before releasing the trigger in the three-round burst setting, on pulling the trigger a second time he will fire only one round. Releasing the trigger again will put the sequence back into cycle once more.

The barrel is fitted with a muzzle brake/compensator which is designed with the ports to vent to the side and upwards. This action reduces the tendency for muzzle climb on this rather short weapon when it is fired on fully automatic.

The weapon is fitted with flip-over type rear sights, which offer either a small aperture for precise target engagement, or two illuminated dots for use in low light levels. The front sight of the carbine version is protected by blades and on the longer assault rifle version is protected by a tunnel-shaped device as fitted to the AK47. The front sight has an illuminated dot on one side

(above) **South Korean troops carrying the K2 assault rifle, a locally-produced weapon.**

(below) **South Korean troops listen to a lecture in the field. They are carrying their K2 assault rifles slung over their shoulders. Note the folding butt stock.**

to allow the firer to line up on his target in low light conditions. The sights for the K2 are graduated out to 600m range, but it is unlikely that an ordinary infantryman using this weapon would ever engage a target at such ranges with ordinary sights.

The K2 can be fitted with an M203-type 40mm grenade launcher, to allow infantrymen to engage targets with indirect fire using explosive projectiles, in the same way as with the M16 rifle.

SPECIFICATIONS:

Calibre:	5.56mm x 45mm; either M193 or SS109
Weight:	3.26kg (unloaded)
Length:	990mm (butt stock extended)
	730mm (butt stock collapsed)
Barrel:	465mm (without muzzle brake/compensator)
Rifling:	Six grooves, right hand
Muzzle velocity:	960m/sec (M193)
	920m/sec (SS109)

The South African-developed 40mm grenade launcher seen here fitted to the muzzle of an AK47 Russian-developed rifle. Note the front sight of the weapon which is well protected by the tube-like fitting.

The Russian-designed AK47 assault rifle is instantly recognisable to many people, due to its high profile in news footage, newspaper features and numerous magazine articles. It is also associated as being the favoured weapon of terrorists and guerrilla forces, from the Philippines to Northern Ireland, the Middle East and South America. It is more commonly referred to simply as the 'Kalashnikov', after the Russian designer Mikhail Kalashnikov who conceived the idea for the weapon in 1947. The weapon entered service in 1951, becoming

the standard rifle of the Russian Army in 1957, and is seen in many quarters as being the benchmark for the development of all current assault rifles.

The AK, or Avtomat Kalashnikova, is the success story of small arms history and has appeared in many shapes and forms. Indeed, most of the former member states of the Warsaw Pact had their own variation of the rifle, which they invariably built under licence from the former Russian State Factory Arsenals. For example, a Polish version, known as the PMK-DGN-60, featured a rifle grenade launcher, the LON-1, on the muzzle and had a fixed wooden butt stock. The Bulgarian Army used a standard version of the AK47 with a fixed wooden butt stock, but some models lacked an integral cleaning rod and bayonet lug. The Romanian AKM version had a forward pistol grip with fixed wooden butt stock, but the former East German Army was issued with the MPiKM version which had a fixed plastic butt stock with a wooden forestock. The Chinese produced their own version of the AK47, known as the Type 56, and this appeared in various forms, including a design which incorporated a fixed bayonet which folded back along the length of the forestock. Other designs of the Type 56 had either a

Russian infantry assault forward from their BMP armoured personnel carrier. They are carrying the AK47 assault rifle.

folding butt stock or fixed wooden butt stock.

It has been estimated that more than 35 million Kalashnikovs had been produced as early as the mid-1970s. Today that number could be doubled, when one takes into account the fact that Iraq produces its own version along with several other major producers, including North Korea which manufactures it as the Type 68.

The AK47 fires the 7.62mm x 39 round, which is a standard Russian-influenced calibre, from 30-round capacity magazines, and has a cyclic rate in the order of 600 rounds per minute. The function of this rifle is well known but, to recap very briefly, it is a gas-operated weapon having the gas piston rod permanently attached to the bolt carrier. A cam-track on the carrier rotates the bolt to lock, and, during the rearward stroke, the hammer is also cocked. The AK47 is laid out in a standard assault rifle design, with the magazine being located in front of the pistol grip. The cocking lever is fixed and moves with the action of the bolt during firing. This has the benefit of acting as a lever to close the bolt, should it not

close properly, to cycle the round during the firing sequence.

The AK47 is manufactured using a combination of pressed parts and machined parts. Parts machined from solid steel are used where extra strength is required. The barrel itself is chrome-plated for increased service life. This robust construction has produced a weapon which can function under the most arduous of conditions, from hot desert terrain to the subzero climates found in the mountainous regions of the Afghan hills.

The AK47 field strips into several parts, including the magazine, very quickly and without the need for tools. Once the magazine has been removed and the weapon cleared to ensure it is unloaded, the end of the return spring guide is pressed into the rear end of the receiver cover, which releases the cover from the receiver. The return spring guide is pushed forward to release it from

A version of the AK47 with a fixed wooden stock. It is seen here being trialled with an optical sight unit which has been developed in Western Europe.

its housing and allow it to be removed from the weapon. By pulling the cocking handle to the rear, the bolt carrier and bolt are moved back and removed from the weapon. This assembly can then be stripped further. By rotating the gas cylinder lock the gas cylinder is freed along with the upper hand guard. Unlike some Western designs, there are no small parts or pins to lose in the debris of a battlefield.

The basic Russian AK47 can be fitted with a knife-type bayonet but others, such as the Chinese Type 56, have a folding spike-type bayonet. The AKM rifle is the upgraded version of the original AK47 with several distinguishing features. For example, there is a groove on the lower hand-guard for the firer's fingers, the bayonet lug is under the gas-tap off point, a small compensator is fitted and the receiver cover has transverse ribs. The cyclic rate of fire remains at 600 rounds per minute, however.

The rifle can be used to launch conventional rifle grenades of Russian origin, including anti-tank and anti-personnel types. A 40mm grenade launcher, known as the Pallad, has been developed to allow an infantryman to fire these explosive projectiles out to ranges between 150m and 250m. A South African defence manufacturer has produced a 40mm grenade launcher known as the Mk 40, which is a single-shot, add-on device. This is compatible with various designs of assault rifle, including the AK47. The design of this launcher features a barrel that swings to the side for launching, which means it can accept the widest possible range of 40mm grenades,

including smoke, illuminating and high explosive.

In summary, the AK47 is a no-frills weapon which even a conscript can use effectively after just a few lessons in basic weapons handling.

SPECIFICATIONS:

AK47

Calibre:	7.62mm x 39
Weight:	4.3kg
Length:	869mm with butt stock extended
	699mm with butt stock folded
Barrel:	414mm
Rifling:	Four grooves, right hand, one turn in 235mm
Muzzle velocity: 710m/sec	

AKM

Calibre:	7.62mm x 39
Weight:	3.15kg
Length:	876mm overall
Barrel:	414mm
Rifling:	Four grooves, right hand, one turn in 235mm
Muzzle velocity: 715m/sec	

The Russian-developed AK47 rifle with fixed wooden butt stock, and fitted with an LS45 laser sight. It is being trialled by a member of the British Army.

Member of the British Army evaluates the Russian AK47, with fixed wooden butt stock, and mounting an LS45 laser sight.

The standard calibre for the Russian Army during the Second World War was the 7.62mm x 39mm, and this was carried over into the post-war era known as the Cold War. However, following a trend in smaller calibres the Russians developed the AK74 rifle which fires a cartridge of 5.45mm x 39mm. It is essentially a reworked Kalashnikov AK47, with some minor but subtle differences. These include a change in muzzle brake design to reduce recoil and force the ejected gases sideways and upwards to reduce muzzle climb when the weapon is fired in fully automatic mode.

Another feature is that the bullet fired by the AK74 has a steel core with a boat-shaped tail. This projectile, which weighs 53 grains, has the unfortunate side-effect that it deforms and tumbles on striking the target. This can produce wounding effects which are worse than the normal type of bullet wound.

The AK74 has been developed into a series of weapons, including the RPK-74 which is similar to a Light Support Weapon, the AKS-74 with a folding butt stock, and the AKR-74 which is greatly reduced in length and intended to fulfil the role of a sub-machine gun. All these types were encountered at one time or another during the Russian involvement in Afghanistan between 1979 and 1988.

The AK74 uses the same receiver, stock, pistol grip and trigger mechanism as the AK47, which it closely resembles. The magazine for the AK74 contains 30 rounds and is manufactured from toughened plastic. The weapon fires at a cyclic rate of 650 rounds per minute. The magazine will also fit the magazine well of the AK47.

Re-created former East German Border Guard infantryman with an AK-74 assault rifle in 5.45mm calibre. Note the compact design of the rifle which comes from the same 'stable' as the more familiar AK-47. Note the brown-coloured plastic butt stock and magazine. This weapon is fitted with a sling which allows the man to carry it in his shoulder whilst performing other tasks.

The Russian-designed and built AK-74 assault rifle as would have been used by the former East German Border Guards. Note brown-coloured butt stock which is manufactured from plastic and the 30-round box magazine, which is also plastic.

The length of the round remains standard at 39mm, but the calibre of the AK74 is actually 2.17mm smaller than the 7.62mm round of the AK47. Some observers claim that the AK47 can fire this smaller round if necessary, but lack of proper gas obturation means there would be considerable falling off in range and accuracy.

The bolt of the AK74 is smaller than that fitted to the AK47, but the carrier and gas piston is the same between the weapons. The lighter bolt gives the weapon a better ratio of bolt to carrier mass, which in turn leads to improved functioning. The fire selector lever is still located on the right-hand side of the weapon and in the top, safe setting, serves the purpose of a dust cover, similar to the AK47. The rifle has a post-type front sight, protected by the usual tunnel-shaped protecting cover, and the rear sights are of the 'U' notch type.

Before the break-up of the Warsaw Pact the former

Detail of the breech of the Russian-designed AK-74 assault rifle. Note the fire selector switch and the rear sight which are made to withstand rough treatment in combat situations. The butt stock is fixed and manufactured from plastic. The 30-round magazine is also manufactured from brown plastic to reduce weight, without altering the weapon's cyclic rate of fire or ruggedness.

Soviet Union supplied quantities of the AK74 to satellite states. These were issued to most branches of the military, including Frontier Guards who would often fit knife-type bayonets. Russia and her former Warsaw Pact Allies have retained the AK74, despite the break-up of the Warsaw Pact and the establishment of the Confederation of Independent States, or CIS. The weapon has been well proven. For the same reason, any former client states in possession of the AK74 are unlikely to re-equip with anything else.

The AK74 has also been fitted with a 40mm grenade launcher, comparable in operation to the American M-203 as fitted to the M16. This allows an infantryman to engage targets such as light vehicles, as well as crew-served weapons like mortars, beyond the range at which he could throw a hand grenade. The AK74 was first seen fitted with this device in Afghanistan during the early 1980s at the time of the Russian invasion. The application of grenade launchers to assault rifles greatly increases the hitting power of an infantryman in close-quarter combat such as street fighting and house clearing.

SPECIFICATIONS:

Calibre:	5.45mm x 39
Weight:	3.6kg
Length:	930mm
	690mm (AKS-74 with butt stock folded)
Barrel:	400mm
Rifling:	Four grooves, right hand, one turn in 196mm
Muzzle velocity:	900m/sec

The Spanish Army at present uses two versions of assault rifle, the Model L which has the straight lines of a conventional rifle with a fixed butt stock, and the Model LC, which is a shorter version of the design and has a retractable butt stock. Both versions fire the standard NATO 5.56mm x 45mm cartridge using a detachable box magazine with a 30-round capacity, and each weapon has a cyclic rate of 600 to 750 rounds per minute. The magazine is of the type used on the American M16 rifle.

The fire selector switch has settings marked 'T' for single shot and 'R' for automatic fire, as well as the usual 'Safe' setting. The safety setting works by locking up the trigger mechanism. The weapons are fitted with conical post front sights, which are protected, and flip-over rear sights which have only two settings, 200m and 400m.

Both weapons work on the delayed blowback principle, which also featured on earlier Spanish weapons. The weapons can be field stripped for cleaning

Spanish infantryman carrying the 'L' version assault rifle with a fixed butt stock.

and maintenance very easily by removing the two securing pins in the butt stock. This allows the butt stock itself to be removed, followed by the return spring and guide which are released from the body. The magazine must be removed prior to this operation to make sure the weapon is in an unloaded state and safe to handle. By pulling the cocking handle back, the bolt assembly can be removed through the rear of the receiver. The fire selector switch may also be removed and the hand grip is removed by withdrawing the pin and sliding it forward and downwards. The bolt assembly can be stripped for cleaning and the firing pin can also be stripped out if required. The weapon can be assembled and stripped without the need for tools.

The Model L weapon is also fitted with a bipod to the fore-end, which allows it to be supported when fired in the automatic mode from the prone position. In this manner it can be used as a Light Support Weapon, as with the British Army's LSW.

SPECIFICATIONS:

(Model LC short assault rifle)

Calibre:	5.56mm x 45mm NATO
Weight:	3.40kg unloaded
Length:	925mm butt stock extended
	665mm butt stock retracted
Barrel:	400mm
Length of rifling:	320mm
Rifling:	Six grooves, right hand, one turn in 178mm
Muzzle velocity:	875m/sec

Although the SIG 540 range of assault rifles was designed and developed in Switzerland, they are manufactured only in Chile. They are all currently in service, in one form or another, with a number of countries including Bolivia, Chile, Gabon, Nigeria, Oman, Senegal and Swaziland.

All the designs in the range use gas operation with a rotating bolt. The cocking handle is of the fixed-type which allows the firer to force the bolt closed if it becomes fouled, in the same way as other rifles with a fixed cocking handle design. The SG 540 and SG 543 both fire 5.56mm x 45 calibre rounds from box magazines of either 20- or 30-round capacity, and have cyclic rates of 650 to 800 rounds per minute. These two weapons are basically the same, the only significant difference being that the SG 543 has a shorter barrel which makes it 0.31kg lighter and 145mm shorter than the fixed butt stock version of the SG 540.

The SG 542 fires the 7.62mm x 51 round from a box magazine with either a 20- or 30-round capacity and, like the SG 540 and 543, has a cyclic rate of 650 to 800 rounds per minute. There is a special hold-open device which engages the follower of the magazine when the last round in that magazine has been fired. The firer inserts a new magazine into the magazine well, then releases the bolt by simply pulling the cocking handle slightly to the rear. This releases the bolt to move forward and chamber a new round, so firing can continue with the minimum of interruption.

All three of these SG assault rifle designs are available in either folding butt stock or fixed butt stock versions, and the 540 and 542 versions can be fitted with a folding bipod. This feature allows these weapons to serve as a light support weapon, when using a 30-round magazine. A bipod also allows them to be used as sniping rifles when equipped with a telescopic sights. The weapons can be fired in semi-automatic and fully automatic settings, with a three-round burst capability.

The weapon range functions perfectly well in all

Accessories for the SG 542 rifle, showing the folding butt stock of tubular design, the carrying sling, barrel cleaning brush and the socket-type bayonet. The optical sight unit is optional and can be fitted for use in place of the normal 'iron sights'.

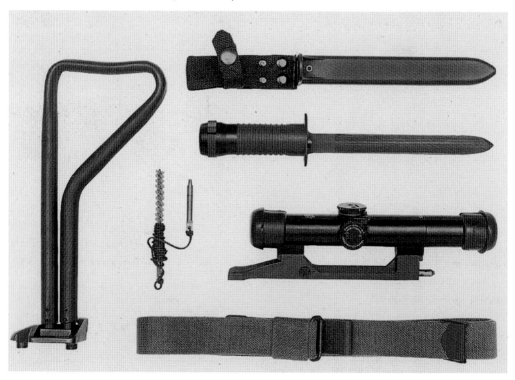

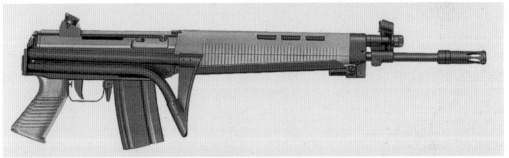

(top) The SG 542 seen from the left-hand side. Note the bipod folded back along the length of the front stock, the magazine release catch in front of the trigger guard and the fire selector switch just above the pistol grip.

(middle) The SG 542 with folding butt stock seen from the right-hand side. Note the gas regulator above the barrel and the bipod which is folded back along the length of the front stock.

(bottom) The SG 542 rifle stripped down for cleaning, showing bolt assembly, return spring and piston rod and the hand guards of the front stock.

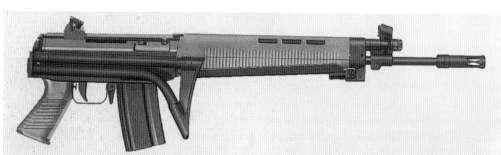

Opposite.

(top) **The SG 542 with the bipod erected and the socket-type bayonet fitted, showing the classic lines of a modern assault rifle.**

(upper middle) **The SG 542 seen from the left-hand side. Note the sturdy construction of the fixed plastic butt stock and the grooves on the pistol grip to assist the firer in grasping the weapon firmly.**

(lower middle) **The SG 540 rifle stripped for cleaning. Similar in detail to the SG 542, it shows all the components which modern assault rifles feature, including rotating bolt assembly.**

(bottom) **The SG 540 seen from the right-hand side. It is fitted with a folding butt stock of tubular design and has a bipod folded back along the length of the front stock.**

(top) **The SG 540 seen from the right-hand side. It is fitted with a folding butt stock of tubular design and has a bipod folded back along the length of the front stock.**

(middle) **The SG 540 seen from the right-hand side. It is fitted with a fixed butt stock, 30-round magazine and bipod, seen here folded, to allow it to be used in the light support role.**

(bottom) **The SG 542 seen from the left-hand side. It is fitted with a standard 20-round magazine and features the fixed butt stock.**

climates and terrain, and to allow firing in sub-zero conditions, when the firer would be wearing gloves or mittens, the trigger guard can be reversed. The trigger guard is also reversed when rifle grenades are fired from the muzzle of the weapon. When firing these munitions the gas regulator is set to 'zero' (fully closed) so that no gas passes into the cylinder – all the gas passes directly through the barrel to give more energy to launching the rifle grenade. The normal firing setting for the gas regulator is '1', with setting '2' reserved for tapping off more gas to cycle the weapon when fouling from sand, dust, water or debris is preventing the weapon from cycling normally.

The sights are identical on all three weapons in this range. The front sight is of the pillar type and is adjusted for zeroing by moving it up and down. The rear sight is a tilted drum which is rotated to the appropriate setting. The rear sights for the 5.56mm versions have increments from 100m to 500m whilst the 7.62mm SG 542 version has increments from 100m to 600m. The weapons can be fitted with a spike-type bayonet which has a tubular shaped handle to fit over the muzzle of the barrel. This means that the bullets are fired through the handle. It makes for a neat design, but results in the same problems as encountered on the British L85A1 rifle – after sustained firing the handle becomes too hot to hold, or even to remove the bayonet.

To field strip the weapons in this series the simple unloading procedure is first carried out. The magazine

View along the length of the SG 540 rifle, with bipod erected, to show the rear and front sights. Note the prominent cocking handle protruding from the right hand side of the weapon, midway down its length.

The SG 540 stripped for field cleaning, showing the main components including bolt assembly, gas cylinder and return spring, and receiver.

is removed and the bolt cocked to the rear to allow the chamber to be inspected and make sure the weapon is unloaded and safe to handle. The take-down pin, located above the pistol grip and slightly to the rear of the fire selector switch, is pressed out to allow the butt stock to be lowered along with the trigger group. The cocking handle is worked to the rear which moves the bolt back in the receiver. The cocking handle is then removed, and the whole bolt action can be withdrawn for cleaning. Further stripping involves removing the return spring and gas rod, along with the fore stock. The SG 540 breaks down into 12 components, counting the take-down pins, bolt assembly and cocking handle as individual items.

SPECIFICATIONS:

	SG 540	SG 542	SG 543
Calibre:	5.56mm	7.62mm	5.56mm
Weight:	3.26kg	3.55kg	2.95kg (with fixed butt stock)
	3.31kg	3.55kg	3.00kg (with folding butt stock)
Length:	950mm	1,000mm	805mm (with fixed butt stock)
	720mm	754mm	569mm (with folding butt stock)
Barrel:	460mm	465mm	300mm (without flash suppressor)
Rifling:	6 grooves	4 grooves	6 grooves
	1 turn in 305mm	1 turn in 305mm	1 turn in 305mm
Muzzle velocity:	980m/sec	820m/sec	875m/sec

The Swiss Industrial Company, SIG, developed the SG 550/551 series of rifles to meet specifications laid down by the Swiss Federal Army. The weapon was well received and accepted into service as the Sturmgewehr 90 assault rifle in 1984. Much use is made of plastic in the design, particularly in the forestock, butt stock, pistol grip and even the magazines. This has led to a dramatic saving in weight, without compromising the serviceability of the weapon.

Like its earlier counterparts, such as the SIG 540 and 550 series, the Sturmgewehr 90 has a three-round burst capability as well as single-shot and fully automatic. Firing a 5.56mm cartridge from either 20- or 30-round capacity magazines, the weapon has a cyclic rate of 700 rounds per minute. The series functions on a gas-operated cycle and uses a rotating bolt.

The SG 550 version is fitted with an integral bipod mounted on the fore-end, and using a 30-round magazine can function like a light support weapon. The SG 551 version is much shorter in length, and both versions have folding skeletal butt stocks. The weapons can be used to fire normal rifle grenades of all natures, including anti-tank and anti-personnel. The trigger guard can be reversed to allow the weapon to be used by the firer when he is wearing gloves or mittens in sub-zero conditions.

The SG 550/551 series features a hold-open device which operates after the last round of a magazine has been fired. When a new magazine is fitted the lock catch is activated and the firer can continue to use the weapon with the minimum amount of time spent in reloading. The transparent plastic magazines allow the firer to keep a visual check on the load status of the weapon. The magazines also feature studs and lugs on their sides which allow the firer to slot three magazines together, to eliminate the need to reach into an ammunition pouch

(left) **Swiss soldier wearing Simlas Torso Harness and carrying laser target pointer mounted on SIG Stgw 90 rifle SG 550. This system allows realistic training in the field.**

(below) **The SG 550 stripped down to show all the sub-assembly units, including the follower spring from the weapon's magazine. The bolt assembly has also been stripped down and the firing pin is visible between the legs of the bipod to the right of the picture. Note the knife-type bayonet and the well-equipped cleaning kit to the left of the picture.**

to retrieve a full magazine. This interlocking facility on magazines is much better than taping them together, because they can be separated easily for stowing.

The weapon series is fitted with a combined dioptre and alignment sight mounted on the breech, and this is fully adjustable in both windage and elevation. The alignment sight has luminous spots as an aiming aid in low light levels. When the daylight alignment sight is adjusted, the low light level sight is automatically adjusted at the same time. The front sight is protected

(top) **The SG 551 short version fitted with a telescopic sight unit and three magazines clipped together. Note the torch fitted underneath the barrel, which is for use when entering darkened rooms during house-clearing operations.**

(middle) **The short-barrelled SG 551 with folding butt stock.**

(bottom) **The long-barrelled SG 550 rifle fitted with a folding butt stock, seen from the right-hand side to show the ejector port and cocking handle.**

by a tunnel-shaped cover, and the rear sights are permanently fitted.

The SG 550/551 series can be fitted with image intensifier units to permit full use in night conditions. The mounting for this feature is standardised for the Swiss Army, but it is understood that a mounting which meets NATO STANAG 2324 can also be fitted. The rifles in this range can be fitted with knife-type bayonets for the assault stage of an infantry engagement.

For training purposes the SG 90 can be integrated with a Laser Target Pointer, with infantrymen wearing

(top) **The short-barrelled SG 551 fitted with telescopic sight. Note folding butt stock and well-shaped pistol grip.**

(bottom) **The short-barrelled SG 551 loaded with three transparent magazines clipped together for speed changing. The weapon is also fitted with a telescopic sight.**

the SIMLAS Torso Harness system. In this role the rifle is fitted to fire an eye-safe laser impulse at an infantryman wearing the receptor harness when a blank round is fired. These systems have been in use for a number of years

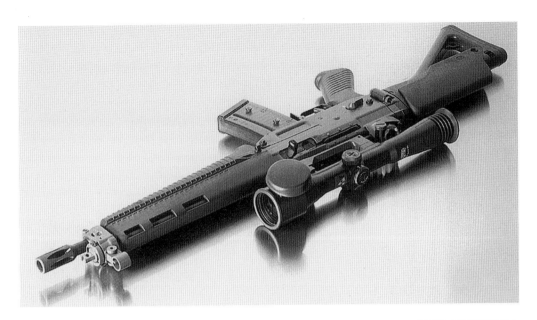

and they allow a level of battlefield training which borders on the realistic. A full magazine is loaded into the weapon and this will allow the firer to engage only those targets which have a coding to allow such engagements. For example, an infantryman can fire and register a 'kill' on another infantryman, but he cannot engage a main battle tank with his rifle. The chest harness which the infantryman wears for the purposes of these exercises mounts a number of sensors and another set for mounting on the helmet. These sensors detect a near miss, normally alerting the wearer with a short 'bleep'.

(top) **The SG 551 showing detail of the cocking handle and telescopic sight mounting unit.**

(middle) **The SG 550 showing the transparent magazine fitted into the magazine well and the folding butt stock extended.**

(bottom) **The SG 550 showing the butt stock folded forward.**

On receiving such an indication the wearer takes cover, as he would if he came under effective enemy fire for real. A direct hit is usually indicated by a continuous bleep

183

and this can only be turned off by an exercise umpire who is monitoring the whole scenario. These devices are now in quite widespread use and can be integrated into most rifle designs, including the G3, M16, sniping rifles and French FAMAS.

There is a commercial design of the SG 550/551 series which has the suffix letters 'SP' after the nomenclature, and fires only in the semi-automatic mode. In Switzerland, this version of the rifle is known as the Sturmgewehr 90 PE and is intended as a sporting weapon for target shooting. The inherent accuracy of

such a weapon means also that it would have a natural role in security or paramilitary forces where it could fulfil the role of a sniping rifle. This model of the SG 550/551

(top) **The SG 550 with a 40mm grenade launcher fitted under the front stock. Note the sights for the grenade are in the raised position by the rear sights. The grenade launcher has its own trigger mechanism for firing the projectile.**

(bottom) **Exploded diagram of the SG 550 assault rifle showing all the component parts.**

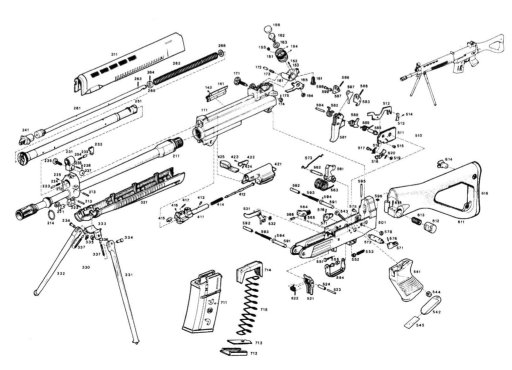

series is ballistically and dimensionally identical to the military version except that it cannot fire in the fully automatic mode.

The SG 550 can be fitted with a 40mm grenade launcher of SIG manufacture. This is an add-on feature and functions in a similar manner to other 40mm grenade launchers, with its own trigger mechanism, and is capable of firing a wide range of ammunition types.

SPECIFICATIONS:

	SG 550	SG 551
	Standard version	Short version
Calibre:	5.56mm x 45	5.56mm x 45
Weight:	4.1kg	3.5kg (unloaded, with bipod)
Length:	998mm	827mm (butt stock extended)
	772mm	601mm (butt stock folded)
Barrel:	528mm	372mm
Rifling:	Six grooves	Six grooves
	Right hand	Right hand

(top left) **British infantryman carrying the L85A1 rifle, also known as the SA80.**

(bottom left) **British infantryman holding the L85A1 rifle. Note the SUSAT sight unit which is used more commonly than the weapon's iron sights.**

(above) **British infantryman taking up the aim using the SUSAT sight fitted to the L85A1 rifle. Note the short length and low profile of the weapon.**

Until the early 1980s the British Army used the venerable L1A1 SLR which was originally designed by Fabrique Nationale of Herstal in Belgium. This rifle fired 7.62mm calibre rounds and had served the British Army through many conflicts, from Aden, Northern Ireland and the Falkland Islands.

In 1987 the British Army was issued with the first units of a new rifle design, which today is known as the L85A1 rifle. The L85A1 is currently in service with the Royal Marines as well as all branches of the British Army, including the Parachute Regiment. The rifle fires the 5.56mm calibre round and is of the bullpup layout. Unlike certain other, similar designs, the L85A1 did not have a smooth transition from experimentation into service issue. During its development trials the rifle was known as the XL70 E3 (Individual Weapon), and was originally designed to fire a round of 4.85mm calibre. There is not much one can say about this rifle that is not already known, and the number of negative reports are almost as legendary as the number of changes made to the weapon's basic design layout.

When the L85A1 first emerged it bore an uncanny

resemblance to the EM2 rifle of 1952 vintage, which fired a 7mm cartridge. The new rifle was for a time referred to as the 'SA80', before being given the reference L85A1, and it is still often known by the shorter term of SA80. The transition for the British Army moving from the L1A1 self-loading rifle, SLR, to the L85A1 was not a simple move. Due to a shortage of supply of the new rifle, the changeover did not happen in one simple process, as should have should have been the case. Difficulties in manufacturing delayed production, which in turn caused further changeover problems. The change in calibre from 4.85mm to allow the weapon to fire the new NATO standard round of 5.56mm calibre also created its own set of problems.

The L85A1 is the rifle version of a series of weapons in a range which includes a version for use by young cadets, who have to cock the weapon after every shot. The Light Support Weapon in the range has a longer barrel than the L85A1, and is fitted with a bipod to allow it to be used as a light machine gun. The two weapons have a high degree of commonality of parts, including magazines and bolt carrier.

The rifle uses box magazines of 30-round capacity and has a cyclic rate of 650 to 800 rounds per minute, which is comparable to other bullpup design rifles. The trigger has a pull weight set between 3.12kg and 4.5kg. A distinguishing feature on the L85A1 rifle is its large carrying handle, comparable to that fitted to the M16, which incorporates the rear sights of the 'iron sights' with the front sight mounted on a removable post protected by blades. The carrying handle can also be removed to allow the fitting of a SUSAT sight with x4 magnification for normal battlefield use. The same mounting bracket, which has a dovetail base, also allows a range of night-vision equipment to be fitted to the L85A1. The rifle has an effective range up to 400m, which is the optimum

British infantryman prepares to use the L85A1 left handed, despite the fact that it cannot be configured to such a role for the safety and comfort of the firer. The FAMAS and AUG, the other two bullpup designs in service, can be configured for left-handed firers.

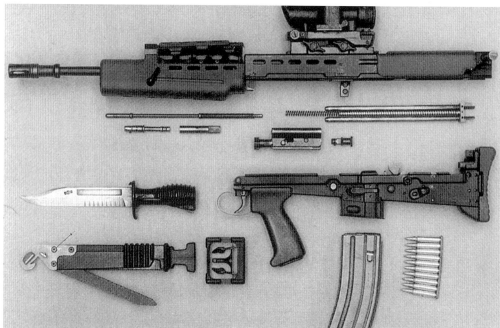

(top) **British infantryman with L85A1 rifle showing detail of the SUSAT sight unit.**

(bottom) **The British Army's L85A1 rifle stripped down to show its rather complicated mechanism. Note the knife-type bayonet which can also be used with the scabbard as a wirecutter.**

Opposite.

(top) **British troops inside the EH 101 troop-carrying helicopter. The compact design of the L85A1 makes it suitable for troops deploying from such confined environments as helicopters and APCs.**

(bottom) **The British Royal Marines also use the L85A1 rifle. It is seen here fitted with SUSAT sights as standard.**

engagement distance for infantrymen on the battlefield.

The rifle is manufactured from stamped and machined parts and plastic material for the pistol grip, forestock and butt plate. The L85A1 is fitted with a carrying sling which is fully adjustable and allows the carrier to place it in a position which allows him to perform tasks with his hands without putting the weapon down. This is similar in practice to the French Army's FAMAS rifle.

The rifle can fire rifle grenades of all natures, but trials into mounting a 40mm grenade launcher were curtailed early on in the development programme. This particular device fired standard 40mm grenades out to a maximum range of 350m and featured all the usual safety mechanisms, with automatic opening and ejection. Unfortunately the launcher added 1.4kg to the weight of the rifle, which was an unacceptable burden, and it never entered service on the L85A1 rifle. A much shortened version of the rifle with a snub-barrel was proposed and trialled to initial development phases. But after some initial interest, that programme, too, was cut short.

The rifle features the familiar gas-operated type of mechanism locked by a rotating bolt which engages in lugs behind the breech and is carried on two guide rods. The cocking handle is on the right-hand side of the weapon. On operating this to load the weapon the ejection port cover – which also acts as a 'dust cover' – is opened. Unlike the Austrian-designed AUG rifle of bullpup layout, the L85A1 cannot be configured to suit left-handed firers. The rifle can be fitted with a blank firing attachment for training in field exercises. A knife-type bayonet can be fitted, but this too has come in for criticism. The design uses a hollow handle, which means it fits completely around the muzzle of the weapon rather than using an adapter ring and mounting lug under the barrel. This means that when the rifle is fired with the bayonet fitted the bullets and hot gases pass through the handle and heat it up. This makes it virtually impossible to remove the bayonet after firing without gloves.

The L85A1 is used by units of the British Army deployed to the Province of Northern Ireland. The weapon was also used by British troops committed to the Coalition forces during Operation DESERT STORM against Iraq in 1990–91, and more recently is used by troops deployed with UN forces conducting peacekeeping missions in areas such as Bosnia.

Overall the weapon appears to function well, but

A member of the British Royal Marines takes aim with his L85A1 rifle using the SUSAT sight.

compared to other bullpup designs, especially the AUG, it is not faultless. The author has fired the L85A1 a number of times and whilst it is comfortable and the SUSAT allows for good target acquisition, he never felt entirely at ease with the weapon. Unofficial reports have filtered out suggesting that troops serving with the Coalition forces during Operation DESERT STORM were far from satisfied with the operational capabilities of the L85A1. Even if one dismisses 90 per cent of these reports as simple moaning, there is still some cause for concern.

The rifle appears to perform well in the temperate climates encountered in Northern Ireland and central Europe, but in more extreme climates it clearly has difficulties. This helps to explain its lack of export success. The Austrian bullpup design, the AUG, has been sold extensively, and even the French FAMAS has been taken in small numbers, although not to the extent of re-equipping entire overseas armed forces. The L85A1, on the other hand, has yet to attract even remote interest from potential overseas clients. Given the continuing adverse reports of the rifle, it looks unlikely that this position will change in the future. The production run of the L85A1 rifle for the British Army is now complete, with over 300,000 units having been built.

SPECIFICATIONS:

Calibre:	5.56mm x 45
Weight:	3.9kg (unloaded and without SUSAT sight)
Weight:	5.04kg (with 30-round magazine and SUSAT sight fitted)
Length:	770mm
Barrel:	518mm
Rifling:	Six grooves, right hand, one turn in 180mm
Muzzle velocity:	900m/sec

There is not much one can say that is new about the US Army's 5.56mm x 45mm M16 rifle. Along with the Russian AK47, the M16 stands as one of the most instantly recognisable rifles of modern times, and has been accepted into service by numerous armies around the world, including Australia, Canada, New Zealand, Israel – even some elements of the British Army have used it.

Since its appearance back in the early 1960s the M16 has influenced many designs of weapon, and has

(top) **M16A2 fitted with the Rifleman's Assault Weapon, RAW, which has a HESH effect on the target. The launching device clips to the muzzle of the rifle and requires no special launching ammunition. Unusually, the M16A2 seen here is fitted with a bipod.**

(bottom) **An American serviceman takes aim with his M16A2 rifle using the RAW HESH system. Note he takes direct aim and the device for launching the RAW is simply clipped to the muzzle of the weapon.**

(above) **An American airborne infantryman takes up firing position with his M16A2 fitted with an M203 40mm grenade launcher.**

(left) **An American airborne infantryman has just landed and is stowing his equipment. He has his M16A2 rifle ready to hand.**

M16A2. Often referred to as 'The Black Rifle' the M16 is a popular service rifle and has been used in countless military engagements around the world from temperate zones to extremes of desert heat and Arctic conditions and still functioned reliably.

The origins of the M16 are as well known as those of the Galil or AK47, but, to recap briefly, the rifle was designed by Eugene Stoner and originally appeared in the early 1960s as the AR-15, with the intention of firing the newly-developed 5.56mm calibre round. Successful trials led to it being adapted and taken into service use by the US Army, which at the time was heavily engaged in the Vietnam War in South East Asia. The rifle was given the service title of M16. The US Air Force quickly followed the lead of the Army and adopted the rifle too, and today there are few American Government agencies which do not have their own stock or access to a stock of M16 rifles, including police forces, FBI, Coast Guard and the Drug Enforcement Agency.

However good any weapon may be, there is always room for improvement, and combat experience in Vietnam showed that some alterations had to be made.

even been copied directly by the Chinese. This last version was termed 'CQ' by the Chinese, which means '16', and was a copy of the M16A1 version of the rifle. It differed from the original only by having a curved pistol grip with some embellishments. If imitation is the sincerest form of flattery, then this was high praise indeed. The M16 has appeared in many authorised versions and been the subject of much experimentation.

The standard version in current service today is the

Opposite.

(top) **A member of the British TA using an M16A1 on an exercise. The British Army has used the M16 for many years and it is regarded as a useful weapon and is very popular with those troops who have used it.**

(bottom) **The American-built M16A2 seen here being trialled by a British serviceman using the LS45 laser sight device. The M16 is capable of being used to mount a great variety of optical sights.**

(right) **Two Guardsmen, of the 1st Battalion Irish Guards of the British Army, patrol the troubled streets of Aden during the crisis in 1966. They are carrying M16A1s, at around the same time that American troops were beginning to receive them for operational use in the Vietnam War.**

The most obvious one was the call for a bolt return plunger, today referred to as 'forward assist', which would allow an infantryman to close the bolt of the weapon if it became jammed through fouling as the result of continued use in combat.

The current M16A2 rifle fires the SS109 round from a detachable box magazine with a 30-round capacity, and has a cyclic rate between 700 and 950 rounds per minute. The effective range of the M16A2 is set at 400m, which is nowadays seen as the optimum engagement range for infantry small arms fire. The different versions of the M16, which have appeared at various times, have included a 'firing port' model for use from inside a Mechanised Infantry Combat Vehicle, or MICV, and the Colt 'Commando' with a collapsible butt stock and shortened barrel. There have also been trials to develop a heavy-barrelled version fitted with a bipod to serve in the role of a squad light support weapon.

The M16 has been used by US service personnel in many engagements, including Grenada in 1983, UN peacekeeping roles around the world, and during Operation DESERT STORM in the Gulf War of 1990–91, against Iraqi forces which had invaded Kuwait.

The M16 can be fitted with a knife-type bayonet and blank firing muzzle attachments for training purposes. The standard M16A2 has a fixed butt stock, manufactured from plastic, the same as the forestock. The flash illuminator is of the type known as a 'birdcage' and the distinctive carrying handle, which also incorporates the rear sights, has been retained.

The M203 40mm grenade launcher was developed to be fitted to the M16. The original design was a rather bulky, heavy affair but it has been refined over the years and greatly reduced in weight. This device can fire all natures of 40mm grenades including high explosive, anti-tank, anti-personnel, smoke and illuminating. Another 'force multiplying' weapon developed for the M16 rifle, was the High Explosive Squash Head – Rifleman's Assault Weapon (HESH-RAW). Developed by the American company of Brunswick Defense, it is seen as a projectile for use in military operations in urban areas (MOUA), or fighting in built-up areas (FIBUA), as it is described in British military terminology. HESH-RAW is a rocket-propelled munition launched from the muzzle of an M16 rifle using a special adapter. The adapter fits easily to the rifle, and the projectile is launched by the firer using his weapon in the direct firing mode from the shoulder. Because it is a line of sight weapon it is aimed at the target using the rifle's ordinary sights. The HESH-RAW projectile is spherical in shape and weighs some 8.5lb with an explosive payload of some 2.5lb. It can be used to destroy light vehicles as well as machine-gun emplacements, mortar sites, and other strengthened positions. It has no backblast, which means an infantryman can use it from the confines of a building – a useful feature in FIBUA operations. In the direct fire mode the infantryman can engage targets out to 200m, and in the indirect fire mode the HESH-RAW will carry out to

2,000m. Although effective, HESH-RAW is a rather bulky munition and if a serviceman were to be given the option between this and several rounds of 40mm grenades for his M203 launcher, he would refuse the HESH-RAW.

The M16 is easy to come to terms with and handling during firing is comfortable, even during the three-round burst sequence. Field stripping for cleaning and maintenance is simple and quick. The take-down pin on the left of the rear of the receiver is pushed through and the butt stock and lower receiver swung down. The bolt carrier assembly and cocking handle can then be slid out and separated. The hand guard is removed, and the buffer and return spring can then be extracted. To reassemble the rifle the stripping sequence is reversed. It takes only a few minutes to achieve and the rifle will function perfectly even under the most arduous of conditions.

SPECIFICATIONS:

Calibre:	5.56mm x 45mm
Length:	990mm overall
Weight:	3.18kg
Barrel:	508mm
Rifling:	Six grooves, right hand, one turn in 305mm
Muzzle velocity:	1000m/sec

The OICW is a revolutionary new rifle that is being developed by the United States to replace the current M16A2 assault rifle and M203 grenade launcher. The programme was begun in 1994, and at the time of writing is well into development and testing. The schedule is for the first units to be equipped with the new weapon in 2005, although it is unusual for such programmes to run to schedule and this may well end up being delayed.

The OICW programme is closely tied in with the US Land Warrior programme, which aims to equip the individual soldier with a range of hi-tech clothing, communications, location/navigation and weapons systems to improve his effectiveness on the battlefield.

The OICW combines a 5.56mm rifle, similar to the M16, with a 20mm cannon and a sophisticated aiming and fire control system. The parameters drawn up for the new system require a 500 per cent increase in the probability of incapacitation, an effective range of up to 1000 metres, and the ability to defeat targets in defilade (for example, an enemy soldier hiding behind a wall). All this is to be achieved with a substantial weight reduction versus the M16/M203 combo, and with an ergonomic design.

The rifle part of the OICW has little about it that is new. The 20mm cannon, arranged piggy-back on top of the 5.56mm receiver and barrel, is a true leap forward, however. It is designed to work closely with a laser targeting and range-finding system, which not only calculates the correct aiming point but also sets a fuse in the projectile, so that it bursts at exactly the right moment for maximum effect on the target.

The soldier, then, can fire a shell to explode directly over the heads of enemy soldiers hiding behind an obstacle, or inside a room or bunker – even a kilometre away. This represents a quantum leap in the effectiveness of the individual soldier. If the contractors can deliver these results in an affordable package, then it will give the United States and its allies a decisive advantage in future conflicts.

Manufacturer:	Alliant Techsystems, Hopkins, MN, USA (Prime Contractor). Heckler & Koch, Germany and UK (5.56mm/20mm weapon). Brashear LP, Pittsburgh, PA, USA (Fire control system)
Model:	OICW (Objective Individual Combat Weapon)
Calibres:	5.56mm assault rifle & 20mm HE cannon
Action:	Selectable semi/full-automatic
Feed:	10-shot detachable box magazine (20mm HE), 30-round detachable box magazine (5.56mm)
Sights:	Red dot night/day sighting system. Laser ranging and fuse setting system for 20mm projectiles
Weight:	12lb.
Length:	33in overall

SNIPING RIFLES

Sniping rifles, like shotguns, have a broad band of users, ranging from police in urban situations to paramilitary forces and the regular military who use snipers on the battlefield for harassment and disruption of the enemy.

The terrorist gunman, erroneously called a sniper, using a semi-automatic weapon, should not be confused with the shooter who has spent many long hours honing his skill to a standard which is second to none.

Historically snipers were excellent shots equipped with well-made rifles fitted with telescopic sights and supplied with special ammunition to engage targets at extreme ranges, well beyond the normal limits of engagement for infantrymen with ordinary rifles. During the American Civil War, for example, sharp-·shooters in the Army of the Confederate States used Whitworth rifles of .450 inch calibre with a hexagonal bore to snipe at Federal troops on the battlefield. The Union Generals Sedgewick and Lytle are believed to have been casualties of such sniping tactics with these rifles.

Sniping in the First World War was much in evidence on both sides of the Western Front Theatre, and by 1918 the British Army was issuing Mk.1* W(T) .303 inch calibre Lee-Enfield rifles at the rate of three per battalion. These weapons were solely for the purpose of sniping and not for an ordinary rifleman's trench warfare. Sniping continued throughout the Second World War and the Russian Army even resorted to using women in the role of battlefield snipers, equipped with the bolt action 7.62mm calibre Mosin-Nagant M1891/30 fitted with a telescopic sight.

The British Army's thinking on the psychology of a sniper at the time was that he should be: '...of above average intelligence, strong, and tireless, have the makings of a good shot, have a liking for being alone and should, for preference, be a countryman'. The fact that this definition of a potential sniper demands only that he should 'have the makings' of a good shot, and not necessarily be an excellent shot indicates that a man can be properly coached in the art of sniping. As a trained sniper at the British Army's Infantry School for Small Arms at Warminster informed the author, the actual taking of the shot is the 'cherry on the cake'. The rest of the engagement, such as the waiting time and the sighting, is equally important. On the battlefield the sniper is a lone wolf. His actions are one-on-one, making sniping one of the most personal of all types of engagement.

In post-war years the requirements for snipers and sniping fell off in most armies, and as a battlefield role it was destined not to regain its former importance until the Korean War. During that conflict both sides employed snipers to good effect, and some individuals made an impressive tally of kills. The British Army was one of the first forces to realise the error of its ways in allowing sniping to deteriorate, and set about remedying its deficiency in battlefield snipers.

The sniper's skills of fieldcraft and marksmanship are as important as his rifle, but naturally snipers are armed with well-made, accurate rifles – usually with a bolt action, fitted with high quality telescopic sights and firing matched ammunition. The sniper's rifle has all manner of features which allow him to 'tailor' it to suit his specific build, including adjustable cheek-plates on the butt-stock, adjustable butt plates, bipods and balancing weights.

The preferred rifle type for police or military snipers for engaging specific, high priority targets, sometimes presenting themselves in an opportune manner, is the bolt action type. There are a handful of very well-designed semi-automatic types which deliver good results. But it must be said that for precise, accurate shooting, rather than volume of fire, the bolt action designs are without equal.

The primary role of the modern military sniper is to create an air of uncertainty in all areas of the battlefield, from the front line to areas extending some several hundred metres to the rear. Troops can never afford to relax their guard if they are aware that snipers are present in the vicinity. A sniper may be anything up to 1,000 metres from the enemy's front line, and he must be able to engage and hit a human-sized target with great precision at this range.

The sniper's skills of concealment and observation also make him a vital ingredient of an army's intelligence-gathering system. With suitable communications, he can report important details of the enemy's strength and movements. The sniper also plays this crucial role in hostage situations involving police or military anti-terrorist forces.

To aid the sniper in his task he is equipped with the finest optical equipment including, for night time, either thermal imaging or passive infra-red sights, to enable him to engage targets 24 hours a day. But even the finest tools will fail if the man is not up to the task, and ultimately the sniper has to rely on his skill, judgment and patience to engage a target successfully.

The TRG sniping rifle from the Finnish company of Sako is available in two models, which share a high degree of commonality in parts, with only the calibres and length of rifling varying between the two models. The TRG rifle has been developed through a highly detailed study of a sniper's requirements. The resulting weapon is one which is primarily for military use and has an accuracy that delivers half a minute of angle. At ranges of 1,000m the rifle in a well trained sniper's hands is capable of consistently placing rounds in a target of some 100mm diameter.

The TRG is a robustly designed weapon, and has substantial weight to match its overall dimensions. The action body of the TRG rifle is triangular in section, with the bottom of the body being flat and the sides angled inwards with flat outer surfaces and rounded inner guides for the bolt. The action is bedded onto an aluminium alloy bedding block. The barrel length of the TRG-21 is 660mm and on the TRG-41 it is 690mm in length. In both cases the barrels are manufactured from cold hammer-forged metal and are free-floating, with some 6.5mm clearance from the bedding block.

The muzzle brake is threaded to permit a suppressor to be fitted if tactical requirements demand it. In this case special subsonic ammunition would be used, such as the 7.62mm x 51 which is full metal jacket with a velocity in the order of 315 metres per second. The projectile of this round weighs 12g and the tip is painted

(top) **The Finnish TRG sniping rifle stripped down to its component parts showing the trigger mechanism, barrel and bolt assembly.**

(bottom) **The Finnish TRG sniping rifle without any added features such as telescopic sight. Note its very plain, almost simple, lines.**

blue for ease of identification. This ammunition demands a barrel with a maximum 435mm twist.

The trigger mechanism is detachable and has a double stage pull. The first take-up pressure can be set at 1kg and the second to 2.5kg, and the trigger can also be adjusted for length of pull and vertical or horizontal pitch. The bolt of the TRG rifle has three forward locking lugs, and the firing pin has a travelling distance of 6.5mm before striking the round. The bolt lift angle in both versions of the TRG is 60 degrees, but the TRG-21 has a bolt throw of 98mm, whilst the TRG-41 has a bolt throw of 118mm. The handle on the bolt is an over-large knob to allow the firer ease of action even in the coldest of conditions. For the best possible stability and rigidity, the aluminium base stock of the rifle is fitted with a polyurethane forestock. The butt stock, also manufactured from polyurethane, has an aluminium skeleton.

The rifle is equipped with a folding bipod and the cheekpiece can be adjusted for height, windage and pitch. The butt plate is also fully adjustable and can be altered to suit individual shooter's requirements in length and horizontal or vertical pitch. The TRG rifle designs have detachable box magazines, which on the TRG-21 model has a capacity of 10 rounds and on the TRG-41 five rounds. The rifles are not supplied with optical sights but the mounting rail will accept most types of sighting units, including night-vision equipment with STANAG 2324.

SPECIFICATIONS

	TRG-21	TRG-41
Calibre:	.308 Win. (7.62mm)	.338 Lapua Mag. (8.58mm)
Overall length:	1,150mm	1,200mm
		(without butt spacers)
Weight:	4.7kg	5.1kg
Barrel length:	660mm	690mm
Muzzle velocity:	760m/sec with 7.62mm x 51 full metal jacket	
Rifling:	Four grooves,	Four grooves,
	right hand, one	right hand, one
	turn in 435mm	turn in 305mm

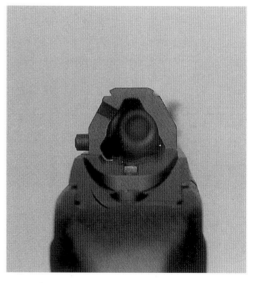

(right) **Close-up detail showing the massive action body of the TRG sniping rifle, which is triangular in shape.**

(below) **The Finnish TRG sniping rifle fitted with both telescopic sight and night-vision device. Note the muzzle brake fitted to the muzzle to give the firer better control of the weapon.**

The French-designed and -built Fusil à Répétition Modèle F1, or FR-F1 sniping rifle, has been declared obsolete in use with the French Army, but like other weapons which have been sold to many users it is still likely to be encountered in many theatres of operation around the world.

This particular rifle can be supplied in either 7.5mm x 54, a round much used by the French before the advent of the 5.56mm, or the 7.62mm x 51, which is NATO standard. To differentiate between the calibres, and avoid costly mistakes, the calibre of the weapon is stamped on the left-hand side of the receiver.

The FR-F1 was designed to replace the ageing Modèle 1936, which was also in 7.5mm calibre, and provided the French Army with a reliable and accurate weapon. The FR-F1 is a bolt-action rifle with a ten-round detachable box magazine, capable of firing out to ranges of 800m at a rate of 10–15 rounds per minute. However, a sniper would seldom be expected to fire that many rounds in the course of one minute, and more selective firing would achieve better results. No left-handed version of the rifle was made, and all models were equipped with basic iron sights.

The locking lugs on the bolt are rear-mounted and on operating the action after firing a cam bears against the surface at the rear of the receiver and full movement of the bolt performs extraction of the spent case, in an action common to many bolt-action rifles. Pushing the bolt forward strips a round from the magazine and feeds it into the chamber, and the locking action of the bolt forces the extractor grips around the rim of the cartridge in readiness to extract the round after firing. At the same time, the sear holds up the firing pin lug to retain the firing pin in the cocked position.

The trigger has the usual two-stage pressure associated with sniping rifles. When the firer takes up the first pressure, the trigger bears on the trigger pin, joining the trigger and sear until the trigger stud reaches the bottom of the receiver. The second take-up pressure pivots the sear and compresses the spring, until the sear releases the lug of the firing pin which moves forward to strike the base of the round.

The FR-F1 is fitted with a bipod which has fully adjustable legs attached to the body of the rifle mid-way along its length to give a good point of balance. The butt

The French FR-F1 sniping rifle has been replaced by the FR-F2, but may still be found in use by various forces around the world. Note the bipod placed at a good point of balance and the adjustable cheek-plate on the butt stock.

stock has fully adjustable butt-plate spacers and cheek-plate. The forestock, butt and pistol grip are all manufactured from wood.

The FR-F1 can accept a wide range of optical sights, including night-vision equipment, but the x4 Modèle 53 telescopic sight is preferred. The magazine of the rifle has a rubber top cover which is removed before inserting into the magazine well and there is the facility to top up the magazine one round at a time, should the sniper feel it necessary.

Snipers of the 2nd Parachute Battalion of the French Foreign Legion (2e Bataillon Etranger Parachutiste; 2 BEP) were equipped with the FR-F1 when they were successfully deployed to the Shaba province in southern Zaire in May 1978. The fighting to restore order to this former Belgian colony was intense, and during this relatively short operation sniping was much in evidence. In fact, one of the first French casualties during the deployment, Corporal Arnold, fell to sniper fire.

SPECIFICATIONS:

Calibre:	7.5mm x 54 or 7.62mm x 51
Weight (empty):	5.2kg
Overall length:	1,138mm (without butt spacers)
Barrel length:	552mm
Rifling:	Four grooves, right hand, one turn in 305mm
Muzzle velocity:	Around 852m/sec, depending on type of ammunition

Just as the FR-F1 sniping rifle was introduced to replace the Modèle 1936, so the Fusil à Répétition Modèle F2, or FR-F2, has been introduced as a modern replacement for the FR-F1. The FR-F2 fires the NATO 7.62mm x 51 calibre, with which it has a firing stoppage rate better than 10^3. The FR-F2 is a bolt-action rifle and its most obvious difference from the earlier FR-F1 is the heavier barrel which is fitted with a flash suppressor, protected by a monobloc stock, and is bolted to the breech casing. The life of the barrel is claimed to be better than 12,000 rounds with no loss of accuracy, and some 20,000 rounds with accuracy remaining better than 90 per cent of the original value.

The breech casing also supports the butt stock and has guide rails on its upper surfaces to accept the mounting for the telescopic sight. The FR-F2 can be supplied in either the wooden monobloc stock design or with a composite material stock. The former serves to protect the barrel and support the integral bipod. The composite material design allows the barrel to be fitted using heat-shrink processes and a ball-jointed bipod to be mounted which makes the tracking of moving targets much easier.

The trigger mechanism comprises the cam action trigger, the sear, and its spring. The cams are fully adjustable and the pull force of the trigger can be set in the order of 2 daN. The safety catch is located to the left of the trigger guard and when applied locks up the trigger action.

The butt stock features an adjustable cheek plate, and insert plates can be fitted or removed to adjust the length to suit individual users. The rifle can accept most optical units and the scope mounting has a simple-to-use cam-type locking lever for quick fitting and removal. A typical daytime telescopic sight of 6 x 42 magnification will allow accurate target engagements out to 800m. For night use the FR-F2 can be fitted with a light-intensified device such as the SOPELEM OB50, which has a x 3 magnification and a ten degree field of view. This night-vision device will allow a sniper to engage targets out to 150m with a light level at 10^3 lux and 400m at 10^1 lux.

The box magazine is identical to the type fitted to the older FR-F1 sniping rifle. It holds ten rounds and can be reloaded one round at a time if required.

The FR-F2 can be used in temperatures ranging from -40°C to +51°C, which makes it versatile enough to equip troops operating in all types of terrain from desert to Arctic warfare.

The French Army's FR-F2 sniping rifle which has replaced the older FR-F1. Here a sniper is seen taking aim showing the rifle's bipod and heavy barrel.

SPECIFICATIONS:

Calibre: 7.62mm x 51

Overall length: 1,200mm

Length of barrel: 650mm.

Weight: 4.45kg (with wooden stock)

                 5.34kg (with wooden stock and telescopic sight)

                 4.84kg (with composite stock)

                 5.74kg (with composite stock and telescopic sight)

Length of rifling: 582mm

Rifling: Three grooves, right hand, one turn in 295mm

The French Army's FR-F2 sniping rifle standing on its bipod. It is fitted with a telescopic sight. Note the flash eliminator on the muzzle.

The G3 SG/1 sniping rifle from the design team of the German company of Heckler and Koch is essentially a modified version of the standard G3A3 semi-automatic rifle. The Scharfschützen Gewehr, SG/1, was developed for the German police, who use the weapon with either a telescopic sight or the weapon's integral iron sights.

The sniping version is not manufactured on a dedicated sniping rifle production line but is the result of standard rifles demonstrating their ability consistently to place their mean point of impact correctly during proof firing trials. Those weapons which meet the high standard required for precision marksmanship are set aside for modification into sniping versions.

Those weapons which qualify for modification are fitted with a special trigger group which incorporates a 'set' trigger with a variable pull. In the 'set' position, the trigger requires only the slightest touch to fire the round. The trigger can only be 'set' when the combined fire selector switch/safety catch is set to the 'E' position, for 'single shots'. The trigger can be reset after firing one round, or the firer can continue to use the weapon without making any adjustment to the trigger which has a full take-up pull in the order of 2.6kg. If the trigger has been 'set' this is automatically released as soon as the fire selector switch is moved from 'single shot' to 'safe' or 'automatic'. However, it is unlikely that a sniper would ever use the latter mode of fire, as single shot is more in keeping with the traditional sniping role.

The G3 SG/1 fires the standard 7.62mm x 51 round and is fitted with a 20-round magazine. It cycles in exactly the same way as the standard G3 rifle, which is based on delayed blowback. This makes it readily familiar to many police and service personnel. Iron sights are fitted as standard on this sniping rifle but an optical sight unit such as a Zeiss variable power 1.5-6x can be clamped to a side rail running along the left-hand side of the receiver for use in the true sniping role. This combination has full windage and range adjustments to ranges between 100m and 600m, which is probably the full

Cut-away diagram showing the trigger mechanism of the G3 SG/1 German sniping rifle.

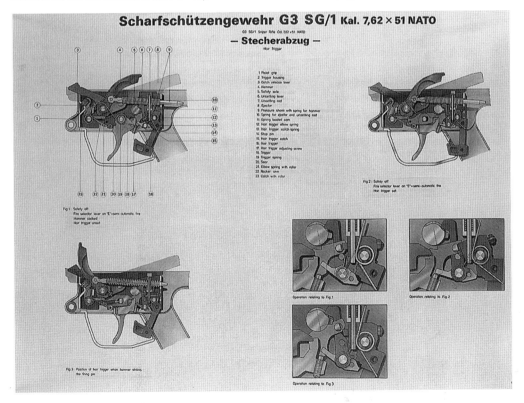

engagement range that police snipers will encounter in urban situations.

The G3 SG/1 sniping rifle has an adjustable bipod fitted to the front end of the forestock and the barrel is equipped with a flash suppressor, as on the standard G3 rifle design. The butt-stock of the SG/1 has an adjustable cheek-plate, and its length can be altered by

(left) **A police sniper takes aim using the G3 SG/1 rifle. He is using the telescopic UA1126 night sight to show the configuration during daylight conditions. Due to his unconventional firing position he has folded the bipod legs back along the length of the forestock.**

(top) **The G3 SG/1 sniping rifle seen from the left-hand side showing the mounting bracket for the standard telescopic sight. Note the adjustable bipod and the cocking handle in the usual position as featured on the normal G3 assault rifle.**

(below) **Exploded diagram of the G3 SG/1 sniping rifle showing all the components, including trigger mechanism and bolt assembly.**

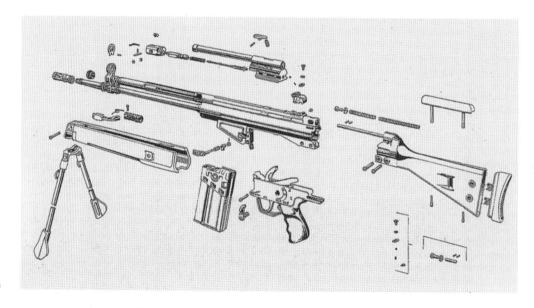

inserting spacers to the butt-plate.

As well as the German police, the SG/1 is in use with several other police forces including the Italian Carabinieri. It should be pointed out, however, that the SG/1 is not the first version of the G3 rifle to be fitted with a telescopic sight. The G3A3Z ('Z' being zielfernrohr for telescope) was an early experimental version, but did not enter general service.

(top) **The G3 SG/1 German semi-automatic sniping rifle seen from the left-hand side with the bipod legs folded and fitted with telescopic sight.**

(bottom) **The G3 SG/1 semi-automatic sniping rifle seen from the left-hand side with bipod erected.**

SPECIFICATIONS:

Calibre:	7.62mm x 51
Overall length:	1,016mm (without spacers)
Weight unloaded:	4.25kg
Barrel length:	450mm
Rifling:	Four grooves, right hand
Muzzle velocity:	Typically in the order of 805m/sec

The Präzisionsschützengewehr (High Precision Marksman's Rifle), or PSG 1, has been developed by Heckler and Koch in response to demands by police and military snipers for high precision weapons. It is one of a handful of semi-automatic rifles to be used in the sniping role, but is limited to delayed blowback, single-fire operation.

As may be imagined, the PSG 1 is a heavy weapon, but the integral bipod and adjustable pistol grip rest plate mean that the firer does not have to support the weight for prolonged periods. The rifle utilises the standard breech mechanism, whereby the bolt is a two-part unit with delayed opening which is achieved through the roller-locked system. The weapon's cycle of operation is familiar to many service personnel. The bolt system, however, has been modified so that when cycling and closing it has a much reduced signature.

The trigger has also been altered so that it has the sniper's favoured two-stage take-up pressure. Adjustments are made by means of a vertically adjustable trigger-shoe to provide variable-width trigger with a take-up pressure of some 1.5kg. The butt stock has fully adjustable cheek-plates and butt-plate to suit the individual anatomy of the shooter.

The PSG 1 fires 7.62mm NATO rounds and is fed by means of a box magazine, which is available in either 5-round or 20-round capacity. Used by an experienced sniper, this weapon is capable of placing ten rounds inside a target area 50mm square at 300m range. The PSG 1 will accept most types of optical sights, including night-vision units. It is normally fitted with a 6 x 42 telescopic sight, which is unusual in that adjustments for windage and elevation are made by movement of

(top) **The semi-automatic PSG 1 sniping rifle showing adjustable plate, cheek-plate and hand grip.**

(bottom) **The semi-automatic PSG 1 sniping rifle stripped for cleaning. Visible are the various components, including trigger assembly, bolt assembly and return spring.**

The German semi-automatic PSG 1 sniping rifle seen here from the left-hand side with telescopic sight fitted and bipod

the internal optical system. There are six settings to allow for ranges between 100m and 600m, and there is also a fine adjustment facility to compensate for any mounting offset angle.

SPECIFICATIONS:

Calibre:	7.62mm x 51 NATO. Also Lapua .308 Winchester Match Ammunition
Weight:	7.2kg
Overall length:	1,208mm
Barrel length:	650mm
Rifling:	Four grooves, right hand
Magazine capacity:	5 or 20 rounds

The Galil assault rifle as used by the Israeli Defence Forces is available in both 5.56mm and 7.62mm calibres, and has been combat proven many times during which the design has stood up well to the rigours of the battlefield. It was only a natural progression that a sniping version of the Galil should be developed, in a comparable move to the SG/1 sniping version of the German G3 rifle. Like that design, the Galil is a semi-automatic weapon and also features iron sights as standard.

The sniping version of the Galil fires a 7.62mm round and was developed in close association with the Israeli Defence Forces. The accuracy of the weapon has been

(top) **The Israeli Galil semi-automatic sniping rifle. Note how closely it resembles the standard Galil assault rifle.**

(bottom) **An Israeli soldier carrying a Galil semi-automatic assault rifle.**

determined to be groupings of 120mm to 150mm at a range of 300m, and 300mm at a range of 600m. The standard optical sight for use with the Galil sniping rifle is the Nimrod 6 x 40, which has a sight radius of 475mm. It is mounted on a side bracket fitted to the left-hand side of the weapon, and with this device the accuracy demands are met repeatedly. Whilst the Nimrod is standard to the weapon, the bracket will accept most optical units, including night-vision equipment.

The barrel is longer and heavier than on the standard version of the Galil and has a muzzle brake and flash suppressor to reduce movement and permit the firer to resight quickly after firing. A silencer can be fitted to this weapon, in place of the muzzle brake, to reduce the firing signature, which will allow a sniper to maintain his vantage point for several shots without revealing his position. When firing the weapon with a silencer fitted it is advised that subsonic ammunition be used, as with the Sako TRG.

The Galil sniping rifle can fire either FN match or M118 match ammunition. The standard bipod rest of sniper weapons is fitted behind the fore-end and is fully adjustable to maintain an excellent balance to the weapon and reduce stress to the firer when holding a firing position. The safety catch is located above the pistol grip on the left-hand side of the weapon and the trigger has a two-stage pull. The weapon is fitted with a 20-round box magazine, and has a rotating bolt, but is limited to firing only single rounds for tactical reasons.

The Galil has a folding butt stock, similar to the Swiss SIG 550 sniping rifle, which when locked in place is completely rigid. A fully adjustable cheek-plate is fitted to the butt, and rubber recoil pads can be fitted to the butt-plate to adjust the length of the weapon.

SPECIFICATIONS:

Calibre:	7.62mm x 51
Overall length:	1115mm (butt extended)
	840mm (butt folded)
Weight:	6.4kg (unloaded)
Barrel length:	508mm (excluding muzzle brake)
Rifling:	Four grooves, right hand, one turn in 305mm
Muzzle velocity:	815m/sec with FN match ammunition
	780m/sec with M118 match ammunition

The Russian Army has always made good use of snipers and the effects that long-range sniping has on enemy morale. The current sniping rifle of the Russian Army is the Dragunov SVD which fires the 7.62mm x 54R round. It features many parts common to the standard AK47 rifle, but due to the fact that the Dragunov fires a cartridge 54mm in length as opposed to the more usual cartridge case of 39mm length, the bolt cannot be interchanged.

The operating cycle of the Dragunov, which can be set to single-shot or semi-automatic modes, utilises a short-stroke gas-operated piston. It has a rotating bolt and is fed by a 10-round box magazine. In operation, the piston is forced back on its short stroke by gases which have been tapped off from the barrel during the firing sequence. This imparts force to the bolt carrier which in turn moves back. A lug on the bolt, which moves freely along a special cam path on the carrier, rotates the bolt to unlock it. The bolt and the carrier move together, the return spring is compressed and the carrier moves forward to lock the bolt, thereby allowing firing to take place. Once the carrier has travelled fully home the safety sear is released which frees the hammer for operating by the trigger and the firing pin is struck to fire the round. The trigger mechanism is set for single shots only and this is partly the reason for the simplicity of the design of this weapon.

The Dragunov does not feature a bipod, and the wooden butt stock, which has a cut-out section, is fitted with a removable cheek-plate, but there is apparently no facility to make adjustments to length using butt-plate inserts.

The telescopic sight used with this weapon is the PSO-1 which has a x4 magnification with a six-degree true field of view but a 24-degree apparent field of view. This sight unit is excellent in daytime use and in low light levels is capable of detecting infra-red sources.

Reports claim that the Dragunov is accurate enough to allow target engagement out to ranges of 1,000m, with an effective range estimated to be in the region of 1,300m.

As with other Russian-designed weaponry the Dragunov has been widely copied. There are two copies worth mentioning here, both manufactured by Iraqi State Arsenals: the Al-Kadisa, which is virtually a straight copy of the Dragunov, and the Tabuk, which is similar to the M76 rifle of the former Yugoslavia.

The Al-Kadisa is termed a sniping rifle and fires the same 7.62mm x 54R cartridge as the Dragunov, with which it achieves a muzzle velocity of 830m/sec – identical to the Dragunov's muzzle velocity. The differences between the two weapons appear to be superficial with no obvious modifications. The Al-Kadisa is a semi-automatic rifle using a rotating bolt and is fed by a 10-round box magazine. It weighs 4.3kg, is 1,230 mm in length and has a barrel length of 620mm.

The Tabuk sniping rifle is based on the standard Kalashnikov design and fires the 7.62mm x 39 rimless cartridge. It features a cut-out butt stock and removable cheek-plate similar to the Dragunov, but has a separate pistol grip, whereas the Dragunov and Al-Kadisa both have the pistol grip incorporated into the design of the butt stock. The Tabuk is 1,110mm in overall length, has a barrel length of 600mm and weighs 4.5kg. The effective range of this weapon is understood to be in the order of 600m and it has a muzzle velocity of 740m/sec.

At the height of the Cold War, the Dragunov was issued at the rate of one weapon per platoon in a motor

The Russian Dragunov SVD semi-automatic sniping rifle. Despite its old-fashioned appearance it is still a useful weapon and remains in widespread use in the CIS and former client states of Russia.

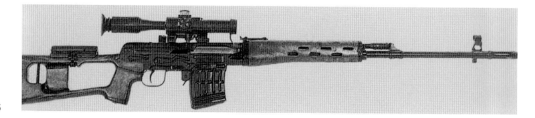

rifle unit. Today, there is no reason to believe this rate of issue to be any different.

SPECIFICATIONS:

Calibre:	7.62mm x 54R (Rimmed)
Weight:	4.3kg with PSO-1 sight fitted
Overall length:	1,225mm
Barrel length:	547mm
Rifling:	Four grooves, right hand, one turn in 254mm
Muzzle velocity:	830m/sec

The SG 550 sniping rifle from the Swiss Industrial Company of SIG is one of a mere handful of semi-automatic sniping rifles, and is made even more unusual by the fact that it has a calibre of 5.56mm x 45, which is more usually associated with combat rifles. However, it must be pointed out that some sniping rifles have calibres as low as .22 inch in order to minimise recoil forces and firing signature. These small-calibre rifles are used mainly for engaging targets in urban areas, however, and are unlikely ever to be used on a battlefield.

The SG 550 sniping rifle has been developed from the standard SG 550 assault rifle in co-operation with special units of the police. It is considered to be an appropriate weapon for use in difficult areas, and has even been adopted for use by the Swiss Army. The basic design of this sniping rifle owes much to the SG 550 combat rifle, but there are differences between the two designs which make the sniping version more inherently accurate. The barrel is a heavy hammer-forged design made to precise dimensions and, coupled with the low recoil forces, makes this an easily controlled weapon. The trigger is a sensitive double-pull type, the first

pressure being in the order of 800g and the second being in the order of 1.5kg. This, combined with the gas operation of the weapon, allows the sniper a rapid response, especially if he is required to fire a second shot at the same target.

The weapon is fitted with an ambidextrous safety catch and a bipod which gives good balance to the weapon. The magazine is detachable and has a capacity of either 20 or 30 rounds. For tailoring the weapon to suit individual users, the SG 550 sniping rifle is fitted with fully adjustable cheek-plates and butt stock, which can be folded. The angle of inclination on the pistol grip can also be altered, as can the hand rest.

A gas-operated weapon, the SG 550 has a rotating bolt and fires the Swiss Army's GP90 cartridge, which has high performance and superior precision characteristics that aid accuracy. The SG 550 sniping rifle can be fitted with a wide range of optical sights, including night-vision equipment such as thermal

Exploded diagram showing the components of the Swiss SG 550 version sniper rifle of semi-automatic design.

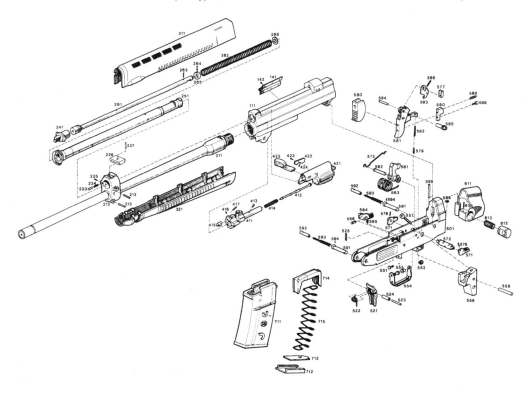

imagers or passive infra-red, to give the sniper a full 24-hour capability. The telescopic sight can be adjusted at right angles to the sight base to give the sniper a more ergonomically designed sighting position. Indeed, the weapon has all the features required to relieve the firer of stress and enable him to remain in a firing position for long periods.

SPECIFICATIONS:

Calibre:	5.56mm x 45
Length:	1,130mm
	905mm with butt folded
Barrel length:	650mm
Length of rifling:	604mm
Rifling:	Six grooves, right hand, one turn in 254mm
Weight:	7.02kg unloaded
Muzzle energy:	Around 1,820J, depending on ammunition

Opposite.

(top) **The SG 550 semi-automatic sniper rifle showing adjustable cheek-plate and butt-plate. The magazine is transparent and the same as used on the infantry's SG 550 assault rifle version.**

(middle) **The SG 550 semi-automatic sniping rifle seen from the left-hand side. Note the adjustable cheek-plate, butt-plate and hand stop on the pistol grip.**

(bottom) **Close-up detail of the bipod and muzzle of the SG 550 semi-automatic sniping rifle.**

Close-up detail of the SG 550 semi-automatic sniping rifle, showing the butt stock in the folded position and the telescopic sight.

Considering the relatively small size of the country, and the fact that it is neutral, Switzerland produces a remarkably comprehensive range of small arms and other weaponry. The SIG-Sauer SSG 2000 sniping rifle is another fine example of this capability and is in widespread use with many police forces, including the Malaysian Police, the Police Force of the Kingdom of Jordan, the Combined Service Forces of Taiwan, some British police forces, and, of course, some Swiss police forces.

The SSG 2000 is a purpose-made sniping weapon available in four calibres including the 7.62mm x 51 cartridge, and is fed from a four-round box magazine. Other calibres in which the SSG 2000 is available are the .300 Weatherby Magnum and the Swiss calibres of 5.56mm x 45 and 7.5mm x 55. It uses a bolt action with hinged lugs mounted at the rear of the bolt which drive outwards to lock into the receiver. This is performed by the action of cams which are driven by the rotation of the bolt handle, the bolt body itself being non-rotating. This latter feature makes for positive case extraction after firing. This might sound like an unusual design feature, but reducing the angular travel of the bolt to some 65 degrees gives a rapid and smooth loading action.

The barrel of the SSG 2000 is manufactured from hammer-forged metal and is fitted with a combination flash suppressor and muzzle brake, which imparts good weapon control and permits the firer to recover his firing position very quickly and compose himself in readiness for a second shot. The trigger mechanism is of the double set type. The standard take-up pull is in the order of 18N, reducing to just 3N when 'set'. The safety catch is a sliding action type which can function in three modes, and can block the sear, the sear pivot and the bolt itself. The bolt can be operated when the safety catch is applied; furthermore the set trigger can be eased by squeezing it when the rifle is in the safe condition, and it is automatically de-cocked when the bolt is opened. To indicate the state of the weapon to the firer there is a signal pin to inform when there is a round in the chamber.

The SSG 2000 rifle can be mounted on a fully adjustable tripod mount to allow moving targets to be tracked. The rifle has a butt stock which incorporates a vestigial thumb hole and features adjustable cheek-plate and butt-plate spacers to allow for length. The rifle does not feature iron sights in its basic form and will accept a wide range of optical sights, including night-vision equipment. A typical telescopic unit would be either the Schmidt & Bender 1.5-6 x 42 or the Zeiss Diatal ZA 8 x 56T.

SPECIFICATIONS:

Calibre:	7.62mm x 51
Weight:	6.6kg (including scope and loaded)
Overall length:	1,210mm
Barrel length:	610mm (excluding muzzle brake)
Rifling:	Four grooves, right hand, one turn in 305mm
Muzzle velocity:	Typically in the order of 750m/sec depending on ammunition

The Swiss-made SSG 3000 from SIG is a precision-made rifle which, in the hands of a well-trained marksman, will produce consistent results of the highest order. The SSG 3000 is a bolt-action rifle firing the standard NATO 7.62mm x 51 calibre round. The bolt itself has six locking lugs to provide a positive gas seal. The weapon uses the very latest in weapon design technology and has been developed using the Sauer 200 STR target rifle as its base.

The rifle is a modular design with the trigger system and five-round capacity magazine forming a single unit which is fitted into the receiver housing, which in turn is joined to the barrel by screw clamps. The receiver housing is machined from a single block with locking between the bolt and the barrel, which minimises the stress transference to the receiver. The stock of the SSG 3000 is made from non-warping wood laminate to

(top) **View along the right-hand side of the SSG 3000 sniping rifle, showing bipod details, bolt handle and telescopic sight.**

(bottom) **The SSG 3000 sniping rifle shown here in its transportation case with compartments for telescopic sight, spare magazines and bolt.**

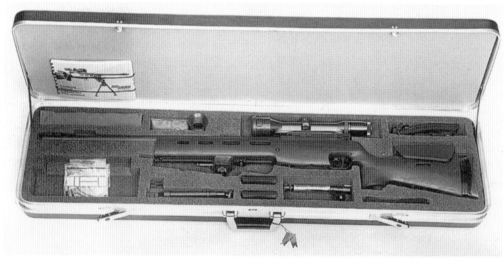

(top) **The SSG 3000 sniping rifle seen from the right-hand side, with bipod removed.**

(middle) **A police marksman takes aim with the SSG 3000 sniping rifle. He is using the rifle resting on a hard surface and has collapsed the bipod legs.**

(bottom) **The SSG 3000 sniping rifle seen from the left-hand side showing the adjustable cheek-plate and bipod which is also adjustable.**

223

produce a weapon that is low maintenance and simple to use.

The trigger has two take-up weights, which can be adjusted to assist in tailoring the weapon to individual firers. The first take-up weight of the trigger is between 13N and 15N, and the second between 13N and 17N. The safety catch is mounted above the trigger and serves to lock the trigger, bolt and firing pin when applied. The firer can release the safety catch without having to change position, which increases his response time. There is a cocking indicator pin with red and white surfaces at the end of the striker head to indicate to the firer the state of the weapon. The firing pin is light and has only a short distance to travel before striking the base of the round, thereby giving an extremely short lock time.

The heavy barrel of the SSG 3000 is manufactured from cold-swaged metal and has a combined muzzle brake and flash suppressor, which has a significant influence on the accuracy and stability of the weapon. It has a fully adjustable cheek-plate and butt-plate and a bipod, all of which can be fitted to suit the anatomy of individual firers. The SSG 3000 is also available in a left-handed version.

The weapon has no iron sights, due to the fact that it is intended to be used solely with telescopic sights. It can accept most optical sights, including night-vision equipment and NATO STANAG equipment, but the Hensoldt 1.5-6 x 42BL has been specifically designed for use with the SSG 3000. This sight unit is attached to the rifle by means of a mounting which allows for axial adjustment to suit individual users' eye relief length. For training or practice purposes a .22 inch conversion kit is available for this weapon.

SPECIFICATIONS:

Calibre:	7.62mm x 51 NATO
Length overall:	1,180mm
Weight unloaded:	5.4kg
	6.2kg (with Hensoldt sight fitted)
Length of barrel:	600mm (excluding flash suppressor)
Rifling:	Four grooves, right hand, one turn in 305mm
Feed:	5-round box magazine
Muzzle velocity:	800m to 830m per second, depending on ammunition
Muzzle energy:	3,500 to 3,750 Joules, depending on ammunition

Exploded diagram of the SSG 3000 sniping rifle.

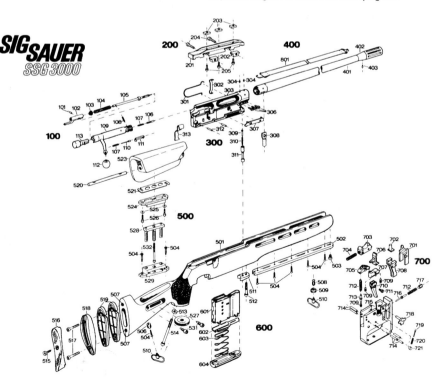

Although no longer in service use with the British Army, the L42A1 sniping rifle, or variants of it, are likely to be encountered from time to time. The L42A1 was introduced into service with the British Army in order to meet the requirements for a specialised sniping rifle. It is essentially a No.4 Lee-Enfield converted to fire 7.62mm ammunition instead of the .303 inch round, and as such is a standard bolt-action rifle.

The rifles converted for the sniping role were either No.4 Mark I (T) or No.4 Mark I* (T), which, as mentioned at the start of this chapter, were already used for the role of sniping, and were fitted with the No.32 Mark 3 telescope. The L42A1 differs from other variants by having its trigger pinned to the trigger guard and not mounted on the receiver as on the L39A1 version. The

trigger has a two-stage take-up, with the first pull being set between 1.36kg and 1.81kg and the second set between 2.27kg and 2.95kg.

The detachable box magazine holds ten rounds of 7.62mm NATO, the same number of rounds as the .303 inch version. The firer can also insert single rounds if necessary to 'top up' the magazine. There are subtle differences between the two types converted, but any differences in the results they deliver are marginal. For example, the bolt head on the No.4 Mk.I has a catch on it which must be depressed to allow the bolt-head to either engage or disengage with the guide rib. The No.4 Mk.I*, on the other hand, has a break in the guide rib, but no catch. The mounting brackets for the L1A1 straight sighting telescopic sight are fitted to the left-hand side of the rifle's body, and these also permit image intensifier

The British L42A1 sniping rifle being shown to visiting delegates at a firepower demonstration before it was replaced by the L96A1 rifle.

A British Army sniper leaves the podium after showing the L42A1 sniping rifle to an audience of visiting delegates.

units to be used. The L1A1 telescopic sight is actually a modified No.32 Mk.3 sight of the No.4 (T) rifle. The open sights of the rifle's original design have been retained and the Mk.1 rear sight is used.

To make allowances for the difference in ammunition types, the datum line has been lowered by 1.78mm and the modified slide marked with an 'm' on the right side. The foresight unit is a spit block sweated onto the barrel, with an adjustment screw to allow the sight blade to be clamped to the block. In fact, there are eight sizes of foresight for zeroing, ranging from 0.762 to 1.905mm in increments of 0.381mm. The safety catch on the L42A1 is exactly the same as for the No.4 Lee-Enfield and is located on the left-hand side of the weapon just above the trigger mechanism.

SPECIFICATIONS:

Calibre:	7.62mm x 51mm
Action:	Manual rotating bolt
Weight:	4.43kg
Length overall:	1,181mm
Barrel length:	699mm
Rifling:	Four grooves, right hand, one turn in 305mm
Muzzle velocity:	838m/sec

The AW series of sniper rifles is produced by the same British company, Accuracy International in Hampshire, who also designed the L96A1 sniping rifle as used by the British Army. On first glance the two weapons bear a remarkable likeness, but investigation reveals them to be completely separate systems.

In the AW series there are three versions of the weapon, all of which use detachable magazines of ten-round capacity, except for the 'SM' version which uses a five-round capacity magazine. The AW and AWS, the 'suppressed' version, both fire the NATO 7.62mm x 51 round (.308 Win) and the AWP also fires a 7.62mm round. The SM, 'Super Magnum', version fires a .338 LAP MAG (.300 Win Mag) round.

The range of rifles in this series can accept many different types of telescopic sight, but there are recommended sights for use with a specific weapon, including night-vision equipment. For example, the AW and AWS are likely to be fitted with a Hensoldt 10 x 42,

(top) **The AW series is the latest design from a British manufacturer of sniping rifles and is based on the earlier, and highly successful, L96A1 design. The Model AWP optimises all that is inherently required of a sniping rifle. It is seen here fitted with a Schmidt and Bender 12x50 variable power scope for excellent target acquisition over all ranges and is currently in service with a large number of military units and law enforcement agencies.**

(bottom) **This is another in the AW series of sniping rifles and is designed to be highly accurate over all ranges, even in low light level conditions, and has a number of reliable safety features. Night vision units can be fitted to permit the weapon to be used in all conditions.**

while the AWP would feature the Schmidt and Bender 3-12V x 50. The type of optical unit fitted to the SM rifle depends on the end user's choice. Each of the designs in this range is fitted with an adjustable bipod, but unlike the Counter Terrorist version of the L96A1, they do not feature a spike in the butt stock.

The AW series of rifles has been designed to permit complete interchangeability of parts, including the barrel and bolt action, with the maintenance of correct head space. The bolt is a three lug design and operates well in adverse conditions such as sub-zero temperatures and heavy fouling, such as sand. In fact, the rifles can be used in conditions with temperatures as low as -40°C. The AWP version has been developed specifically to meet the requirements of Special Forces units and other groups mounting internal security operations. The AW version has been NATO codified and the action can be supplied with either a three or six forward lug bolt system.

Test firings using four weapons have revealed very little wear even after 10,000 rounds. Only the barrel, which is stainless steel throughout the series, showed some wear. The tests were conducted without maintenance being carried out on the weapons and resulted in few, if any, part failures and misfeeds, or other malfunctions.

The AWS 'suppressed' version is basically an AW rifle with an integrated barrel and suppressor interchanged for the normal barrel. This action takes some three minutes to perform and full power ammunition can be used. With the suppressor the AWS can be used out to ranges of 300m, with a signature noise less than the report of a .22LR round.

The 'SM' Super Magnum version is available in 8.60mm x 70 calibre, which usefully closes the gap left between the conventional calibres of 7.62mm and the much larger .50 inch calibre 'anti-material' rifles. The SM is usually supplied with a Bausch and Lomb Tactical 10x telescopic sight, but it can be fitted with whichever sight unit the firer prefers. The inherent accuracy and high power of this rifle extends the effective range for serious anti-personnel sniping by some 35 per cent, to ranges of 1,100m and beyond.

The SM is also available in .300 Win Mag and 7mm Rem Mag, and is interchangeable between calibres by

(top) **The AWS is a fully suppressed version of the AW series of sniping rifle and has been developed to give law enforcement agencies a low signature weapon for use in urban situations. A number of sniping rifles can be fitted with suppressors, but the signature of the AWS is comparable to the report from a .22 inch LR round, which is virtually negligible. Full power ammunition can be used with the AWS without unduly shortening the service life of the suppressor. However, the re-calibration of sights is highly advised.**

(bottom) **This version of the standard AW series sniping rifle is fitted with the Hensoldt 10x42 scope to illustrate the versatility of the weapon's design in being fitted with various types of optical units which increase its usefulness in all situations.**

changing the bolt head, magazine and barrel. The stock is formed from reinforced nylon and is fitted over the entire length of the rifle, with the two halves being held together by Allen screws, in the same manner as the L96A1. The butt stock can be adjusted in length by inserting or removing spacer plates and the pistol grip is formed into part of the butt stock to provide a vestigial thumb hole.

SPECIFICATIONS:

	AW & AWS	AWP	SM
Calibre:	7.62mm x 51	7.62mm x 51	.338 LAP MAG
	(.308 Win)	(.308 Win)	(.300 Win Mag)
Weight:	6.4kg	6.8kg	7.0kg
Length:	1,180mm (AW)	1,100mm	1,200mm
	1,200mm (AWS)		
Barrel:	660mm	610mm	610–686mm

All sniping rifles are transported, where practical, in a specially constructed transportation box. This box is capable of absorbing normal handling during transportation to the site of deployment and contains all the necessary items required for use and maintenance, such as spare magazines, cleaning kit, butt stock spacers for length adjustment and other ancillary items. The box protects the rifle and the delicate telescopic sight unit when being moved over long distances.

The British Army's latest sniping rifle is termed the L96A1 and fires the 7.62mm x 51 cartridge. It is designed by a British company and was chosen for service over the Parker-Hale M85 rifle following a competitive series of trials and field shoot-offs.

The L96 is designed to be effective, yet have a straightforward operating system without compromising safety. The whole stock furniture of the rifle comprises two halves bolted together, but is so designed as to allow access to component parts for maintenance and cleaning. The trigger assembly is fully adjustable, having a take-up pull of between 1kg and 2kg, and can be removed without the need to dismantle the whole rifle. The entire stock can be stripped away in approximately

five minutes using only a screwdriver and an Allen key.

The barrel is manufactured from stainless steel and is fitted to the body of the rifle by means of a threaded breech end, and is of the type known as 'floating'. This means that it is unsupported along its entire length and is fixed to the body of the rifle only at the breech. This design is well accepted for sniper rifles and does not upset the zeroing of the rifle under normal handling conditions. On the L96A1 barrel changing can be completed in less than five minutes without having to strip the rifle down.

The L96A1 is bolt-action with multi-lug design and uses detachable box magazines with ten-round capacity. The rifle is fitted with a detachable bipod, which is fully adjustable and can be used in conjunction with a retractable spike in the butt stock to form a tripod base for use if the sniper has to maintain his position for prolonged periods. The butt stock is adjustable in length by fitting or removing spacers and the overall configuration has been designed for ambidextrous use.

The L96A1 has iron sights as standard but in the military sniping role is usually fitted with PM 6 x 42 telescopic sights. The 'Counter Terrorist' version of the

(left) **A British Army sniper in his firing position takes aim with the L96A1 sniping rifle.**

(bottom) **A British Army sniper takes position behind a tree for camouflage whilst using the L96A1 sniping rifle.**

rifle, for use by law enforcement agencies, is usually fitted with the PM 21/2-10 x 56 telescopic sight. The rifle is capable of accepting most night-sight units, including the Pilkington 'Kite', and other sighting units such as the KN250 and OE 8050 Individual Weapon sight. The weapon can also be supplied in the 'moderated' or low signature version for use in urban situations.

SPECIFICATIONS:

Calibre:	7.62mm x 51
Weight:	6.50kg
Length:	1,124mm to 1,194mm
Barrel:	655mm

A British Army sniper emerges from his hide holding the L96A1 sniping rifle. He is wearing a Ghillie suit to aid him in concealing himself when firing at the enemy in the combat area.

Close-up detail of the bolt action and telescopic sight of the British Army's L96A1 sniping rifle.

The Parker-Hale M85 sniping rifle was designed by the British company bearing that name with the intention of supplying the British Army. However, it was pipped at the post by the L96A1 in a final shoot-off. According to one source from the British Army's Small Arms School at Warminster, in Wiltshire, there was not a great deal between the two weapons. The weapon is no longer manufactured in the United Kingdom. In 1990 Parker-Hale sold the manufacturing rights to the Gibbs Rifle Company in America, who are still manufacturing the weapon and supplying various end users.

The M85 was designed to give the firer a 100 per cent first-round hit capability out to ranges of 600m. It is fitted with a specially designed action, which has a built-in aperture rear sight – adjustable for ranges out to 900m – for use in an emergency. The M85 features an integral dovetail mounting to allow a wide variety of telescopic sights and night-vision equipment, such as the Simrad KN250, to be fitted, which will permit combat sniping in all conditions, 24 hours a day. The weapon also features a positive return-to-zero and recoil stop.

The M85 fires the standard 7.62mm x 51 round using a detachable ten-round box magazine, and uses the bolt action typical of most sniping rifles of this type. The trigger mechanism is all steel and has the double pull action set between 0.9kg and 2.25kg. The safety catch is silent in operation and when applied it locks the bolt sear and trigger.

An adjustable bipod is fitted to the fore-end of the rifle and allows the firer to track a moving target. The bipod folds back along the forestock when not in use and has provision for both swivel and cant adjustments of approximately 14 degrees in each direction, without moving the leg positions. The butt stock is fully adjustable in length by means of insert plates, and the cheek-plate, as well as being adjustable, is also ambidextrous. The M85 sniping kit comes with five insert plates supplied in the carrying box, along with other ancillary items, including spare magazines and cleaning kit. The whole stock of the M85 is cast in one piece from fibreglass

(left) **Close-up detail of the bipod fitted to Parker-Hale's M85 sniping rifle.**

(bottom) **The Parker-Hale M85 sniping rifle seen from the right-hand side, showing the bolt action and detachable ten-round box magazine.**

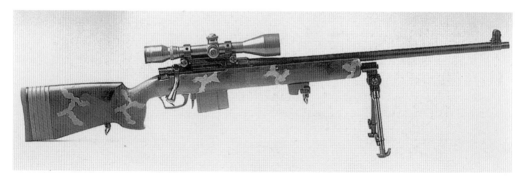

and is available in NATO green, jungle and desert disruptive pattern, an Arctic disruptive pattern and an urban disruptive pattern. This last design uses dark colours and would be ideal for law enforcement agencies who wish to place their snipers, or 'marksmen', in a low-profile location.

The M85 can also be fitted with a suppressor, for which purpose the muzzle is threaded. The suppressor will handle both supersonic and reduced velocity ammunition and all but eliminates muzzle flash and firing signature. To allow a suppressor to be fitted the firer has only to remove the front sight assembly, by means of an Allen key, which is achieved in very little time. Use of a suppressor on the M85 has the added benefit of reducing the recoil energy when fired, which means a sniper does not have to make adjustments to his aiming position if he is required to fire another shot in quick succession.

When the company of Parker-Hale was manu-facturing the M85 it developed the M86 version of the rifle, which fired 7.62mm rounds from a detachable box magazine but with a five-round capacity. This model was fitted with a micro-adjustable aperture rear sight suitable for ranges in excess of 1,000m. The action of the M86 was also drilled and tapped to receive standard Unertl-type bases for mounting a long tube telescopic sight.

SPECIFICATIONS:

Calibre:	7.62mm x 51
Weight:	5.7kg to 6.24kg, depending on telescopic sight fitted, and with magazine
Length:	1,150mm overall
Butt length:	Adjustable from 315mm to 385mm
Barrel:	700mm
Rifling:	Four grooves, right hand, one turn in 305mm

Opposite.

(top) **The Parker-Hale M85 sniping rifle fitted with an SS80 night-vision sight.**

(middle) **The Parker-Hale M85 sniping rifle with urban camouflage stock. Note the well-constructed bolt action and the fully adjustable bipod.**

(bottom) **The Parker-Hale M85 sniping rifle in its carrying case, complete with cleaning kit, spare magazines and sights.**

(below) **The M86 from Parker-Hale was a development of the M85 sniping rifle and could engage targets out to 1,200m range.**

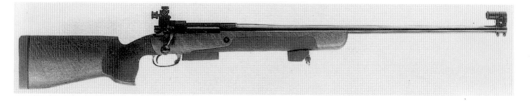

The Barrett 'Light Fifty' is the heavyweight among sniper rifles, and one with an awesome reputation. It fires the devastatingly effective .50 calibre Browning Machine Gun (.50 BMG) round, with an effective range of nearly 2 kilometres and the power to stop a soft-skinned vehicle in its tracks or demolish a lightly fortified position. Needless to say the effect on the human body is more than lethal, regardless of any body armour worn.

The rifle is a semi-automatic, air-cooled, box magazine fed weapon which operates on the short-recoil principle. It has standard iron sights, but is normally fitted with a telescopic sight and a bipod. It is considered to have an effective range of around 1800 metres.

The 'Light Fifty' was conceived as an anti-materiel weapon, that is to say a weapon that could be used to knock out enemy assets such as trucks and aircraft from a distance of over a kilometre, and deny ground to enemy forces. In this role it has certainly proved its worth, but experience has shown it is a valuable tool in other ways too.

In peacekeeping operations, such as those in the Balkans towards the end of the twentieth century, the 'Light Fifty' was used as an effective anti-sniper weapon. Snipers armed with standard .30 calibre weapons would hide up in buildings or lightly-fortified positions giving a commanding view of an area, and cause havoc among the opposing civilian population. With one or two well place .50 rounds, a peacekeeping force sniper could effectively discourage this and make the sniper's position untenable. In the Gulf War and elsewhere, EOD operators have found the 'Light Fifty' useful for neutralising unexploded ordnance from a safe distance.

The weapon has been shown to have a significant psychological factor, causing a serious loss of morale among troops who know that their enemy possesses a .50 calibre sniping capability. When the IRA obtained a small number of 'Light Fifties' in the 1980s, the weapon was much feared by British troops stationed in Northern Ireland, and for a while even conventional sniper attacks were attributed to the .50 calibre weapon.

Manufacturer:	Barrett Firearms Manufacturing Inc., Tennessee, USA
Model:	M82A1 ('Light Fifty').
Calibres:	.50 BMG (12.7 Y 99mm NATO)
Action:	Recoil-operated semi-automatic
Feed:	10-shot detachable box magazine
Sights:	Normally fitted with telescopic sights.
Weight:	28.5lb.
Length:	57in overall
Barrel:	29in, rifled 1 turn in 15in.

COMBAT SHOTGUNS

Despite the fact that the shotgun has been used by the military at various times, it has never been readily adopted into service use as an infantry weapon. It is instead seen primarily as a weapon used by police and paramilitary forces, mainly for security purposes.

It was US servicemen serving in the trenches of the First World War who first popularised the use of the shotgun as an effective military weapon for use in confined spaces. Known as the 'Trench Gun M1917' the US Army originally bought several thousand short-barrelled riot guns which had been modified to accept bayonets and were fitted with sling swivels. The original cardboard-based cartridges were far too flimsy for conditions in the trenches and brass cases, like rifle cartridges, were soon developed. After the First World War the shotguns were consigned back to the arsenals, re-emerging only when America entered the Second World War following the attack on Pearl Harbor in December 1941. The shotgun was used by US troops in the Pacific theatre of operations, but in Europe it was rarely used by regular troops in combat.

The shotgun in military use is an ideal close-quarter weapon, well suited to use in jungle fighting, house clearing and perimeter security at sensitive military bases. The British Army used shotguns to good effect against the Communist guerrillas during the Malayan campaign in the 1950s. However, it must be pointed out that British troops had to learn from the Malayan police how valuable a shotgun could be in an ambush situation. The British Army at the time purchased several thousand shotguns from the American companies of Browning and Remington. With typical British thoroughness and attention to detail, a report into the effectiveness of shotguns in a combat situation was prepared. With equally British contempt, the report, considered by those who have seen it to be the definitive work of its type on combat shotgun use, was ignored. Even today, this report has only ever been studied by America with any great seriousness.

The use of shotguns by US troops in Vietnam was influenced more by results achieved during the Pacific theatre of the Second World War than anything else. As a result they had to re-evaluate the position of the shotgun in a combat role. The Americans produced their own assessment and it came as no surprise to find that it echoed the British report.

Whilst America is historically seen as the home of the shotgun, relatively little has been done in the US in the way of research into finding means of developing the shotgun into a truly useful combat weapon. Most US military shotguns are simply 'militarised' versions of police models. In Italy, however, the shotgun has been the subject of much research and development, which has concentrated on improving magazine capacity and rate of fire.

Most designs of shotguns used by the military are pump-action, which is to say the slide action has to be pumped in a rearward motion by the firer's forward supporting arm in order to feed and chamber a round from the tubular magazine under the barrel. This means that the number of cartridges held in the tubular

Tear gas grenade, the muzzle attachment for launching and the special propelling cartridge for firing the tear gas grenade. This shows how versatile shotguns can be.

magazine is dictated by the length of the weapon. Conversely, the length of the weapon was determined by the number of cartridges a manufacturer or customer wished to load into the tubular magazine.

The Italian company of Beretta still manufactures a range of conventional shotguns using the slide or pump-action. These weapons have either fixed or folding stocks and are in widespread use with police and paramilitary forces. However, another Italian company, Luigi Franchi, has developed a range of semi-automatic shotguns and even a box magazine-fed weapon, the SPAS 15, which have resulted in the most militarily developed shotguns to date.

Ammunition for shotguns, usually referred to as cartridges, has also been developed way beyond the standard load of lead pellets. A range of non-lethal ammunition has been developed for internal security and riot control use. These include cartridges which discharge a payload of non-penetrating rubber balls, which hurt but lack the kinetic energy of conventional 'rubber bullets'. Another feature for riot control involves a grenade-launching device which is fitted to the muzzle of a shotgun and allows CS gas anti-riot grenades to be fired. More specialised cartridges for police and military roles include 'slug' and 'rifled slug', essentially a heavy ball round capable of penetrating to great depth, and a CS gas-filled cartridge known as 'Ferret' which can be used against fixed or moving targets. The Ferret projectile comprises a plastic carrier which can penetrate glass to deliver its payload of CS gas into a room or a moving vehicle. Other rounds known or believed to be under development for use from a shotgun include a

High Explosive Anti-Tank (HEAT) round for engaging lightly armoured vehicles, and flechette for anti-personnel use. These specialised rounds are in addition to the usual cartridges which can be fired from a shotgun. The typical anti-personnel cartridge carries a payload of spherical lead balls approximately 8.4mm in diameter. The terminology is not standardised, and these may be referred to as SG in Britain, or 00 Buck in the United States. The Belgians and Dutch know this size as 9G and the Italians refer to it as 11/0. A 3-inch magnum 12-bore cartridge, containing $1\frac{5}{8}$ oz of shot, will fire 13 of these pellets – each one roughly as lethal as a 9mm pistol round.

Today, shotgun cartridges are manufactured from plastic – a material which is lightweight and water-resistant, but stands up well to the rough handling associated with combat situations. The most common shotgun calibre in use with current in-service weapons is referred to as 12-gauge, also known to some users as 12-bore. The gauge or bore size was originally defined by the number of lead balls, fitting exactly in the barrel, which would weigh 1 lb – so a smaller 'gauge' or 'bore' number denotes a larger calibre weapon. A 10-gauge shotgun, for instance, is larger than a 12-gauge.

Range of shotgun cartridges, including slug, non-lethal rubber ball types, conventional pellets and the tear gas 'Ferret' round.

The Beretta RS200 12-gauge shotgun is a conventionally laid out pump-action weapon designed specifically for use by law enforcement agencies. This is a well-made weapon capable of withstanding rough handling under most circumstances. The tubular magazine for the RS200 can accommodate up to six rounds of any nature of 12-gauge ammunition, and with one round ready in the chamber this gives the firer a capacity of seven shots ready for immediate use. The RS200 is fitted with a fixed wooden butt stock, and a special sliding-block locking mechanism prevents accidental discharge before locking is complete. A double bent on the hammer is a further safety precaution to prevent premature discharge of a round and a bolt catch allows the firer to extract a chambered round without firing it.

The RS200 has been declared obsolete but its usefulness and ruggedness mean it is still likely to be encountered. The RS200 can fire all natures of 12-gauge ammunition, including CS gas cartridges, non-lethal rubber balls, ordinary shot and slug.

SPECIFICATIONS:

Calibre:	12-gauge
Operation:	Manual repeating, pump-action
Locking:	Sliding block
Feed:	5 to 6 rounds in tubular magazine
Weight:	3kg
Length Overall:	1,030mm
Barrel length:	520mm
Chamber length:	70mm

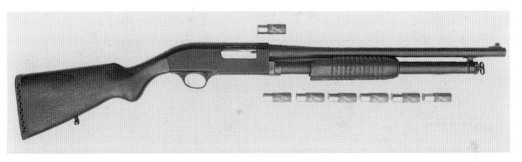

This is another Italian-designed shotgun from the manufacturers of the RS200 and is primarily intended for use by law enforcement agencies. In fact, the RS202P is a natural development from the earlier RS200 model and most specifications of that weapon also apply to this one. The main difference between the two designs is the fact that the RS202P has a 'cartridge latch button', which allows the bolt to be operated without releasing the next round from the magazine. This allows the user to load a special purpose round without first emptying the magazine. Furthermore, loading and unloading with the RS202P is easier than on the RS200 shotgun.

There are various designs which make up a range of models available in the basic RS202P pump-action shotgun, each with the capability of being fitted with interchangeable chokes to alter the pattern of shot. One variation is a folding stock version which allows ease of handling in the interior of a vehicle. The model RS202PM3 features a folding stock and barrel cover with rifle sights and an attachment for fitting a telescopic sight and a muzzle diffuser. A telescopic sight is, in fact, rarely fitted to a shotgun. It can make for greater accuracy with rifled slug cartridges, but even then accuracy with these types of cartridge never matches that of a rifle. However, the telescopic sight fitting will also permit other types of sight to be used, including night-vision types.

(top) **The Beretta RS202P shotgun showing its rugged design.**

(middle) **The Beretta RS202P shotgun showing details of the trigger, ejector port for spent cases and the loading 'gate' on the underside just in front of the trigger guard.**

(bottom) **The Beretta RS202P shotgun with folding butt stock.**

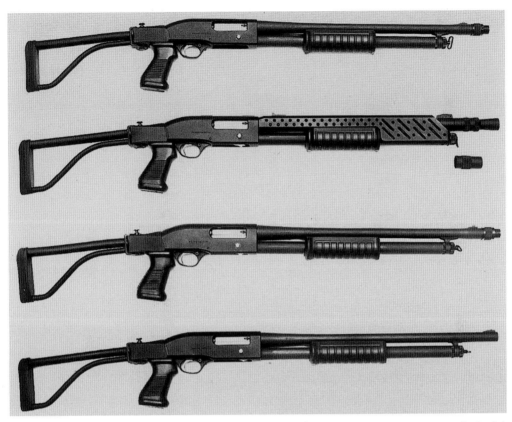

SPECIFICATIONS:

As for Beretta RS200

(top) **Top: The Beretta RS202P with folding butt stock extended.**
Bottom: The Beretta RS202PM3 with folding butt stock, barrel
cover and special sights and diffuser.

(middle) **The Beretta RS202P with interchangeable chokes and**
folding butt stock.

(bottom) **The Beretta RS202P with folding butt stock in extended**
position.

The PA3 range of shotguns was designed and developed by the Italian company of Luigi Franchi and these weapons represent very compact designs of shotguns. The PA3 range comprises the 215 and 345, which have three- and five- round magazine capacity respectively, with an extra cartridge ready in the chamber. Both designs are manufactured from high strength alloy with double operating rods which are made from all-machined drawn alloyed steel. Apart from the usual safety catch, which is located on the right-hand side of the trigger plate, the weapon will not function until the breech block is completely locked, and the breech mechanism can only be operated after the hammer has been released.

Both designs are fitted with pistol grips for the firing hand, and the safety catch can be operated without having to remove the hand from the firing position, which makes for a rapid response. The PA3/215 version is a no-frills design, lacking butt stock and sights, which gives it an appearance not dissimilar to the Ithaca 'Stakeout' Model 37. However, unlike that weapon the PA3/215 has a forward pistol grip to assist with the pump-action to eject spent cartridges and rechamber a new round. It has an overall length of only 470mm which makes it an ideal weapon for close quarter protection and possible use by special forces units to remove hinges from doors during rapid entrance operations.

The PA3/345 is a more conventional pump-action shotgun design with a five-round capacity and folding butt stock. This weapon has basic sights and its robust design lends it to being used by either police or paramilitary forces for a wide range of uses, including road blocks, perimeter security and dynamic entry techniques by counter-terrorist forces.

The PA3 range. Top: PA3/215 with forward pistol grip. Bottom: PA3/345 with folding butt stock and standard pump action.

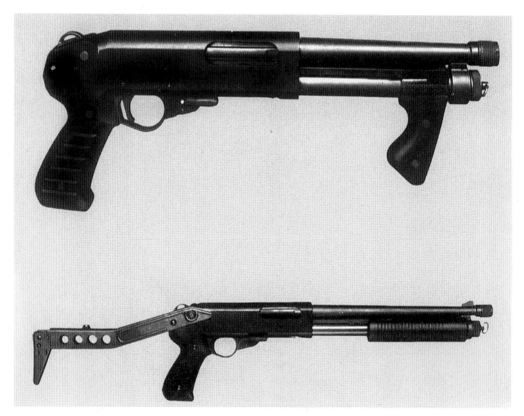

SPECIFICATIONS:

	PA3/215	PA3/345
Calibre:	12-gauge	12-gauge
Magazine capacity:	3 + 1	5 + 1
Barrel length:	215mm	345mm
Overall length:	470mm	840mm
Width	46mm	46mm
Weight unloaded:	2.3kg	2.8kg

Despite the modern appearance of the two designs in this range of shotguns, the models PA7 and PA8 are actually well-established weapons from the Italian company of Luigi Franchi, who also designed the PA3 series and the SPAS 12 and SPAS 15. The main difference between the PA7 and PA8 designs lies in the fact that the former design lacks a pistol grip, giving it a rifle-like appearance.

The PA8 shotgun is available in either the 'E' series or 'I' series, which have a fixed or folding butt stock respectively. The weapons in the series can be fitted with either a 475mm or 610mm Magnum Variomix barrel, with a two-round magazine extension also available. The basic weapons already have a five-round tubular magazine capacity, with one in the chamber, and so the ability to have up to eight rounds ready to fire makes this range of shotguns one of the most powerful in service.

All three weapons in this range are conventional pump-action types, and are well-constructed to withstand punishing treatment. Each of the weapons is fitted with rifle sights and features a double safety device within the trigger group as found on the SPAS 12 shotgun.

Variomix chokes, with a barrel extension from 50mm to 150mm, can also be fitted to all three weapons to alter the pattern of the shot.

This range of shotguns can fire all natures of 12-gauge ammunition, including slug. However, when using slug the Variomix choke cannot be fitted. The PA7 and PA8 shotguns are high-profile weapons and are well-suited to the roles of perimeter security and road blocks. In this last role, the weapons could be used to fire CS gas cartridges to penetrate the windscreen to incapacitate, in a non-lethal manner, those drivers who are reluctant to stop.

Top: PA7 with fixed butt stock.

Centre: PA8E with fixed butt stock and pistol grip.

Bottom: PA8I with folding butt stock and pistol grip.

The Italian company of Luigi Franchi has a reputation for producing high-quality shotguns for police and paramilitary use, but when they unveiled their design for the SPAS 12 the company took the shotgun fraternity by storm.

Despite its bulky appearance, the SPAS 12, or Special Purpose Automatic Shotgun, still fires only the standard 12-gauge cartridge of 70mm in length. The tubular magazine capacity can be either six or seven rounds, plus one in the chamber, and the weapon can fire all natures of shotgun ammunition, including slug, non-lethal and anti-vehicle rounds. This is a high-profile weapon of sturdy construction, making it an excellent all-round weapon for both offensive and defensive purposes. It can be supplied with either a folding or fixed butt stock, depending on the operational role.

The SPAS 12 has the normal functions of standard pump-action type shotguns, but it can be switched to gas-operated semi-automatic fire simply by depressing a button on the forestock. This feature is particularly useful in allowing the firer rapidly to fire heavy loads to suppress a target, although at the cost of the weapon being difficult to control.

The very nature of the SPAS 12's appearance makes it a psychological deterrent in most situations. Indeed, it has often been considered by special forces, due to its versatility and high rate of fire. A practical rate of fire with the SPAS 12 is considered to be in the region

The Italian SPAS 12 shotgun.

(top) **Overall view of weapon with folding stock.**

(bottom) **Close-up detail of the barrel and forestock.**

of 24 to 30 rounds per minute, but in the semi-automatic mode it is capable of 250 cyclic rounds per minute.

The SPAS 12 has front and rear sights fitted, and the bodywork is manufactured from a special anti-shock resin.

The SPAS 12 is a purpose-built shotgun, not one which has been militarised from a design which started life as a sporting weapon. The author has experience in firing this weapon, and whilst it is quite a 'fistful', after a few rounds it felt comfortable once the firing sequence had been accepted as being so much different from ordinary pump-action shotguns.

Safety features on the SPAS 12 include the normal safety catch by the trigger mechanism, plus there is also a lock-up safety with plunger in order to block the hammer, and a safety on the trigger lever to make it doubly safe when operating from a vehicle.

SPECIFICATIONS:

Calibre:	12-gauge x 70mm
Type:	Pump-action slide and semi-automatic
	gas-operated (selectable)
Feed:	6-7; plus one in chamber
Barrel length:	460mm or 550mm
Overall length:	710mm (460mm barrel and stock folded)
	930mm (460mm barrel and stock extended)
Weight:	4.1kg

Following on the success of its SPAS 12 design, the Italian company of Luigi Franchi once more turned its attention to perfecting a shotgun which was more in keeping with military requirements. The result was the SPAS 15, or Special Purpose Automatic Shotgun 15, which is as far removed from tubular magazine shotguns as these are in turn from double-barrel shotguns.

With the SPAS 15, the company of Franchi has overcome the problem of how pump-action shotguns could be quickly reloaded, which was one of the stumbling blocks with other designs. Franchi simply looked at alternative methods and came back to the reliable box magazine method which is fed from underneath, in the same manner as a conventional rifle. Indeed, the SPAS 15 has the appearance of a bulky rifle, with its integral top-mounted carrying handle and box magazine in place.

The SPAS 15 can be operated by the usual pump-action method but, like its predecessor, the SPAS 12, it can be converted to gas-operated semi-automatic fire simply by engaging a conversion button located on top of the forestock. In this mode, the SPAS 15 taps gas from the barrel and feeds it into the gas chamber mounted above the barrel to operate the working parts in the same way as an assault rifle functions. The bolt is a rotating-head design to give the best and most reliable feeding and ejection action possible.

The SPAS 15 is available with either a fixed or folding stock and can fire all natures of 12-gauge ammunition,

including smoke, CS gas, non-lethal rubber ball, slug, steel anti-vehicle piercing, and standard buckshot. The weapon can also be fitted with discharger cups to allow smoke and CS gas grenades to be launched into buildings or to project them to longer ranges than possible with hand-thrown projectiles.

The SPAS 15 is a dual-purpose weapon, being well-suited to both offensive and defensive roles. It can be fitted with a laser-designating device mounted on the top carrying handle to identify positively selected targets. It is marginally lighter in weight than the SPAS 12 and its dimensions are comparable to that weapon. However, the practicalities of it being magazine-fed, and therefore easier to reload, make it a more viable military choice than most other shotguns. There are other magazine-fed shotguns available, but the SPAS 15 has the appearance and rugged endurance required of a real combat shotgun.

The weapon has a double safety feature, the first being the normal safety catch by the trigger guard, which is positively operated. The second safety feature is fitted into the pistol grip and is released by the gripping action of the firing hand. The magazine, which has a capacity

The advanced design of the Italian SPAS 15 with box magazine feed. It has a folding butt stock and is an ideal weapon for use in house-clearing operations.

of six rounds, is loaded into the weapon from underneath, as on a rifle, and the cocking handle is located on the upper surface of the receiver under the carrying handle, in a manner similar to the French FAMAS rifle.

The magazine release catch is located behind the magazine and just in front of the trigger guard, which makes for speedy reloading in combat situations. Magazines can be colour-coded, so that the firer can instantly identify the nature of the ammunition in each magazine and can load his weapon according to the situation. The rigid stock is manufactured from anti-shock resin material and the folding stock is manufactured from pressed alloys.

SPECIFICATIONS:

Calibre:	12-gauge x 70mm
Type:	Pump-action slide and semi-automatic gas-operated (selectable)
Feed:	6-round box magazine, plus one round in the chamber
Barrel length:	406mm
Overall length:	1,000mm with fixed stock
	980mm with folding stock extended
	700mm with folding stock folded
Width:	49mm
Weight:	3.90kg (unloaded)
Weight of empty magazine:	0.45kg

The security forces in South Africa have a long history of using shotguns to break up and disperse rioters. The types of shotguns used in these situations tend to be conventionally laid out weapons, but local arms manufacturers have invested time and effort to produce some very forward-thinking firearms.

In the early 1980s the 12-gauge 'Striker' made an appearance, and its design left no-one in any doubt that it was intended for use as an offensive weapon during operations involving street fighting or house clearing. The Striker utilised a spring-wound 12-shot rotary magazine which could be pre-loaded to allow the firer to use various natures of ammunition. The Striker was cylinder-bored to permit the firing of either shot or slug cartridges. Some 13 years after Striker was intended to enter production, the author saw at a major defence exhibition a weapon on a South African defence manufacturer's stand with startling similarities to the Striker. It emerged that the weapon in question was called the 'Protecta' and was indeed based on the layout of the Striker.

Whilst the Striker had good potential and hitting power, the Protecta was seen as its natural successor, with improved safety features. The Protecta has a 12-shot revolver action which eliminates the need to wind the driving spring to impart the rotary action required to align the cylinder with the breech. The underlying safety feature of the Protecta is the fact that it cannot be fired unless the double-action trigger is fully depressed in a positive action. This feature, along with the drop-safe hammer-lock, prevents accidental discharge through trigger snagging if the safety catch is disengaged in readiness for use.

It is claimed that the Protecta can be fired single-handed from the hip, but this would produce poorly aimed shots. The weapon has a metal skeleton butt stock which folds up and over along the top of the weapon, and a forward pistol grip. With the butt stock extended the user can fire the weapon from the shoulder in a more controlled manner. With the special Occluded Eye Gunsight (OEG) sight, which is used with both eyes open, the firer can track and engage a moving target, from a man-sized target to a motor vehicle.

The barrel length of the Protecta is only 300mm,

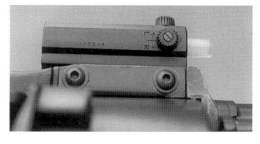

(right) **Close-up detail of the Occluded Eye Gunsight as fitted to the South African Protecta.**

(below) **Overall view of the South African Protecta, showing its two pistol grips, folding butt stock and rotary drum magazine.**

but the manufacturers claim the pattern of shot to be comparable to weapons with barrel lengths twice this size. The Protecta fires standard 12-gauge shotgun cartridges, including non-lethal types such as the 'Thundershot' which produces a loud report and flash, the Baton Single and the Baton Double which discharge one and two rubber balls respectively and are for use in anti-riot situations.

Spent cartridges are automatically ejected from the cylinder which allows the firer to load single rounds to replenish the ammunition capacity as required, with the nature of ammunition appropriate to the situation.

The 'Roadblocker' MAG-10 shotgun from Ithaca has been designed for law enforcement agencies with the sole purpose of providing a force-multiplier to deal effectively with criminals in vehicles. The Roadblocker is unusual in that it is of 10-gauge, which gives it considerably greater power than the standard 12-gauge shotgun cartridge. The cartridge for the Roadblocker is 3.5 inches in length and the tubular magazine holds only three rounds, with a round in the chamber, to give a capacity of four rounds ready to use.

The weapon is gas-operated and considerably heavier than its Model 37 counterparts. The force of the recoil with such a weapon might be considered excessive, but Ithaca has overcome this problem by developing a recoil compensator known as 'Countercoil'. This acts by extending the period during which the recoil force is maintained, reducing it to more controllable levels.

In military terms the Roadblocker has limited usefulness, due largely to its heavy weight and limited ammunition capacity, and is therefore more likely to be used by mobile police and paramilitary forces.

SPECIFICATIONS:	
Calibre:	10-gauge x 3.5 inch
Type:	Gas-operated semi-automatic
Feed:	3 rounds in tubular magazine, plus 1 in chamber
Barrel length:	558mm
Weight:	4.87kg

The Ithaca MAG-10 'Roadblocker' showing its heavy construction.

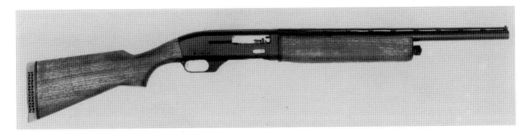

Of all the American-designed shotguns the Ithaca range of Model 37 shotguns is perhaps the most comprehensive. They all follow the straight-line layout of the conventional shotgun design, but the variations in calibre (gauge) and stocks are what make them different.

The Model 37 M&P is available with either a five-shot or eight-shot capacity tubular magazine, with an extra cartridge in the chamber in each case. This version is a 'no-frills' shotgun and is built to withstand punishing treatment. The Model 37 M&P is chambered to accept all natures of standard 12-gauge cartridges of 2.75 inch length. The 'DS' version in the Model 37 range is also available in five- and eight-shot versions, with the standard 'one in the chamber' to increase the

ammunition capacity to six and nine rounds respectively. The 'DS' stands for 'Deerslayer', indicating that this started as a sporting version of the company's range of hunting shotguns. The progression of such a highly

(top) **The Ithaca Model 37 'Deerslayer' Police Special with eight-shot magazine.**

(middle upper) **The Ithaca Model 37 'Deerslayer' Police Special with five-shot magazine.**

(middle lower) **The Ithaca Model 37 Special Los Angeles Police Department Model.**

(bottom) **The Ithaca Model 37 M&P five-shot.**

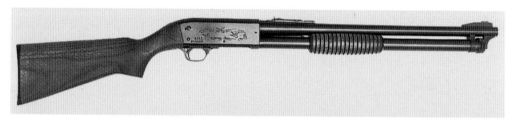

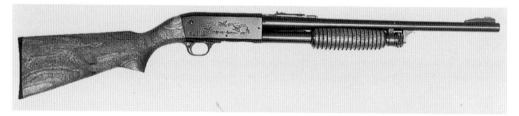

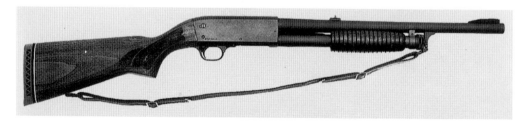

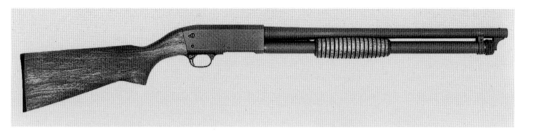

(top) **The Ithaca Model 37 M&P 8-shot.**

(bottom) **The Ithaca Model 37 'Stakeout' 20 gauge.**

reliable and well-made weapon from sporting roles to law enforcement and military use was a natural evolution.

The action and specifications of the 'DS' are the same as for the basic Model 37 M&P, with the only difference being that the 'DS' is fitted with rifle-type sights. The 'Special LAPD' version of the Model 37 has been developed specifically for use by the Los Angeles Police Department and is available in the five-round version. It features sling swivels for a carrying strap, a recoil pad on the butt stock, fire-interruptor and a special drive-in rear-block sight.

The Ithaca Model 37 'Stakeout' version of the standard Model 37 is a very compact design, lacking a butt stock entirely, and is available in either 20-gauge or 12-gauge calibres. Of these two sizes the 12-gauge is the preferred calibre, with the 20-gauge calibre being developed for personal protection services and intended for use at close quarters. Such roles would include the movement of important personnel from vehicles to buildings by law enforcement agents. Its compact design makes it an ideal weapon for carrying in a concealed manner or for deploying from a light motor vehicle, yet still having a capacity of five rounds in the tubular magazine and an extra round in the chamber.

SPECIFICATIONS:

	Calibre	Action	Capacity	Barrel	Weight
Model 37 M&P	12-gauge	Pump-action	5 or 8 + 1	470mm (5-shot)	2.94kg (5-shot)
and Model 37 'DS'			508mm (8-shot)	3.06kg (8-shot)	
Special LAPD	12-gauge	Pump-action	5 + 1	470mm	2.95kg
Stakeout 12	12-gauge	Pump-action	5 + 1	336mm	2.26kg
Stakeout 20	20-gauge	Pump-action	5-round	336mm	1.58kg

FIGHTING KNIVES AND DAGGERS

Fighting knives are the stuff of legend. Who has not read some gripping tale of adventure, or watched a blockbuster movie, in which the hero sneaks up on a sentry and dispatches soundlessly him with a swift stroke of his trusty fighting knife?

Stories are one thing; real life is another. No soldier with an ounce of common sense would tackle an enemy with a knife unless he had no alternative. It is just too damn dangerous. Unlike the tales of derring-do, a real knife fight is a messy, noisy, bloody business in which winner and loser alike will probably emerge badly wounded and physically exhausted.

The phrase 'taking a knife to a gun fight' has become a cliche to describe going into a situation woefully under-equipped – and with good reason. In fact, the man armed with a knife can also be defeated with a chair-leg, baton, and a host of other objects, provided the defender has had suitable training. Police men and women in the UK do not routinely carry firearms, but they do carry a variety of batons, such as the Asp extending baton. They are trained to use these batons very effectively to disarm and subdue an attacker armed with a variety of possible weapons, including knives.

Given the unpredictable nature of combat, the soldier cannot know how his opponent may be armed. Col. Rex Applegate, in the classic *Combat Use of the Double-Edged Fighting Knife*, concedes: 'One-on-one knife-fighting incidents – where both men are forewarned, similarly armed, and engaged – are extremely rare.'

The fact is that soldiers do not use fighting knives – at least not for fighting with. A knife would be useless against an enemy armed with any sort of firearm. Against an enemy armed with a knife, the first choice would be a pistol or assault rifle; 'overkill' is not something that troubles the professional soldier. Failing that, the next best thing would be an entrenching tool, axe, even a chair or a pickaxe handle – anything that allows him to strike without coming within reach of the blade.

Knife fighting was taught to British soldiers as a specific skill during the Second World War, and the Fairbairn-Sykes knife was developed specifically for use by British Commandos. This has ensured its place in combat legend and mythology, but we should beware of taking such stories too literally; even in the 1940s the War Office understood the value of propaganda to boost its soldiers' morale and undermine that of the enemy.

The fighting knife cannot have been all that valuable to the average British soldier, as its issue and training in its use were discontinued not long after the war. For many years, the British army has not issued any sort of fighting knife.

Peter Ratcliffe DCM, who was the RSM of the British SAS during the Gulf War, nails the lie in his excellent book, *Eye of the Storm*: 'There is no such thing in the British Army, never mind the Regiment [SAS], as an official fighting knife. The only knives issued are small clasp knives which are used mainly for opening ration packs and removing or replacing screws in your rifle. I have known a few SAS guys who carried larger knives, but only for doing ordinary things – not for stabbing people and dogs or slitting sentries' throats. . . if you have to kill someone, or some animal, in combat or otherwise when on active service, then you use your rifle or pistol.'

All generalisations are dangerous, as a famous writer once said, and no doubt someone will complain that yes, they did use a fighting knife in such-and-such an operation, and no other weapon would have done the job. If so, I would be most interested to hear from them: write to me c/o this book's publishers.

Despite the fact that a soldier is most unlikely to use a fighting knife, there is a great proliferation of fighting patterns, and fighting knives make up a significant proportion of the manufactures' knife sales. We would do well to remember, however, that this tells us more about the legendary status of the fighting knife than its value in real-life combat.

A development of the famous Second World War Fairbairn-Sykes Commando Knife, the Applegate Fairbairn Fighting Knife was designed by Colonel Rex Applegate (of the US OSS) and Captain WE Fairbairn (of the British Royal Marines, and who had co-designed the F-S Dagger).

The A-F is a significant improvement on the F-S, which, despite its fame, had a number of shortcomings: it lacked strength at the tip and the tang, and the grip shape did not lend itself to alternative holds.

The A-F knife has a broader, stronger blade than the F-S, and the more rounded spear point gives much better strength at the tip. Also, the tang is considerably wider and stronger than that of the F-S. The blade is made of stainless steel, a considerable improvement on the basic carbon steel used in the wartime dagger.

The handle, too, has been improved beyond all recognition. Made of Lexan plastic, it is oval in cross-section and fills the hand well. The recess near the guard provides good control and aids withdrawal. The double guard is angled away from the hand, allowing alternative holds and minimising the chance of the guard's catching in clothing and the like.

The knife also has adjustable lead weights in the handle, so that one may alter the knife's balance to suit the particular style and preference.

All in all, this is a highly sophisticated fighting knife and a worthy successor to the famous F-S knife.

The design is manufactured by several makers, including Blackjack, Yancey and Mar. The specifications here refer to the model made by Bill Harsey, but are virtually identical in other makes.

Manufacturer:	Bill Harsey, Creswell, Oregon, USA
Model:	Applegate-Fairbairn Fighting Knife
Length overall:	11in.
Blade length:	6 1/2in.
Blade shape:	Parallel-sided blade with spear point
Blade material:	145CM stainless steel
Edge:	Double-edge bevel ground
Grip:	Moulded Lexan in waisted shape with longitudinal grooves and lanyard hole; separate double guard
Construction:	Handle screwed to full length tang
Features:	Lead weights in handle adjustable for balance

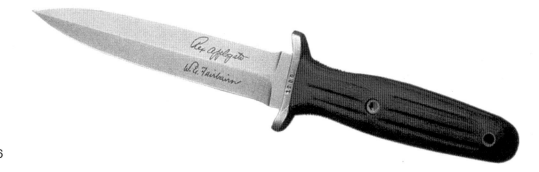

The Blue Devil is a specialised sleeve dagger intended to be worn concealed and deployed rapidly when needed. It is basically a single piece of steel, measuring 8in. overall, with a symmetrical 3 1/2in. dagger blade. This blade length is misleading, since the shape of the knife allows it to stab deeper than the length of the blade. The handle is formed by shaping the other end of the steel, with milled depressions for grip and finger grooves for the first finger and thumb.

The result is a thin, flat knife that may be worn in its sheath on forearm or leg without restricting movement or showing unduly through clothing. However, it can be rapidly drawn when required and provides a lethal fighting blade which can be used for stabbing or slashing.

Not a knife that would be particularly useful for field chores, but highly practical for its intended purpose, offering a larger effective blade length and better grip than many boot and concealment knives.

Manufacturer:	Blackjack Knives Ltd, Effingham, Illinois, USA
Model:	Blue Devil
Length overall:	8in.
Blade length:	3 1/2in.
Blade shape:	Spear point
Blade material:	1085 carbon steel, Rc 55-57
Edge:	Bevel-grind, double-edge
Grip:	Milled holes in plain steel tang
Construction:	One-piece steel
Sheath:	Nylon sheath designed to be worn concealed on forearm or calf

The American military knife supplier Camillus offers two sizes of boot knife which are identical in design. The standard model measures 7in. overall, with a 3 1/8in. blade, while the large model is 8 5/8in. overall and has a 4 1/2in. blade.

The blade is a symmetrical, convex, dagger shape, sharpened both sides to give a double edge. It has extended choils both sides which provide a double guard. The knife is a full tang design, with black chequered Valox scales pinned to either side to form the handle. The blade is made of 440 stainless steel, with a parkerised matt finish.

The knife comes in a black leather sheath with stainless steel boot clip.

Manufacturer:	Camillus Cutlery Co, Camillus, New York, USA
Model:	CM-CP75 Boot Knife
Length overall:	7in. (large version 8 5/8in. overall)
Blade length:	3 1/8in. (large version 4 1/2in.)
Blade shape:	Double-edged, spear point
Blade material:	440 stainless steel with parkerized matt finish
Edge:	Bevel grind
Grip:	Black chequered Valox scales; guard formed from extended choils
Construction:	Scales pinned to full tang
Sheath:	Black leather sheath with boot clip

Based on the traditional Scottish skean dhu, the Cold Steel Culloden measures 8 1/2in. overall and has a 5in. serrated edge with a 1 3/4in. jimped section on the back edge which provides extra purchase for the thumb or forefinger. The blade is sharply pointed but ground on one edge only. True to type, there is no guard, and the handle is waisted and has a flared pommel. The handle is made from moulded Kraton rubber, with a pin (with decorated head) holding it to the full-length tang. Two versions are available: in stainless steel and in carbon V steel. An attractive piece which combines a traditional design with modern materials, this knife nevertheless has considerable limitations, both as a fighter and as a general purpose tool.

Manufacturer:	Cold Steel Inc, Ventura, California, USA
Model:	11SS Culloden
Length overall:	8 1/2in.
Blade length:	5in.
Blade shape:	Single-edged convex curve to sharply-angled point
Blade material:	400 series stainless steel (carbon steel version also available)
Edge:	Hollow ground with serrations on main edge, and 1 3/4in. jimped section on back edge
Grip:	Chequered, black Kraton rubber handle in traditional waisted pattern with flared pommel
Construction:	Handle riveted to tang; no guard
Sheath:	Cordura belt sheath

The Cold Steel Peacekeeper I is a double-edged dagger measuring 12in. overall, and with a 6 1/2in. spear point blade. The blade - which is available in either stainless or carbon V steel - has its widest part about one-third of its length back from the tip. This gives excellent penetration and also provides a slight reverse curve cutting edge; making this a superb fighter well suited to stabbing and slashing. The handle is black Kraton moulded in a coffin shape and chequered for extra grip. The double guard is moulded with the handle and is radiused at the base, making this a particularly comfortable knife to use. The double edge limits this knife's usefulness for general camp chores, but there is no doubt that it excels as a pure fighter. In the circumstances, the name 'Peacekeeper' has an ironic ring to it.

Manufacturer:	Cold Steel Inc., Ventura, California, USA
Model:	10D Peacekeeper I
Length overall:	12in.
Blade length:	6 1/2in.
Blade shape:	Spear point
Blade material:	Stainless steel and carbon steel versions available
Edge:	Double-edged, hollow-ground
Grip:	Symmetrical, chequered, black, Kraton rubber, one-piece handle incorporating double guard and lanyard hole
Construction:	Handle moulded to full-length tang
Sheath:	Black Cordura sheath with leg tie

Cold Steel's Peacekeeper II is a smaller version of the Peacekeeper I. All the comments made about the Peacekeeper I apply equally to this model, with the proviso that the smaller and lighter blade will be marginally less effective at both stabbing and slashing. Still a highly effective fighting knife, however, and one that comes with a boot clip sheath so it can be worn semi-concealed.

Manufacturer:	Cold Steel Inc., Ventura, California, USA
Model:	10B Peacekeeper II
Length overall:	9 3/4in.
Blade length:	5 1/4in.
Blade shape:	Spear point
Blade material:	Stainless steel and carbon steel versions available
Edge:	Double-edged, hollow-ground
Grip:	Symmetrical, chequered, black, Kraton rubber, one-piece handle incorporating double guard and lanyard hole
Construction:	Handle moulded to full-length tang
Sheath:	Black Cordura sheath with boot clip

The Delta Dart is a particularly nasty or useful weapon, depending on one's point of view. Made entirely of Zytel glass-reinforced nylon, it has no metal parts and so is extremely hard to detect with conventional search aids such as X-ray equipment and magnetometers. Its 8in. length can be readily concealed in clothing or on the person, and even when held ready for use it does not catch the eye in the same way as a conventional knife blade.

Skilfully used, however, the dart is as lethal as any knife. Its blade is triangular in cross-section and comes to a very sharp point. It is not suitable for slashing, but penetrates deeply, even through clothing. The rounded pommel allows it to be held between the second and the third finger, in the manner of a push dagger, allowing much deeper penetration.

The triangular blade shape leaves a particularly serious wound which tends to remain open, causing rapid blood loss. A puncture in the abdomen will allow air to be sucked into the chest cavity, collapsing the lungs. If the victim survives, the wound is difficult to treat and does not heal easily.

Manufacturer:	Special Projects Division, Cold Steel Inc., Ventura, California, USA
Model:	92DD Delta Dart
Length overall:	8in.
Blade length:	3 1/2in.
Blade shape:	Triangular-section spear point
Blade material:	Zytel glass-reinforced nylon
Edge:	Moulded
Grip:	Round section, chequered Zytel with rounded pommel
Construction:	One-piece moulded
Features:	No metal parts

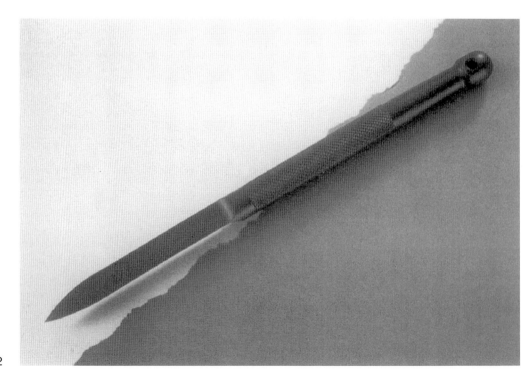

The CAT, or Covert Action Tanto, is made entirely of Zytel glass-reinforced nylon, making it difficult to detect by X-ray or magnetometer search. While the unusual materials limit its usefulness for general tasks, it still makes a highly effective weapon, with all the legendary penetrating power of the conventional steel Tanto blade. Although less easily concealed than the Delta Dart, the CAT does allow the use of a slashing stroke as well as stabbing, and offers the psychological advantage of having an appearance just as intimidating as a conventional knife.

Manufacturer:	Special Projects Division, Cold Steel Inc., Ventura, California, USA
Model:	92CAT Tanto
Length overall:	11 1/in.
Blade length:	5 3/4in.
Blade shape:	Tanto
Blade material:	Zytel glass-reinforced nylon
Edge:	Bevel ground with chisel tip
Grip:	Oval section, chequered Zytel handle with integral single guard and lanyard hole
Construction:	One-piece moulded
Features:	No metal parts

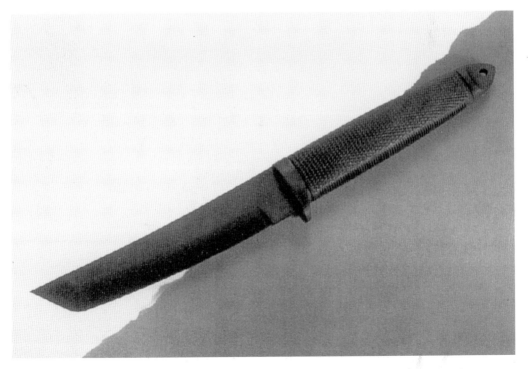

The Tai Pan from Cold Steel measures 13in. overall, it has a broad, straight-sided, double-edged 7 1/8in. dagger blade with a spear point which is effective for stabbing, slashing and hacking at an opponent. The handle is similar to the Tanto - a tapering oval-section handle covered with chequered black Kraton rubber, with a stainless steel double guard, bolster and pommel. The knife is completely symmetrical, and can be used either way up in the hand.

The Tai Pan is similar in many ways to the Applegate Fairbairn fighting knife. Although capable of being used for general chores, the Tai Pan is primarily a fighting knife and excels for this purpose.

Manufacturer:	Cold Steel Inc., Ventura, California, USA
Model:	13D Tai Pan
Length overall:	13in.
Blade length:	7 1/8in.
Blade shape:	Spear point
Blade material:	8A stainless steel
Edge:	Double-edged, hollow-ground
Grip:	Round, tapered, chequered, black Kraton rubber, one-piece handle, brushed stainless guard and pommel with lanyard hole
Construction:	Handle moulded to full-length tang
Sheath:	Black leather belt sheath

The unique characteristics of the Tanto design make it particularly useful as a fighter, and it is preferred by some exponents to the more familiar dagger and Bowie-style blades.

The Tanto blade shape was developed in the Far East to pierce metal body armour and its penetrating power is legendary. The angled chisel point pierces amazingly well through all types of material - several Cold Steel catalogues show the blade pushed through a car door from the outside, for instance, having penetrated the sheet steel of the door panel.

The 6in. stainless steel blade is single-edged, with the full thickness of the steel retained almost to the tip for extra strength. The main edge is almost straight, and the blade has a slight upsweep towards the tip.

The grip consists of a tapering oval-section handle covered with chequered black Kraton rubber, with a stainless steel, single guard, bolster and pommel. The pommel incorporates a lanyard hole, and comes to a point which can also be used against an opponent, by bringing it down on his skull.

Manufacturer:	Cold Steel Inc., Ventura, California, USA
Model:	13BN Master Tanto San Mai
Length overall:	11 1/4in.
Blade length:	6in.
Blade shape:	Tanto
Blade material:	San Mai III steel
Edge:	Bevel-ground with chisel tip
Grip:	Round section, tapered, chequered, black Kraton rubber, one-piece handle, brushed stainless single guard, and pommel with lanyard hole
Construction:	Handle moulded to full-length tang
Sheath:	Black leather belt sheath

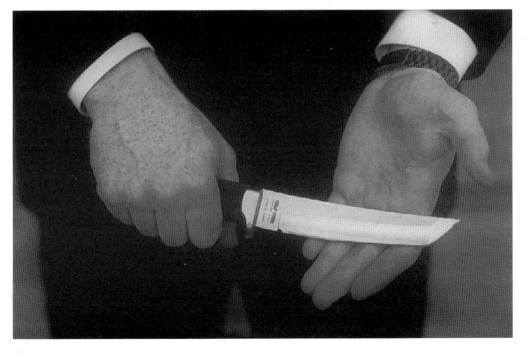

The Recon Tanto is a development of Cold Steel's standard Tanto design, which matches the proven effectiveness of the Tanto blade shape with a Westernised grip shape and black powder coated Carbon V steel blade.

The blade of the Recon Tanto is 7in. long, giving an overall length of 11 3/4in. The coating helps to protect the steel from the elements, as well as avoiding the reflections of the brightly polished stainless steel of the standard Tanto. This might reduce the psychological effect of a flashing blade in certain situations, but is a positive advantage in covert and night-time operations.

The grip is a single piece moulded from black Kraton rubber and incorporates a single guard. It is more rectangular in cross-section than the more traditional Tanto type, which helps the user to keep track of the knife's position, as well as to resist any twisting of the knife in the hand.

Manufacturer:	Cold Steel Inc., Ventura, California, USA
Model:	13RT Recon Tanto
Length overall:	11 1/4in.
Blade length:	7in.
Blade shape:	Tanto
Blade material:	Black coated Carbon V steel
Edge:	Bevel-ground with chisel tip
Grip:	Chequered, black Kraton rubber, one-piece handle with integral single guard, and lanyard hole
Construction:	Handle moulded to full-length tang
Sheath:	Black Cordura belt sheath

The Colt Black Diamond series is advertised as 'the ultimate in knife technology... a perfect back-up tool for military, police, swat, customs inspectors and other law enforcement personnel.' These knives certainly make use of modern materials and manufacturing methods, with 6 1/8in. 420 J2 stainless steel blades and handles that combine grey Zytel with black Kraton rubber for strength, comfort and a sure grip.

The handle is based on a solid 'interframe' of Zytel with a recess for the full length tang. The tang has a hole at the end which matches up with a corresponding hole in the Zytel piece; a stainless steel tube is driven through to anchor the interframe firmly to the tang. This construction gives strength and rigidity and the softer Kraton rubber provides a comfortable hold. Ridges and chequered panels of Zytel show through the rubber, giving the handle a distinctive look as well as providing added grip.

The Black Diamond series offers three blade options: a double-edged dagger with central fuller, a spear point design based on the M7 bayonet, and a Tanto shape. Also available for these knives is a lightweight, black nylon, shoulder harness and sheath which allows the knife to be worn concealed under a jacket or coat. Removed from the harness, the sheath has a stainless steel clip that can be attached to a boot or belt. Alternatively, there is a black leather sheath with a belt loop and press-stud, quick-release strap. It is a versatile system that enables the knife to be worn in a number of different ways - overtly or concealed - to suit the user's requirements.

Manufacturer:	United Cutlery, Sevierville, Tennessee, USA
Model:	CT8 Black Diamond Liberator
Length overall:	10 3/4in.
Blade length:	6 1/8in.
Blade shape:	Dagger blade with fuller (also available: tanto and bayonet type blades)
Blade material:	3/16in. thick 420 stainless steel
Edge:	Bevel-grind
Grip:	Solid grey Zytel with chequered panels and black Kraton partial covering
Construction:	Zytel interframe pinned to full-length tang by stainless steel lanyard tube
Sheath:	Black leather belt sheath. Shoulder harness and black nylon sheath with boot/belt clip also available

The origins of the Combat Smatchet may be traced back to Celtic short swords, but the modern design is attributed to Colonel Rex Applegate and Captain WE Fairbairn. Applegate worked for the Office of Strategic Services during the Second World War, while Fairbairn was one of the designers of the Fairbairn Sykes Fighting Knife used during the War by British Commandos. A single-edged smatchet was issued to OSS operatives in Europe.

In his wartime classic *All-In Fighting*, Captain Fairbairn says of the Smatchet: 'The psychological reaction of any man, when he first takes the smatchet in his hand, is full justification for its recommendation as a fighting weapon. He will immediately register all the essential qualities of a good soldier - confidence, determination and aggressiveness.' His recommended blows with the smatchet include driving the point into an enemy's stomach, chopping to the neck, wrist or arm to sever the main arteries, and smashing the pommel into the face.

In combat, the smatchet is very effective for stabbing, hacking and slashing. Its weight and blade shape create deep, debilitating wounds with the minimum of effort. Although ostensibly a close-quarter combat weapon, the smatchet is also effective as a general-purpose camp and survival tool; it may be used for chopping, digging and even paddling a raft or canoe.

The blade is a broad leaf shape, with a spear point. It measures 10in. long, and 3in. wide at its widest point. The blade has serrated sections on either edge for more effective cutting of difficult materials such as rope and webbing. There is a hole drilled through the blade near the guard, so that one may identify the edges even in total darkness by feel. This allows one to use one side as a 'working edge' and keep the other razor sharp for emergency use.

Several manufacturers offer a version of the Combat Smatchet, including Bill Harsey and Wells Creek Knife & Gun Works of Oregon, USA. The model shown here, and described in the specifications, is by Al Mar.

Manufacturer:	Al Mar Knives Inc., Lake Oswego, Oregon, USA
Model:	Combat Smatchet
Length overall:	15in.
Blade length:	10in.
Blade shape:	Wide leaf shape with spear point
Blade material:	T425 stainless steel, Rc 54-56
Edge:	Bevel-ground
Grip:	Black Lexan plastic with longitudinal grooves and lanyard hole
Construction:	Handle pinned to full-length tang
Sheath:	Black leather sheath with leg tie

The Boot Knife from John Ek is a post-war design incorporating all the characteristics which have made Ek knives some of the most highly regarded by servicemen - a full tang, cord-wrapped design, a thick, strong blade of surgical stainless steel, and a reinforced spear point.

The Boot Knife is the smallest of the Ek knives and is designed to be carried covertly as a back-up weapon, in a black leather boot-clip sheath. It measures 7 1/2in. overall, with a 3 1/2in. blade with the distinctive waisted shape that is seen in other Ek blades. The waisted blade aids deep penetration when used for stabbing and provides a reverse curve edge for efficient cutting.

The Boot Knife is of simple design, being basically a single piece of steel shaped to provide blade and handle. The grip is formed from a six-foot length of black military paracord wrapped around the handle. This provides a secure and comfortable grip, and may be unwrapped for emergency use if necessary, leaving the knife fully functional although slightly less comfortable to hold.

Manufacturer:	Ek Commando Knife Co., Richmond, Virginia, USA
Model:	Ek Boot Knife
Length overall:	7 1/2in.
Blade length:	3 1/2in.
Blade shape:	Spear point, waisted
Blade material:	High carbon, surgical stainless steel
Edge:	Double-edge bevel-grind
Grip:	Paracord
Construction:	One-piece steel with 6ft. of black military specification parachute cord wrapped around tang
Sheath:	Black leather sheath with boot clip and tie holes

The Ek Warrior is the modern version of the legendary Commando Combat knife developed in the Second World War by John Ek. This knife is conservatively estimated to have sold 100,000 to American servicemen during the Second World War, and continued to be a popular private military purchase through the Korean and Vietnam wars.

The Ek knife is a highly functional design, with no frills. It is built around a single piece of thick steel, with a tang the full width and length of the handle. This makes the knife exceptionally strong - far stronger than a 'rat tail' or partial-length tang. The grips are made of contoured hardwood scales, riveted through the tang, and the tang extends beyond the grips to provide a round ended 'skull crusher' pommel (a more pointed pommel might appear more effective, but would endanger the user when carried in a sheath). This pommel may also be used for prying and hammering.

The blade is bevel-ground to a waisted spear point shape, with the back edge on this model extending roughly half way along the length of the blade (Bowie blade model illustrated). The spear point is very strong and provides excellent penetration for stabbing, while the waisted shape helps the blade to penetrate deeper into the opponent's body.

The knife balances well in the hand, and may be held in a variety of grips for different fighting styles and strokes.

Manufacturer:	Ek Commando Knife Co., Richmond, Virginia, USA
Model:	Warrior
Length overall:	12 1/2in.
Blade length:	6 5/8in.
Blade shape:	Spear point, waisted
Blade material:	High carbon stainless steel, with sandblasted non-reflective finish
Edge:	Bevel-ground
Grip:	Wood, with extended tang forming 'skull crusher' pommel
Construction:	Wood handles secured to full-size tang by three large rivets
Sheath:	Nylon web sheath

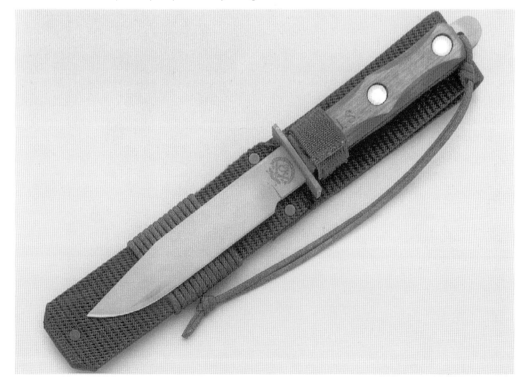

The Ek Paragrip range of knives have the same distinguished history and rugged design as the Ek Commando knives, but with paracord wrapped around the full-size tang to provide the grip in place of the riveted wood scales of the Commando models.

The paracord can be unwrapped if required, to provide 18ft. of military specification cord which is enormously versatile and useful for all manner of jobs in a survival situation. With the paracord removed, the knife is fully functional, the only drawback being a slightly less comfortable grip.

Ek Paragrip models come in a range of blade shapes, including part double-edged and full double-edged spear points, and a clip point Bowie design. The knives are around 12 1/2in. long overall, with a 6 5/8in. blade. The paracord may be black or green, and the knives are available with black or green nylon web sheaths.

Manufacturer:	Ek Commando Knife Co., Richmond, Virginia, USA
Model:	S/F 3, 4, 5 and SWAT 4 and 5
Length overall:	12 1/2in.
Blade length:	6 5/8in.
Blade shape:	Spear point, waisted, or Bowie-style clip point
Blade material:	High carbon, surgical stainless steel
Edge:	Bevel-grind
Grip:	Paracord, black or green
Construction:	One-piece steel with 18ft. of military specification parachute cord wrapped around tang
Sheath:	Nylon web sheath, black or green

The legendary Fairbairn-Sykes is perhaps the most widely known military knife of all time, a classic that has become synonymous with daring Second World War Commando raids and still adorns the cap badges and insignia of elite British units.

The Commandos were formed in 1940 to 'carry out raids... to destroy enemy installations and obtain information'. Captains Fairbairn and Sykes had served with the Shanghai Municipal Police and were experienced in martial arts and hand-to-hand combat. They were put in charge of teaching close-combat fighting skills at the Commando Basic Training Centre at Achnacarry in Scotland.

Fairbairn and his colleagues in Shanghai had worked on fighting knife designs, modifying British bayonets. For the Commandos they wanted a knife that was grip-heavy, and could be held in the fencing position. This is why the F-S knife handle is bottle-shaped - it is based on fencing foil designs. The grip is shaped to fall into the natural crease between the palm and the ball of the thumb, with the narrow neck of the grip fitting against the ball of the hand and the thumb and index finger grasping the forward part of the grip.

The double-edged tapered dagger blade is intended to provide excellent penetration for stabbing, but with two good edges for slashing. The full length tang gives good strength to the knife.

Sykes taught that the knife should be used delicately, 'as an artist uses his paint brush', making incisions with almost surgical precision. Fairbairn's wartime book, *All-In Fighting*, describes with anatomical detail the positions of the brachial, radial, carotid and subclavian arteries, and the techniques by which these may be cut with the F-S knife. A table details the depth of the arteries below the surface, and the length of time a man will take to lose consciousness when each one is cut.

During the War years, the original First Model F-S knife was developed, both to increase its effectiveness and to speed production with the materials and manufacturing technology available in wartime Britain. The early 3in. S-shaped guard was reduced to 2in. in production models to make it less likely to snag in clothing, and later became straight rather than S-shaped. Early examples have a ricasso or flat to the blade close to the hilt; more common, later F-S knives are bevelled all the way to the hilt. The grip was originally made of lathe-turned brass and chequered for added grip. As brass was needed for shell casings, this was replaced in the Third Model by a die-cast, zinc alloy handle, with rings for grip.

An enormous number of variations on the F-S design were produced by official and unofficial makers, some of which are highly prized by modern collectors. Genuine wartime F-S knives command a premium, and many

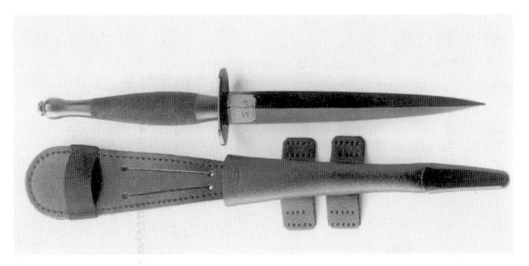

replicas and deliberate fakes have been produced since - so collectors should take care to ensure they know the true history of any example they are thinking of purchasing.

Manufacturer: British War Office contractors

Model: Fairbairn-Sykes Fighting Knife, Third Model

Length overall: 11 5/8in.

Blade length: 7in.

Blade shape: Tapered diagonal-section dagger blade

Blade material: Carbon steel

Edge: Bevel-ground

Grip: Cast zinc alloy, ringed, with characteristic bottle shape

Construction: Full-length, rat-tail type tang, with rounded nut at pommel screwed on to threaded end of tang

Sheath: Brown leather sheath with metal chape, belt loop and tabs for attachment to clothing or equipment, and black elastic strap to hold knife in position

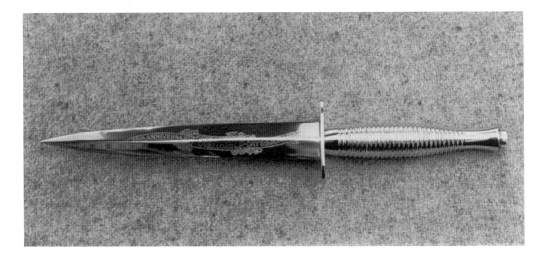

Gerber's Guardian Back-Up is a small boot knife which manages to combine small size and concealability with an effective fighting blade. The knife measures 7 1/4in. overall, with a 3 3/8in. blade of high carbon stainless steel. The blade is a double-edged tapered dagger shape, rather like a foreshortened Fairbairn-Sykes. It is bevel-ground to a sharp point, and finished with a black powder coating which matches the black handle. The handle is made of black Santoprene rubber with integral double guard and a textured surface for improved grip. There is a grooved portion at each edge of the grip, and a thumb recess on either side just behind the hilt. The butt is flared slightly.

As a pure fighting knife, the Guardian is rather small, but then it is designed to be used as a concealed last resort defensive weapon, and its small size is part of that concept.

The sheath is part of the system, and consists of a rigid, moulded black plastic unit with a stainless steel clip that may be reversed to permit the knife to be worn either way up on belt or boot. Slots in the sheath also allow it to be strapped to the user's arm, leg or equipment. The sheath features an adjustable retention system which holds the edges of the double guard. Sliding buttons may be set to hold the knife relatively loosely, to allow easy withdrawal, or tightly for security - or any position in between. A hole at the tip of the sheath serves both as a drain hole and to allow a leg tie to be fitted.

Having used this knife, I may say that the sheath works very effectively, and the knife itself balances well in the hand and is more effective than its size might suggest. My only complaint is that the sheath is inclined to be noisy, when one withdraws or inserts the knife, and if it knocks against other equipment.

Manufacturer:	Gerber (a division of Fiskars Inc.), Portland, Oregon, USA
Model:	Guardian Back-Up
Length overall:	7 1/4in.
Blade length:	3 3/8in.
Blade shape:	Dagger
Blade material:	0.156in. thick, high carbon stainless steel, with black epoxy coated finish
Edge:	Double, bevel-ground
Grip:	Grooved and textured Santoprene rubber
Construction:	Santoprene grip moulded on to full-size tang
Sheath:	Rigid black plastic sheath with adjustable tension locking system and belt/boot clip

The Gerber Mk I was actually developed after the Mk II, and was designed in conjunction with military-knife-fighting experts during the Vietnam War. The Mk I shares the basic shape and concept of the Applegate Fairbairn fighting knife, with its tapered dagger-shaped blade, forward-angled double guard, and oval-section handle which is fattest in the centre of the palm.

The Mk I is 8 3/4in. overall, with a 4 3/4in. 440A stainless steel blade which can be supplied bright or epoxy-coated black. The handle is made of cast aluminium with a black epoxy finish with a non-slip texture. The butt is slightly flared and has a lanyard hole.

The Mk I is a serious, no-frills fighting knife. It is a little shorter than some would prefer (hence the alternative of the Mk II), but is well balanced and an efficient and effective fighting tool.

Manufacturer:	Gerber (a division of Fiskars Inc.), Portland, Oregon, USA
Model:	Mk I
Length overall:	8 3/4in.
Blade length:	4 3/4in.
Blade shape:	Dagger
Blade material:	1/4in. thick, 15/16in. wide 440A stainless steel, Rc 57-59. Finish either satin or black epoxy-coated
Edge:	Double, bevel-ground
Grip:	Cast aluminium, contoured, incorporating double guard, textured black epoxy-coated, with lanyard hole
Construction:	Guard and handle formed as one piece
Sheath:	Black Cordura belt sheath with leg tie loop

Developed during the Vietnam War with the advice of military-knife-fighting experts, the Mk II is a development of the Fairbairn-Sykes concept of a fighting dagger. A no-frills design, it has a 6 1/2in. blade made of 1/4in. thick 440A stainless steel, hardened to Rc 57-59. The blade is a parallel-sided dagger type, with a strong spear point and a serrated section on each edge for extra cutting power. This blade is excellent for stabbing, slashing, ripping and cutting, making the Mk II a highly effective fighting weapon.

The handle is a single aluminium casting, incorporating a double guard and contoured to fit the hand well. It has a truncated cone pommel which may be used as a 'skull crusher'.

Manufacturer:	Gerber (a division of Fiskars Inc.), Portland, Oregon, USA
Model:	Mk II
Length overall:	11 1/2in.
Blade length:	6 1/2in.
Blade shape:	Dagger, with serrated sections near hilt
Blade material:	1/4in. thick 440A stainless steel, Rc 57-59. Finish either satin or black epoxy coated
Edge:	Double, bevel-ground, with serrated section
Grip:	Cast aluminium incorporating double guard, black epoxy-coated, with lanyard hole
Construction:	Double guard and handle formed as one piece
Sheath:	Black Cordura belt sheath with leg tie

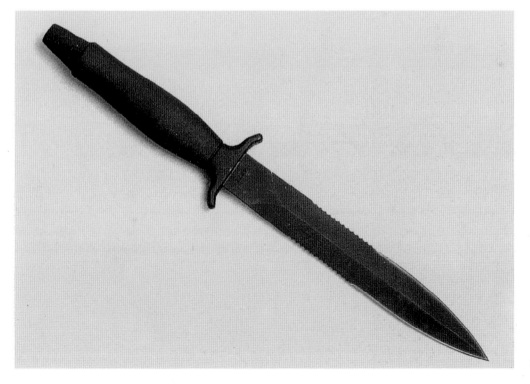

The Sleeve Dagger is one of the notorious weapons of clandestine operations during the Second World War. It is basically a steel spike, made of a single piece of stainless steel. Measuring 7in. long overall, it has a 3 1/2in. 'blade' ground into a triangular section culminating in a sharp spear point. The three flats of the blade have deep fullers or 'blood grooves'. The edges of the blade are sharpened, although because of the blade profile they cannot be as sharp as a normal knife blade.

Stabbing with the triangular blade creates a devastating wound which allows rapid blood loss and does not heal easily (see also Cold Steel Special Projects Delta Dart). Although the blade can also be used for slashing, it is less effective than a knife and is best used for stabbing.

The handle is rectangular in section, with rounded edges, measuring 3/8in. wide and 1/4in. thick. The butt is grooved just before the end forming a hammer head which may be used to deliver a blow.

The Sleeve Dagger is carried in a brown leather sheath which has a strap to hold it to the forearm or leg, where it can be worn concealed but drawn quickly when needed.

Manufacturer:	HG Long & Co., Sheffield, England
Model:	OSS Sleeve Dagger
Length overall:	7in.
Blade length:	3 1/2in.
Blade shape:	Triangular cross-section spike with fullers ground into flats
Blade material:	Stainless steel with sandblasted, non-reflective finish
Edge:	Sharpened spike point. The three edges are also sharp
Grip:	Bare steel
Construction:	Machined from one piece of steel
Sheath:	Leather sheath with strap for wear on forearm, concealed by sleeve

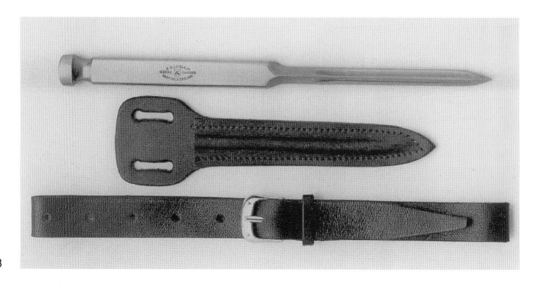

The Smith & Wesson Military Model Boot Knife is basically a miniature version of the Combat Smatchet - comparison of the photograph of this knife with those of the Smatchet earlier in this chapter will show the obvious similarity. Like the Smatchet, the S&W Boot Knife has a broad, symmetrical, leaf-shaped blade ending in a spear point. It has a similar handle, with longitudinal grooves for grip and integral, forward-angled, double guard. There is a hole in the ricasso to identify the 'working' edge, even by feel in the dark.

The dimensions are much smaller, however - the S&W Boot Knife measures 9 3/4in. overall, with a 5in. blade (compared with the massive 10in. blade of the Smatchet). This gives the Boot Knife completely different handling characteristics - it balances and handles much more like a conventional knife. The Smatchet blade shape still has certain advantages even at this size, however. It still offers what is effectively a reverse curve cutting edge, and the spear point is immensely strong.

The blade shape keeps much of the weight forward, giving better chopping performance than one might expect from such a relatively short blade.

This is one of a number of 'mini-Smatchets' offered by different makers, including Harsey and Mar. These models are in effect a variation on the Applegate-Fairbairn Fighting Knife design, bringing some of the advantages of the Smatchet blade shape to this highly effective fighter.

Manufacturer:	Smith & Wesson, Springfield, MA, USA
Model:	Military Model Boot Knife
Length overall:	9 3/4in.
Blade length:	5in.
Blade shape:	Smatchet
Blade material:	440 stainless steel
Edge:	Double-edged, bevel-ground
Grip:	Moulded black Kraton rubber with longitudinal grooves
Construction:	Handle screwed to full-length tang
Sheath:	Black leather boot clip sheath

SOG's Desert Dagger was developed in response to military personnel needs, and aims to provide a more versatile tool than the regular dagger-type fighting knife. It has a typical dagger-type blade, with parallel sides and a strong spear point, but with the addition of a central fuller or 'blood groove', and two types of serrated edge for a short section on either side - fine serrations on one side, and larger, deeper serrations on the other. The knife also has an enlarged, flat-ended, stainless steel pommel which may be used for hammering in the field.

The grip is of Kraton rubber, contoured and with chequering for extra grip. One notable feature of this knife is the soldered crossguard, something that is generally found only on the most expensive knives.

Whether the different serration types are really needed is debatable, but there is no doubt that this is a serious fighting knife, and one that is also capable of taking on a range of general chores in the field.

Manufacturer:	SOG Knives, Edmonds, Washington, USA
Model:	Desert Dagger
Length overall:	12in.
Blade length:	6 1/2in.
Blade shape:	Parallel-edged, dagger blade with spear point
Blade material:	0.18in. thick 440A stainless steel, Rc 57-58
Edge:	Double, bevel-ground, with fuller and serrated sections on both edges near hilt
Grip:	One-piece Kraton grip, with all-round chequering. Flat steel pommel suitable for hammering.
Construction:	Full tang, with soldered crossguard
Sheath:	Black nylon belt sheath with leg tie

Designed as a back-up weapon for law enforcement personnel, the Pentagon has a 5in. tapered dagger blade with one plain edge and one serrated. The waisted handle is made of Kraton, with chequering for grip. There is no guard as such, the bolster fitting flush with the handle. There are thumb notches on either side of the ricasso, so the knife can be used equally well with the serrated or the plain edge uppermost.

The Pentagon comes with a black leather boot clip sheath with press studded retaining strap.

Manufacturer:	SOG Knives, Edmonds, Washington, USA
Model:	Pentagon
Length overall:	9 3/4in.
Blade length:	5in.
Blade shape:	Tapered dagger
Blade material:	0.16in. thick 440-A stainless steel, Rc 56-57
Edge:	Double, bevel-ground, with one edge serrated
Grip:	One-piece flared Kraton grip, with all-round chequering
Construction:	Full tang
Sheath:	Black leather scabbard with boot/belt clip

Although not a current design, this knife is included here since it illustrates a type of fighting knife which still influences some modern designers and is still manufactured in reproduction form and therefore may be encountered in certain theatres of operation.

The Trench Knife is a particularly versatile weapon, combining not just a blade but also a heavy brass knuckle-duster and a pointed steel 'skull crusher'. The loops of the knuckle-duster have points to make a blow more damaging.

The modern reproduction of this First World War knife measures 11in. overall, with a 6 1/2in. polished blade of stainless steel. The handle is cast brass and is held in place by a threaded nut which screws on to the end of the full-length tang. The nut is hexagonal at the base and is extended into a point to form the 'skull crusher' pommel spike.

All in all, this is a crude but effective weapon, well suited to hand-to-hand fighting in confined spaces.

Manufacturer:	Replica distributed by United Cutlery, Sevierville, Tennessee, USA
Model:	WWI Trench Knife
Length overall:	11in.
Blade length:	6 1/2in.
Blade shape:	Dagger
Blade material:	5/32in. thick 420 J2 stainless steel
Edge:	Bevel-ground
Grip:	Solid brass one-piece handle incorporating guard and knuckle duster, with conical 'skull crusher' pommel
Construction:	Full-length tang
Sheath:	Metal sheath with non-glare black finish

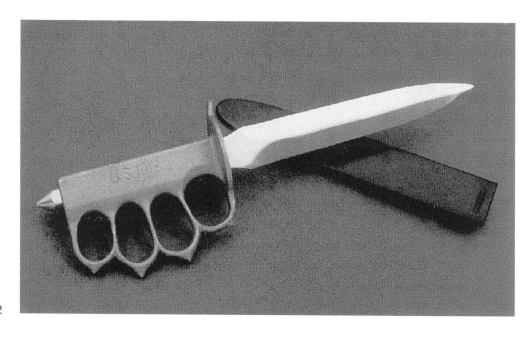

BAYONETS

In the introduction to the previous chapter, I argued that the 'fighting knife' is of little use to the professional soldier. There is little call for soldiers to get involved in knife fights, and the 'fighting' knife's specialisation renders it unsuitable for many other tasks.

The bayonet is at the other end of the scale. It is a highly useful and versatile tool with many practical uses for the soldier on and off the battlefield. Whilst virtually no modern army issues its troops with an 'official' fighting knife, it is hard to think of an army that does not issue a bayonet.

The obvious use of a bayonet is for close-quarters battle with the bayonet fixed on the soldier's rifle. In the final stages of an assault on an enemy position, soldiers might use their bayonets to clear trenches and bunkers, for instance.

However this is just one of the bayonet's many uses – and ironically one of the rarest. Whereas a soldier may go through his entire career without once bayoneting an enemy, he will use his bayonet as a general purpose tool several times a day while in the field. In this respect, the bayonet is simply a combat knife, with the added advantage that it can be fitted to a rifle when required.

Removed from the rifle, the bayonet is carried in a sheath on the soldier's webbing, in the manner of a normal sheath knife. It has a conventional handle and blade, very much like a regular combat knife, and can be used for all the typical camp and field tasks: cutting undergrowth, preparing wood for a fire, dispatching, skinning and preparing game for food, prying open ammunition crates, and many more.

In conjunction with a cleverly designed sheath, the bayonet becomes an even more versatile tool. Many bayonets are designed to combine with their sheath to form a powerful, electrically-insulated wire-cutter, to help in breaching wire obstacles. Other tools may be built into the sheath: often there is a sharpening stone on the rear face, while the British Army bayonet sheath includes a folding saw. Some bayonets also include notches for opening bottles and the like.

Once fitted to the rifle, a bayonet can be used for a number of tasks. It makes a useful probe to search haystacks, thatched roofs, piles of rubbish and the like. The rifle can be fired immediately a target is exposed, while the sharp blade prevents an adversary grabbing the muzzle and pulling the rifle from the soldier's hands.

A bayonet can also be a powerful deterrent in crowd control, work which is increasingly a feature of modern 'peacekeeping' operations. To quote from the marketing literature of one bayonet manufacturer: 'The thought of cold steel sliding into one's body is more horrific and real than the thought of a bullet doing the same'. This psychological effect may help to contain a crowd and prevent the situation escalating to the point where shots are fired.

There are many different bayonet designs, but the one thing they all have in common is some means of attaching them to the muzzle end of a rifle. The very earliest bayonets had a simple plug at the hilt, and were rammed into the barrel of a muzzle-loading rifle like a cork in a wine bottle. This had the disadvantage that the rifle could not then be fired – not a significant problem when loading was a long, drawn-out process, but clearly unacceptable for a modern breech-loading assault rifle.

The typical modern bayonet has a ring and clip mechanism. The ring fits over the muzzle, and the clip holds the bayonet firmly in position under the barrel, so that the rifle can be loaded and fired normally. The bayonet can be removed quickly if required by manually operating the catch and sliding the bayonet forward off the muzzle.

One notable exception is the British Army's SA80 bayonet, in which the entire handle is a hollow tube that fits over the muzzle; the bullets are fired literally through the centre of the handle. This has been criticised because the handle becomes extremely hot, and can cause serious burns if the soldier tries to remove it with bare hands after firing.

The Kalashnikov assault rifle in its various forms (AK47, AK74 and derivatives) remains the standard infantry weapon of former Communist bloc states and their allies. Consequently, the corresponding bayonet is still in widespread service, and may be encountered in just about any part of the world, whether in the hands of government troops or rebel and guerrilla forces.

The bayonet has been manufactured in several countries over the years, and a number of minor variations exist which are significant to collectors but have little relevance here. Suffice it to say that most examples are substantially the same in materials, design and dimensions.

The AK47 bayonet is a relatively crude but effective tool. Measuring 11in. overall, it has a 6in. clip point blade, with a serrated sawback edge. There is an oval hole in the blade which engages a knob on the scabbard, to form a scissor-type wire cutter. The steel sheath often has a latex grip to provide electrical insulation, so that the cutters may be used to breach electrified wire obstacles.

The bayonet's handle is formed from moulded plastic grip scales, fixed to the tang with machine screws. The guard is extended to form a muzzle ring, which fits around the rifle's muzzle. At the butt end is a clip with a catch mechanism which engages on a protrusion beneath the barrel of the Kalashnikov rifle. This attaches the bayonet firmly to the rifle until the catch is released with the push-button. The bayonet typically has a thin webbing strap which extends from the guard to the butt.

This bayonet is conceived as a multi-purpose combat knife which will be useful to soldiers for many chores in the field, as well as for hand-to-hand fighting and use as a bayonet when necessary. Like most multi-purpose tools, it does an adequate job of most tasks, but does not really excel in any one. As a general purpose field knife, however, it is hard to beat.

Manufacturer:	Former Communist bloc state factories
Model:	Bayonet, AK47
Length overall:	11in.
Blade length:	6in.
Blade shape:	Clip point, Bowie-type
Blade material:	Stainless steel, Rc 56-58
Edge:	Bevel-ground
Grip:	Black or brown plastic scales with chequered pattern
Construction:	Scales attached to tang with machine screws; butt incorporates clip to attach to fitting on Kalashnikov assault rifle and derivatives
Sheath:	Steel sheath with attachment for bayonet blade to form scissor-type wire cutter

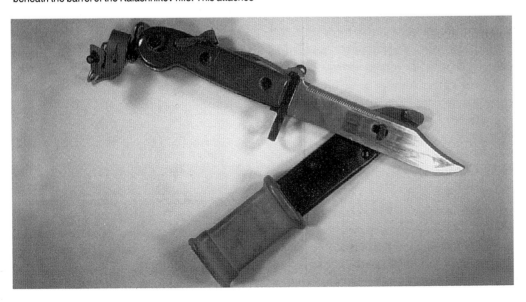

A Eickhorn GmbH are one of the leading manufacturers of military knives in the world and supply bayonets and combat knives to a number of NATO armies. Their leading bayonet/combat knife system is the KCB 77 - a modular system which allows a government to specify the features and fittings to meet its requirements in a combat knife or bayonet.

The example shown here is the USM9, a bayonet which at first glance resembles the AK47 design with its clip point blade, rectangular section handle, and rigid sheath that combines with the bayonet to form a scissors-type wire cutter.

There is much more to this bayonet than meets the eye, however. Quite apart from the stringent testing and quality control employed by Eickhorn, the USM9 has a number of additional features which add to its usefulness in the field.

For instance, the knife and bayonet are electrically insulated, and the knife handle incorporates a voltage tester that will illuminate a small bulb if the blade touches an electrified conductor. This warns the soldier that the fence or obstacle he is facing is electrified.

The guard is hooked forward to form a bottle opener, which may also be used for various prying and levering tasks. The catch has a lubrication point, which applies a small squirt of grease to the moving parts each time the bayonet is fitted or removed from the rifle. There is a protective cap to keep the catch free of dirt and debris when the bayonet is not attached to the rifle.

The scabbard may be unclipped from its nylon webbing hanger, so that the wire cutters can be quickly deployed without the soldier removing his webbing. On the back of the scabbard is a sapphire sharpening stone. The scabbard has an adjustable retaining spring to hold the bayonet blade in place; this can be set to release easily if the bayonet may be needed in a hurry, or screwed down tightly so that vigorous activity will not dislodge the bayonet.

A plastic cap protects the wire cutter end of the scabbard. This is not only to prevent the wire cutter from snagging in clothing or undergrowth, but also allows the bayonet in its scabbard to be used as a baton (with the retaining system adjusted to its tightest position), for example, for riot control or by military police. For riot control, an 80,000-volt piezo-electric 'cattle prod' type attachment can be fitted to the end of the scabbard, and used either in the hand or attached to a rifle.

Altogether, the KCB 77 is a versatile and well-thought-out system which effectively meets the needs of modern soldiers

Manufacturer:	Eickhorn GmbH, Solingen, Germany
Model:	USM9 (KCB 77 system)
Length overall:	11 11/16in.
Blade length:	6 5/8in.
Blade shape:	Clip point
Blade material:	Carbon steel with corrosion-resistant black finish
Edge:	Bevel-ground
Grip:	Ribbed and contoured plastic scales, rectangular section, incorporating voltage tester
Construction:	Scales fitted to full-length tang; extended guard forms muzzle ring; catch in butt fits to rifle
Sheath:	Sophisticated rigid plastic sheath with multiple features, including wire cutter, screwdriver tip, adjustable tension blade retention and clip attachment to belt hanger. Optional accessories include protective end cap and 'cattle prod' attachment for riot control

Eickhorn's USM series is based on the M7 design, but is available in a variety of configurations to fit almost any military rifle in use today, including the M16 A1 and A2, FN-FAL, SIG and H&K G3. The basic blade shape is a parallel-sided dagger with spear point. Handles are of moulded plastic (glassfibre-reinforced polyamide), contoured to fit the hand and chequered for grip. The handles are fixed to the tang with machine screws. Muzzle rings and butt catches vary to suit the particular rifle the bayonet is intended for.

Eickhorn take pride in the quality of their materials and manufacturing methods, and their USM series, used by a number of NATO armies, is no exception. Components undergo rigorous testing for strength, resilience, hardness and other characteristics, under extreme conditions of temperature and humidity. The knives and scabbards are insulated against high voltage electricity and are tested for resistance to fungal growth, corrosion and chemical agents.

Manufacturer:	Eickhorn GmbH, Solingen, Germany
Model:	USM 4, 5, 6, 7
Length overall:	11 11/16in.
Blade length:	6 5/8in.
Blade shape:	Spear point
Blade material:	Carbon steel, with corrosion-resistant black finish
Edge:	Bevel-ground
Grip:	Moulded plastic, contoured shape with chequering
Construction:	Grip scales screwed to full-length tang
Sheath:	Rigid plastic sheath, with nylon web hanger and wire clip for attachment to military web belt. Some sheaths incorporate wire-cutter attachment and screwdriver tip

Now superseded by the M9, the M7 was the standard US Army issue bayonet for the M16 A2 assault rifle. It is a relatively simple design, measuring 11 3/4in. overall with a 7in. spear point blade. The handle is formed from black plastic grip scales, with moulded chequering, screwed to the tang. The double guard is extended one side to form a muzzle ring, and the butt incorporates a spring-loaded catch to clip on to the dovetail attachment point on the M16 rifle.

The sheath is made of plastic, with a Cordura hanger with a wire clip for attachment to a military pattern web belt.

Manufacturer:	Ontario Knife Co, Franklinville, New York, USA (also manufactured by other US Department of Defense contractors such as Camillus)
Model:	M7 Bayonet
Length overall:	11 3/4in.
Blade length:	7in.
Blade shape:	Spear point
Blade material:	Black finished carbon steel
Edge:	Bevel-grind
Grip:	Moulded black plastic with black chequering
Construction:	Grips screwed through tang. Butt and guard designed to fix to attachment points on rifle muzzle
Sheath:	Rigid plastic sheath with Cordura hanger and wire clip for attachment to military web belt

Designed as a bayonet for the M16 A2 rifle, the M9 has been adopted by the US Army and Marine Corps as well as the Australian Army, and has also proved popular with civilian users as a general field knife. Around 1995 it was estimated that Buck had produced well over 300,000 M9s for the US Army alone.

This is a hefty knife, weighing 14oz, with an overall length of 12 1/4in. and a 7 1/8in. blade of 7/32in. steel. The blade is a clip point shape, with a hollow ground main edge and a fine-toothed saw section on the back edge. On the right side of the blade is a fuller or 'blood groove'. The clip edge is partly sharpened to give a sharp point to the blade and to act as the wire cutter blade when the knife is fitted to its sheath by means of the oval hole in the blade.

As with most bayonet designs, the guard incorporates a muzzle ring, and there is a catch in the butt to attach to the appropriate fitting on the rifle.

The handle is circular in cross section and made of Zytel. It is deeply grooved and chequered to provide a sure grip even in extreme conditions. This handle may be rather hard on unprotected hands, however, and due to its circular profile may turn in the hand during use,

despite the grooves and chequering.

The knife is heavy enough for chopping and hacking, but it can also be used for more delicate work - although, as with most bayonets, the extended guard/muzzle ring makes it difficult to choke up the grip. The saw is less effective than it might appear and is better for cutting materials such as rope and webbing than for sawing wood and bone.

The rigid plastic sheath is a hefty item in its own right, weighing as much as the knife. It incorporates the wire cutter mentioned above, plus a sharpening stone and screwdriver. There is a webbing pouch that can be used for carrying small items such as a flint striker or water purification tablets. The sheath has two retaining straps for the knife, together with a retention spring inside the sheath which holds the blade. There is a Bianchi clip which allows the sheath to be attached or removed from webbing without removing other items such as water bottle and ammunition pouches which is covenient when regulations state that knives must be removed on board an aircraft, for instance.

See also Buckmaster, a combat knife based on the M9.

Manufacturer: Buck Knives, El Cajon, California, USA

Model: M9

Length overall: 12 1/4in.

Blade length: 7 1/8in.

Blade shape: Bowie-style clip point with fuller on right hand side, and serrated sawback

Blade material: 7/32in. thick forged steel, Rc 56-58. Black oxide finish available

Edge: Hollow-ground main edge, clip false edge, and serrated-type saw back

Grip: Grooved and chequered olive drab Zytel, circular section, with flared butt. Fittings for attachment to M16 A2 rifle

Construction: Tubular Zytel grip fitted over circular section handle

Sheath: Plastic and Cordura sheath incorporates sharpening stone, and fits to knife to form wire-cutters

The current British Army issue bayonet was designed specifically for the SA80 assault rifle. Like its counterparts in other armies, the SA80 bayonet is a versatile tool, capable of being used as a general purpose field knife or fighting knife when not attached to the rifle.

The blade is a clip point design, with a deep fuller or 'blood groove' on the left-hand side. The clip edge is sharpened, and the keyhole for the wire cutter is set back from this edge so that the spine of the knife acts on the wire, not the clip edge. The main edge is bevel-ground, with widely spaced serrations for the first half of its length.

The handle is unusual for a bayonet in that it is a metal tube open at both ends, designed so that the rifle's muzzle passes right through the centre. A catch on the underside at the butt end clips on to a ring on the rifle barrel to hold the bayonet in position. There are slots cut into the handle to align with the slots in the flash suppressor at the muzzle.

The scabbard is made of rigid plastic with steel fittings and has a Fastex buckle to attach to the belt hanger. It incorporates a wire-cutter attachment, with a peg that fits into a keyhole in the knife blade to form a scissors-type cutter. There is also a folding saw blade in the scabbard and a sharpening stone set into the rear face.

Manufacturer:	Royal Ordnance, UK
Model:	SA80 bayonet
Length overall:	10 3/4in.
Blade length:	7in.
Blade shape:	Clip point
Blade material:	Stainless steel
Edge:	Bevel-ground, with widely spaced serrations for first half of main edge
Grip:	Contoured hollow tubular steel handle to fit over rifle muzzle, with flash suppressor slots and attachment clip; grooves to provide extra grip
Construction:	Steel handle continuous with blade
Sheath:	Rigid plastic sheath with wire-cutter attachment, folding saw blade, and Fastex buckle attachment for belt hanger

COMBAT AND SURVIVAL KNIVES

The combat knife is the Jeep of knives: a simple, rugged tool that will survive all the use and abuse of life in the combat zone, and still come back for more. It is a true multi-purpose tool which can be used for any number of practical outdoor tasks by the soldier living and working outdoors. Most of these tasks will be straightforward camp chores – preparing food, making a fire, hammering in tent pegs and the like. However the combat knife must also be capable of use as a fighting knife if the situation demands.

Any combat knife is therefore a compromise. There can be no 'perfect' design, because a knife that is specialised for one task becomes less good for another. For instance it is useful to be able to chop quite heavy branches – to build a shelter or provide materials to construct obstacles. This requires a heavy knife with a thick, strong blade of relatively soft steel. However such a knife would be too heavy and clumsy for delicate tasks such as gutting a fish.

Similarly, a good fighting knife is double-edged so it will cut in either direction, but for many ordinary cutting tasks it is helpful to have a flat, blunt back edge, so that you can press down with a finger, or even use a piece of timber as a mallet to drive the edge into the work.

This is why there is such a wide variety of combat knives available. Each one is the result of many different compromises being struck, depending on the designer's view of the likely uses to which the knife will be put.

Perhaps the classic combat knife is the Ka-Bar, a good, solid knife with a clip point Bowie-style blade of around 7in. The original version was issued to US troops in the Second World War. It was still being issued to some units in Vietnam, and became a popular private purchase with others. Today it is still widely used and respected by US and other forces' personnel, and the Ka-Bar company has now developed an updated model with an almost identical profile.

The other category of knives covered in this section is survival knives. This is generally taken to mean a knife carried in case the user finds himself in a survival situation – perhaps an aircraft crash or other disaster leaves him in hostile territory with no supplies and a long walk to safety ahead. Such knives are designed to be even more versatile than a combat knife, often with extra gizmos and gadgets fitted, or concealed inside, to do specific jobs.

This is fine as far as it goes. If I were stuck in the woods for an uncertain length of time, I would be very pleased to have a few fish-hooks and a compass in addition to a good, strong knife. In practice one needs to exercise extra care when selecting a knife with extra survival tools. Some are excellent quality, but there are others designed to appeal to the 'gadget freak', with the maximum number of items crammed in without regard to quality and function.

I have seen so-called survival knives that are so weakened by the hollow handle that they would be virtually useless in a real survival situation. By contrast, knives such as the Chris Reeve series are excellent knives in their own right, and the hollow handle allows you to make up your own survival kit to store inside – choosing the items most likely to be of use in the circumstances and terrain where you may find yourself.

I mentioned that, in theory, a survival knife is kept in a dedicated survival kit and not used for everyday chores. While this may be true of knives in aircraft survival kits and the like, most soldiers will carry one knife on their webbing to be used everyday, and for survival chores if the need arises. This need not be a problem, but it is important to replace any items used, so that they are not missing if the time comes when your life depends on them – just as items removed from a first aid kit should always be replaced without delay.

Based on Second World War military knife designs, the Al Mar Grunt I measures 9 3/4in. overall, with a 5 1/8in. Bowie-type blade of 6A steel hardened to Rockwell 57-59. The clip of the blade is straight and ground to a false edge which extends all the way along the length of the blade to the depression just in front of the guard. This depression looks as though it could be used as a thumb rest for a 'choked-up' grip, but in fact the double guard makes this hold all but impossible.

The handle is made of stacked leather washers. The washers are threaded on to the rat-tail type tang and held in place with a pinned stainless steel butt cap. The handle thus formed is then cut to shape, including three deep grooves for added grip in wet and slippery conditions. The knife comes with a brown leather belt sheath.

This knife is a good, solid, no-frills design which is excellent for general chores, and could be used effectively as a fighter if required.

Manufacturer:	Al Mar Knives Inc., Lake Oswego, Oregon, USA
Model:	Grunt I
Length overall:	9 3/4in.
Blade length:	5 1/8in.
Blade shape:	Bowie
Blade material:	6A steel, Rc 57-59
Edge:	Deep bevel-ground with false back edge
Grip:	Grooved, stacked brown leather, with brass guard and stainless butt
Construction:	Stacked washers on full-length tang
Sheath:	Brown leather belt sheath

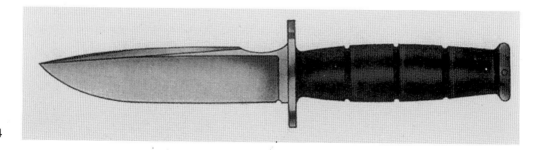

The Al Mar Grunt II is a Bowie-style fighting knife, with a long 7 3/4in. clip point blade made of 6A steel hardened to 57-59 Rc. The clip point is extended and slightly concave, giving a sharp point that penetrates exceptionally well, although there is some trade-off in tip strength: using this knife for heavy prying work would risk damaging the tip.

The blade shape makes this knife less suitable than some for general camp chores, but its length, weight and handling make it excellent for fighting - a good knife for stabbing, slashing and hacking.

Like the Grunt I, this knife has a military-style, stacked leather washer handle, with brass double guard and stainless steel butt pinned through the end of the tang. This handle is similar to that found on the USMC-type combat knifes. It provides a good chunky contoured grip that fills the hand well and is comfortable in use. The only real drawback to this type of handle is that it is round in cross-section and may turn in the hand if considerable twisting force is applied to the blade.

Manufacturer:	Al Mar Knives Inc., Lake Oswego, Oregon, USA
Model:	Grunt II
Length overall:	13in.
Blade length:	7 3/4in.
Blade shape:	Bowie with pronounced clip
Blade material:	6A steel, Rc 57-59
Edge:	Bevel-ground with sharpened clip edge
Grip:	Grooved, stacked brown leather, with brass guard and stainless butt
Construction:	Stacked washers on full-length tang
Sheath:	Brown leather belt sheath

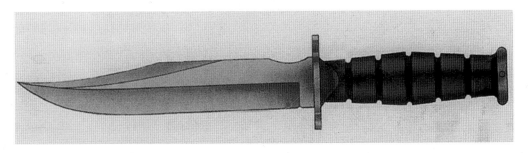

Al Mar's SERE series of knives were designed as multipurpose blades for special forces personnel (SERE stands for Survival, Evasion, Resistance, Escape). They are exceptionally good-looking knives, but immensely practical too. There are three basic models of fixed-blade knife and three folders. The fixed-blade knives are the SERE IV, SERE V and SERE VIII. The IV and V are essentially the same, except that the IV has a plain false back edge, while the V has a 2 5/8in. serrated section on the back edge. Both knives measure 10 1/2in. overall, with a deep, heavy 5 3/4in. spear point blade made of 6A steel hardened to 57-59 Rc. The model VIII is larger, at 12 1/2in. overall, with a 7in. blade.

The green micarta handles are contoured, with the lines flowing smoothly into the contoured stainless steel double guard, which has a forward-angled shape. One drawback noted by users of these knives is that the polished micarta handles offer little grip and may turn easily in the hand. This can be overcome by having the handle grooved or chequered to provide better grip.

The SERE knives are a little light for heavy chopping, but otherwise are versatile enough to tackle most field chores. They are a popular private purchase among elite military units, who recognise their value not only as a rugged and dependable field tool but also as lethally effective fighters.

Manufacturer:	Al Mar Knives Inc., Lake Oswego, Oregon, USA
Model:	SERE - Models IV, V and VIII
Length overall:	12 1/2in. (SERE VIII)
Blade length:	7in. (SERE VIII)
Blade shape:	Spear point with serrated back
Blade material:	6A steel, Rc 57-59
Edge:	Bevel-ground with false top edge and serrated back
Grip:	Green micarta; brushed stainless guard; 3 lanyard holes
Construction:	Micarta scales pinned to full tang with three hollow brass tube rivets
Sheath:	Black leather belt sheath with sharpening stone

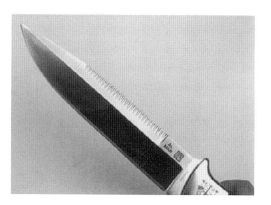

Al Mar's SF-Sog Special Ops is an impressive fighting knife design, with an extended clip point blade. Like most of Al Mar's fixed-blade knives, the blade is of 6A steel, with a hardness of 57-59 Rc. The blade of this model has a double concave back edge, which gives it a distinctive profile similar to that of the SOG Tech knives.

The handle is full and contoured, with shallow finger grooves. It is made of black micarta, with lines that flow smoothly into the contoured brass double guard and butt. Coloured spacers add to the distinctly up-market appearance, which despite its good looks is an immensely practical blade, highly effective as a fighter and good for general field and camp tasks as well. As with any clip point design, however, this blade is not well suited to digging or prying.

Al Mar also make a larger knife under the SF-Sog Special Ops name, with a 'B' suffix to the product code. This measures 12in. overall, with an 8in. blade of the Randall Mk I style. The micarta handle is of a more utilitarian design, with deeper finger grooves and a plainer stainless steel guard. Although not so pretty to look at as its namesake, it is a fearsome fighting weapon and practical field tool.

Manufacturer:	Al Mar Knives Inc., Lake Oswego, Oregon, USA
Model:	SF-Sog Special Ops (A1 model)
Length overall:	11 3/4in. ('B' model 13in.)
Blade length:	6 5/8in. (('B' model 8in.)
Blade shape:	Clip point
Blade material:	6A steel, Rc 57-59
Edge:	Hollow ground with false top edge
Grip:	Black micarta; brass guard and butt; lanyard hole
Construction:	Full-length tang
Sheath:	Black leather belt sheath

Alan Wood is a custom knifemaker based in Cumbria, England, who makes a range of well-regarded hunting knives as well as a small selection of military patterns. His Model 14 'Serviceman' is a full-sized combat knife on the Randall theme, with a straight clip point 7in. blade. Wood describes this knife as 'primarily a heavy duty field tool, but one that will cope with use as a last ditch weapon'. The handle is contoured, and the lines flow continuously into the contoured double guard and butt.

A shorter 'Pilot' version of this knife is also available, with a 5 1/2in. blade. This also has a flatter handle so it may be carried less obtrusively.

Being a custom knife, the Model 14 is available in a number of variations to the customer's order. The handle, for instance, may be of micarta, exotic hardwood or other material, and a sub-hilt may be added. Guard and butt may be brass, nickel silver, bronze, blued steel or stainless steel, and engraving can be arranged to order. Blade finish may be satin, mirror polish or matt beadblasted.

Wood also makes other knives intended for military use, including an 8 1/4in. concealment boot knife, an 11in. dirk, and a 10 1/4in. modern fighter named the 'Sentinel'.

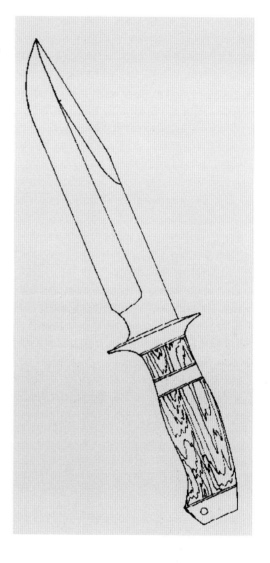

Manufacturer:	Alan Wood, Carlisle, Cumbria, England
Model:	Mod 14 Serviceman
Length overall:	11 3/4in.
Blade length:	7in.
Blade shape:	Bowie
Blade material:	Steel
Edge:	Hollow-ground
Grip:	One-piece hardwood handle with lanyard hole
Construction:	Full-length narrow radiused tang with buttcap; guard pinned and soldered
Sheath:	Handmade knife. Choice of sheaths possible

Blackjack's AWAC is a knife designed to withstand the most extreme conditions, hence the name AWAC: All Weather, All Conditions. It is a medium-sized knife, measuring 10 1/2in. overall with a 6in. blade. The materials used in its construction are chosen to live up to the name - 440A stainless steel for the blade and furniture, and black micarta for the handle.

Unusually for a military knife, the blade is flat ground, and has a drop point shape. The blade follows the line of the ricasso, with a small choil separating the two. This type of blade is good for food preparation and similar jobs involving slicing and skinning, but is less well suited to heavy chopping, prying and similar jobs. It is also not the blade of choice for fighting, although a good deal better than nothing in a tight spot.

The AWAC's handle is contoured, with a straight back and a finger groove. It is flared towards the butt, giving a firm hold. There is a lanyard hole, formed from a stainless steel tube which pins the handle to the tang, and the knife comes in a black leather belt sheath.

Manufacturer:	Blackjack Knives, Effingham, Illinois, USA
Model:	AWAC
Length overall:	10 1/2in.
Blade length:	6in.
Blade shape:	Drop point
Blade material:	440A stainless steel, satin finish
Edge:	Flat-grind
Grip:	Black micarta with finger groove for index finger, and lanyard hole
Construction:	Full-length tang
Sheath:	Black leather belt sheath

The acronym HALO stands for High Altitude Low Opening - a parachuting tactic used by special forces for covert insertion into enemy-held territory. The use of this term as a name for this Blackjack knife clearly implies that it is intended for special forces use and its general design would appear to confirm this.

The Blackjack HALO is a solidly built, medium-sized combat knife, measuring 10in. overall, with an extended clip blade in the Randall style.

The handle is a solid, rectangular section, slab of micarta, with four deep finger grooves and a thick, straight brass double guard. The knife comes with a lined black Cordura belt sheath with leg tie.

This is a hefty general purpose combat knife, well suited to most field chores, and which would prove effective as a fighter when needed.

Manufacturer:	Blackjack Knives, Effingham, Illinois, USA
Model:	HALO
Length overall:	10in.
Blade length:	5 1/2in.
Blade shape:	Clip-point with extended false back edge
Blade material:	Carbon steel, satin finish
Edge:	Bevel-grind
Grip:	Black micarta with four pronounced finger grooves, and lanyard hole
Construction:	Brass double hilt
Sheath:	Black Cordura belt sheath with leg tie

Blackjack Knives produce a number of knives in their 1-7 series, all of which are modern copies of the famous Randall Model 1 combat knife.

The story goes that Walter Doane 'Bo' Randall began making knives in 1937, when he could not find another knife like one he had seen made by Bill Scagle. What began as a hobby became a flourishing business after Captain Zacharias of the US Navy asked Randall to make him a fighting knife, shortly before the USA entered the Second World War. The design became known as the Model 1, or 'All Purpose Fighting Knife'. As Randall's reputation spread, he received orders from US servicemen all over the world - including Captain Ronald Reagan of the USAAF.

Later designs included the Model 2 'Fighting Stiletto', inspired by the Fairbairn-Sykes Fighting Knife, the Bowie bladed Model 14 'Attack', and a hollow-handled sawback survival knife, the Model 18 'Attack Survival'.

Randall's Model 1 was offered with a 6in., 7in. or 8in. blade of 1/4in. stock, in a choice of carbon steel or stainless. Blackjack's modern reproductions are carbon steel, with a 7in. blade.

Randall's original knives had stacked leather washer or micarta handles. The current Blackjack models offer these options as well as staghorn. As with the originals, the Blackjack 1-7 may be obtained with or without a steel butt; decorative spacers are used between the handle itself and the guard and/or butt. One model, the Subhilt, has a single guard 1 1/8in. back from the double guard. This acts as a finger groove and provides extra grip.

The Randall Model 1 and its modern copies is one of the most highly prized fighting/combat knife designs among US and other servicemen around the world, which have seen extensive use in conflicts since the Second World War.

Manufacturer:	Blackjack Knives, Effingham, Illinois, USA
Model:	Classic Model 1-7
Length overall:	12in.
Blade length:	7in.
Blade shape:	Randall-style Bowie
Blade material:	Carbon steel
Edge:	Bevel-grind
Grip:	Stacked leather washer (micarta or staghorn also available)
Construction:	Handle on full-length tang with brass double guard and duralumin butt
Sheath:	Leather belt sheath

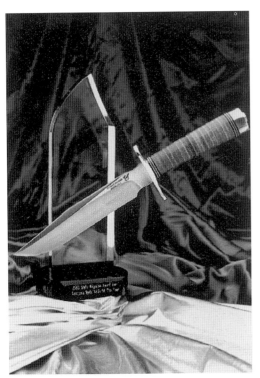

The Buck Master is perhaps the most widely known of the combat/survival knife type, encompassing popular features such as a hollow handle and sawback in a big, hefty knife. Measuring a little over 12in. overall, the Buck Master is based on the M9 bayonet design. It is a Bowie-style knife, with a 7 1/2in. clip point blade, a wide double guard, and a grooved and chequered steel tube handle with screw-on butt cap.

The blade has a plain convex main edge and a heavily serrated clip edge. On the spine of the blade is a saw-toothed edge, with rear-facing teeth. It is a versatile blade which, although not really suited to heavy chopping, will tackle most jobs required of a big knife in the field, and may also be used for fighting if necessary. The serrated clip edge can be useful for tough materials like hide and webbing, but the saw edge is much less effective than a purpose-made saw for cutting wood, bone and the like - the teeth hang up in the work and clog quickly. The saw teeth are also a distinct disadvantage if the knife is used as a fighter, as they tend to hang-up in the opponent's body, making withdrawal difficult.

The handle's grooved and chequered surface gives good grip, although being plain steel it is cold to the touch and may freeze to a bare hand in sub-zero conditions. It is also not very forgiving when the knife is used for heavy work, transmitting all the shock of heavy chopping strokes to the hand, wrist and arm. Some users wrap the handle of this knife in paracord, which not only makes the grip more comfortable but also provides a handy length of cord for emergency use.

The butt is a screw-on cap, under which is a hollow where are stored the two anchor pins. These screw into threaded holes in the guard, allowing the knife to be used as an anchor or grapple, with a line attached to the lanyard point at the butt. While this could conceivably be a useful feature in certain circumstances, users should bear in mind the consequences if the knife breaks free from its hold while there is tension on the line. A conventional grapple coming towards you at speed is bad enough, but one with a 7 1/2in. blade is doubly unpleasant.

There is sufficient space in the hollow handle to store

small survival items along with the anchor pins. If the anchor pins are discarded, of course, one may then carry considerably more survival gear.

The sheath and its accessories are an important part of the Buck Master system. The sheath is similar to that for the M9 bayonet, although it lacks the wire-cutter attachment. The sheath itself is made of rigid plastic, with a nylon webbing belt hanger and attachment slots for a webbing pouch which may be used to store small items, including a Silva compass which is available as an accessory. The sheath also incorporates a sharpening stone and has a cord leg tie.

This knife has proved popular with the civilian market and with some soldiers. My personal opinion is that the compromises necessary to provide this number of features in a knife reduce its usefulness for general tasks, and I would choose to carry a knife with a more conventional and simpler design.

Manufacturer:	Buck Knives, El Cajon, California, USA
Model:	Buck Master
Length overall:	12 1/2in.
Blade length:	7 1/2in.
Blade shape:	Bowie
Blade material:	Stainless steel. Satin or parkerised finish available
Edge:	Hollow-grind main edge; serrated clip edge; saw back
Grip:	Steel tube with grooves and chequering
Construction:	Hollow steel tube handle with screw-on butt cap; double guard
Features:	Anchor pins - stowed in handle - screw into threaded holes in guard for use as grapple. Lanyard attachment ring under pommel.
Sheath:	Plastic and Cordura sheath includes sharpening stone and attachment points for accessory pouch

The Nighthawk is a relatively recent addition to Buck's range, and one that has quickly found favour with military users. It is a medium-sized combat/field knife, with a sharply pointed 6 1/4in. straight clip blade shaped a little like the Randall Model 1. The blade is well suited for stabbing, piercing and cutting, but lacks heft and forward weight for chopping. The tip is fine enough for quite delicate work, but is not really strong enough to be used for prying. The blade has a barely discernible reverse curve, which gives it a little more cutting power.

The handle of this knife is unusual in design and proves to be very effective. It is formed of a skeleton made of hard, black, Kevlar-reinforced Zytel, with infills of soft Alcryn with a textured and pimpled surface. One large Alcryn insert forms the contoured belly of the handle, while another smaller insert is placed on top of the handle just behind the guard, where the thumb falls. The textured surface and contoured shape of the handle by themselves would give excellent grip, but added to this is the softness of the Alcryn, which yields slightly to the pressure of the hand, essentially moulding itself to the contours of the fingers. The soft handle material has another useful feature - it helps to absorb the impact of a chopping stroke, dulling any vibrations that are set up in the knife rather than transferring them to the bones of the hand and wrist. This allows the knife to be used for extended heavy tasks with comfort.

It is worth noting that, despite its contoured shape, the handle lends itself to alternative holds. It sits well in the fencing hold advocated by Fairbairn and Sykes (see entry for the Fairbairn Sykes Fighting Knife) and may also be reversed in the hand for a downward stab to the carotid or subclavian artery. The shape of the handle means that one remains aware of the knife's orientation in the hand - unlike a simple round handle which does not transmit this sense. The grip can be choked up for fine work, although the short ricasso and lack of choil mean that the first finger must remain hooked around the lower guard to avoid its being cut on the edge of the blade.

The Nighthawk comes with a well-fitted Cordura sheath, with a plastic insert for stiffness. It holds the blade well, keeping it firmly in place even if turned upside down

and shaken, and there is a press-studded retention loop for added security.

Manufacturer:	Buck Knives, El Cajon, California, USA
Model:	Nighthawk
Length overall:	11 1/4in.
Blade length:	6 1/4in.
Blade shape:	Sharply-pointed clip point design with false back edge
Blade material:	425 steel with black oxide finish
Edge:	Hollow-grind
Grip:	Kevlar reinforced Zytel ST-801, with contoured dimpled Alcryn inserts and thumb rest
Construction:	Handle moulded on to tang
Sheath:	Black Cordura belt sheath

Now being partially replaced by Eickhorn's ACK, this knife has for many years been the issue combat knife of the German *Bundeswehr*. Measuring 10 3/8in. overall, it has a relatively plain looking 5 11/16in. drop point blade of 420 stainless steel. The guard is made of steel and is extended at the bottom for extra protection of the hand. The grip is made of green plastic scales, which are held on the tang by screws, the rear one of which incorporates a lanyard hole. The handle is contoured, with a central bulge, and flares out again at grip and butt. The scabbard is made of steel, with a leather frog for attachment to the soldier's belt.

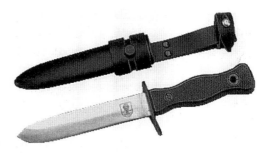

Manufacturer:	Distributed by United Cutlery, Sevierville, Tennessee, USA
Model:	UC855 Bundeswehr Knife
Length overall:	10 3/8in.
Blade length:	5 11/16in.
Blade shape:	Drop point
Blade material:	1/8in. thick 420 stainless steel
Edge:	Bevel-ground
Grip:	Green impact-resistant plastic with lanyard hole; steel crossguard
Construction:	Grip pinned to full-length tang with threaded screws
Sheath:	Metal scabbard with leather frog

The 1219C2 USMC Fighting/Utility knife has become the definitive American combat knife. It was first issued to US troops during World War II, and early models were manufactured by Union Cutlery under the Ka-Bar trademark. Consequently the design became universally known as the 'Kabar', although over the years the knife has been made by several US companies, including Case and Ontario, to Department of Defense specifications.

Camillus Cutlery Co. produced the first knives of this pattern in 1942, and their version of the 'Kabar' has long been widely respected by US soldiers. During the Vietnam War, it was issued to many personnel and was a popular private purchase for those who were not issued with it. In Vietnam and other conflicts, servicemen used the Kabar for all manner of field chores, from shelter building to preparing food, and it was widely recognised as a versatile and reliable tool.

The knife is utilitarian in looks and design. It consists of a 7in. Bowie type clip point blade, with a fuller or 'blood grove' on both sides. The clip edge is slightly concave and is sharpened. The blade is made of carbon steel, with a Parkerised protective finish. There is a straight double guard made of steel, and the handle is made of leather washers stacked on the tang and held in place with a steel butt cap pinned through the end of the tang. This cap may be used as a light hammer for tent pegs and the like.

The grooved leather handle gives a good grip, although being of a natural material it will eventually degrade in jungle conditions, despite the preservatives added by the manufacturers.

The knife comes with a black leather welted, stitched and riveted sheath, with belt loop, press studded retention loop, and a hole at the tip for a leg tie.

The Marine Combat is a compromise design, as any combat knife must be. The blade is a little light for chopping, and does not have the strength needed for heavy prying, but its relative thinness (0.16in.) helps it to cut better than a thick blade. It also keeps the knife's total weight down - an important factor for a soldier who must carry his equipment on his body. Kabars have been known to break when used for prying and throwing, but there are many reports of their effectiveness in combat. Here again, the design's compromises show up: it is not an ideal shape either for stabbing or for hacking/slashing, but combat experience has proved that it is more than capable.

An almost identical knife is available, with a brown leather grip, in a tan leather sheath stamped with the USMC initials and the globe, anchor and eagle device of the US Marine Corps

Manufacturer:	Camillus Cutlery Co., Camillus, New York, USA
Model:	Marine Combat
Length overall:	12in.
Blade length:	7in.
Blade shape:	Bowie with fuller
Blade material:	Carbon steel with protective black phosphate finish
Edge:	Bevel-ground, with sharpened clip edge
Grip:	Black leather, grooved
Construction:	Stacked leather washers on full-length tang, with steel butt-cap
Sheath:	Black leather welted sheath

The Mk 3 Trench Knife is a simple utility/fighting design, based on the M4 bayonet, but without attachments to fit it to a rifle. The blade is a parallel-sided spear point, measuring 6 3/4in. long. It has one sharp edge and a false back edge. Construction is similar to that of other US military knives, such as the Marine Combat, with a simple oval steel guard and leather washers stacked on a narrow tang and finished off with a steel butt cap pinned through the end of the tang.

This is a good, dependable utility/fighter, with the added advantage that its relatively cheap construction makes it dispensable and consequently, easily replaced. It is rather too light for heavy duty chopping and prying but is otherwise reliable for general jobs.

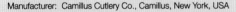

Manufacturer:	Camillus Cutlery Co., Camillus, New York, USA
Model:	Mk 3 Trench Knife
Length overall:	11 5/8in.
Blade length:	6 3/4in.
Blade shape:	Spear point
Blade material:	Carbon steel with black phosphate finish
Edge:	Bevel-grind with false back edge
Grip:	Brown leather, grooved
Construction:	Stacked leather washers on full-length tang
Sheath:	Brown leather belt sheath with leg tie

Similar in construction to that of the well-known Kabar, the USAF Pilot Survival Knife is carried by aircrew and other personnel for survival use in the event of an aircraft being forced to land in inhospitable or enemy-held territory. The knife is shorter than the Kabar types, at 9 1/2in. overall, with a 5 1/8in. blade. The blade is slightly bellied, with a concave clip edge, and has a saw-tooth back. It is coated with a protective black phosphate finish. The handle is formed from stacked brown leather washers and topped off with a hexagonal pommel which may be used for hammering.

This knife is smaller and lighter than the standard Kabar types, making it easier for aircrew to carry on their clothing without its getting in the way. However, it is a strong and versatile knife which has proved invaluable, both for survival tasks like shelter building and as a last-ditch fighting weapon. It should be noted, however, that any saw back may hang-up in an opponent's body and be difficult to withdraw, with potentially disastrous consequences.

The Camillus version comes with a light tan leather belt sheath, with a pouch for a sharpening stone. Many service personnel dispose of the stone, and replace it with a small Swiss Army type knife for delicate tasks, creating a highly versatile package which occupies little space and weight.

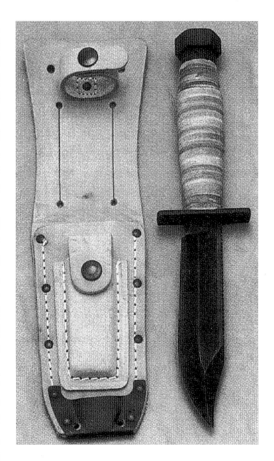

Manufacturer:	Camillus Cutlery Co., Camillus, New York, USA
Model:	Pilot Survival Knife
Length overall:	9 1/2in.
Blade length:	5 1/8in.
Blade shape:	Bowie with saw back
Blade material:	Carbon steel with protective black phosphate finish
Edge:	Bevel-ground, with false clip edge and saw-tooth back edge
Grip:	Brown leather, grooved, with hexagonal steel pommel
Construction:	Stacked leather washers on full-length tang
Sheath:	Brown leather sheath with sharpening stone in pouch

The Chris Reeve Aviator is based firmly on the USAF-issue Pilot Survival knife, and at first glance closely resembles it in size and blade shape. Indeed, the Aviator is made for the same purpose, but any similarity ends there. Chris Reeve knives are made from a single piece of steel, a design trait which completely side-steps any problems of strength at the join of tang and blade; the handle and blade are one continuous piece of steel. Like all Chris Reeve knives, the Aviator is also finished to a much higher standard than is possible in a mass-produced, military-issue knife.

The Aviator is made from A2 steel, measures 8in. overall and weighs 5 1/2oz. The 4in. blade is a Bowie style, with a straight false edge clip, and there is a saw-toothed edge on the spine. This saw is said by Reeve to be designed for versatility rather than excellence in any one task - 'it can be used to saw most material, although none perfectly'.

The handle is tubular and has a chequered surface for extra grip. A narrow section near the guard allows the knife to be grasped firmly by the thumb and first finger. The handle is hollow and capped by a hexagonal, screw-on pommel with a lanyard hole. The pommel is designed to screw up to the shoulder of the threaded section, so that it may be used for hammering without damaging the threads. A neoprene O-ring seals the recess inside, which may be used to store matches and other small survival items.

The Aviator, like other Chris Reeve designs, is highly regarded, and a popular private purchase item with military personnel. Users report that one of its few drawbacks is the grip, which being bare steel is cold to the touch in low temperatures and may turn in the hand owing to its round cross-section.

The knife comes with a pancake-style leather sheath with belt slots.

Manufacturer:	Chris Reeve, Boise, Idaho, USA
Model:	Aviator
Length overall:	8in.
Blade length:	4in.
Blade shape:	Clip point with saw back
Blade material:	A2 steel, Kal-Gard coated
Edge:	Bevel-ground with false clip edge, and saw-tooth back
Grip:	One-piece chequered, tubular section steel, with lanyard hole in hexagonal pommel
Construction:	Ground from single piece of steel; hollow handle with screw-on pommel
Sheath:	Flat 'pancake' leather sheath with twin slits for webbing or belt

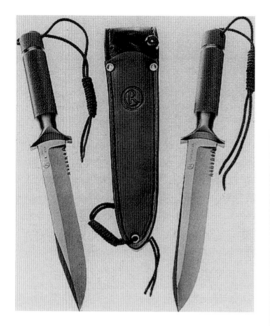

a nylon stud for retention, which holds the knife firmly in place even when it is worn inverted on webbing, but can be pushed out of engagement with the thumb as the knife is withdrawn. The stud can be fitted on the right or the left of the sheath for the correspondingly handed user.

Manufacturer:	Chris Reeve, Boise, Idaho, USA
Model:	Project I
Length overall:	12 3/4in.
Blade length:	7 1/2in.
Blade shape:	Spear point with serrated section near hilt (Project II has clip point blade shape)
Blade material:	A2 steel, Kal-Gard coated
Edge:	Bevel-ground
Grip:	One-piece chequered, tubular section steel, with lanyard hole in matching pommel
Construction:	Ground from single piece of steel; hollow handle with screw-on pommel
Sheath:	Leather sheath with leg tie and nylon retaining stud

The Chris Reeve Project I and II were designed in conjunction with Sgt Karl Lippard, who served with the USMC and wrote *The Warrior*. Like the Aviator, they are one-piece designs, made from a single piece of A2 steel. This makes them immensely strong, while leaving a hollow handle which may be used for the storage of small survival items (see the Aviator, for a description of the general construction).

The Project I and II were designed to fulfil all the functions that Sgt Lippard felt were vital for a knife carried by a Marine. The 7 1/2in. blade will chop, dig and cut, and has sufficient 'meat' up front for maximum strength and good balance. The wave serrations on the main edge are shaped to cut easily through nylon cord or webbing. The 2in. cross guard has a night index which tells the user by touch which way up the knife is in the hand.

The Project I has an immensely strong spear point blade, which gives a particularly strong tip for digging and prying. The Project II has a more traditionally styled clip point blade, giving a finer point which is still more than strong enough for most jobs. Both knives are 12 3/4in. long overall, have 7 1/2in. blades, and weigh 14oz.

The Project knives come with a stitched and riveted black leather sheath with belt loop and leg tie. There is

The Shadow III and IV are two more in Chris Reeve's one-piece knife range; see the descriptions of his Aviator and Project knives for details of their general construction. The Shadow III is 8in. overall, with a 4in. spear point blade, and weighs 6oz. The Shadow IV is larger at 10 1/2in. overall, weighing 11 1/2oz with a 5 1/2in. blade. Both knives have double guard and are noted for the strength of the spear point tip. Reeve says that this design 'has been used by professional soldiers all over the world, who have found them to be extremely good weapons as well as rugged dependable tools.'

Manufacturer:	Chris Reeve, Boise, Idaho, USA
Model:	Shadow IV
Length overall:	10 1/2in. (Shadow III 8in.)
Blade length:	5 1/2in. (Shadow III 4in.)
Blade shape:	Spear point
Blade material:	A2 steel, Kal-Gard coated
Edge:	Bevel-ground, with false back edge
Grip:	One-piece chequered, tubular section steel, with lanyard hole in matching pommel
Construction:	Ground from single piece of steel; hollow handle with screw-on pommel
Sheath:	Slim symmetrical sheath with snap loop over crossguard and snap fastener on belt loop. (Shadow III has flat 'pancake' leather sheath with twin slits for webbing or belt)

Cold Steel's Black Bear Classic is a sub-hilt design first developed by Bob Loveless. It is primarily intended as a fighter, with an 8in. blade that gives good reach and excellent penetration. The sub-hilt gives a very firm hold, and aids withdrawal of the knife from an opponent's body, although restricting the use of alternative holds.

The blade is almost a dagger shape, with a diamond-shaped cross-section, but with a vestigial clip point. The knife is available with the back edge sharpened or unsharpened. It is made from the same high carbon stainless steel that is used in Cold Steel's Tanto series.

The handle is formed from micarta scales, which are pinned to the full tang, and the whole knife is buffed to a lustrous shine.

This is an impressive looking fighting knife but it is versatile enough to be used for a variety of jobs in the field.

Manufacturer:	Cold Steel Inc., Ventura, California, USA
Model:	Black Bear Classic
Length overall:	13 1/2in.
Blade length:	8 1/4in.
Blade shape:	Double-edged, close to dagger style, but with slight clip point (unsharpened back edge model available)
Blade material:	3/16in. thick, high carbon stainless steel
Edge:	Double edged, hollow-ground
Grip:	Black micarta handle with stainless guard and single guard subhilt; lanyard hole
Construction:	Micarta scales pinned to full tang
Sheath:	Black leather belt sheath with sharpening stone in pouch

The Bush Ranger was designed by Lynn C Thompson to fulfil the need for a rugged but light sheath knife that was large enough to be useful in a real emergency, but light enough to be worn on the belt every day in the field. Its performance belies its light weight of 8.8oz, and size of 12 1/2in. overall.

The blade is Bowie shaped, and is flat ground for maximum cutting performance. The main edge is curved continuously from the choil to the tip, giving a highly efficient draw cut. There is extra belly at the tip which is a bonus for field dressing and the skinning of game. The concave clip gives a sharp tip for piercing, which is nonetheless remarkably strong and resistant to breaking or bending.

The handle has a deep belly which fills the hand well, and its chequered Kraton rubber surface gives excellent grip, even in wet conditions.

The Bush Ranger comes with a black Cordura nylon sheath with a leg tie and double retaining straps. The knife is available with a black epoxy powder coated Carbon V steel blade, or a bright AUS 8A stainless steel version.

Manufacturer:	Cold Steel Inc., Ventura, California, USA
Model:	Bush Ranger
Length overall:	12 1/2in.
Blade length:	7 1/2in.
Blade shape:	Deep-bladed Bowie style
Blade material:	Available in AUS 8A stainless steel or black epoxy coated Carbon V steel
Edge:	Flat-ground with false clip edge
Grip:	One-piece black Kraton rubber handle in deep bellied shape, incorporating double guard and lanyard hole
Construction:	Kraton handle moulded to full-length tang
Sheath:	Black Cordura belt sheath

Cold Steel's R1 Military Classic is a modern copy of the Randall Model 1; see Blackjack Model 1-7 for details of this classic military knife.

Cold Steel make their model R1 from the same stainless steel used in their famous Tanto series. The double guard is fashioned from 300 series stainless steel, and the handle is black linen micarta with coloured fibre spacers.

The knife comes with a brown leather belt sheath, a long press-studded retaining strap and a pocket for a sharpening stone.

Manufacturer:	Cold Steel Inc., Ventura, California, USA
Model:	R1 Military Classic
Length overall:	11 7/8in.
Blade length:	7in.
Blade shape:	Randall-style straight-clip Bowie
Blade material:	3/16in. thick 400 series stainless steel
Edge:	Bevel-ground
Grip:	Contoured black linen micarta handle
Construction:	Handle fitted to full-length tang, with stainless double guard and coloured fibre spacers
Sheath:	Brown leather belt sheath with sharpening stone in pouch

The Cold Steel Recon Scout is essentially a scaled-down version of the company's Trail Master Bowie. Measuring 12 1/2in. overall, it has a 7 1/2in. Bowie-style clip point blade which is flat ground. The back edge is false ground and slightly concave. The blade is made from Carbon V steel, and has a baked-on black epoxy finish which resists corrosion and minimises reflections.

There is a straight double guard, and the handle is made of Kraton rubber, chequered for extra grip, with a brass-lined lanyard hole.

Cold Steel describe the Recon Scout as 'the strongest, toughest 7 1/2in. combat knife in the world' - not a claim that a company with their reputation would make lightly. Certainly the 'torture tests' shown in their catalogue photographs would appear to bear this out.

Manufacturer:	Cold Steel Inc., Ventura, California, USA
Model:	Recon Scout
Length overall:	12 1/2in.
Blade length:	7 1/2in.
Blade shape:	Clip point
Blade material:	5/16in. thick Carbon V steel, black epoxy powder coated
Edge:	Flat-ground with false back edge
Grip:	One-piece chequered black Kraton rubber with lanyard hole
Construction:	Kraton handle moulded to full-length tang
Sheath:	Black Cordura belt sheath

The Cold Steel SRK was designed by Lynn C Thompson as a versatile knife for survival/rescue operations - a knife that would be able to withstand extreme abuse. The blade is made of 3/16in. thick Carbon V steel, finished with black epoxy powder coating. It measures 6in. long, and has a Bowie-style clip point blade, bevel-ground in a sweeping curve for good cutting performance. The clip shape gives a fine point for good penetration and detailed work, while the blade is also heavy enough for light chopping.

The handle is Kraton rubber, with a contoured shape and integral single guard. This allows the grip to be 'choked up' for fine work. The soft, chequered surface gives a good grip in virtually any conditions and helps to absorb the shocks of use rather than transmit them to the bones of the hand and wrist.

The knife comes with a black Cordura belt sheath with a leg tie.

Manufacturer:	Cold Steel Inc., Ventura, California, USA
Model:	SRK
Length overall:	10 5/8in.
Blade length:	6in.
Blade shape:	Clip point
Blade material:	Carbon V steel, black epoxy powder coated
Edge:	Bevel-ground with false back edge
Grip:	One-piece chequered black Kraton rubber with lanyard hole
Construction:	Kraton handle moulded to full-length tang
Sheath:	Black Cordura belt sheath

Cold Steel's Trailmaster Bowie is a large, high performance knife designed by Lynn C Thompson. It measures 14 1/2in. overall and weighs just over 1lb, with a 9 1/2in. Bowie blade of 5/16in. thick Carbon V steel. The blade is hardened and tempered to give exceptional strength and flexibility. The false clip edge is slightly concave, with extra thickness near the tip, making it extremely resistant to breaking or bending. The blade is flat-ground for good cutting and slicing performance, and honed to a very sharp edge. The balance of the knife is approximately 3/4in. in front of the guard, which gives a blade-heavy feel that increases the power of chopping and slashing strokes.

The handle is 5in. long and made of chequered Kraton rubber, which gives it a non-slip, shock-absorbing grip. The cross section is contoured to help in preventing the knife turning in the hand. The double guard is relatively short so that it does not tend to become snagged in clothing or equipment.

The Trailmaster is a big, powerful knife with quite astonishing chopping and slashing performance - a photo-sequence in Cold Steel's catalogue shows Thompson chopping clean through a rope as thick as his arm with a single stroke. The knife is also extremely robust, yet remains capable of quite delicate work. It makes a highly versatile, heavy-duty field knife, which also has awesome capabilities as a fighter.

Manufacturer:	Cold Steel Inc., Ventura, California, USA
Model:	Trailmaster Bowie
Length overall:	14 1/2in.
Blade length:	9 1/2in.
Blade shape:	Bowie
Blade material:	5/16in. thick triple tempered carbon V steel
Edge:	Flat-ground with false clip edge
Grip:	One-piece chequered black Kraton rubber with lanyard hole
Construction:	Kraton handle moulded to full-length tang
Sheath:	Black Cordura belt sheath with leg tie

The Collins/Parry Knife was the result of collaboration between Steve Collins, a designer and martial artist, and Mel Parry, who served with British special forces. Their aim was to produce the definitive combat survival knife - a true working tool. The knife is fairly simple at first glance, with a bellied Bolo-type clipped blade. But on closer inspection it offers several different cutting edges and holds, making it extremely versatile.

The knife is strong and heavy, with the blade made from 1/4in. thick high tensile carbon spring steel hardened to 57-58 Rc. The main edge is bevel-ground for strength. The deep belly shape takes the weight forward, giving the knife a powerful chopping stroke. The point looks clipped in shape but is ground as a spear point, which is strong enough for digging and prying. Near the choil is a hollow-ground section which can be honed to razor sharpness for fine cutting and whittling jobs such as making fire sticks. On the spine of the blade is a serrated edge which may be used for sawing through rope, webbing or gristle.

The knife is of full-tang construction, with micarta scales screwed to the tang. These are contoured with a deep belly and chequered for extra grip. The steel double guard is also contoured, with its lines flowing continuously into the scales, to be kinder on the hand. It is designed with relatively short guards so that one can choke up the grip for fine work - the ricasso is extended and has finger grooves which make the choke grip firm and comfortable.

The steel butt is squared off on two sides so that it may be used as a hammer in either direction. The flats are file-cut to reduce any tendency for them to skid off the work on striking. The butt also incorporates a lanyard hole.

A variation on the original design has the blade angled downwards, in the manner of a kukri.

I first handled this knife at the COPEX show in 1995 and was immediately impressed with its heft and handling. It is a true working tool, designed by people who use knives professionally and know what is needed in a combat survival knife. I was told that the knife had been selected for Richard Branson's attempt at a round-the-world balloon flight, and that several special forces units had shown interest. At the time of writing, however, the knife has not gone into production and only a few pre-production models exist. With the current British political climate, it is doubtful whether the Collins/Parry Knife will ever become widely available, which would be a loss to military and civilians alike.

Manufacturer:	Portfolio Section V, Stockport, Cheshire, UK
Model:	Collins/Parry Knife
Length overall:	13 3/4in.
Blade length:	8 3/4in.
Blade shape:	Bolo/Bowie-type with serrated back edge
Blade material:	1/4in. thick high tensile carbon spring steel EN9
Edge:	Main edge bevel-ground; hollow ground section near choil for extra sharpness
Grip:	Chequered and contoured micarta scales. Contoured double guard and butt, the butt squared off and file-cut for use as hammer
Construction:	Scales screwed to full tang
Sheath:	Leather belt sheath with leg tie

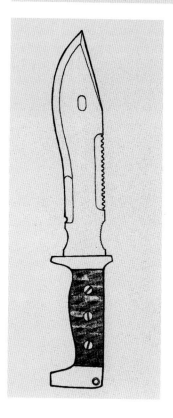

Developed for the German *Bundeswehr* in the late 1980s, Eickhorn's ACK is a modern, multi-function combat knife with many advanced features. As well as the *Bundeswehr*, it has since been adopted by a number of other military forces around the world.

The knife is basically a Bowie-type combat knife with a moulded plastic handle. It is remarkably light, at around 220g, or a total of 430g with sheath. The blade is carbon steel, with a black chemical finish, and has a bevel-ground main edge and concave false clip edge. The spine has a sophisticated saw edge, with teeth set alternately left and right to remove material to the thickness of the blade; this avoids the blade's jamming as it saws through wood, bone or the like.

The moulded plastic handle is contoured and grooved for grip and incorporates a double guard. The handle is flattened at the sides, giving the knife a thinner profile so that it rides less obtrusively on the belt. Set into the top guard is a steel extension which may be used as a bottle opener and has a notch for wire stripping. The handle has a hollow compartment which can store small survival items.

The scabbard has a quick-release clip so that it may be removed from the belt and used in conjunction with the knife to form a scissor-action wire cutter. There is also a screwdriver at the tip of the scabbard.

The knife is electrically insulated and resistant to fungal and NBC agents. It is tested to between -40 and +80°C, and may be decontaminated.

Manufacturer:	Eickhorn GmbH, Solingen, Germany
Model:	ACK (Advanced Combat Knife)
Length overall:	11 11/16in.
Blade length:	6 5/8in.
Blade shape:	Bowie-type clip point
Blade material:	Carbon steel with black chemical finish
Edge:	Bevel-ground
Grip:	Moulded contoured, glass-reinforced plastic with grooves, incorporating double guard
Construction:	Plastic grip moulded on to tang
Sheath:	Rigid plastic sheath incorporating wire-cutter attachment and sharpening stone, with detachable hanger with clip for military web belt

The Eickhorn KCB 77 CS is identical to the company's KCB 77 bayonet, except that it does not have the fittings for attachment to an assault rifle. Refer to the relevant entry earlier for details.

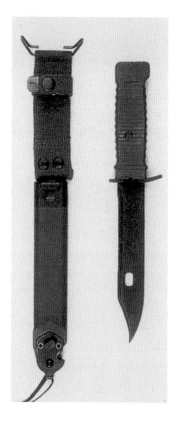

Manufacturer: Eickhorn GmbH, Solingen, Germany

Model: ACK (Advanced Combat Knife)

Length overall: 11 11/16in.

Blade length: 6 5/8in.

Blade shape: Clip point

Blade material: Carbon steel with corrosion-resistant black finish

Edge: Bevel-ground

Grip: Ribbed and contoured plastic scales, rectangular section

Construction: Scales fitted to full-length tang

Sheath: Sophisticated rigid plastic sheath with wire cutter, screwdriver tip, and clip attachment to belt hanger

Carried by the Swedish National Defence forces, the F1 is a small utility knife with a Kraton handle and a 3 3/4in. drop point, flat ground blade. It comes in a flapped leather belt sheath.

This knife is handy for light work, but would be of little use for fighting, or for chopping or slashing. It is no bigger than many pocket folders, but offers more strength and rigidity due to its non-folding design. It is a good quality item, made from modern materials which offer high performance and resistance to corrosion.

Manufacturer:	Solingen, Germany
Model:	F1
Length overall:	8 1/4in.
Blade length:	3 3/4in.
Blade shape:	Drop point
Blade material:	ATS 34 stainless steel
Edge:	Flat-ground
Grip:	Black chequered Kraton rubber grip with lanyard hole
Construction:	Kraton grip moulded on to tang
Sheath:	Full black leather pistol flap style sheath

Gerber's BMF is a big, solid knife well capable of the heaviest chopping, hacking and slashing. Designed as 'the ultimate survival knife system', it makes a versatile field tool, as well as an effective close-combat weapon. The initials BMF stand for Basic Multi-Function, although the troops often refer to it as the 'Big Mother F***er'.

The knife is a massive 14in. overall, with a heavy 9in. Bowie-type blade with a long, straight, false edge clip. The blade is 1/4in. thick high carbon stainless steel, with a bevel-ground edge. The blade comes to a fine point at the tip, offering good penetration. A saw back version is available, although the saw has been criticised as being relatively ineffective, jamming and clogging too easily.

The handle is Hypolon rubber, which offers a soft, comfortable grip that absorbs vibration, although its smooth surface can slip in the hand under extreme conditions. The double guard has two holes, with another hole in the single butt guard. These can be used for lashing the knife to a pole for use as a spear, or to attach a lanyard. There is a truncated cone pommel which can be used as a hammer or in combat as a 'skull crusher'.

The sheath is a strong unit of Cordura, with a belt loop and Bianchi clip. There is a pouch for a Silva compass (included with the knife), and a leg tie.

The Gerber BMF is a popular private purchase among military personnel. It is a good looking and rugged field tool which can also serve as a close-combat weapon if necessary. It is immensely practical for survival tasks such as shelter building, trap making, clearing brush and heavy undergrowth, and dressing out all sizes of game. If anything it is too big for some more delicate jobs and is best carried in conjunction with a good small knife or multi-tool.

Manufacturer:	Gerber (a division of Fiskars Inc.), Portland, Oregon, USA
Model:	BMF
Length overall:	14in.
Blade length:	9in.
Blade shape:	Bowie style clip point
Blade material:	1/4in. thick, high carbon stainless steel with satin finish
Edge:	Angle-ground, clip false edge. Saw back version available
Grip:	Hypolon rubber, contoured, with double guard and single guard at butt, truncated cone pommel
Construction:	Full- length tang
Sheath:	Black Cordura lined belt sheath with leg tie, compass, and diamond sharpening stone on rear

Gerber's Bowie is a traditionally shaped, big Bowie knife, with a 9 1/2in. flat ground blade made from 5/16in. thick, high carbon stainless steel. The knife measures 14 1/2in. overall, and weighs 18oz. The handle is a 'coffin' shape and is made of Kraton rubber moulded on to a full-length tang. It has a brass double guard and a lanyard hole. The knife comes with a Cordura sheath with belt loop and leg tie.

This is a big, well-balanced, heavy knife which is well up to heavy hacking, chopping and slashing. It would make an effective survival or field tool, as well as an effective and intimidating combat weapon.

Manufacturer:	Gerber (a division of Fiskars Inc.), Portland, Oregon, USA
Model:	Bowie
Length overall:	14 1/2in.
Blade length:	9 1/2in.
Blade shape:	Bowie clip point
Blade material:	5/16in. thick, high carbon stainless steel with satin finish
Edge:	Flat ground, clip false edge
Grip:	Coffin-shaped Kraton rubber grip with brass double guard and lanyard hole
Construction:	Handle moulded on to full-length tang
Sheath:	Black Cordura belt sheath

The Gerber LMF is a scaled-down version of the BMF. The initials stand for Light Multi-Function. The basic style and construction of the knife are the same as for the BMF. The LMF measures 10 5/8in. overall, with a 6in. blade, so it is by no means a small knife, even though it is dwarfed by its big brother.

The LMF is not simply a sized-down version of the BMF, however; there are some significant differences, especially in the handle. Here there is no butt guard, and the guard and butt are shaped so that their contours are continuous with the shape of the Hypolon rubber grip, which, unlike the BMF, also has finger grooves.

Blade shape is similar to that of the BMF, and there is the same option of a saw back. The sheath is black Cordura nylon, with a belt loop and leg strap assembly, but lacks the diamond sharpening hone which is found in the BMF sheath.

Manufacturer:	Gerber (a division of Fiskars Inc.), Portland, Oregon, USA
Model:	LMF
Length overall:	10 5/8in.
Blade length:	6in.
Blade shape:	Bowie style clip point
Blade material:	1/4in. thick, high carbon stainless steel with satin finish
Edge:	Angle-ground, clip false edge. Saw back version available
Grip:	Hypolon rubber, with two finger grooves, double guard, and matching stainless pommel
Construction:	Full-length tang
Sheath:	Black Cordura lined belt sheath with leg tie

The Gerber Patriot is a solidly made and straightforward combat survival knife, with the distinctive feature that it is intended for airborne troops - it is one of the few 'jump certified' knives for paratroopers. Designed by Blackie Collins, it has a 6in. blade and measures 10 5/8in. overall. The blade is a Bowie-style, with a long clip false edge. It is made of stainless steel with a black finish. The handle is made from moulded Zytel, with chequering and longitudinal grooves for extra grip. It is contoured to provide a finger groove for the first finger. The handle is screwed through the full-length tang and there is a cylindrical butt piece with a lanyard hole.

Perhaps the most remarkable feature of this knife is its sheath. This is made of rigid black plastic which gives a high level of protection to the blade, so that the blade will not break through and injure the user if he falls on it upon landing. There is a two-stage locking mechanism which comprises a clip and locking latch.

When the knife is slid into the sheath, the clip catches the tip of the guard and clicks into place, holding the knife securely. A violent movement could cause the knife to break free, however, so the locking latch can be moved up with the thumb into the locked position. This holds the clip so that it cannot open, ensuring that the knife remains in its sheath even if it is knocked hard in a heavy fall.

I have tried the system and found it very effective. My only reservation was that the knife rattles loudly in the sheath when it is withdrawn or replaced, making it unsuitable for close observation patrols and similar types of operation.

Manufacturer:	Gerber (a division of Fiskars Inc.), Portland, Oregon, USA
Model:	Patriot
Length overall:	10 5/8in.
Blade length:	6in.
Blade shape:	Bowie-style clip point
Blade material:	0.240in. thick, high carbon stainless steel with black oxide finish
Edge:	Angle-ground, clip false edge
Grip:	Moulded Zytel handle with chequering and lateral grooves, finger groove
Construction:	Full-length tang
Sheath:	Rigid black plastic sheath incorporates safety-catch locking device that holds knife securely in an inverted position on webbing or during violent physical activity

The kukri may seem an odd knife to include in this section; it is known and feared world-wide as the fighting weapon of the Gurkhas. However, the kukri is much more than a weapon, it is a highly effective field tool which is favoured by many experts besides the Gurkhas themselves for jungle survival use.

The kukri comes in many variations, but the one described here is fairly typical of the type issued to Gurkha soldiers in the British Army. It has a heavy, downward curved blade of thick carbon steel, measuring 7/16in. at the spine. This thins towards the sharpened edge, which is bevelled. The handle is hand-carved from buffalo horn, with a pronounced flare at the butt and is fitted to a full-length tang, with brass bolster cap and butt cap. The knife comes in a wooden block sheath which is covered with black leather. It has a brass chape and a leather frog for attachment to a belt.

The kukri's weight and blade shape provide superb chopping, hacking and slashing performance. The heavy blade chops powerfully through logs and branches, and the reverse curve edge cuts deeply with little effort. The kukri is almost unmatched for heavy survival tasks such as shelter building and clearing vegetation and can also be used for surprisingly delicate work. It also excels as a close-combat weapon, where the power of its chopping stroke is legendary - tales abound of Gurkhas lopping off the heads of their enemies with a single stroke. Some of the legend and mystique surrounding the kukri is fantasy, but there is no denying that it is a very useful jungle survival tool and a highly effective weapon.

Manufacturer:	Nepalese workshops
Model:	British Army issue type
Length overall:	15 3/4in.
Blade length:	11in.
Blade shape:	Bolo type, with pronounced downward curve
Blade material:	7/16in. max. thickness carbon steel
Edge:	Bevel
Grip:	Hand-carved buffalo horn with brass bolster and butt
Construction:	Full-length tang
Sheath:	Leather-covered wooden block sheath with leather belt frog

The Aitor Jungle King II was one of the first hollow-handled survival knives and spawned many imitators. The type has rather lost credibility over the years, owing to the many cheap and inferior hollow handled knives that were sold to unsuspecting users and failed to live up to expectations. The Jungle King II, however, remains a useful knife which is considerably stronger and more practical than many of its imitators.

The knife measures approximately 10 3/4in. long, with a 5 1/2in. hollow-ground Bowie type blade with a bellied main edge and a saw back. The bellied blade provides an effective reverse curve cutting edge, but the saw teeth are not so effective, clogging and jamming too easy to be very useful. The handle is an alloy tube, with chequered bands for grip. It has an integral double guard and screw-on butt cap which gives access to the compartment inside. This contains a basic survival kit of sticking plasters, safety pins, tweezers, pencil, sewing needles and thread, scalpel blade, fishing hooks, weights and line, and a flint striker.

The rigid plastic sheath is part of the 'system', incorporating a catapult, mini heliograph, sharpening stone, and 4m of black paracord. Basic ground-to-air signalling instructions are moulded into the plastic of the sheath. Also contained in the sheath is a small skinning knife/tool which has a 1 1/2in. main blade,

gutting hook, shackle wrench, can/bottle opener and screwdriver.

The Jungle King II is often written off as a gimmicky survival knife, but it deserves more serious consideration: it is a surprisingly robust and practical tool which is perfectly capable of general camp and field tasks, with a useful array of survival items which would be welcome in an emergency.

Manufacturer:	Aitor Cuchilleria Del Norte SA, Ermua, Spain
Model:	Jungle King II
Length overall:	10 3/4in.
Blade length:	5 1/2in.
Blade shape:	Bowie, with bellied main edge
Blade material:	4mm thick chrome molybdenum vanadium stainless steel, 56-57 Rc
Edge:	Hollow-ground main edge, false clip edge, and 2 1/2in. saw toothed section on spine
Grip:	Black anodised alloy, tubular section, with chequered bands
Construction:	Short stub tang set into recess in handle
Sheath:	Green polyamide sheath with webbing belt loop, incorporating catapult, 4m paracord wrap, heliograph, sharpening stone and survival signalling instructions

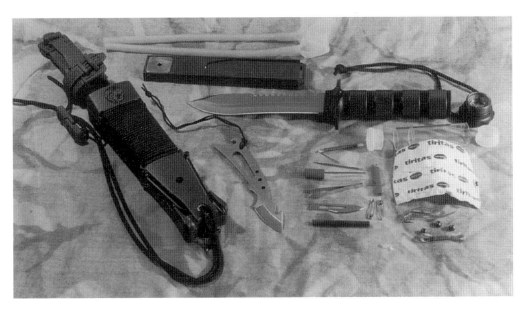

The knife universally known as the 'Ka-Bar' is the 1219C2 USMC Fighting/Utility knife which was first issued to US troops during the Second World War. Early models were manufactured by Union Cutlery under the Ka-Bar trademark, but over the years the knife has been made by several American companies, including Camillus, Case and Ontario, to Department of Defense specifications.

The background to this knife is covered in more depth earlier in this section, under the entry 'Camillus Marine Combat'

The Ka-Bar has a 6 7/8in. Bowie-type clip point blade, with a fuller or 'blood grove' on both sides. The clip edge is concave. The blade is made of carbon steel with a black protective finish. There is a straight double guard made of steel and the handle is made of brown leather washers stacked on the tang and held in place by a steel butt cap pinned through the end of the tang. This cap can be used as a light hammer.

The sheath is of brown leather, stitched and stapled, with the initials USMC and the US Marines globe, eagle and anchor symbol.

Manufacturer:	Ka-Bar Knives, part of Alcas Corp., Olean, New York, USA
Model:	USMC Fighting Knife
Length overall:	11 7/8in.
Blade length:	6 7/8in.
Blade shape:	Bowie with fuller
Blade material:	Carbon steel with protective black finish
Edge:	Bevel-ground, with false clip edge
Grip:	Brown leather, grooved, with steel butt-cap
Construction:	Stacked leather washers on full-length tang
Sheath:	Brown leather sheath with USMC logo

Ka-Bar developed their 'Next Generation' Fighting Knife as the successor to their famous USMC Fighting Knife, which has been a favourite of US servicemen for over 50 years. The Next Generation closely follows the dimensions and shape of the original Ka-Bar, but uses modern materials to provide superior performance and high resistance to corrosion.

The blade is made of high carbon stainless steel which is highly corrosion resistant. The handle is moulded Kraton, with a contoured shape and deep lateral grooves to improve the grip. The guard is single and is contoured to flow smoothly into the line of the handle. Likewise the stainless steel butt piece follows the curve of the handle and provides a surface for hammering as well as a lanyard hole.

The sheath has been brought up to date, too. It is made of moulded black Kydex in a rectangular shape and has a belt hanger and holes for a leg tie.

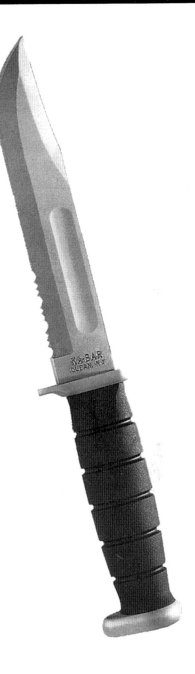

Manufacturer:	Ka-Bar Knives, part of Alcas Corp., Olean, New York, USA
Model:	Fighting Knife - The Next Generation
Length overall:	11 7/8in.
Blade length:	6 7/8in.
Blade shape:	Bowie
Blade material:	High carbon stainless steel
Edge:	Bevel-ground, with wave-form serrations on 1 3/4in. section near ricasso
Grip:	Moulded black Kraton rubber, contoured and grooved for grip
Construction:	Kraton grip fitted to full-length tang, with stainless steel single guard and butt
Sheath:	Black moulded Kydex belt sheath with leg tie

The MPK or Multi-Purpose Knife is unusual in that it is made of non-magnetic titanium alloy. It is used by US Navy SEALs and others for EOD work, as it will not affect magnetically-triggered 'influence mines'. The titanium alloy is also immensely strong, extremely resistant to corrosion, and holds a good edge, although it is so hard that it is unaffected by conventional sharpening stones and steels and must be sharpened with a special diamond hone.

The blade is 7 1/8in. long, and has a Bowie-type shape, although the clip is straight, resulting in a point almost of spear type. The edge is flat-ground, giving good cutting and slicing performance. While this type of grind is normally associated with a weaker blade, in this case the titanium is so strong that the problem does not arise. US Navy SEALs, notorious for giving their kit a hard time, used the knives for three years and never broke one. There is a 2in. serrated section near the handle which features special wave-form serrations designed to slice easily through rope, weed and the like.

The handle is made of high-performance Hytrel, a fire-resistant synthetic material, reinforced with Kevlar fibres. It is contoured to be held easily and firmly, even by a diver wearing gloves, and has longitudinal grooves for extra grip. The sheath is also made of Hytrel/Kevlar and has fittings so that it can be worn on a belt, strapped to a leg, or attached to webbing in an inverted position.

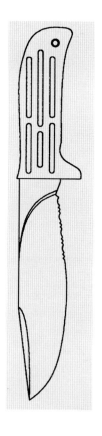

Manufacturer:	Mission Knives Inc., San Juan, California, USA
Model:	MPK
Length overall:	12 1/8in.
Blade length:	7 1/8in.
Blade shape:	Bowie with straight clip and bellied main edge
Blade material:	Mission Knives proprietary Beta-Titanium alloy
Edge:	Flat-grind, with wave-form serrations on 2in. section near handle
Grip:	Hytrel fire-resistant synthetic, reinforced with Kevlar, longitudinally grooved for grip
Construction:	Hytrel handle moulded on to full-length tang
Sheath:	Hytrel and Kevlar moulded sheath may be worn on belt, strapped to leg, or attached to webbing

The MoD Survival Knife is about as simple as a knife can be. It is basically a thick steel bar, with a sharpened edge at one end and wooden scales riveted on to the other to form a handle. The design is much like the British Army Golok, but with a shorter, stubbier blade.

It is a heavy, bulky knife, measuring 12 1/4in. long and weighing a little over 1lb 2oz. The blade is made of 1/4in. thick carbon steel, 7in. long and 1 5/8in. from spine to edge. The edge grind is quite steep, leaving plenty of meat in the blade for strength and heft. The weight is well forward, making this a good chopping and hammering tool, and the broad shape and strong tip make it excellent for digging and prying too. There is an oval double guard, which is spot welded to the tang at top and bottom.

The knife has a couple of drawbacks. First the handle, which is rather hard on the hands when used for heavy work: the large rivet holes, the less than perfect fit between wood and metal, and the lack of any vibration-absorbing ability combine to make this knife uncomfortable to use for extended periods with unprotected hands. Wrapping the handle with paracord helps to alleviate this and also provides a reserve supply of cordage for emergencies. Secondly, the knife is a purely heavy-duty

tool and is too clumsy for fine work. It really needs to be carried in conjunction with a Swiss Army Knife or Leatherman type multi-tool.

As a basic heavy chopper, this knife takes a lot of beating, however, and proves excellent at survival tasks from shelter building to digging a solar still or butchering large game. For these sorts of task, it is favoured by many of Britain's special forces.

Manufacturer:	Wilkinson Sword, England
Model:	Survival Knife
Length overall:	12 1/4in.
Blade length:	7in.
Blade shape:	Drop point
Blade material:	Carbon steel
Edge:	Bevel-ground
Grip:	Wooden scales
Construction:	Scales riveted to full tang with three large copper rivets
Sheath:	Simple brown leather sheath, stitched and riveted, with belt loop and press-studded retaining strap

This knife is Ontario's version of the Ka-Bar, officially designated the 1219C2 USMC Fighting/Utility knife, which was first issued to US troops during the Second World War. Ontario is one of several manufacturers who have made this knife to Department of Defense specifications.

The background to this knife is covered in more depth earlier, under the entry Camillus Marine Combat.

Manufacturer:	Ontario Knife Co., Franklinville, New York, USA
Model:	Marine Corps Combat Knife
Length overall:	12in.
Blade length:	7in.
Blade shape:	Bowie with blood groove. Saw back version available
Blade material:	Black-finished carbon steel
Edge:	Angle-grind
Grip:	Black leather
Construction:	Stacked leather washer handle secured by steel butt cap
Sheath:	Black leather belt sheath

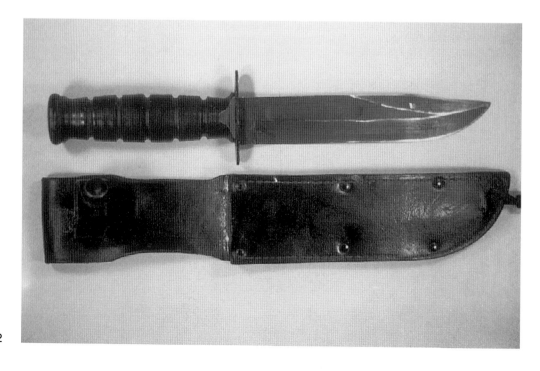

This knife is Ontario's version of the Navy Knife issued to US troops for many years. Ontario is one of several companies who have made this knife to Department of Defense specifications.

The knife is similar to the US Marine Corps Combat Knife, but has a number of differences to make it more suitable for use by the US Navy. The blade is made of stainless steel and finished with a protective black coating. The blade is shorter than that of the USMC Knife, at 6in., and has a pronounced concave sharpened clip edge which results in a very fine point. There is a saw back which is useful for cutting through weed, rope and the like.

Clearly a stacked leather washer handle would not survive long in marine conditions, and on the Navy Knife the handle is made of moulded black plastic pieces, contoured and chequered for grip and screwed to the full-length tang.

The sheath is made of rigid black plastic, with a Cordura hanger and a clip for a military web belt.

Manufacturer:	Ontario Knife Co., Franklinville, New York, USA
Model:	Navy Knife
Length overall:	10 7/8in.
Blade length:	6in.
Blade shape:	Bowie with serrated back and deep clip
Blade material:	Black finished stainless steel
Edge:	Angle-grind
Grip:	Moulded black plastic
Construction:	Grip screwed through tang
Sheath:	US Navy issue knife

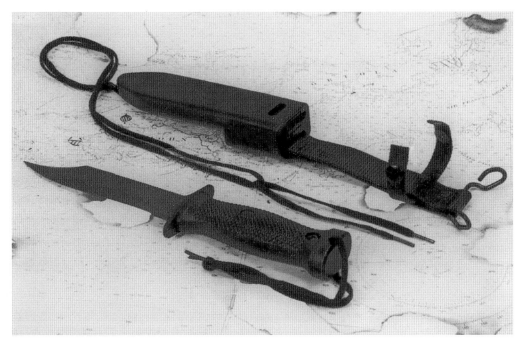

This knife is Ontario's version of the Navy Knife issued to US troops for many years. Ontario is one of several companies who have made this knife to Department of Defense specifications.

The knife is similar to the US Marine Corps Combat Knife, but has a number of differences to make it more suitable for use by the US Navy. The blade is made of stainless steel and finished with a protective black coating. The blade is shorter than that of the USMC Knife, at 6in., and has a pronounced concave sharpened clip edge which results in a very fine point. There is a saw back which is useful for cutting through weed, rope and the like.

Clearly a stacked leather washer handle would not survive long in marine conditions, and on the Navy Knife the handle is made of moulded black plastic pieces, contoured and chequered for grip and screwed to the full-length tang.

The sheath is made of rigid black plastic, with a Cordura hanger and a clip for a military web belt.

Manufacturer:	Ontario Knife Co., Franklinville, New York, USA
Model:	Navy Knife
Length overall:	10 7/8in.
Blade length:	6in.
Blade shape:	Bowie with serrated back and deep clip
Blade material:	Black finished stainless steel
Edge:	Angle-grind
Grip:	Moulded black plastic
Construction:	Grip screwed through tang
Sheath:	US Navy issue knife

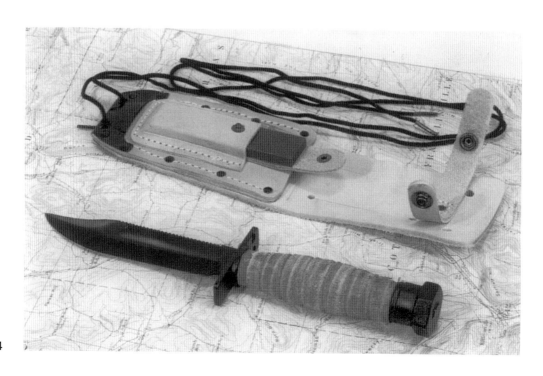

The SOG Bowie is the company's original flagship model and was developed for the US 5th Special Forces in the Vietnam War for reconnaissance, infiltration and behind-the-lines operations.

The knife measures 10 3/4in. overall, with a blade of unusually thick (0.28in.) SK5 carbon tool steel hardened to Rc 57-58. The main edge has a deep hollow grind and there is a distinctive double concave clip on the back edge. The tip is faceted to give superb penetration and fine point work. The blade is engraved with the crest and logo of US Special Forces in Vietnam.

The handle is made of stacked leather washers, with white fibre spacers at either end. The double guard and butt are made of blued steel and are contoured to follow the lines of the grip. This gives the knife a more comfortable grip, as well as adding to its fine looks.

Manufacturer:	SOG Knives, Edmonds, Washington, USA
Model:	Bowie
Length overall:	10 3/4in.
Blade length:	6 1/4in.
Blade shape:	Bowie
Blade material:	SK-5 carbon tool steel, with blued finish
Edge:	Hollow-ground; false back edge
Grip:	Natural leather
Construction:	Stacked leather washer grip on full-length tang; blued steel crossguard and butt, held in place by aircraft spanner nut
Sheath:	Leather pouch with sharpening stone

The SOG Government model is a Bowie-type knife with a 6 1/4in. blade of 440A stainless steel and a chequered Kraton handle (Kraton has a slightly 'tacky' feel in wet conditions, and tends to adhere to the hand, giving a sure grip). The crossguard and pommel are of stainless steel, and the guard is soldered to the blade to keep out moisture. The blade is bevel-ground with a straight clip.

The SOG Government is a straightforward design which uses advanced materials for superior performance. It is a good, all-round, field knife, which is capable of being used as a fighter if necessary.

Manufacturer:	SOG Knives, Edmonds, Washington, USA
Model:	Government (Recon Government version available with deep blued finish to all metal parts)
Length overall:	11 1/4in.
Blade length:	6 1/4in.
Blade shape:	Bowie
Blade material:	440-A stainless steel, Rc 57-58
Edge:	Bevel-ground
Grip:	One-piece Kraton grip with wrap-round chequering
Construction:	Full-length tang
Sheath:	Nylon belt sheath

Designed for the US Navy SEALs, the SOG Seal Knife 2000 is a strong, high-performance knife which is highly resistant to sea water. It measures 12 1/4in. overall, with a 7in. Parkerised 440-A stainless steel blade hardened to Rc 55-56. The blade shape is along similar lines to SOG's successful Bowie and Trident models, with a double concave clip which extends almost the full length of the back edge. There is a 1 1/2in. serrated section on the main edge near the hilt.

The handle is made of contoured black Zytel, with chequering and finger grooves for grip and an integral guard. The knife comes with a black nylon belt sheath with leg tie.

Manufacturer:	SOG Knives, Edmonds, Washington, USA
Model:	SEAL Knife 2000
Length overall:	12 1/4in.
Blade length:	7in.
Blade shape:	Bowie with double concave clip
Blade material:	1/4in. thick 440-A stainless steel, Rc 55-56, Parkerised
Edge:	Bevel-ground, with 1 1/2in. serrated section near hilt
Grip:	One-piece Kraton grip with chequering and finger grooves
Construction:	Handle moulded to full-length tang
Sheath:	Black nylon belt sheath with leg tie

The SOG Tech is a knife that combines an established blade and handle shape with modern materials for good looks and performance. There are two models, the 5 3/4in. blade Tech I, and the 7 1/4in. blade Tech II. Both models feature the double concave clip blade seen on SOG's highly respected Bowie and Trident models.

The handles are of contoured black Kraton rubber, with a chequered non-slip surface, and brass guard. Each knife comes with a black nylon belt sheath, with leg tie.

These are multi-purpose knives which may be used for most field tasks and will also serve as effective fighters when circumstances require.

Manufacturer:	SOG Knives, Edmonds, Washington, USA
Model:	SOG-Tech II (SOG-Tech I similar but 11in. overall, and with 6in. blade)
Length overall:	12 1/2in.
Blade length:	7 1/4in.
Blade shape:	Clip point
Blade material:	1/4in. thick 440-A stainless steel, Rc 56-57
Edge:	Bevel-ground
Grip:	One-piece Kraton grip with wrap-round chequering and lanyard hole
Construction:	Full-length tang construction, with brass crossguard
Sheath:	Nylon scabbard

The SOG Tigershark follows the same lines as the company's famous Bowie and Trident models, but is considerably larger at 14in. overall with a 9in. carbon steel blade. It has a one-piece, contoured Kraton rubber handle, with integral double guard and non-slip chequered surface.

This is a big, powerful knife that offers useful chopping, hacking and slashing performance, while remaining capable of more delicate work. Penetration by the sharply pointed tip is excellent.

The Tigershark is a versatile knife which will cope admirably with most tasks requiring a big knife, and makes a formidable fighter as well as a highly effective combat survival knife. It is also available with a gun-blue finish as the Midnite Tiger.

Manufacturer:	SOG Knives, Edmonds, Washington, USA
Model:	Tigershark
Length overall:	14in.
Blade length:	9in.
Blade shape:	Clip point
Blade material:	1/4in. thick carbon steel, Rc 56-57
Edge:	Bevel-ground
Grip:	Moulded Kraton grip with wrap-round chequering and lanyard hole
Construction:	Handle moulded to full-length tang
Sheath:	Nylon belt sheath

The SOG Trident is a development of the company's renowned Bowie, with almost identical dimensions and lines. However, it makes use of more modern materials for better all-round performance and resistance to corrosion.

The blade is hand ground from 440C stainless steel, hardened to Rc 57-58. The handle is black micarta with white spacers, and the contoured double guard and pommel are of stainless steel. The knife comes with a waterproof black nylon sheath with leg tie.

Manufacturer:	SOG Knives, Edmonds, Washington, USA
Model:	Trident
Length overall:	10 3/4in.
Blade length:	6 1/4in.
Blade shape:	Clip point
Blade material:	0.28in. thick 440-C stainless steel, Rc 57-58
Edge:	'Surgical'-ground, faceted tip
Grip:	Stacked Micarta handle, steel pommel with lanyard hole
Construction:	Full-length tang construction
Sheath:	Nylon scabbard

Ontario Knife Co. are one of a number of manufacturers who make the US forces issue knives such as the Marine Combat, Air Force Survival and Navy Knives.

Spec Plus is the company's vision of the next generation of military knives, offering the same proven blade shapes but with improved handles of Kraton rubber, with integral guards. Blade material is generally thicker and the general standard of construction higher than with standard issue knives.

This is the Spec Plus version of the Marine Combat Knife, with the same fullered Bowie blade, but in a thicker (3/16in.) steel, and with a contoured Kraton handle. It comes with a black nylon belt sheath.

Manufacturer:	Ontario Knife Co., Franklinville, New York, USA
Model:	SP1 Marine Combat
Length overall:	12 1/8in.
Blade length:	7in.. Blade depth 1 1/4in.
Blade shape:	Bowie with blood groove
Blade material:	3/16in. thick 1095 carbon steel, black epoxy powder coated
Edge:	Bevel-ground
Grip:	Black Kraton grooved handle with lanyard hole
Construction:	Handle moulded on to full-length tang
Sheath:	Black nylon belt sheath

The SP2 is the Spec Plus version of the Air Force Survival Knife, with the same fullered Bowie blade shape and saw back, but deeper at 1 1/4in., and made from a thicker (3/16in.) steel. It has a contoured Kraton handle, and comes with a black nylon belt sheath.

Manufacturer:	Ontario Knife Co., Franklinville, New York, USA
Model:	SP2 Air Force Survival
Length overall:	10 5/8in.
Blade length:	5 1/2in.
Blade shape:	Bowie, with saw back and blood groove
Blade material:	3/16in. thick 1095 carbon steel, black epoxy powder coated
Edge:	Bevel-ground
Grip:	Black Kraton grooved handle with lanyard hole
Construction:	Handle moulded on to full-length tang
Sheath:	Black nylon belt sheath

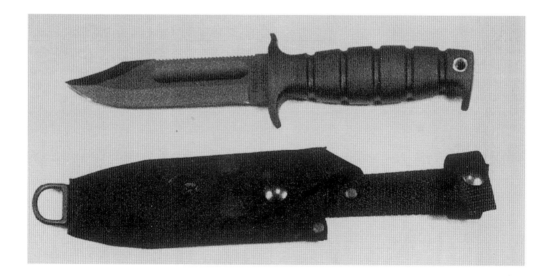

The SP3 is the Spec Plus version of the Trench Knife based on the M7 bayonet. It has the same spear-point blade shape with half-length sharpened back edge, but is made from thicker (3/16in.) steel and has a contoured Kraton handle with integral double guard.

The knife has a sharply pointed, steel 'skull crusher' pommel, which is black powder coated. This feature is felt by some to be useful in close combat, but may give the user a nasty poke if he sits down carelessly with the knife in a belt sheath. Some users take a file and round off the point.

Manufacturer:	Ontario Knife Co., Franklinville, New York, USA
Model:	SP3 M7 Bayonet Knife
Length overall:	12 1/2in.
Blade length:	6 3/4in.
Blade shape:	Spear point
Blade material:	3/16in. thick 1095 carbon steel, black epoxy powder coated
Edge:	Bevel-ground
Grip:	Black Kraton grooved handle with 'skull crusher' pommel
Construction:	Moulded Kraton handle; pommel screwed to tang
Sheath:	Black Cordura belt sheath

The SP4 is the Spec Plus version of the Navy Knife, with the same concave clip Bowie blade shape and serrated back, but made from thicker (3/16in.) 440A stainless steel. It has a contoured Kraton handle with integral double guard, and comes with a black nylon belt sheath.

Manufacturer:	Ontario Knife Co., Franklinville, New York, USA
Model:	SP4 Navy Knife
Length overall:	11 1/8in.
Blade length:	6in.
Blade shape:	Bowie, with serrated back and deep clip
Blade material:	3/16in. thick 440A stainless steel, black epoxy powder coated
Edge:	Bevel-ground
Grip:	Black Kraton grooved handle with lanyard hole
Construction:	Kraton handle moulded on to tang
Sheath:	Black Cordura belt sheath

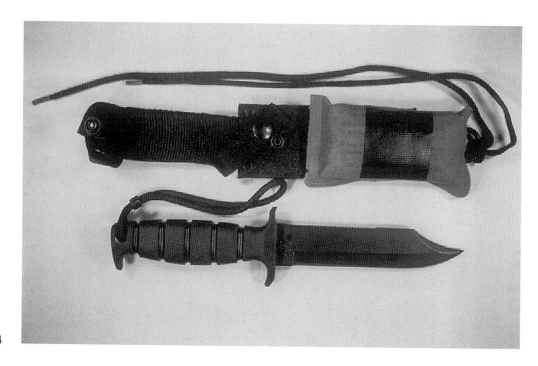

The Spec Plus Survival Bowie is a massive blade with dimensions and handling more like those of a machete than a knife. It has a flat ground 10in. blade of 1/4in. thick 1095 carbon steel, with an upturned clip point. Overall the knife measures 15 1/8in. from tip to butt. The heavy, flat-ground blade has immense cutting and chopping power, and makes short work of dense brush and undergrowth. Despite its size, this big Bowie is also capable of remarkably delicate work. It slices well, and the point is quite fine.

Although not its main purpose, this knife would also make an effective fighting weapon, with good stand-off, an intimidating appearance, and the ability to stab, slash and cut.

Like all the Spec Plus range, the Survival Bowie has a moulded Kraton handle, with integral guard and deep lateral grooves for extra grip. It comes with a Cordura sheath with a leather belt loop attached to a pivot ring, and there is a loop at the tip for a leg tie.

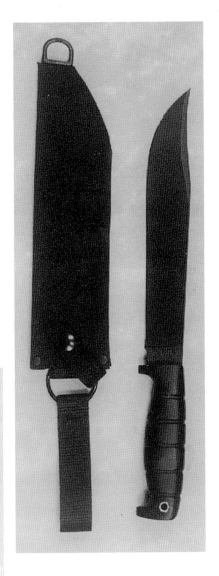

Manufacturer:	Ontario Knife Co., Franklinville, New York, USA
Model:	SP5 Survival Bowie
Length overall:	15 1/8in.
Blade length:	10in.
Blade shape:	Bowie
Blade material:	1/4in. thick 1095 carbon steel, black epoxy powder coated
Edge:	Flat-ground, with concave false clip edge
Grip:	Black Kraton grooved handle with lanyard hole
Construction:	Handle moulded on to full-length tang
Sheath:	Cordura sheath with pivot ring and tie cord

The Spec Plus SP6 Fighting Knife is based on the Randall R1 blade shape described earlier, under the heading Blackjack Model 1-7. A proven and versatile design, it works well in the Spec Plus guise, with a black epoxy coating and moulded Kraton handle.

This is a big, powerful knife, with an 8in. blade and measuring 13 1/8in. overall. The blade is 3/16in. thick, and has a sharpened straight clip edge. Like the other Spec Plus knives, it has a bellied handle with deep grooves for added grip.

Although described as a fighter, this knife is much more versatile, with the ability to cope well with medium chopping, slashing, cutting and piercing. It makes a useful field tool.

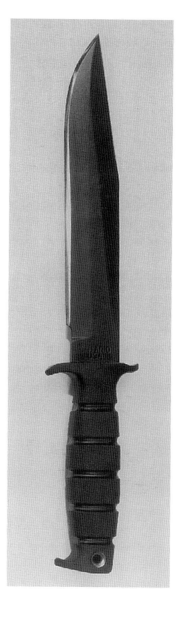

Manufacturer:	Ontario Knife Co., Franklinville, New York, USA
Model:	SP6 Fighting Knife
Length overall:	13 1/8in.
Blade length:	8in.
Blade shape:	Randall R1 type straight clip Bowie
Blade material:	1/4in. thick 1095 carbon steel, black epoxy powder coated
Edge:	Bevel ground
Grip:	Black Kraton grooved handle with lanyard hole
Construction:	Handle moulded on to full-length tang
Sheath:	Cordura belt sheath

The Spec Plus SPC20 USMC Parachutist knife and SPC21 Navy Mark 1 are relatively recent additions to the Spec Plus range. They mark a departure from the established Spec Plus look, with bright brush finished metalwork rather than the deliberately sombre black powder coating that had come to be associated with these knives.

The quality is entirely characteristic of Spec Plus, however, with a 1095 carbon steel blade, full-length tang, and contoured moulded Kraton handle with the familiar bellied shape, deep lateral grooves and integral double guard.

The USMC Parachutist has a straight clipped, flat ground blade, with a tip that is almost a spear point. The blade is relatively small, at 4 1/8in. long, with a thickness of 1/6in.. It is a handy utility blade, good for cutting and piercing, but does not have the size and heft to tackle heavy chopping and slicing. For cutting tangled parachute cords it would be ideal.

The Navy Mark 1 is very similar, but with a slightly longer 4 3/4in. blade, giving it an overall length of 9 1/4in.. The extra length makes this knife slightly more versatile, but it is still not enough to allow for heavy work.

The Kraton handle is common to both knives. It gives good grip and flares to a milled butt cap which is screwed on to the full-length tang. This can be used for hammering and pounding

Manufacturer:	Ontario Knife Co., Franklinville, New York, USA
Model:	SPS20 USMC Parachutist/SPC21 Navy Mark 1
Length overall:	8 3/4in./9 3/4in.
Blade length:	4in./4 3/4in.
Blade shape:	Straight clip point with false top edge
Blade material:	1/6in. thick 1095 carbon steel with bright brushed finish
Edge:	Flat-grind
Grip:	Black Kraton grooved handle
Construction:	Stainless steel butt cap screwed on to threaded tang
Sheath:	Leather and Cordura belt sheath with leg tie

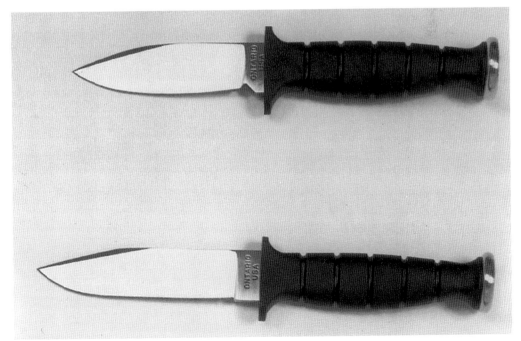

'SPC 20 USMC Parachutist' and 'SPC 21 Navy Mark 1'.

Like the USMC Parachutist and Navy Mark 1, the Patrol and Ranger stand apart from the rest of the Spec Plus range, owing to their bright brushed blades and butt caps.

The two knives differ in blade shape only. The Patrol has a spear point blade which is basically a shortened version of the M7 bayonet, while the Ranger's blade is a straight clip Bowie-style. Both blades are made of 1/6in. thick 1095 carbon steel.

The handles are identical, made of Kraton rubber moulded to a contoured shape that incorporates deep lateral grooves and double guards. The handles flare at the butt to accommodate the butt cap, which is screwed on to the full-length, threaded tang.

Manufacturer:	Ontario Knife Co., Franklinville, New York, USA
Model:	SPC22 Patrol/SPC23 Ranger
Length overall:	9 3/4in.
Blade length:	5in.
Blade shape:	Spear point/straight clip Bowie
Blade material:	1/6in. thick 1095 carbon steel with bright brushed finish
Edge:	Bevel-ground
Grip:	Moulded Kraton rubber, contoured, with grooves and integral double guard
Construction:	Steel butt cap screwed on to threaded end of full-length tang
Sheath:	Black Cordura and leather belt sheath with lanyard

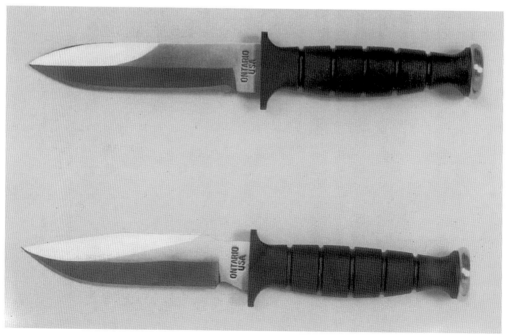

'SPC 22 patrol' and 'SPC 23 Ranger'.

The Timberline Specwar knife was designed by Ernest Emerson to meet US Special Warfare Group specifications. It is a high-tech knife, made of modern, high-performance materials, and with an unusual blade and handle profile. This is not what some would call an attractive knife to look at, but its performance is exceptional.

The blade is angular, with a clipped chisel point reminiscent of the Tanto shape, and a straight main edge. The grind is one side of the blade only, giving good strength and cutting efficiency. The chisel point has exceptional penetration and may also be used for quite fine work when necessary. The blade material is ATS-34 steel and unusually hard at Rc 60.

The handle is contoured nylon, with a belly and single guard. The top edge extends well along the back of the blade, allowing one to place the thumb well forward to exert a powerful downward cutting pressure. There is a deep finger groove choil, so that one may choke up the grip for fine work, and the shape of the butt allows the grip to be extended for hacking and slashing.

This is an unusual, futuristic-looking knife which develops some interesting ideas and offers outstanding performance in important areas. It is perhaps a little specialised for general field use, but would tackle most camp chores with ease and could also serve well as a fighter if necessary. It is available with either a grey bead blasted finish, or black titanium nitride coating.

Manufacturer:	Timberline, USA
Model:	Specwar
Length overall:	11 7/8in.
Blade length:	6in.
Blade shape:	Chisel point
Blade material:	ATS-34 stainless steel, Rc 60, with bead blasted grey finish or black titanium nitride coating
Edge:	Bevel-ground one side only
Grip:	Moulded black nylon
Construction:	Nylon handle moulded to full-length tang
Sheath:	Rigid Kydex sheath with 'jump safe' features

The United Special Operations Utility Knife is an unusual design, consisting of a single flat piece of ATS-34 stainless steel machined to form a blade and handle. The blade is a spear point design, with a convex main blade and a sharpened back edge with serrations cut into it. The serrations are, in fact, notches which do not need sharpening individually - the blade is simply sharpened on a flat hone.

The handle is a skeleton design, simply shaped from the full tang of the knife. It has two finger grooves, and the tang is drilled through in four places. These holes serve to lighten the knife, as well as providing a means of lashing it to a pole to form a spear. A smaller hole at the butt end allows one to attach a lanyard. Also in the butt is a notch for cutting wire. This is not so much a wire cutter as a wire breaker, and is claimed to work on wire up to 1/8in. thick.

The sheath is made of black nylon web, with a rigid plastic insert that is held in place by a Velcro strip, allowing it to be removed if required. The sheath allows various carrying options: it may be attached to a belt with a loop or Alice clips, worn on a leg or arm with rubber diving straps, or attached to webbing via the six impact resistant grommets.

Manufacturer:	United Cutlery, Sevierville, Tennessee, USA
Model:	Special Ops Utility Knife
Length overall:	8 7/8in.
Blade length:	4 3/8in.
Blade shape:	Spear point
Blade material:	ATS-34 stainless steel with black finish
Edge:	Bevel-ground main edge, serrated back edge
Grip:	Bare full tang with finger grooves
Construction:	Single piece of steel, ground and milled to shape
Sheath:	Black nylon web sheath with removable plastic insert

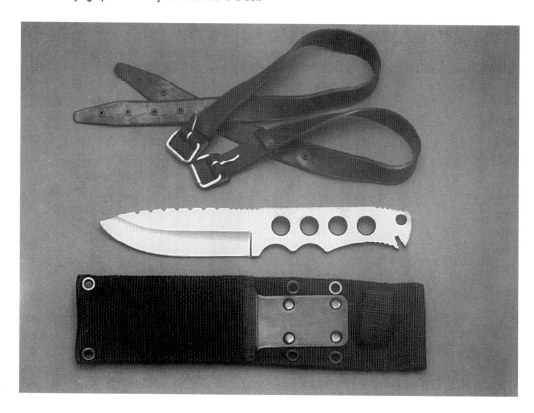

MULTI-TOOLS

When Leatherman introduced the first multi-tool, it was an instant hit with soldiers as well as civilian users. Before the Leatherman, there was really only the Swiss Army knife that offered a useful collection of tools in a pocket-sized package. The various models of Swiss Army knife are enormously versatile and well made, but the tools are simply too lightweight for daily use on full-sized jobs.

The Leatherman changed all that. Here was a tool that would fit unobtrusively in your webbing or a combat jacket pocket, yet contained a selection of full-sized tools capable of serious work – pliers, various screwdrivers, tin opener, file and a useful knife blade. The original Leatherman Tool had its disadvantages: it lacked a saw, and the screwdrivers had an unfriendly habit of folding over just as you applied maximum torque to a difficult screw. But it was the best thing on offer, and a great deal better than nothing at all.

Then came the clones. SOG, Gerber and a host of others saw the potential, and each applied their considerable design and manufacturing skill to the challenge of packing the maximum number of useful and useable tools into a pouch-sized package. Leatherman themselves, determined not to be left behind, developed several variations on their original design.

Before long there was a host of multi-tools to choose from, in various sizes and with different combinations of tools to suit different users. True to the original concept, the tools were generally truly multi-purpose, with useful additions such as various types of saw, scissors, alternative knife blades, and fittings to accept standard 'hex' tool bits. This last development allows the user to select from commercially available bits, to put together a pocket tool set that matches the screw heads and nuts that he knows he is most likely to come across in his work.

One of the major design problems to overcome was providing an effective locking mechanism for the tool in use, whether a knife blade, saw or screwdriver bit. The mechanism needed to be quick and easy to operate, but still lock the tool firmly in the extended position, so that it could not snap shut on the user's hand. I know personally of a couple of people who suffered unpleasant injuries to the hand as a result of this happening with simple, non-locking multi-tools. This is undesirable at any time, but in a survival situation it could lead to serious loss of function and even infection.

A number of different locking mechanisms have been developed and are now offered by the various manufacturers. They inevitably slow down the process of using the tool, even if only to operate a simple catch, but I would always advise selecting a tool with locking blades. The minor inconvenience is well worth the safety improvement. Another problem for the designers is making the tool comfortable to use. The most simple designs have the tools hinged in two handles formed of steel bent into a U-shaped profile. If the handles attach to the pliers by a simple hinge, as in the original Leatherman, this places the open part of the U against the palm and ball of the thumb when using the pliers. Although the back edges of the folded blade help to even out the surface, it can still be quite uncomfortable in prolonged or heavy use. Various designs have approached this problem in different ways. Gerber turned the U-pieces around and adopted a sliding mechanism for storing the pliers; SOG and others have used a more complicated hinge mechanism for the pliers so that they swing out sideways from the handles, keeping the rounded back of the U against the user's hand. In choosing a multi-tool, it is best to try a number of different designs to see which one offers, for you, the best compromise between weight, comfort, ease of use, and the right selection of tools for the tasks you expect to need to tackle. Finally, be aware that as with other types of knives, multi-tools have been extensively copied by manufacturers in the Far East. These copies are often made to minimum specifications to provide a very attractive price, but will not stand up to serious work.

The Multi-Plier is Gerber's answer to the various multi-tools that have appeared in recent years, but it is not just a copycat item - it brings some completely new ideas of its own to answer the challenge of cramming as many tools as possible into a pocket-sized package.

Most multi-tools fold the plier head away into the handle, in the manner of the Leatherman, whereas the Gerber's Multi-Plier has a unique sliding mechanism, so that the plier head retracts into the handles when not in use. This makes the pliers easy to deploy with a quick flick of the wrist, with centrifugal force throwing the plier head out until the sprung buttons lock in place. The mechanism also means that the handles are not reversed when using the pliers, so the palm of the hand presses against the rounded outside edge of the handles - a feature that makes the pliers more comfortable to use than some other types. The tool is designed so that the handles cannot quite come together when the pliers are in use, preventing any painful trapping of a fold of skin between the handles. The Multi-Plier is available with either square-ended or needlenose pliers.

The other tools are located in the handles, hinged at the bottom end of each in the same way as a folding knife blade. There are two main blades, both 2 5/8in. long - one a drop point, the other a serrated sheepsfoot type. Also in the handles are three straight screwdriver blades, a Phillips screwdriver, a metal file, a fold-out lanyard ring, and a can/bottle opener. The tools all click into place with an over-centre spring mechanism, but do not lock. With the handles held together, however, the blades are able to fold only partly, and cannot close on to the hand holding the tool. The handles are marked in inches and centimetres for measuring up to 3in. or 7cm.

The Multi-Tool comes in a black ballistic nylon belt pouch. As an optional accessory, one may also buy a tool kit which includes an adapter that fits on the Phillips screwdriver, together with a selection of 1/4in. hex bits for several screw head types.

Having tested all the various multi-tools available, I have carried a Gerber Multi-Plier for the past two years in preference to other models. It is not always the strongest, lightest, most powerful or easiest to use, but I have found that it offers the best compromise. The deciding factor was the ease and speed with which the plier head can be deployed, even with only one hand free.

Manufacturer:	Gerber (a division of Fiskars Inc.), Portland, Oregon, USA
Model:	G-55800 Multi-Plier
Length overall:	4 3/8in. (closed), 6in. (open)
Blade length:	2 5/8in. main and serrated blades
Blade shape:	Drop point main blade, sheepsfoot serrated blade
Blade material:	All stainless steel, bead blasted finish (black finish version available)
Edge:	Hollow-ground
Grip:	Plier handles form grip
Construction:	Slide-out pliers with hinged knife blades and tools in handles
Features:	Pliers (needlenose or square-ended versions available) with wire cutter, file, three straight-head screwdrivers, Phillips screwdriver, lanyard ring, can/bottle opener, blades as above, ruler, black ballistic nylon belt pouch. Supplementary tool kit available with coupler and assorted screwdriver heads in pouch

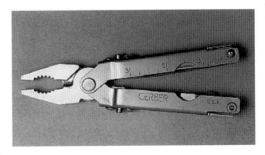

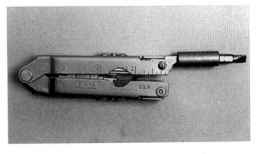

353

Gerber's MPT, or Military Provisional Tool, was developed to meet a US military specification. Unlike the company's Multi-Plier, the MPT follows the Leatherman design in which the plier handles are hinged on the base of the pliers and fold out for use. This means the edges of the U-section handles bear on the palm of the hand and so Gerber have folded these edges to increase the surface area in contact with the hand in an attempt to make them more comfortable to use. Like the Multi-Plier, the plier jaws of the MPT are narrower than those in some other tools, but are still strong enough for most jobs. I have used the MPT and prefer the Multi-Plier or the Leatherman - but to be fair the MPT is a rugged and effective tool made to tight price constraints. It has been adopted by a number of US and other military forces.

Manufacturer: Gerber (a division of Fiskars Inc.), Portland, Oregon, USA

Model: MPT (Military Provisional Tool)

Length overall: 4 1/2in. closed

Blade length: 2 5/8in.

Blade shape: Drop point main blade

Blade material: All stainless steel, bead blasted finish (Black finish version available)

Edge: Hollow-ground

Grip: Plier handles form grip

Construction: Folding construction with hinged knife blades and tools in handles

Features: Needlenose pliers with wire cutter, file, two straight-head screwdrivers, Phillips screwdriver, lanyard ring, can/bottle opener, main blade as above, small utility blade, ruler

The Leatherman Tool was the original multi-tool - the first tool, to my knowledge, to apply the principle of a folding plier with tools and blades located in the handles. Certainly it was the one that popularised the multi-tool idea and spawned numerous imitators.

Although other models have come along, the original Leatherman Tool is still hugely popular, both with military personnel and civilians. It consists of a plier head with two U-section stainless steel handles. These fold around a hinge pin near the plier head, so that they completely enclose the plier head when closed. The plier head is the needlenose type and incorporates a wire cutter. One minor drawback of the design is that, when using the pliers, the open side of the U is against the palm, which makes it uncomfortable to use force on the work.

Hinged at the bottom end of the handles are a selection of tools: a hollow-ground clip point blade, a metal file, three sizes of slot-head screwdriver, a Phillips screwdriver, an awl, and a can/bottle opener. The tools are held in place by an overcentre flat spring when opened, but do not lock. However they cannot close on the hand when in use, as they are stopped by the opposing handle.

On the outer edge of the handles is a ruler scale marked in centimetres and inches and by aligning the handles in the partly folded position the scale will measure up to 20cm or 8in..

The Leatherman Tool comes with either a leather or ballistic nylon belt pouch, and has a lanyard ring attachment.

The original Leatherman is a simple and effective tool which packs enormous versatility into a small space. It is still deservedly one of the most popular multi-tools and is an ideal addition to a survival kit or tool kit.

It is available in either bright stainless steel or a black finish. There is also a military version, with a detonator crimp tool incorporated into the plier head, which has proved popular with combat engineers, ATOs and EOD.

Manufacturer:	Leatherman Tool Group Inc., Portland, Oregon, USA
Model:	Leatherman Tool
Length overall:	4in. (closed)
Blade length:	2 5/8in.
Blade shape:	Clip point
Blade material:	All stainless steel, satin finish (also available in black finish)
Edge:	Hollow-ground main blade
Grip:	Plier handles form grip
Construction:	Folding construction with hinged knife blades and tools in handles
Features:	Needlenose pliers with wire cutter, main blade as above, ruler, can/bottle opener, three sizes of slot-head screwdriver, Phillips screwdriver, file with saw-type edge, awl, leather belt sheath

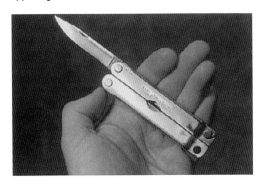

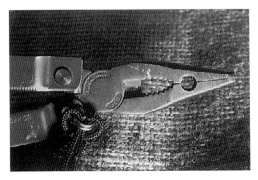

Leatherman's Mini Tool takes the already small, original Leatherman and makes it smaller still - just 2 5/8in. long when closed. This was achieved by having the handles fold in half before closing them on to the plier head - a second piece of U-section handle folds into the first. This restricts the space available for tools in the handle, but even so Leatherman have managed to fit in a hollow-ground clip blade and a file/screwdriver. The handle extensions incorporate a can opener and a bottle opener.

The Mini Tool comes in bright stainless or black finish and has a small ballistic nylon belt pouch. Although the selection of tools is limited, and the small size restricts the power of the pliers, it is still a robust and practical tool and is useful where space is limited - in a belt-mounted survival pack, for instance.

Manufacturer:	Leatherman Tool Group Inc., Portland, Oregon, USA
Model:	Mini Tool
Length overall:	2 5/8in. (closed)
Blade length:	1 1/2in.
Blade shape:	Clip point
Blade material:	All stainless steel, satin finish (also available in black finish)
Edge:	Hollow-ground main blade
Grip:	Plier handles form grip
Construction:	Double folding construction with hinged knife blades and tools in handles
Features:	Needlenose pliers with wire cutter, main blade as above, ruler, can opener, bottle opener, file with screwdriver tip, black Cordura belt sheath

Based on the original Leatherman Tool, the PST II (Pocket Survival Tool II) offers an uprated tool selection in the same sized package. Like the original tool, the PST II has a needlenose plier head with wire cutters and folding U-section handles. Tools in the handles include the familiar Phillips and slot-head screwdrivers and can/bottle opener. In addition, however, the PST II has a very sharp serrated main clip blade, scissors and a diamond-coated crosscut file with a sharpening groove for needles, fish hooks and the like.

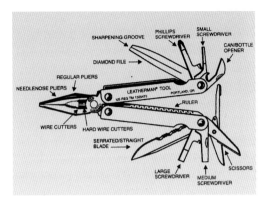

One of the few complaints about the original Leatherman was its lack of scissors, which are more suitable for some fine cutting jobs than a knife blade. The PST II puts this right and at the same time offers an uprated file and main blade - the serrated section is very effective in cutting tough materials such as rope and webbing.

These improvements have been achieved within the same overall size as the original Leatherman, at just 4in. x 1in. x 7/16in. when closed, making it a very handy, lightweight and versatile item. It is available with a leather or ballistic nylon belt pouch.

Manufacturer:	Leatherman Tool Group Inc., Portland, Oregon, USA
Model:	PST II
Length overall:	4in. (closed), 6 1/4in. (open)
Blade length:	2 5/8in.
Blade shape:	Clip point with serrated section
Blade material:	All stainless steel, satin finish
Edge:	Hollow-ground, with serrated section
Grip:	Plier handles form grip
Construction:	Folding construction with hinged knife blades and tools in handles
Features:	Needlenose pliers with wire cutter, main blade as above, scissors, ruler, can/bottle opener, three sizes of slot-head screwdriver, Phillips screwdriver, file with diamond-coated side and cross-cut side, awl, leather belt sheath

The original Leatherman Tool was such a useful and practical item that it was inevitable that people would ask for more - more power, more tools and more features. These could be provided only at the expense of greater bulk and weight, but for some users a bigger, heavier tool was acceptable if it would tackle heavier work.

The Supertool addressed this by offering a number of extra items, notably a second blade with a very effective serrated edge, and a high-performance wood/bone saw. Making the tool bigger also allowed the plier head and other tools to be bulked up, offering more power and strength to cope with heavier work.

The other major addition in the Supertool was a locking mechanism on all the fold-out tools and blades. This is achieved with a catch in the spring back, which engages in a notch on each blade when it is fully opened. The blade is then held firmly in the open position and cannot fold regardless of the direction of the force on it. This is particularly valuable for the knife and screwdriver blades, which in the original Leatherman may fold suddenly when force is applied to the work.

The downside is that releasing the locking mechanism may be fiddly. This requires one to open another blade in the same handle half-way - raising the

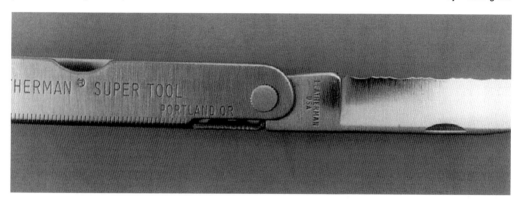

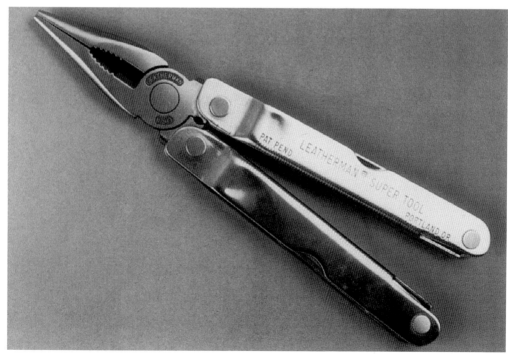

catch out of the notch and allowing both blades to be closed. In practice this may be awkward, not to mention risky with cold, slippery hands, since one is opening the second blade towards an open sharp edge. Provided that this is done carefully there is no need for a mishap, however, and in two years of using the Supertool I have not had an accident - indeed, it becomes easier as the blades wear and the hinge mechanism frees up.

The Supertool is altogether bigger and heavier than the original Leatherman, at 4 1/2in. x 1 1/4in. x 5/8in. With heavier work, however, the extra weight and bulk are well worth it - the tools are better able to cope and the locking mechanism makes the job safer. The wood saw in particular is valuable outdoors, cutting branches for a shelter or trap with ease - something that would not be possible with a standard multi-tool. The knife blades are big and strong enough to dress medium-sized game, and would even serve for fighting in a dire emergency. If one is going to depend on a multi-tool alone for survival then the Supertool is the one to choose.

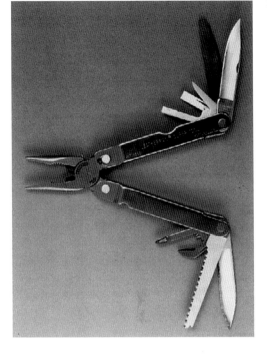

Manufacturer:	Leatherman Tool Group Inc., Portland, Oregon, USA
Model:	Supertool
Length overall:	4 1/2in. (closed)
Blade length:	3in.
Blade shape:	Clip point main blade, drop point serrated blade
Blade material:	All stainless steel, satin finish
Edge:	Hollow-ground
Grip:	Plier handles form grip
Construction:	Folding construction with locking hinged knife blades and tools in handles
Features:	Needlenose pliers with wire cutter and wire crimper, main blades as above, wood saw, ruler, can/bottle opener, file, three sizes of slot-head screwdriver, Phillips screwdriver, awl, brown leather belt pouch

The Mauser Officer's Knife is made under licence by Victorinox of Switzerland - makers of the famous Swiss Army Knives. A simple folding pocket knife, it incorporates a few extras that bring it into the multi-tool category.

The knife measures 4 1/4in. long and has green plastic scales with moulded chequering for extra grip. There are two main blades - a flat-ground drop point blade, and a clip point, also flat-ground, which bears the Mauser logo and text which declares that the Mauser name is being used under licence.

Next to the main blades is a third, of the same length, which has a 2 1/4in. saw edge, plus a bottle opener and a screwdriver at the tip. The saw teeth are very aggressive, and set alternately right and left to remove material to the thickness of the blade, so the saw does not jam as it cuts through wood or bone. This saw is extremely effective on softwood and will even do a decent job on hardwood, although it is inclined to bite too deep if any downward pressure is applied. Its only real drawback is its length, which means that one may only use very short strokes. The saw comes with a thin metal cover to protect the fingers when using the bottle opener or screwdriver on the same blade.

On the back of the knife are an awl/reamer and a corkscrew. There is a hole through one end of the knife where a lanyard may be attached.

A good, sturdy, pocket knife with an impressive saw blade, the Mauser Officer's Knife nevertheless offers fewer tools than the equivalently sized Swiss Army Knives and has never become a very popular private purchase item for the military.

Manufacturer:	Victorinox, Switzerland
Model:	Mauser Officer's Knife
Length overall:	4 1/4in. (closed)
Blade length:	3 1/4in.
Blade shape:	One drop point blade, one clip
Blade material:	Stainless steel
Edge:	Flat-ground (both blades)
Grip:	Green plastic scales with moulded chequering
Construction:	Standard folding pocket knife construction, with blades sandwiched between metal scales held by pins
Features:	Two blades as above, wood saw/bottle opener/ screwdriver blade, awl/reamer, corkscrew, lanyard hole

SOG's development of the Leatherman idea was the ParaTool. Designed by Blackie Collins and Spencer Frazer, it is a folding plier/multi-tool with some innovative ideas. For a start, the handles do not have to be folded round to expose the plier head. Instead, the plier head is hinged sideways in the handles, and is flipped into position by pressing on a tab which doubles as a lanyard ring. This enables one to deploy the pliers single handedly, which is useful when one hand is occupied. The design also means that the palm of the hand is pressing against the rounded side of the U-section

handles, which gives greater comfort than some other multi-tool designs. The handle surfaces are drilled with a pattern of small holes to give a better grip.

The selection of tools is a good one, with a 3in. straight blade, 3in. serrated sheepsfoot blade, file, three slot-head screwdrivers, a Phillips screwdriver, a can/bottle opener, an awl, and a coarse/fine file. Unlike other multi-tools of this type, the SOG ParaTool's hinge pins have hex heads, and may be unscrewed so that the user can alter the tool configuration – optional accessory blades include a seat belt/gutting hook and a double tooth wood/bone saw.

The ParaTool has an injection moulded black plastic belt pouch with a locking mechanism to prevent the tool falling out while being carried.

Manufacturer:	SOG Speciality Knives Inc., Edmonds, Washington, USA
Model:	ParaTool
Length overall:	4in. closed, 6 2/5in. open
Blade length:	3in. standard blade, 3in. serrated blade
Blade shape:	Drop point standard blade, sheepsfoot serrated blade
Blade material:	420 stainless steel, satin finish, also available in black finish
Edge:	Hollow-ground
Grip:	Plier handles form grip
Construction:	Folding construction with hinged knife blades and tools
Features:	Needlenose pliers with wire cutter, three sizes of flathead screwdriver, Phillips screwdriver, metal file, awl, can/bottle opener, ruler, lanyard hole and two blades as above. Optional saw blade and seat belt cutter/gutting blade. Moulded plastic belt sheath

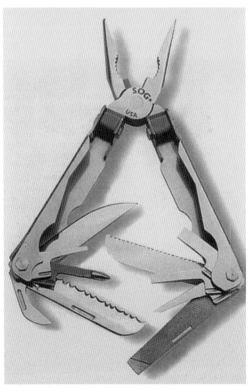

With the Power Plier, SOG have reverted to the folding-handle system pioneered by Leatherman, but have built in a gear mechanism that increases the leverage on the plier head. The Power Plier has similar tools to the ParaTool, and the same hex bolt construction that allows one to add optional blades and to adjust the ease of opening to the personal preference.

The main blade is a drop point with a partially serrated edge; other tools are the same as those in the ParaTool, and are listed below. The Power Plier comes with a heavy duty nylon belt pouch.

A smaller version, the Mini Pocket Power Plier, is also available, measuring 4in. when closed. This has fewer blades but retains the main blade, two slot-head screwdrivers, Phillips screwdriver, can/bottle opener, and file.

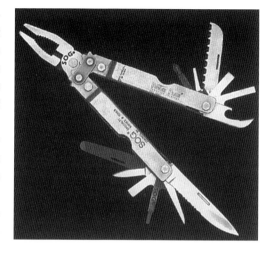

Manufacturer:	SOG Speciality Knives Inc., Edmonds, Washington, USA
Model:	Power Plier
Length overall:	4 1/4in. x 1/4in. x 5/8in. (closed), length 6 3/4in. (open)
Blade length:	3in.
Blade shape:	Drop point blade with serrated section
Blade material:	All stainless steel, polished finish
Edge:	Hollow-ground
Grip:	Plier handles form grip
Construction:	Folding construction with hinged knife blades and tools. Gear mechanism provides added leverage for pliers
Features:	Pliers with wire cutter, three sizes of flathead screwdriver, Phillips screwdriver, square drive, double tooth saw, fine-coarse file, awl, chisel, can/bottle opener, ruler, small blade, and main blade as above. Nylon belt pouch

The SOG Toolclip represents an alternative approach to the multi-tool idea, being built more along the lines of a conventional folding pocket knife. The plier head forms an extension of the handle, with the knife itself providing one handle and the other being hinged out of the back of the knife. The plier head is very square in shape, and incorporates a wire cutter.

Between the stainless steel scales are a drop point main blade, a serrated blade with screwdriver tip and wire-stripping notch, a bottle opener/small utility blade, and a small screwdriver/chisel. The plier handle is held in the closed position by a bail, and may also be used as a light pry bar.

The Toolclip has a spring steel clip attached to one side, so that it may be clipped to pocket or belt

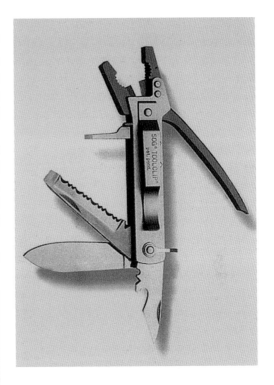

Manufacturer:	SOG Speciality Knives Inc., Edmonds, Washington, USA
Model:	Toolclip
Length overall:	5 1/4in. (closed)
Blade length:	3in.
Blade shape:	Drop point (main blade)
Blade material:	All stainless steel
Edge:	Flat-ground
Grip:	Stainless steel scales, with single plier handle at edge
Construction:	Blades and tools sandwiched between pinned stainless steel scales
Features:	Pliers with wire cutter, utility blade with bottle opener and wire stripper, serrated edge blade with metal file and screwdriver, small screwdriver, pocket/belt clip

The Micro Toolclip takes the theme of the Toolclip, but in a smaller overall size. In addition to the plier/wire-cutter head, there are three blades - a drop point, a serrated edge sheepsfoot, and a file with screwdriver tip and wire-stripper notch. As with the Toolclip, the hinged plier handle may be used as a light duty pry bar.

The Micro Toolclip has polycarbonate scales and is available in a range of colours including black, yellow, green and red. On the back of the handle is a pocket/belt clip.

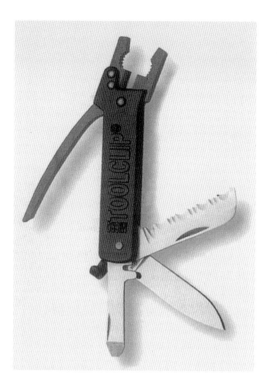

Manufacturer:	Made in Japan for SOG Speciality Knives Inc., Edmonds, Washington, USA
Model:	Micro Toolclip
Length overall:	3 3/4in. (closed)
Blade length:	2in.
Blade shape:	Drop point main blade, sheepsfoot serrated blade
Blade material:	Stainless steel
Edge:	Flat-ground
Grip:	Polycarbonate scales in choice of colours, with single plier handle at edge
Construction:	Blades and tools sandwiched between pinned stainless steel liners and polycarbonate scales
Features:	Pliers with wire cutter, two blades as above, file with screwdriver tip and wire stripper, pocket/belt clip

The Spyderco SpydeRench marks a departure from the now familiar multi-tool design of pliers with a variety of folding blades stored in folding handles. It is a very different looking tool, with an appearance more like a small adjustable spanner.

It consists of two main parts, which can be separated and used individually. One is basically an adjustable spanner or wrench (hence the name); the other contains a folding knife blade and has a hexagonal hole to take a screwdriver bit – a selection of these are stored in the handle.

Locked together in the manner of a bayonet and its sheath, with a lug passing through a hole, the two parts form another, plier-like spanner. The jaws are rounded in shape, which rather limits their potential uses – they cannot tackle the same range of delicate work that you might get from, say, the Leatherman's electrical pliers. They also offer no wire-cutting facility.

The screwdriver bits stored in the handle offer a range of common sizes, and are standard bits that can easily be replaced at any hardware store. If you commonly tackled a particular type of non-standard screw in your work, the appropriate bits could easily be substituted.

A small, separate screwdriver/file is located in the handle, and holds the bits in their storage slots. It also provides the 'click' mechanism that holds the tool shut when not in use. On the face of it, this is an efficient multiple use of a single component; in practice however it means that when the small tool is deployed, it is easy to lose the screwdriver bits.

The single knife blade has a serrated 'Spyderedge' which is supplied extremely sharp and gives astonishing cutting power for its size, although it can be difficult to keep sharp without a special tool for sharpening serrated edges.

Having used this tool for some time, I feel that its value is more in its contribution to the development of the multi-tool idea, and its interesting design innovations, than as a practical everyday tool. Having said that, if the particular selection of tools is well suited to your work, it could be just what you need.

Manufacturer: ....Spyderco, Golden, Colorado, USA
Model: ....SpydeRench
Length overall: ...112mm closed, 180mm extended.
Weight:...217g
Blade length: 63mm
Blade material: ....440C stainless steel
Edge:.....Hollow ground with serrated 'Spyderedge' (plain edged version also available).
Construction:.....Multi-tool construction with hinged handles that can be separated at the pivot pin so that tools can be used separately.
Features: ....Adjustable wrench, selection of four screwdriver bits stored in handle, small screwdriver with slot-head and Phillips-type head, diamond-coated file, locking knife blade, pocket clip.

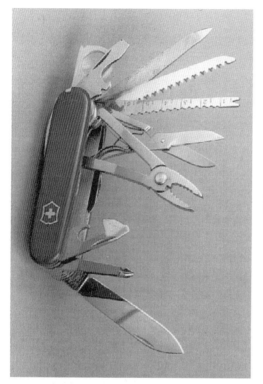

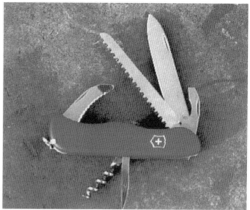

Before the Leatherman and its imitators came along, there was really only one multi-tool to choose from - the Swiss Army Knife. This distinctive knife, with its red plastic scales and enormous selection of stainless steel tools, has been a favourite of soldiers, boy scouts, campers and outdoorsmen for years and still has much to commend it. A well chosen Swiss Army Knife will tackle just about any light job and is handy for everyday chores as well as invaluable in a survival situation.

It is important to remember, however, that the Swiss Army Knife is essentially a light duty tool and cannot tackle the heavy jobs that are essential in a survival situation, such as shelter building, fire preparation and digging, etc. It is of no use for fighting. The ideal combination for survival would be a Swiss Army Knife or similar multi-tool, carried together with a big knife or machete for chopping, hacking and digging.

The standard Victorinox Swiss Army Knife is 3 1/2in. long and 1in. deep. The width of the knife depends on the number and types of tool in any particular model - further tools are accommodated by .adding layers in the sandwich of scale/liner/blade/liner/blade/liner/scale. Shorter and thinner tools are paired within a single blade space - the standard blade and small blade, for instance, sit together between two liners. Larger tools, like the scissors or the pliers, require a space to themselves.

A knife with half a dozen or so tools may still be regarded as a pocket knife, but above this size it becomes too heavy and bulky to slip into a pocket and is best carried in webbing or a belt pouch. Some of the

larger models come with a black leather belt pouch with pockets for additional small items, including a sharpening stone, compass/ruler, pencil, sticking plasters and needle and thread.

Victorinox also produce smaller Swiss Army Knives, measuring 2 1/4in. when closed, with a small main blade, scissors and nail file. There is a larger range, measuring 4 3/8in. closed, which has a locking mechanism for the main blade.

There is not space here to list all the possible combinations of tools available in the many Swiss Army Knives. Instead, as an example, here is a list of the tools and blades found on the Swiss Champ, one of the larger models:

Main blade 2 3/4in. drop point, small blade 1 5/8in. drop point, metal file/saw, woodsaw, fish hook disgorger/descaler, scissors, light pliers/wire cutters, Phillips screwdriver, magnifying glass, bottle opener/medium screwdriver, can opener/small screwdriver, awl/reamer, small screwdriver, light chisel, corkscrew containing separate fine screwdriver, tweezers, ballpoint pen, toothpick, lanyard ring. In the knife's separate leather belt pouch are found: sharpening stone, clutch pencil, ruler/compass, length of fine nylon twine, matches, safety pins, writing paper, sticking plasters, needles and thread. All this fits into a belt pouch which measures 4 1/4in. x 2 1/2in. x 1 3/4in.. Combined with a good sized knife or machete, and with a few minor additions, it would make a sound survival kit in a remarkably compact package.

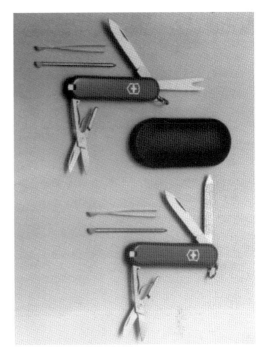

Manufacturer:	Victorinox, Switzerland
Model:	Swiss Champ
Length overall:	3 1/2in.
Blade length:	Main blade 2 3/4in.
Blade shape:	Drop point
Blade material:	Stainless steel
Edge:	Flat-ground
Grip:	Red plastic scales with Swiss flag logo
Construction:	Blades/tools sandwiched between pinned steel liners
Features:	Huge variety of blade/tool options available

The name of Victorinox tends to be associated most firmly with Swiss Army Knives, but Wenger of Switzerland have an equally good claim to be a maker of 'genuine' Swiss Army Knives, and produce a similarly wide range of multi-function knives with red plastic scales.

At first glance the knives are identical, but a closer look reveals vital differences. The first clue is the Swiss cross symbol - on Wenger's knives this is set in a rounded box, instead of the shield seen on the Victorinox knives. Wenger knives also have a short length of chain on the lanyard ring, whereas Victorinox knives do not.

Wenger's tools are very similar to those of Victorinox - the knife blades, reamer, can and bottle openers, for instance, are virtually identical. Other tools, however, show some improvements. The Phillips screwdriver and bottle opener/screwdriver have a patented safety lock mechanism that locks them open when pressure is applied to the tip. This prevents their folding closed at the vital moment when the maximum pressure is applied. The scissors have micro-grooved edges which grip difficult materials like fishing line to give better cutting performance. They also make use of a clever lever system to dispense with the vulnerable flat steel spring, using instead the spring in the knife back to return them to the open position when the pressure is released. This system is also employed on the pliers, which have a slot so the gape may be extended to tackle larger items.

Wenger knives tend not to be so widely marketed as Victorinox, at least in the UK, but if one is planning to buy a Swiss Army Knife it is well worth looking for them, in case the slight differences in the tools appear preferable.

Manufacturer:	Wenger, Switzerland
Model:	Supertalent
Length overall:	3 1/2in.
Blade length:	Main blade 2 3/4in.
Blade shape:	Drop point
Blade material:	Stainless steel
Edge:	Flat-ground
Grip:	Red plastic scales with Swiss flag logo
Construction:	Blades/tools sandwiched between pinned steel liners
Features:	Huge variety of blade/tool options available

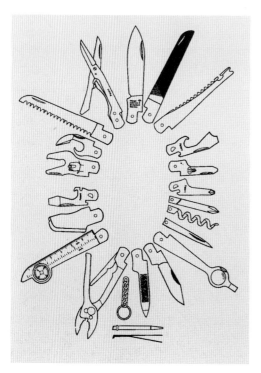

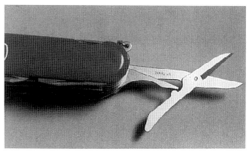

Manufacturer: ToolLogic Inc.

Model: Credit Card Companion

Length overall: 3 3/8in. x 2 1/8in. x 3/16in.

Blade length: 1 7/8in.

Blade shape: Drop point

Blade material: Stainless steel

Edge: Serrated

Grip: Truncated, square-ended grip with deep finger groove

Construction: Credit-card sized unit incorporates compass and lens, with pull-out blade and small tools

Features: Compass, x8 magnifying lens, can/bottle opener, awl, tweezers, toothpick, screwdriver

The ToolLogic Credit Card Companion is an extraordinarily light and compact item that manages to cram a useful knife blade plus a surprising number of tools into a package little bigger than a credit card.

The whole thing is just 3/16in. thick, and measures the same as a credit card - 3 3/8in. x 2 1/8in.. The case is made of black Zytel, and incorporates a compass, x8 magnifying lens and lanyard hole. Separate tweezers and a toothpick are located in holes in the card, and can be pulled out with a fingernail.

At the top of the card is housed a combined can/bottle opener and screwdriver. The main part of the card forms the sheath for a knife with a 1 7/8in. serrated drop point blade. The restricted size of the knife means that it does not have a conventional handle. Instead the handle is cut off square and there is a deep finger groove which enables the knife to be held firmly between thumb and first finger. Alternative holds are possible - the knife may be inverted for cutting upwards, or held in the manner of a push-dagger. The shortened tang is covered with black Zytel, to match the card and to provide a better grip.

This knife is too small for anything but very light work, and would not provide a serious alternative to a conventional knife. However, it is small and unobtrusive enough to be carried anywhere, and in an emergency with nothing else available it would be invaluable.

United Cutlery's Utili Tool is one of several credit-card sized survival/utility tools which consist of a flat piece of steel with sharpened edges, points and cut-outs to tackle a range of light jobs such as cutting, piercing and removing bottle tops.

This one has its own slim case of black ABS plastic to protect it when carried in a wallet or pocket.

Its functions include: can opener, knife edge, screwdriver, bottle opener, wrench, magnifying lens and ruler.

As with the ToolLogic Card, the Utili Tool is too small to be useful for anything but the lightest jobs, and is no alternative to a knife - but unlike a knife it can be carried anywhere and provides the ability to tackle a number of jobs that would otherwise be impossible in an emergency.

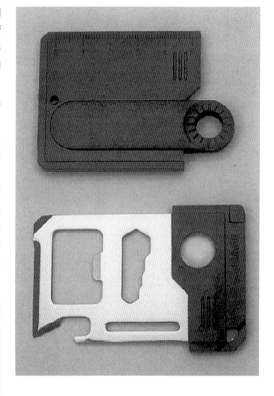

Manufacturer:	Made in Taiwan for United Cutlery, Sevierville, Tennessee, USA
Model:	Utili Tool
Length overall:	3 1/8in. x 2in.
Blade length:	1 3/4in.
Blade shape:	Sharpened straight edge of rectangular piece of steel
Blade material:	420J2 stainless steel
Edge:	Bevel-ground
Grip:	ABS plastic cover on one end of steel rectangle
Construction:	Plastic grip moulded on to steel
Features:	See text

FOLDING KNIVES

A folding knife has much to commend it, and only two real drawbacks. On the plus side, a folder is smaller and more compact than a comparable rigid knife. It can be carried safely without the slightest risk of injuring the user even in a heavy fall. It can be carried covertly, or at least unobtrusively – avoiding the need to draw attention to oneself or being called on to explain why one is carrying a knife.

On the minus side, a folder is not so easy to deploy. Opening out the blade, and locking it into the extended position, takes a finite amount of time and may be tricky when your movements are restricted – perhaps when one hand is occupied or you are wearing gloves. This is certainly true of the old-fashioned penknife with its thumbnail notch on the blade. Many of the most popular folders today have some ingenious design to simplify opening. The Spiderco range, for instance, have a distinctive large round hole in the blade, while the Timberlites have a plastic stud with a milled edge.

This means you can hold the knife in the palm with all four fingers, and use a flicking movement of the thumb to throw the blade open, whereupon the locking mechanism takes over and pushes the blade the last few degrees until it locks into place ready for use. With practice this can be done quickly with one hand, overcoming what is otherwise a significant disadvantage of a folding knife.

Another potential problem with a folding knife is the inherent weakness of the hinge mechanism. A hinge can never be as strong as a solid bar of steel, and so a folder cannot ever have the strength of a fixed-blade, full-tang knife of the same weight and dimensions. Having said this, the best of the modern designs are extremely strong and lightweight, and knives such as the SERE series are plenty strong enough for any task the user is likely to throw at them.

The blades of folding knives tend to be limited in size, due to the need for the handle to fully contain the blade when the knife is closed. Compare the Applegate-Fairbairn folding fighter, for instance, with the fixed version of the same knife. It is immediately apparent that, without the restriction of needing to fit the blade inside the handle, the designers – both highly respected experts in fighting techniques – preferred a longer blade. Clearly, then, the folder is a compromise, reducing the ideal blade length for the benefit of portability, and perhaps, to a degree, concealability.

Within this section there are folding knives of every type: I have not attempted to divide folders into fighting knives, combat and survival knives, etc as I did with fixed knives. There are clear examples of each type here, however. The SERE series, for example, are clearly the folding equivalent of a combat and survival knife, while the Applegate-Fairbairn referred to above is intended for fighting and little else.

Many of the knives in this section are truly general-purpose, and might be carried as a utility pocket knife by soldiers, police, search-and-rescue teams and the like, as well as by ordinary civilians. This is an area where folding knives really come into their own. I carry a Timberlite folder as a general pocket knife, and although it sometimes attracts comment it has never once received the unwelcome attention that would come from carrying an equivalent-sized fixed-blade knife around the streets of London.

If there is one piece of advice to anyone choosing a folder, it is to pay close attention to the locking mechanism. This is not one of the more obvious features of a folder, but should be inspected carefully, as it will make an enormous difference to the knife's ease of use. A good one will make the knife a pleasure to use; a bad one will cause nothing but trouble and could even cause you an injury by failing at a critical moment. One type to avoid, in my opinion, is the lockback type where the release button lays along the back of the handle: this is all too easily released unintentionally by a firm grip around the handle.

Manufacturer: Al Mar Knives Inc., Lake Oswego, Oregon, USA

Model: SERE Attack Models I and II

Length overall: SERE Attack II 6in. closed, SERE Attack I 5in. closed

Blade length: SERE Attack II 4in., SERE Attack I 3in.

Blade shape: Spear point

Blade material: Stainless steel, Rc 57-59

Edge: Bevel-ground with false top edge

Grip: Green micarta or neoprene; brushed stainless bolster; lanyard hole

Construction: Scales pinned through liners; blade swivels on hinge pin; springback lock mechanism

Features: Black leather belt sheath

Like Al Mar's fixed-blade SERE knives, the folding models - the SERE Attack I and II - were conceived by Col. Nick Rowe, a Special Operations Commando based at Fort Bragg in North Carolina. The initials SERE stand for Survival, Escape, Resistance, Evasion and those are exactly the situations these strong little folders are intended for.

The Attack II is the bigger of the two, with an overall length of 6in. when closed, and a blade length of 4in.. The blade has a spear point, with a false back edge for half its length, and the main edge is bevel-ground. There is a thumbnail slot for opening. It is a sturdy blade which gives good penetration and cutting performance.

The handle has inner brass liners, with stainless steel bolsters, spine and locking mechanism. The grip is contoured neoprene or green micarta, with longitudinal grooves, and an inset square brass medallion featuring the Al Mar logo. The bolster on the left hand side has a 'special forces' logo of crossed arrows and a sword. There is a tubular steel rivet at the butt which forms a lanyard hole.

The Attack I is similar, but slightly smaller, at 5in. overall, with a 3in. blade.

Either knife would make a useful field tool, although neither has the length or weight for chopping and is too small to be a serious fighter - although well capable of serving the purpose if the occasion demands. For other general tasks, though, these knives are an excellent choice.

The Applegate Combat Folder was developed by Col. Rex Applegate from the Applegate-Fairbairn fixed blade fighting knife, to provide an effective fighter which can be carried discreetly in a pocket or a small pouch or sheath.

The knife shares a number of features with its fixed-blade cousin, as well as having the same look and feel. The blade is very similar, with a spear pointed dagger shape, and the basic shape of the grip is close to that of the original A-F Fighter. Obviously some changes were necessary to turn the fixed blade model into a folder - the wide double guard of the A-F has gone, and in its place is a waisted section on the handle to keep fingers off the blade. The blade itself, at 4 1/2in., is considerably smaller than the 6 1/2in. of the A-F Fighter - after all, it has to fold away into the handle - but Applegate has managed to fit a surprisingly large blade snugly into a comfortably shaped handle.

The blade shape is designed to provide excellent penetration and stabbing performance, with a diamond-shaped cross-section for strength since a knife blade may break surprisingly easily when used for stabbing, either through striking bone or through the massive sideways forces exerted as the muscles go into spasm. The knife's blade is also effective for slashing: the serrated section on the main edge helps to rip through clothing etc. and create a deep, debilitating wound. The blade is not big and heavy enough for hacking and chopping, however.

The blade has a thumb stud so that it can be deployed quickly and surely with one hand - allowing the user to keep one hand free, either for defence as the knife is deployed, or to keep hold of another weapon. Once the blade is opened, it locks firmly in place by means of a liner lock mechanism. This is preferable to a springback in a fighting folder, since it is stronger and less likely to be released inadvertently by the hand holding the handle.

The handle is similar to that of the A-F Fighter, made of glass-filled nylon and contoured to fit the hand, with longitudinal grooves for extra grip. The finger/thumb grooves are ridged to reduce the chance of the hand slipping on to the blade.

This knife is unusual in being designed primarily as a fighter - most folding knives are basically general-purpose blades, although some have features intended to make them more suitable for fighting. Although the Applegate Combat Folder excels at its intended purpose, it is also versatile enough to make a handy general purpose blade which could be used for a multitude of everyday tasks.

Manufacturer:	Gerber (a division of Fiskars Inc.), Portland, Oregon, USA
Model:	Applegate Combat Folder
Length overall:	5 3/4in. closed, 10 1/4in. open
Blade length:	4 1/2in.
Blade shape:	Spear point dagger
Blade material:	425 modified stainless steel, 57 Rc
Edge:	Bevel-ground, with serrated section
Grip:	Contoured glass-filled nylon handle with longitudinal grooves
Construction:	Blade swivels on hinge pin; grip scales on liners, with locking mechanism
Features:	Thumb stud for easy deployment of blade

Designed in conjunction with Chris Caracci, a former US Navy SEAL, Benchmade's AFCK - or Advanced Folding Combat Knife - is a strong and handy general purpose blade. Although not primarily designed as a fighter, it is nevertheless up to that job if the occasion demands.

The knife has a 3 9/10in. blade of ATS-34 stainless steel, with a Rockwell hardness of 59-61, and a satin finish. The main edge is convex, with an aggressive, serrated section near the handle. There is an extended straight clip with a false edge, giving a very sharp point which is excellent for penetration and for fine work.

The blade has a thumb hole so that it can be opened quickly and easily with either hand. This is the same as the Spyderco system and is licensed by that company for use in this knife. The blade locks with a titanium liner-lock mechanism, which provides a strong lock-up which is not easily released accidentally when the knife is in use - a knurled section of the liner must be pushed sideways with the thumb to release the lock.

The handle is made of bead blasted G-10 laminate, with a chequered surface for grip. It is a slim, contoured handle with a deep finger groove, which gives a good firm hold. The finger groove is set back from the hilt, effectively increasing the blade length but still allowing the grip to be choked up for fine work. A stainless steel clip allows the knife to be clipped to a belt or pocket. The handle has an inset medallion with Benchmade's butterfly logo and there is a lanyard hole.

The knife is also available with the blade finished in a proprietary Black-T finish which is highly resistant to salt water corrosion. A Mini AFCK is also available, with an overall length of 7in. (open) and a blade length of 3 1/4in..

Manufacturer:	Benchmade Knife Co Inc., Clackamas, Oregon, USA
Model:	AFCK - Advanced Folding Combat Knife
Length overall:	9in. open, 5.7/10in. closed
Blade length:	3.9/10in.
Blade shape:	Clip point with opening hole
Blade material:	ATS-34 stainless steel, satin finish, Rc 59-61
Edge:	Bevel-ground with false back edge and serrated section near grip
Grip:	Black chequered G-10 laminate scales, with bead blasted finish; deep index finger groove
Construction:	Scales fitted to 6AL-4V titanium liners; inset medallion with butterfly trademark
Features:	Easy opening Spyderco type thumb hole; liner locking mechanism; belt/pocket clip

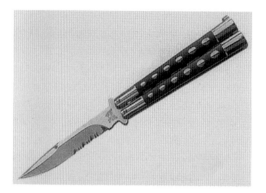

Manufacturer:	Benchmade Knife Co Inc., Clackamas, Oregon, USA
Model:	Bali-Song range
Length overall:	9 1/4in. open, 5 1/4in. closed
Blade length:	4in.
Blade shape:	Large range available, including several clip point and drop point designs
Blade material:	Stainless steel
Edge:	Range includes flat- and bevel-grind, types, with and without serrations
Grip:	Several styles available, including die-cast skeleton designs
Construction:	Two-part handle hinged at ricasso, folds out to expose blade
Features:	Illegal in UK

The 'Butterfly' knife or Bali-Song has become notorious as a favoured weapon of criminals and is banned in the UK and certain other countries. It is unfortunate that misuse has led to this type of knife being unavailable to many legitimate users, since it is a good practical design which is equally effective for legitimate purposes.

The basic principle of the Bali-Song is that the handle is formed of two parts, hinged separately at the blade. With the knife closed, the blade is completely enclosed by the handles, which are held together by a clip at the butt end. To open the knife, one unlatches the clip and swings the handles in opposite directions through 180°, so that they come together and can be clipped together with the latch. This provides a knife almost as rigid as a fixed blade, with no possibility of the blade's folding shut in use; yet when closed the blade is totally enclosed and completely safe. The system is one of the few folding designs that allows a double-edged blade to be used without risk of injury when the knife is folded.

Benchmade produce a wide range of Bali-Song knives, with an enormous variety of blades including clip points, drop points, spear points, chisel points, and a 'weehawk' blade - a type of spear/clip blade which combines tip strength with good penetration. Blades are of stainless steel, with Zamak die-cast handles, some with black or wood inserts. Blade lengths are generally 3in. or 4in., with overall lengths of 7 1/2in. or 9 1/4in. when open, 4 3/8in. or 5 1/4in. closed.

The CQC7, or 970, was designed by Ernest Emerson as a tough, lightweight, folding combat knife. Since its introduction it has become Benchmade's most popular folding tactical knife and with good reason. The 970 is an immensely strong and rugged knife which offers excellent performance in a convenient and lightweight package.

The knife measures 4 5/8in. long when closed, and has a 3 3/8in. blade with a thumb stud for one-handed opening. The blade is a clipped chisel point design, ground on one side only for added strength. It is made of 1/8in. thick ATS-34 stainless steel, hardened to Rc 59-61, with a bead-blasted finish. It has a serrated section near the handle on the main edge and there is a raised and grooved thumb section on the back of the blade, allowing one to exert a powerful downward pressure for cutting and penetrating.

The handle is formed of titanium liners with flat bead-blasted G-10 laminate scales, chequered for extra grip. The right-hand liner is sprung to form a strong liner lock to keep the blade firmly in the open position until the lock is released.

The 970 is an extremely rugged and versatile knife which will tackle a multitude of general chores and may also be used for fighting - although any folder is very much a last resort to be used when other weapons are unavailable.

Variations on the 970 include a pocket clip version, a long-bladed model with 3.95in. blade, and an 'automatic' model which utilises a coil spring to deploy the blade simply by pressing a release button in the handle (this latter model is subject to legal restrictions in many countries).

Manufacturer:	Benchmade Knife Co Inc., Clackamas, Oregon, USA
Model:	970
Length overall:	8in. (open), 4 5/8in. (closed)
Blade length:	3 3/8in.
Blade shape:	Clipped chisel point
Blade material:	ATS-34 stainless steel, bead blasted finish, Rc 59-61
Edge:	Bevel-ground one side only, with serrated section near grip
Grip:	Black chequered G-10 laminate scales, with bead blasted finish
Construction:	Scales fitted to 6AL-4V titanium liners
Features:	Easy opening thumb stud; liner locking mechanism

Britain and other NATO armies issue a simple, rugged, stainless-steel folding utility knife which incorporates a main blade and a small selection of tools. The main blade is 2 1/2in. long, of a flat-ground sheepsfoot design. This is good for simple cutting jobs, but is not suitable for fine point work, piercing or chopping, etc.

Typical models also include a can/bottle opener blade, and there is often a thick marlin spike hinged at the back of the knife.

Construction is simple, with the blades sandwiched between pinned stainless steel scales; a stainless steel spring snaps the blades into the open position but does not lock them. One scale is extended to form a screwdriver blade, and there is a bail which may be used to attach a lanyard.

The knife is immensely strong and corrosion resistant, but is not particularly comfortable to use owing to the lack of contoured grip scales.

Manufacturer:	Ministry of Defence contractors, UK
Model:	Folding Knife
Length overall:	3 11/16in. closed, 6 1/2in. with main blade open
Blade length:	2 1/2in.
Blade shape:	Sheepsfoot main blade
Blade material:	Stainless steel
Edge:	Flat-ground
Grip:	Stainless steel scales
Construction:	All stainless steel, pinned through scales
Features:	Marlin spike, can/bottle opener, lanyard bail

Made in France, Opinel knives are of a long-established design admired for its simplicity. There is a range of sizes, from the tiny 2 1/4in. model up to the 6 1/4in. model 12, but the most popular are the models 6 and 8, with closed lengths of 3 3/4in. and 4 1/4in., respectively.

The design is basic, with a simple drop point blade hinged in a turned wooden handle. The blades are of carbon steel, although the models 6 and 8 are also available in stainless steel. The bolster is strengthened with a steel collar and there is an outer collar which is turned to lock the blade in position. The blade features Opinel's 'crowned hand' logo.

The blade may often be stiff to open - especially since the wooden handle shrinks and swells depending on atmospheric temperature and humidity - and owners soon get into the habit of giving the butt of the knife a smart tap on a hard surface to free the blade and partly open it, rather than risk a broken fingernail by using the notch.

Although this somewhat dated design has considerable drawbacks, it has a loyal following of users who are looking for a simple, reliable knife. As a general purpose folder it has a certain appeal, with the advantage that being inexpensive it can be treated as disposable.

Manufacturer:	Opinel, France
Model:	Dimensions below are for Model 8
Length overall:	4 1/4in. closed
Blade length:	3 1/8in.
Blade shape:	Drop point
Blade material:	Carbon steel (stainless version available)
Edge:	Flat-ground
Grip:	Contoured rounded wooden handle
Construction:	Blade hinged on pin through handle, strengthened at joint with steel collar and locking collar
Features:	Range of sizes available; also specialist blades including pruning saw and hooked pruning blade

Designed for wartime parachutists, this unusual knife has the advantage that it is effectively a fixed-blade knife when opened, but folds down so that the blade is totally enclosed in the handle and cannot cause injury.

It is an ingenious design, using two handle halves hinged at the bolster and connected to the base of the blade by hinged linkages. To open the knife and extend the blade, one first releases a clip that holds the two handle pieces together. The handles are then pulled apart at the middle, so that the linkages begin to pull the blade out through the slot in the bolster. The base of the blade must be pushed past the centre position, after which the handles can be squeezed together to push the blade fully out. With the hand holding the handles, the blade cannot then retract into the handle again, and by reclosing the clip the knife effectively becomes a fixed blade.

The blade is a spear point design, made of 420 J2 stainless steel, and measures 5 1/4in. long. When folded, the knife is 6 7/8in. long.

This type of knife is banned from sale in the UK, although one suspects this is largely due to the fact that its design is easy to define in law; it is no more dangerous or prone to misuse than a simple butcher's knife and it has considerable safety advantages for legitimate users.

This knife is more than just a gimmick. It is a useful all-round field tool, although a little too light and small to be good for heavy chopping work. The all-steel construction makes it unsuitable for use in extreme cold without some form of protection for the hands.

Manufacturer:	Distributed by United Cutlery, Sevierville, Tennessee, USA
Model:	Paratrooper
Length overall:	6 7/8in. (closed); small version 5in., with clip point blade
Blade length:	5 1/4in.
Blade shape:	Spear point
Blade material:	420 J2 stainless steel
Edge:	Bevel-ground
Grip:	Pentograph design hinged at guard allows blade to be retracted into handle by swinging handle halves outwards
Construction:	Folded sheet steel handles with steel pin hinges
Features:	Safety latch holds knife in open or closed position. Illegal in UK

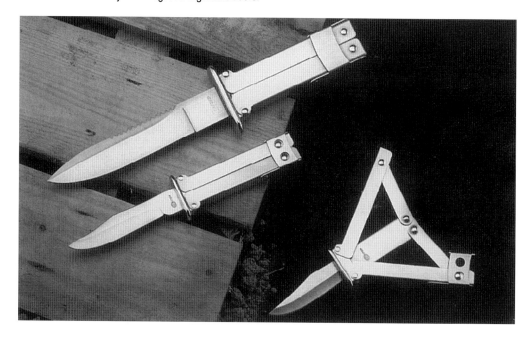

Designed by Blackie Collins, the Smith & Wesson First Response knife is intended to be carried by paramedics, traffic police and others who may be first on an accident scene and need to free trapped casualties.

It has a spring-loaded glass-breaker punch tool built into the handle. This is cocked by pulling a tab back against spring pressure and folding it over to engage in a slot. To break a vehicle or aircraft window, the butt of the knife is held against the glass, and the tab pushed out of engagement, releasing a pointed punch which smashes into the glass with considerable force, causing it to crack - something which is remarkably hard to do without a heavy implement.

The knife blade has a serrated edge which is good for cutting through seat belts, rope, etc. It has a screwdriver tip which can be used for prying window seals, for instance.

This is a special purpose knife which excels at rescue work, but is severely limited by its specialist design for more general tasks.

Manufacturer:	Smith & Wesson, Springfield, MA, USA
Model:	First Response
Length overall:	4 1/2in. closed
Blade length:	3 3/4in.
Blade shape:	Slightly convex edge with screwdriver tip
Blade material:	440 stainless steel
Edge:	Bevel-ground
Grip:	Moulded black Zytel with chequered panels
Construction:	Liner lock mechanism
Features:	Spring-loaded glass-breaker tool in handle. Black Cordura sheath with boot/belt clip

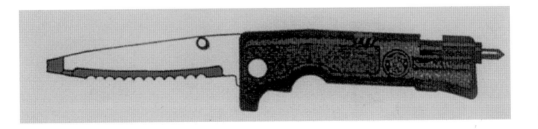

The SOG Tomcat is a modern, high-tech folding knife which makes use of stainless steel and Kraton for high performance. It is a relatively small but sturdy knife, with a 3 3/4in. blade of 1/5in. thick 440C stainless steel. The blade is a double clip design, derived from SOG's fixed-blade knives such as the Trident. It is very strong for its size, with excellent penetration and good cutting performance.

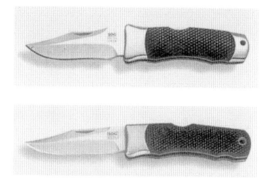

The handle is chequered black Kraton rubber, with stainless steel bolsters, and there is a lockback mechanism to hold the blade open in use.

This is a solid little knife, well suited to a range of tasks, and strong enough to be used as a last resort fighter.

Based on the Tomcat are SOG's Stingray and Sogwinder folding knives, which offer different blade shapes and sizes in a similar design.

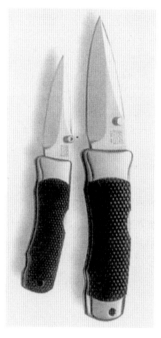

Manufacturer:	SOG Knives, Edmonds, Washington, USA
Model:	Tomcat
Length overall:	8 1/4in. open
Blade length:	3 3/4in.
Blade shape:	Double clip Bowie
Blade material:	1/5in. thick 440-C stainless steel, Rc 57-58
Edge:	Bevel-ground, with false double clip edge
Grip:	Chequered Kraton scales
Construction:	Induction welded bolsters
Features:	All stainless steel construction. Dual mounting nylon scabbard

The SPF50 Marine Combat is a lockback folder based on the US Marine Corps combat knife. Like that knife, it has a clipped Bowie-style blade; the fuller of the USMC knife is retained to provide a thumb notch, which allows one-handed opening. The folder's blade measures approximately 4in., and has a serrated section for about half the length of the main edge.

Like many of the Spec Plus fixed-blade knives, the SPF50 has a 1095 carbon steel blade with a black epoxy powder coating to minimise shine and protect the blade from corrosion.

The handle is similar to those of Spec Plus fixed-blade knives also. Made of 'Gnvory' - a reinforced nylon material - it is black in colour and has deep lateral grooves for added grip. The handle incorporates a lanyard hole, and there is a thumb-operated lockback mechanism to lock the blade open when in use.

The SPF51 Navy Survival and SPF52 Jump are similar knives, but with different blade shapes derived from well established military service patterns.

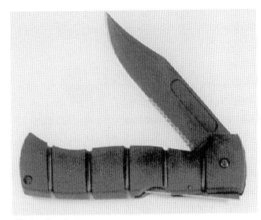

Marine Combat.

Navy Survival.

Jump.

Manufacturer:	Ontario Knife Co., Franklinville, New York, USA
Model:	SPF50 Marine Combat
Length overall:	5 1/4in. (closed)
Blade length:	4in.
Blade shape:	Bowie-style clip point
Blade material:	1095 carbon steel with epoxy powder coated black finish
Edge:	Bevel ground, part serrated
Grip:	Black Gnvory grooved handle
Construction:	Springback-type locking mechanism
Features:	Leather and Cordura belt sheath

Spyderco's Military folder is a development of their popular Police Model, designed to offer more heft but with little extra weight. It measures 5 1/4in. overall, with a 4in. blade of high performance CPM 440V steel. The blade is typical Spyderco - a convex main edge, with a straight back rising to incorporate a thumb hole for easy one-handed opening. The hole is larger than usual, at 9/16in., so that it may be used with a gloved hand.

Just behind this hole is a ridged portion which the thumb falls naturally into for extra cutting power. The blade is available with a plain edge or with Spyderco's SpyderEdge serrations, renowned for their ability to slice through difficult materials such as webbing or rope.

The handle is made from Spauldite G-10 epoxy filled glass composite, and is contoured to fit the hand well. It has a clip on the right-hand side, which may be used to clip the knife on belt, boot or pocket. Inside is a Walker Linerlock, which holds the blade firmly when in use, but which may be readily released by pushing the knurled section inwards with the thumb.

This is a high performance folder from a company with a strong reputation among service personnel. It is available with a black non-reflective finish to blade, lock, clip and pivot pin.

Manufacturer:	Spyderco Inc., Goldon, Colorado, USA
Model:	C36 Military
Length overall:	5 1/4in.
Blade length:	4in.
Blade shape:	Straight back convex edge, with 9/16in. thumb hole at rear of top edge
Blade material:	CPM 440V steel, black titanium finish available
Edge:	Flat-ground; plain or serrated edge versions available
Grip:	Spauldite G-10 scales
Construction:	Walker liner lock mechanism
Features:	Pocket/belt clip

Timberline's Timberlite range has proved popular with service and civilian users due to the knives' light yet strong and rugged design. The Police range offers two sizes of knife - 4in. and 4 1/2in. when closed - with a strong spear point blade.

The blade has a convex main edge, with a high performance serrated section near the handle. The main edge is ground with a slight hollow. A false back edge is then ground to provide what is effectively a spear point, giving a tip that is strong but penetrates well and is fine enough for delicate work.

The blade has a plastic thumb stud which enables it to be opened one-handedly with either hand. Locking is by a patented Neeley Lock mechanism. This is an unusual but effective system in which the pivot pin sits in a slot in the blade, rather than the usual round hole. As the blade comes into the fully open position, a spring pulls the blade back into the handle, engaging it into a shaped recess in the handle. The blade is then firmly locked open until the blade is pulled directly away from the handle in the direction of the tip; any pressure on the tip or edge of the blade simply locks it more firmly.

The handle is a single piece moulded from Zytel, with chequered panels for grip.

There is a belt/pocket clip, also made from Zytel, on the right-hand side. The knife is available with a polished or matte stainless finish, or black titanium coating.

Manufacturer:	Timberline, USA
Model:	Police Model Folder
Length overall:	4 1/2in.
Blade length:	3 1/8in.
Blade shape:	Spear point
Blade material:	425 stainless steel, Rc 58, black titanium finish available
Edge:	Hollow-ground main edge with serrated section, false back edge
Grip:	Chequered, black reinforced nylon
Construction:	One-piece moulded handle, patented Neeley lock mechanism
Features:	Thumb stud on blade for easy opening. Belt/pocket clip on handle

UTILITY AND SPECIAL PURPOSE BLADES

This is perhaps the most contentious section of this book. There are blades in the following chapter which are certain to have some readers cringing in embarrassment. There are knives here that appear designed to appeal to all the wrong people for all the wrong reasons.

Why should the modern soldier, armed with some of the most efficient firearms man has ever devised, feel the need to tuck a tomahawk into his belt? Or carry a blade derived from an ancient African war-spear? It would suggest not just that he has worryingly little understanding of what modern warfare is like, but also that he carries an even more worrying image in his head – a boy's adventure with himself as anti-hero, hacking and slashing his way through the hordes of evil enemies.

Let us leave aside such weapons with the comment that, for the sake of completeness, it is necessary to include them in a book such as this. Some readers will study this book to discover what they may be up against on the streets, or in some treacherous corner of a foreign land. To ignore such weapons would do these readers a disservice; their inclusion in this book should not be taken to imply some sort of tacit approval or fitness for a particular purpose.

Other knives and tools listed here are more down-to-earth and practical. Take for example one of the two Russian 'special forces' weapons, the Spetsnaz shovel. This shovel is much the same as entrenching tools carried by soldiers world-wide, and a vital piece of kit. The soldier uses his entrenching tool every day in the field, for tasks as mundane as burying his excrement and digging a cooking pit, to making a trench for concealment or protection against enemy fire. A versatile tool, its sharpened edge can also be used as an axe for light chopping of firewood and the like.

In a masterpiece of Cold War propaganda, Russia managed to turn this humble tool into a weapon to strike fear into the hearts of her potential Western enemies. 'Leaked' footage showed Russian Spetsnaz troops practising deadly fighting techniques with the shovel – hacking, slashing, stabbing, and even throwing the tool into tree-trunks with potentially lethal force. And so a legend was born.

The shovel's counterpart, the Spetsnaz machete, never achieved this legendary status, but it is a splendid example of a truly multi-purpose tool – one designed to tackle a wide variety of specific tasks as well as others that its makers never thought of. This one rugged blade will chop or saw wood, dig a pit, remove bottle-tops, paddle a raft, measure angles like a protractor, and much more besides. It will not do any of these things as well as an axe, saw, shovel, bottle opener, etc. But to carry each of those items separately would be impossible, and who could predict which ones would be required?

This is the essence of a multi-purpose tool – by carrying it, one is equipped to face whatever the enemy or the environment may throw in your way. Another fine example of this principle is the survival knife designed by former SAS trooper and survival instructor Lofty Wiseman. This knife has a blade that is deigned to chop timber like a machete or small axe, yet remain capable of lighter, more precise work such as feathering fire-sticks, and skinning and preparing game.

Other tools in this chapter are designed for specific environments: the Royal Navy diver's knife for the marine environment; various machete types for a jungle environment; and so on. Each has its own specialisations, with a blade shaped to tackle the particular tasks most commonly required. In the case of the diver's knife this means cutting rope and weed, and prying wood, rock and metal. For a jungle knife the most common uses will be hacking and slashing through heavy vegetation, and preparing natural materials to build a shelter.

Many of the knives here are specially good at one or two particular tasks. But the best of them achieve this specialisation while retaining the versatility that is the mark of a truly good knife.

The Cobra is intended as a multi-purpose survival tool, capable of the various heavy tasks required by the survivor in a hostile environment. The unusual blade shape can be used to clear vegetation, chop and split wood for a raft, fire or shelter, dig, gut and butcher large animals, hammer nails, and much more besides. Advertisements for the Cobra claim that it will cut all the requirements for a raft, and then be used as a paddle.

The unique curve of the blade provides different types of edge for specific tasks. The hooked curve near the tip is good for clearing light vegetation, as it catches the stems and then cuts them as it is dragged through. The tip itself is sharply pointed, unlike the more traditional machete-shaped blades and so may be used for quite delicate piercing jobs - opening a carcass, for instance. Used in conjunction with the hook, this is particularly useful for gutting fish and animals.

For heavier duty chopping and splitting tasks, the deep bellied curve comes into its own. The sheer weight of the blade allows a powerful chopping stroke, and the convex-belly edge provides a reverse curve that cuts particularly well.

The story goes that the knife's designer discovered by accident that the Cobra also works as a decoy - when chopped into a fencepost at an upright angle, it has a silhouette similar to that of a crow or hawk and will attract other birds.

Manufacturer:	Bay Knife Co., USA. Distributed in the UK by Resource Services, Bracknell, Berkshire
Model:	Cobra
Length overall:	16in.
Blade length:	11in.
Blade shape:	Deep-bellied, hook-ended machete-style blade
Blade material:	Carbon steel, Rc 48-55, Teflon coated
Edge:	Bevel-ground
Grip:	Black composite with guard and lanyard hole
Construction:	Handle pinned to full-length tang
Features:	Multi-purpose survival tool

The name and appearance of the Cold Steel Special Projects Bad Axe suggest that it was intended more as a weapon than a tool, although it is difficult to imagine many soldiers choosing to carry such a weapon in preference to a more versatile tool, or even a few extra rounds of ammunition.

The double-edged bat-wing style head is equally effective at chopping in either direction, which would make this a fearsome weapon in close quarter combat. The flat steel blades have ridges to provide extra strength and resist any tendency for them to fold over in heavy use.

However, as a survival tool its uses are limited: it would no doubt be handy for shelter building and clearing undergrowth and could be used as a paddle, but it would be unsuitable for digging or food preparation.

Manufacturer:	Special Projects Division, Cold Steel Inc., Ventura, California, USA
Model:	92BX Bad Axe
Length overall:	20in.
Blade length:	7 1/4in. edge length x 8 1/8in. width
Blade shape:	Butterfly-shaped double-sided axe
Blade material:	Carbon steel with black finish
Edge:	Bevel-ground
Grip:	Straight round-section hardwood handle
Construction:	Handle pinned into hollow tubular section of head
Features:	Strengthening ridges in blade flats

The Gurkha kukri, with its heavy, downward-curved, forward-weighted blade, has earned a reputation as a wickedly effective combat weapon as well as a versatile survival tool. This Special Projects version from Cold Steel offers all the advantages of the traditional kukri blade, but in a purely practical stylised form which omits features such as the blade notch, and takes advantage of modern materials including Kraton and Cordura.

The Special Projects kukri has a high carbon blade of 1/8in. thick steel - somewhat thinner than that of the Gurkha kukri. It has a deeper belly than the traditional shape, however, which goes some way towards making up the weight lost in the thickness. Like the traditional kukri, the Special Projects version has most of its weight in the forward portion of the blade, allowing a powerful chopping stroke.

The reverse curve of the edge provides phenomenal cutting performance.

The handle is softer and more rounded than in the Gurkha version, making it more comfortable for extended heavy use, such as constructing a raft or shelter. The black finish on the blade cuts down reflections, as well as helping to protect the steel from the elements.

Manufacturer:	Special Projects Division, Cold Steel Inc., Ventura, California, USA
Model:	35LTC Kukri
Length overall:	17in.
Blade length:	12in.
Blade shape:	Kukri (traditional notch omitted)
Blade material:	1/8in. thick, high carbon steel, black epoxy powder coated
Edge:	Bevel-ground
Grip:	Chequered and contoured one-piece, black Kraton rubber handle with flared butt and lanyard hole
Construction:	Kraton handle moulded to full-length tang
Sheath:	Black Cordura belt sheath

During the Cold War, legend had it that the elite Soviet *Spetsnaz* forces trained in the use of several exotic weapons, including a special entrenching shovel with sharpened edges which could be swung like a battle axe or thrown at an enemy. No doubt there was an element of truth in this, but suggestions that *Spetsnaz* troops would use their shovels to eliminate sentries from a distance sound like pure propaganda.

The Cold Steel Special Projects Special Forces Shovel is modelled after the original *Spetsnaz* version and is a relatively crude but effective tool with a multitude of uses.

Every soldier needs a shovel or entrenching tool, and the design of this one allows it to be used as a paddle, hammer, hatchet and battle axe as well as for the more mundane tasks of digging trenches and latrines. It is relatively light to carry, at 28.6oz, but still solid enough to be useful as a weapon and multi-purpose field tool. For survival purposes it would be best carried along with a good knife.

Manufacturer:	Special Projects Division, Cold Steel Inc., Ventura, California, USA
Model:	92SF Special Forces Shovel
Length overall:	20 1/2in.
Blade length:	7 1/2in.
Blade shape:	Shovel with sharpened edges
Blade material:	Carbon steel with black finish
Edge:	Bevel-ground
Grip:	Straight round-section hardwood handle
Construction:	Handle pinned into hollow tubular section of head
Features:	Modelled on Soviet *Spetsnaz* shovel, intended for multiple uses including digging, paddling, hammering, chopping, throwing and close quarter combat

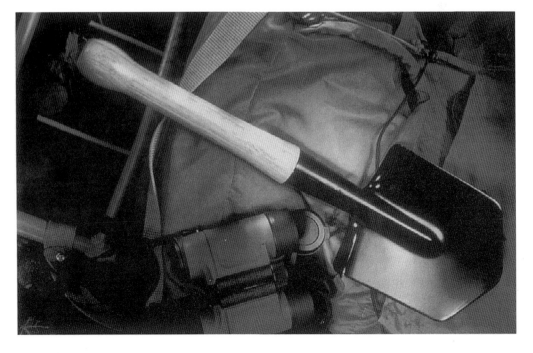

Knife throwing may look good in the cinema, but there is little call for it in real life battle, or for that matter in special operations. Nevertheless, Cold Steel have produced their True Flight Thrower for those who wish to practise the art.

The knife is 10 3/4in. overall, and consists of a single flat piece of steel, with a simple cord wrap for a handle. The balance is designed to be suitable for throwing, with the moment of inertia well forward, and the steel used is a relatively soft high carbon type to resist any tendency to chip on striking a hard surface at speed.

Unlike some specialist throwing knives, the blade is a conventional drop point shape, making this knife also suitable as a general purpose tool.

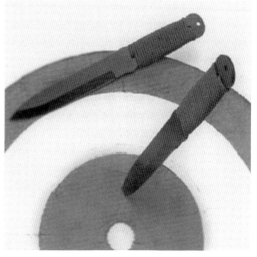

Manufacturer: Special Projects Division, Cold Steel Inc., Ventura, California, USA

Model: 80TFT True Flight Thrower

Length overall: 10 3/4in.

Blade length: 6 1/2in.

Blade shape: Drop point

Blade material: High carbon steel, black finished

Edge: Bevel-ground

Grip: Cord wrapped around metal tang; lanyard hole

Construction: One-piece steel, with simple cord-wrap for handle

Sheath: No sheath

The Cold Steel Special Projects Tomahawk is a modern replica of a weapon which was favoured by certain troops in Vietnam for close quarter combat. The main blade is an effective chopping hatchet type, with a partially sharpened lower edge for hooking. The reverse side provides a fiendish spike which has tremendous penetrating ability and is capable of penetrating a steel helmet and still inflicting a lethal wound to the skull.

The Tomahawk weighs approximately 1lb, with a straight-grain, hickory shaft which effectively extends the user's reach by a foot or so. Although very much a weapon of last resort, it can be lethally effective even in untrained hands. It may be swung at an enemy like a hammer or thrown.

Manufacturer:	Special Projects Division, Cold Steel Inc., Ventura, California, USA
Model:	90VT Vietnam Tomahawk
Length overall:	13 1/2in.
Blade length:	6 1/2in., with 2 3/4in. cutting edge
Blade shape:	Tomahawk shape blade, with spike on reverse edge
Blade material:	Carbon steel, black finished
Edge:	Bevel-ground
Grip:	Straight grain, hickory handle
Construction:	Handle passes through hole in head and is secured by a wedge driven into top of shaft
Sheath:	Oxblood-stained leather sheath to cover head only

Like the Vietnam Tomahawk, the Rifleman's Hawk is a close-quarter combat weapon with a straight shaft and axe-type head. This weapon is around double the weight of the Vietnam version, at 2lb, and is 6in. longer overall.

The hawk head is forged from a single piece of medium carbon 5150 steel, and has a 3 1/2in. cutting edge, with a hammer-head butt.

The weapon may be swung in the hand or thrown at an enemy several yards away. However, throwing is not recommended unless you are confident of hitting the target - otherwise you simply disarm yourself and hand your enemy the means to retaliate!

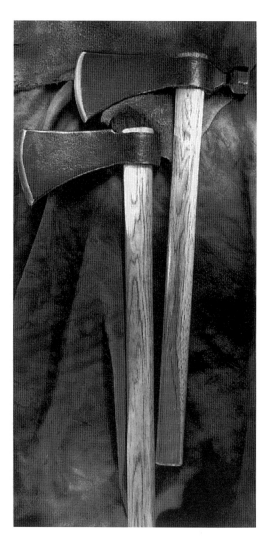

Manufacturer:	Special Projects Division, Cold Steel Inc., Ventura, California, USA
Model:	90RH Rifleman's Hawk
Length overall:	19 1/2in.
Blade length:	8 1/8in., with 3 1/2in. cutting edge
Blade shape:	Tomahawk-shape blade, with hammer head on reverse edge
Blade material:	Medium carbon 5150 steel, black finished
Edge:	Bevel-ground
Grip:	Straight-grain, hickory handle
Construction:	Head forged from single piece of steel. Handle passes through hole in head and is secured with wedge driven into top of shaft
Sheath:	Oxblood-stained leather sheath to cover head only

The Assegai was a short spear used by Zulu warriors in southern Africa. In the absence of firearms, it revolutionised tribal warfare.

This type of weapon has little relevance in modern warfare, but Cold Steel Special Projects have nevertheless produced this modern version, using a black finished carbon steel blade and American ash handle.

The narrow leaf-shaped spear point blade is sharpened along the full length of its 13 1/2in. double edge, and is effective for both stabbing and slashing - the shaft allowing a single- or double-handed hold.

Manufacturer:	Special Projects Division, Cold Steel Inc., Ventura, California, USA
Model:	95F Assegai
Length overall:	37 1/2in.
Blade length:	13 1/2in.
Blade shape:	Spear
Blade material:	Carbon steel, black finished
Edge:	Bevel-ground
Grip:	Straight ash handle
Construction:	Handle pinned into hollow tubular section of head

The LL 80 is a parachutist's knife developed in 1980 by A. Eickhorn GmbH. It has been developed and improved over the years. Its primary use is for a parachutist to cut himself free if his parachute cords become entangled in a tree, fence or other obstacle. The knife is designed so that the blade falls out under gravity when the lock is operated and the knife held upside-down. This means that the knife may be used one-handedly in an emergency.

As an additional safety feature, the mechanism allows the blade to slide freely back into the handle if there is pressure on the tip. This prevents the parachutist from stabbing himself inadvertently. It also makes the blade virtually useless for self-defence, but there is a fold-out awl at the other end of the handle which may be used for this purpose. The handle also incorporates a bottle opener.

The LL 80 is designed to be disassembled and reassembled without the need for tools, to facilitate cleaning. It will work in any weather conditions, and resists pressure and impacts even up to being run over by a vehicle.

The LL 80 has also proved useful to special forces, police units, tank and aircraft crews.

Manufacturer:	Eickhorn GmbH, Solingen, Germany
Model:	LL 80
Length overall:	
Blade length:	
Blade shape:	Drop point
Blade material:	Stainless steel
Edge:	Flat-ground
Grip:	Green plastic
Construction:	Gravity-operated blade stored in handle, with lock mechanism
Features:	Awl, bottle opener, lanyard bail

The Golok has been a standard British Army issue item for jungle operations for some years and has proved its worth many times over. A basic but effective piece of kit, it consists of a simple flat steel blade with wooden handle. The slight belly to the blade has two functions: the curve improves the cutting performance, and places the weight of the blade well forward. The Golok balances about 4in. in front of the handle, producing a powerful chopping stroke.

The Golok is effective for clearing undergrowth, and performs well at chopping fair sized branches. It may also be used for splitting - preferably by jamming the blade in the grain and then driving it down by hammering with a short section of thick branch. When necessary it can also be pressed into service as a digging tool and pry-bar.

The blade is made of relatively soft carbon steel. This reduces its tendency to chip and makes it easy to sharpen, but it does mean that the Golok loses its edge quite quickly and needs regular sharpening.

The wooden handle is not very forgiving on the hands, and many users bind the handle with cord or twine to give a better grip. For extended periods of use, gloves are advisable.

Manufacturer:	R. Martindale & Co., Birmingham, England
Model:	No. 2 Golok
Length overall:	18in.
Blade length:	13in.
Blade shape:	Bellied machete type with drop point
Blade material:	5/32in. thick carbon steel
Edge:	Bevel-ground
Grip:	Wooden handle
Construction:	One-piece slotted wooden handle riveted to three-quarter length tang, with lanyard hole
Sheath:	Composite belt sheath

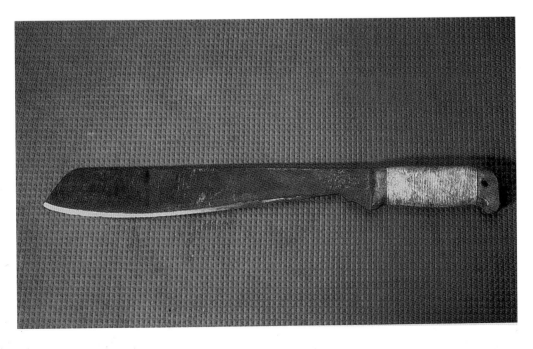

The Hook was conceived as a knife with one purpose: rescue. It is designed to be used to free accident victims quickly and with little chance of causing further injury, as would be all too possible with a normal, straight-bladed knife.

The blade can be hooked round a rope, seat belt or clothing and yanked through, the razor-sharp edge slicing through the toughest materials with relative ease. Speed is of the essence in rescue work, and operators have little time to worry about the blade's follow-through as they slash through obstructions. The advantage of the Hook is that it is virtually impossible to cause an injury with it - the rounded tip will not penetrate flesh and the edge itself is protected.

The Hook is deliberately simple in construction, to keep costs down. It is basically a single piece of 5mm high tensile surgical steel, with contoured grips of beech wood screwed on either side of the tang. The tang extends to form a heavy duty screwdriver/pry bar, which also serves as a windscreen breaker if required, and there is a hole for attaching a lanyard so the Hook can not get lost in the heat of a rescue operation.

The manufacturers claim that the Hook has proved popular with the emergency services in Britain as well as with the prison service, where it is used to cut down prisoners who attempt to commit suicide by hanging.

Manufacturer:	Portfolio Section V Ltd, Stockport, Cheshire, UK
Model:	The Hook
Length overall:	7 7/8in.
Blade length:	2 3/4in.
Blade shape:	Hooked blade with edge on inside, blunt safety tip
Blade material:	5mm thick high tensile surgical steel
Edge:	Hollow-ground
Grip:	Contoured beech wood scales
Construction:	Scales pinned to full-size tang with threaded screws
Features:	Heavy duty screwdriver/windscreen breaker pommel with lanyard hole
Sheath:	Leather or nylon belt pouch

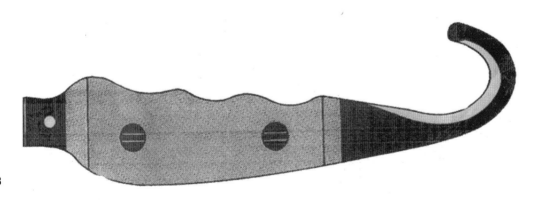

Although designed and marketed as a general purpose knife, Lansky's 'The Knife' has - perhaps unfairly - acquired a reputation as a clandestine fighting weapon because of its all-plastic construction, which makes it difficult to find with conventional detection methods such as X-ray and magnetometer search.

The Knife is moulded in one piece from black ABS plastic. It measures 7in. overall, with a double-edged 3 1/2in. spear point blade. One side has a plain bevel edge, the other is serrated. The grip is chequered, with a finger groove and thumb rest for added grip.

Although its materials and light weight do not particularly lend The Knife to either general field chores or fighting, because of the ease with which it can be hidden it may be used as a clandestine or escape and evasion weapon in situations where the alternative might be no knife at all.

Manufacturer:	Lansky Sharpeners, Buffalo, New York, USA
Model:	LS-17 The Knife
Length overall:	7in.
Blade length:	3 1/2in.
Blade shape:	Spear point
Blade material:	ABS plastic
Edge:	Double-edge bevel-grind, with serrated section on one edge
Grip:	Chequered black plastic with finger groove and thumb rest
Construction:	One-piece moulded plastic
Features:	Lanyard hole. Sheath available

This tool was developed by John 'Lofty' Wiseman, a former survival instructor with the British Special Air Service Regiment and author of several books on survival, in conjunction with designer Ivan Williams. The design shows influence from a variety of edged tools around the world (including the kukri, Machax and Golok), and draws on Wiseman's considerable experience of the tasks that are most important in a survival situation.

'What you need in the wilderness is a knife you can rely on, that does a variety of jobs, and is safe to use', explains Wiseman in an advertisement for his knife. He designed it to tackle a wide range of tasks, ranging from heavy work such as cutting down trees, to preparing game and feathering fire sticks.

The blade is heavy, with the weight forward, which makes it excellent for chopping. The spear point is strong enough for digging and prying, and the back edge is steeply ground for chopping and splitting. At the widest part, the edge is convex, which is good for slashing as well as chopping. Near the handle, the blade narrows and provides a fine edge that can be kept razor sharp for jobs such as feathering sticks for fire-starting.

The handle is moulded Zytel, on a full tang. This sits comfortably in the hand, and is angled downwards to provide a good angle for chopping. There is also a lanyard hole moulded into the grip.

Finally, the sheath has been designed as part of the system. Made of black leather, it has a hanging belt loop and a leg tie. It encases the knife securely, and has a double poppered strap which holds the knife in place until required.

Wiseman's experience really is apparent in the design of this knife and sheath, and anyone who has been in a real life survival situation will appreciate the care and thought that have gone into its design and manufacture.

Manufacturer:	Oakwood Sports, UK
Model:	Lofty Wiseman Survival Tool
Length overall:	15 1/2in.
Blade length:	11in.
Blade shape:	Spear point, upswept machete type
Blade material:	Steel
Edge:	Bevel-ground
Grip:	Moulded Zytel, stainless steel bolster
Construction:	Handle moulded to full length tang
Sheath:	Black leather sheath with belt drop loop and leg tie

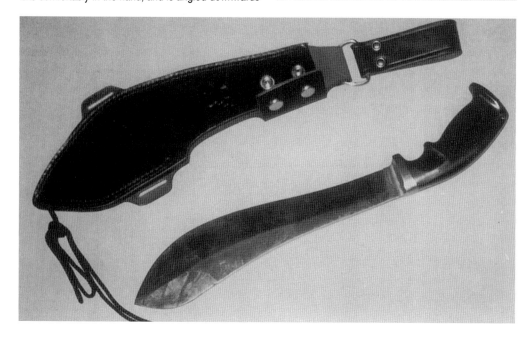

A vital military tool for jungle operations, a machete is used for a wide range of jobs including clearing vegetation for paths and landing sites, constructing shelters, gathering and preparing food. In extremis it may be used as a close-quarter combat weapon.

Ontario's model ON-18 Military Jungle Machete is a typical example, with an 18in. carbon steel blade with a black composition handle fixed to the full tang with three large copper rivets. The blade has a black finish which protects against the elements, as well as cutting down reflections which could give away a soldier's position.

The blade broadens towards the tip, finishing in an upswept edge which meets the straight spine at the tip. This gives the forward-weighted characteristics which make the machete such an effective hacking and chopping tool. In addition to the plain version, there is a sawback model which is identical in all respects except for a saw edge along the middle section of the spine.

The machete comes with a choice of scabbard - a canvas type in olive drab with a belt loop, or a rigid black plastic one with steel clips to fit a military duty belt.

Other models supplied by Ontario offer a similar design but with a variety of blade shapes, including a rounded, partly hooked beak shape (ON-CT3), and a round-ended beavertail (ON-CT4) both 17 1/4in. overall.

Manufacturer:	Ontario Knife Co., Franklinville, New York, USA
Model:	ON-18 Military Jungle Machete
Length overall:	23in.
Blade length:	18in.
Blade shape:	Convex edge with straight spine
Blade material:	Carbon steel with black finish
Edge:	Bevel-ground (sawback version also available)
Grip:	Black composition, with lanyard hole
Construction:	Scales riveted to full-size tang
Sheath:	Choice of OD canvas belt sheath or black plastic sheath with webbing clip and built-in sharpener

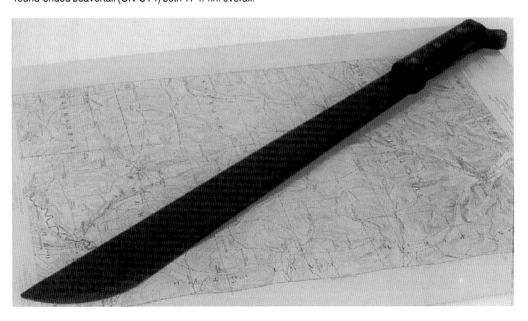

This is a relatively new addition to the Ontario product line, and includes several models with different blade sizes and shapes, based firmly on the conventional machete styles. The main difference between these and the regular machete designs is the full knuckle guard which forms a loop from butt to hilt, and gives these machetes a distinctly cutlass-like appearance. The ON-1495 has a clip point Bowie-style blade, which reinforces this impression. The clip point serves the useful purpose of providing a sharp point, while not reducing the machete's effectiveness for chopping, etc.

Manufacturer:	Ontario Knife Co., Franklinville, New York, USA
Model:	ON-1495 Blackie Collins Machete
Length overall:	18in.
Blade length:	12in.
Blade shape:	Clip point Bowie-style machete
Blade material:	Carbon steel with black finish
Edge:	Bevel-ground with false clip edge
Grip:	Black composition, with full knuckle guard
Construction:	Handle riveted to full-size tang
Sheath:	Heavy duty black nylon belt sheath

This is a design that may be seen in bush and jungle areas all over the world, where it is used as an everyday field and agricultural tool. In the hands of paramilitaries and guerrilla forces it becomes a brutal, close-quarters weapon wielded in the same way as a sword, and has been used, for instance, in tribal massacres and repression in central and southern Africa.

The examples shown here are manufactured by Tramontina in Brazil. They are simply made, with hardwood or rubber handle scales riveted to a carbon steel blade. The blade steel is deliberately quite soft, which minimises any tendency for the blade to chip or shatter when used for chopping and hammering, and also makes it easy to sharpen.

The name 'Panga' is sometimes applied to a shorter machete with an upswept blade, such as the 16in. model made by Ralph Martindale & Co. of Sheffield, England.

Manufacturer:	Tramontina, Brazil
Model:	TT-524 Machete
Length overall:	28in. (19in. and 23in. models also available)
Blade length:	22in. (14in., 17in. and 18in. in other models)
Blade shape:	Upswept, convex edge
Blade material:	Carbon steel
Edge:	Bevel-ground
Grip:	Wooden or black rubber
Construction:	Scales riveted to full-size tang
Sheath:	Supplied with or without sheath

This British Royal Navy issue diver's knife was designed by the RN diving school, and is made in Sheffield to Ministry of Defence specifications. It measures 12 4/5in. overall, with a 7 11/16in. double-edged blade made of corrosion-resistant stainless steel. One side of the blade has a plain bevel-ground edge, while the other has deep serrations for cutting rope, webbing, etc. The blade ends in a strong spear point which can be used for prying.

The handle is made of black rubber, and features lateral ridges for extra grip. It has a lanyard hole, and there is a flat stainless steel pommel which can be used for hammering.

The knife comes with a black rubber sheath with leg straps, for wearing on the thigh.

A vital survival and rescue tool for divers, this knife also serves as a lethally effective combat weapon when required.

Manufacturer:	UK Ministry of Defence contractors, Sheffield, England
Model:	RN3
Length overall:	12 4/5in.
Blade length:	7 11/16in.
Blade shape:	Parallel-edge spear point, with serrated back edge
Blade material:	Stainless steel
Edge:	Bevel-ground
Grip:	Black rubber with three lateral ridges, lanyard hole
Construction:	Full-length tang, grip secured with stainless steel pommel
Sheath:	Black rubber sheath with leg straps

line. An ice-pick attachment can be fitted to the butt, where it is retained in place by the pommel.

Users report that this machete performs extremely well at all chopping, slashing and digging tasks, and has proved to be an invaluable camp and field tool. It would also be an effective combat weapon if so required.

Manufacturer:	Saratov Military Factory, Russia
Model:	*Spetsnaz* Machete
Length overall:	15in.
Blade length:	10in.
Blade shape:	Broad square-ended bolo machete style with sawback
Blade material:	High carbon steel
Edge:	Bevel ground
Grip:	Grooved moulded polymer grip, with hollow cavity for survival items; lanyard hole
Construction:	Short tang to allow for hollow handle
Features:	Screw-on pommel cap allows access to handle cavity containing matches, hooks and line; ice-pick attachment

Said to be a standard issue item of the former Soviet Union's elite *Spetsnaz* units, this multi-purpose camp and field tool will chop, dig, cut, pry and much more besides.

The machete weighs 1 1/2 lb and measures 15in. long with a 10in. blade. It has a broad, square-ended machete blade weighted towards the tip. There is a sawback, and a serrated section on the reverse curve cutting edge. A plain edge on the broadest part is suitable for chopping wood, etc., and the square end is also sharpened for digging, etc. The blade features degree markings and a measuring rule.

The blade material is high carbon steel, which the marketing literature rather optimistically claims will never need sharpening. This steel is hard, but any edge will lose its sharpness with use, never mind abuse. However, the machete's edge can quickly be restored with a good sharpening stone.

The handle is made of orange-brown-coloured polymer, and has a hollow section capped with a screw-on pommel. The compartment contains a small collection of survival items, including matches, fishing hooks and

The Spec Plus SP7 is a specialist diver's knife, designed to fulfil a wide range of uses required by military and civilian divers. The blade is double-sided with serrations on both sides for 1 3/4in. near the hilt. These serrations give extra cutting power for rope, webbing, weed and the like. The tip is cut off square, with a false edge which is suitable for prying. The flat-ended pommel allows one to pound the tip into a crevice with the flat of the hand or a rock, using the knife like a chisel.

Materials are chosen to be resistant to salt water and corrosion: the blade is 440A stainless steel, and the handle is black Kraton. The knife comes with a rigid, moulded, black plastic belt sheath, with a stainless steel clip to attach to a military duty belt.

Manufacturer:	Ontario Knife Co., Franklinville, New York, USA
Model:	SP7 Diver Probe
Length overall:	11in.
Blade length:	5 3/4in.
Blade shape:	Spear truncated with chisel point
Blade material:	0.187in. thick 440A stainless steel, black epoxy powder coated
Edge:	Double. Bevel-ground, with 1 3/4in. serrated section either side
Grip:	Black Kraton grooved handle with flat oversized pommel incorporating lanyard hole
Construction:	Kraton handle moulded on to tang
Sheath:	Rigid plastic sheath with nylon loop and clip for military duty belt

This Spec Plus machete is a versatile tool which deserves to be used more regularly in the field than its 'survival' tag implies. The simple, rectangularly shaped blade measures 10in. long, and is made from a solid bar of 1/4in. thick carbon steel. This is sharpened along one edge and across the end, leaving plenty of meat in the blade for work like prying and digging. The blade retains weight too, giving a powerful chopping action - good for clearing brush, cutting materials for a shelter or raft, and preparing wood for a fire.

On the spine of the blade is an effective saw edge, with the teeth set to cut on the away stroke. The teeth are cut like a proper saw blade, alternately set right and left. This ensures that the saw removes its own thickness of material, so that the blade does not jam as it cuts into wood or bone.

The Kraton rubber handle is shaped to fill the hand well, with guards at front and back for protection. The lateral grooves give added grip, and the soft Kraton rubber cushions the hand against the shock of heavy chopping.

The belt sheath is made from black Cordura nylon, with leather press-studded straps to hold the machete firmly in place until required. A leg tie prevents the sheath from flapping against the leg when the wearer runs.

Manufacturer:	Ontario Knife Co., Franklinville, New York, USA
Model:	SP8 Survival Machete
Length overall:	15 1/8in.
Blade length:	10in.
Blade shape:	Rectangular
Blade material:	1/4in. thick 1095 carbon steel, black epoxy powder coated
Edge:	Double milled, bevel-ground, with saw back
Grip:	Black Kraton grooved handle incorporating lanyard hole
Construction:	Kraton handle moulded on to tang
Sheath:	Black Cordura and leather belt sheath with leg tie

A relatively new addition to the Spec Plus line, the Broad Point Survival has a symmetrical, double-edged spear point blade which is shaped like a smaller version of the Combat Smatchet. This gives good chopping and slicing characteristics for what is a relatively short blade, and may also be used for prying and digging. Although not its primary purpose, this blade would also be effective as a close-quarters combat weapon.

The handle is made of black Kraton rubber, with lateral grooves for extra grip. The pommel is flat-ended, and is screwed on to the threaded end of the full-length tang. It may be used as a hammer, or pounded with a rock, log or the flat of the hand to drive the spear point of the blade into an object. The shape of the spear point provides the strength necessary to stand up to this kind of use.

Manufacturer:	Ontario Knife Co., Franklinville, New York, USA
Model:	SP9 Broad Point Survival
Length overall:	11 3/8in.
Blade length:	6in.
Blade shape:	Leaf-shaped spear point
Blade material:	1095 carbon steel, black epoxy powder coated
Edge:	Bevel-ground
Grip:	Black Kraton grooved handle with flat-ended pommel incorporating lanyard hole
Construction:	Milled butt cap screwed on to threaded tang
Sheath:	Black Cordura and leather belt sheath with lanyard

The large, forward-weighted, downward-curved blade of the Spec Plus Bolo owes a great deal to the Gurkha kukri, but is combined with a straight grip of black Kraton rubber in the familiar Spec Plus style. The end result is a hefty knife with immense cutting and chopping power - equally effective for camp and field tasks or for combat.

Like the kukri, the Bolo's blade broadens out towards the last third of its 10in. length. This places the bulk of its weight well forward for a powerful chopping stroke. It also provides a reverse curve cutting edge nearer the grip. The reverse curve is acknowledged as one of the most effective edge shapes for cutting and slashing - like a scythe, it keeps the edge pressed tightly against the work as the blade is drawn through. The drop point is less sharply angled than a clip point style but still gives effective penetration for stabbing.

Like other heavy knives in the Spec Plus range, the well shaped rubber Kraton handle provides excellent grip and cushions the hand against the shock of chopping.

Manufacturer:	Ontario Knife Co., Franklinville, New York, USA
Model:	SP11 Bolo
Length overall:	15 1/8in.
Blade length:	10in.
Blade shape:	Drop point bolo style
Blade material:	1095 carbon steel, black epoxy powder coated
Edge:	Flat-ground
Grip:	Black Kraton grooved handle incorporating lanyard hole
Construction:	Kraton handle moulded on to tang
Sheath:	Black Cordura and leather belt sheath with lanyard

The Spec Plus Marine Raider takes the old 'iron mistress' Bowie style and applies modern materials and manufacturing techniques to produce a distinctive looking knife with a multitude of uses.

The deep, 9 5/8in. clip point blade is heavy enough for chopping, but still effective for more delicate slicing and cutting. The clip point provides a sharp point which may be used for surprisingly delicate jobs. A good all-round camp and field tool, this knife is also a fearsome combat weapon with a shape that is as intimidating as it is effective.

Where the traditional Bowie would have a plain blade and natural wood or bone handle, this modern version has a protective black epoxy powder coating on the blade and a moulded Kraton rubber handle. These modern materials provide better performance in adverse conditions, with extra resistance to the elements.

Manufacturer:	Ontario Knife Co., Franklinville, New York, USA
Model:	SP10 Marine Raider
Length overall:	15in.
Blade length:	9 5/8in.
Blade shape:	Deep 'iron mistress' style Bowie
Blade material:	1095 carbon steel, black epoxy powder coated
Edge:	Bevel-ground
Grip:	Black Kraton grooved handle incorporating lanyard hole
Construction:	Kraton handle moulded on to tang
Sheath:	Black Cordura and leather belt sheath with lanyard

The United Cutlery Special Ops Jungle Machete is said to have been designed specifically for the US Navy SEALs by custom knifemaker George Lainhart. Smaller and more compact than a regular machete, it aims to retain all the weight and chopping power of a full-sized machete.

This machete has a deep, straight backed blade of 3/16in. thick ATS34 stainless steel, hardened to 56-57 on the Rockwell scale. ATS34 is renowned for its strength and edge holding. The blade is coated with a high tech black polymer called 'Roguard' to protect the steel and reduce reflections.

The handle is moulded from black Kraton rubber, with chequered panels for extra grip. It has a bellied shape, and large guards at hilt and butt to protect the hand. The lanyard hole is formed from a stainless steel tube which also serves to pin the handle to the full-length tang.

This is a hefty chopping tool which would be highly effective both for camp and field chores and for combat. Its modern materials offer excellent resistance to adverse conditions and should continue to provide superior performance for many years.

The sheath is made from black Latigo leather which is treated with a fungicide to resist mildew in jungle conditions. It has several attachment options, so that it may be worn on a belt, attached to webbing with Alice clips, or tied to load-carrying equipment using the four grommet holes.

Manufacturer:	United Cutlery, Sevierville, Tennessee, USA
Model:	UC934 Special Ops Jungle Machete
Length overall:	14 11/16in.
Blade length:	9 3/8in.
Blade shape:	Straight back convex edge machete
Blade material:	3/16in. thick ATS34 stainless steel, 56-57 Rc, black 'Roguard' polymer coated
Edge:	Bevel-ground
Grip:	Chequered black Kraton handle with lanyard hole
Construction:	Kraton handle moulded on to full-length tang and secured with tubular stainless steel pin which also forms lanyard hole
Sheath:	Black Latigo leather treated with fungicide; includes belt strap, grommets and Alice clip slots

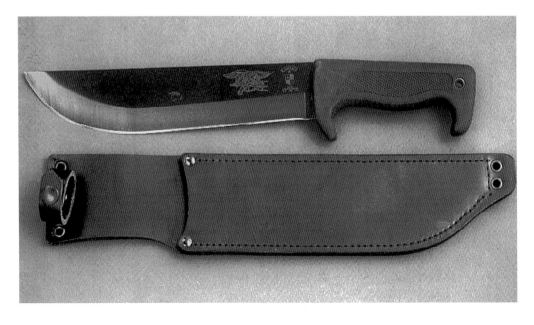

ACR: Advanced Combat Rifle.

AK: Avtomat Kalashnikova (Russian).

AK: Automatische Karabiner (Swiss).

AKM: Avtomat Kalashnikova Modernizirovannyi.

AKS: Avtomat Kalashnikova Skladyvayushchimsaya.

Ammunition: Unit fired by a rifle, comprising a cartridge case (often made of brass}, containing propellant (powder), projectile (bullet) and primer cap.

AP: Armour piercing. Some small arms ammunition is of the armour piercing type to allow the engagement of light armoured vehicles. This type of ammunition may also be used to defeat body armour.

APDS: Armour piercing discarding sabot.

APDSFS: Armour piercing discarding sabot fin stabilised.

Apers: Anti-personnel.

Aperture sight: Type of sight that uses a small hole (aperture) as the rear element.

ASARS: Army Small Arms Requirements Studies.

ATO: Ammunition Technical Officer.

AUG: Armee Universal Gewehr.

Ball: Standard rifle ammunition with a single projectile.

Ballistics: The science of understanding and measuring the performance of the primer, propellant and projectile.

Ballistite: Propellant used in blank cartridge which may be used to launch a rifle grenade from the muzzle of a rifle.

Barleycorn (sight): Front sight in the shape of a grain of wheat or barley.

Barrel: Tubular part of a rifle, pistol or other weapon through which the projectile is fired and given direction.

Barrel band: Band of steel or other material used to attach the weapon's barrel to the fore-end of the stock.

Basha: Temporary sleeping shelter.

Belt kit: Webbing belt and pouches worn by soldier to carry items of equipment. May also include equipment so carried.

Bent: A notch cut in the weapon's bolt, striker or hammer into which the sear engages to hold the component in readiness to fire.

Bergen: Soldier's rucksack.

Bevel ground: Knife blade formed by machining the sides in a V cross-section to produce an edge (c.f. hollow ground, qv).

Bolt: Moving part of a rifle which closes against the breech end of the barrel to load a round and hold it in place as it is fired.

Bolt-action: Type of rifle in which the breech bolt is operated by hand – most commonly found on sporting and sniping rifles.

Bore: The hole down the length of the barrel along which the bullet is propelled. The term 'bore' can also describe the internal diameter of the barrel, as in '12-bore shotgun' (see also 'Calibre').

Bottle-necked: A cartridge case in which the diameter is reduced at the opening to accommodate the bullet, which has a smaller

Box magazine: A fixed or detachable metal box which holds ammunition ready to be fed into the breech.

Breech: The rear end of a barrel into which the ammunition is loaded.

Bullet: A projectile fired from a rifle – usually made from lead with a jacket of copper, sometimes with a core of another metal such as steel.

Bullpup: A rifle in which the mechanism is laid out to reduce the overall length of the weapon. The magazine is generally located behind the pistol grip and the receiver is set against the firer's shoulder.

Butt: Part of the rifle held against the firer's shoulder.

CAL: Carabine Automatic Légère.

Calibre: Diameter of weapon's bore measured across the rifling lands (See also 'Bore', qv). May also refer to the type of cartridge used, as in '7.62 ¥ 51mm'.

Cam: Camouflage.

Cam & con: Camouflage and concealment.

Cap: Primer assembly at the rear of the rear of a cartridge case, which is struck by the firing pin to fire the round.

Carbine: Term used to denote a short rifle. No longer in military usage.

Cartridge: A round of ammunition comprising case, cap, propellant and projectile.

Cartridge case: Brass shell used to contain propellant and primer cup.

diameter than the body of the case.

Cartridge headspace: The distance between the face of the bolt or breech-block and the base of the cartridge case when the weapon is loaded.

Caseless ammunition: A cartridge that has no metal casing. The propellant is formed into a solid block which also serves to hold the bullet and primer.

Centre fire: Cartridge case which has the primer cap located centrally in its base; rifle or pistol designed to fire such ammunition.

Chamber: Part of the barrel into which the cartridge is loaded ready for firing.

Choil: Small notch in knife blade at the proximal end of the edge proper, i.e. between the edge and the ricasso. Helps to prevent damage to sharpening stones etc. when working on the edge.

Choke: Constriction in shotgun barrel causing shot to disperse less than it would if the barrel was unchoked (or cylinder bored).

Chronograph: Electro-optical device used to measure the velocity of a projectile such as a rifle or pistol bullet.

Click: A kilometre (soldiers' slang)

Clip point: A knife blade shape in which the back edge is cut away, often in a concave shape, in the typical Bowie knife style, offering improved penetration and the ability to cut on the upward stroke.

Cook-off: Premature ignition of round due to high barrel temperature.

Cordite: Propellant used in rifle cartridges.

CTR: Close target reconnaissance (usually shortly before an operation or assault).

Cycle of operation: Process of semi-automatic rifles. pistols, shotguns, etc., whereby a round of ammunition is fed, chambered , and fired, the empty case is ejected, and the weapon re-cocked ready to fire the next shot.

Cyclic rate of fire: Theoretical rate of fire, usually expressed in rounds per minute, if the weapon could be fired continuously without the need to replenish magazine.

Cylinder: Shotgun barrel with the same internal diameter along its entire length, i.e. without choke (qv) – suitable for firing solid projectiles.

DPM: Disruptive pattern material – the distinctive camouflage pattern of brown, black and green used for British Army combat clothing

Drop point: Knife blade shape in which the back edge curves smoothly down towards the point.

DZ: Drop zone – the area for a parachute landing.

Ejector: Component which throws the empty cartridge case away from the weapon after firing.

Elevation: The vertical angle between the line of sight and the bullet's trajectory or intended point of impact.

EOD: Explosive Ordnance Disposal.

Extractor: Component which pulls cartridge case from chamber after firing, or when slide or bolt is drawn back.

FAL: Fusil Automatique Léger.

FAMAS: Fusil Automatique de Manufacture d'Armes de St Etienne.

Feed: Portion of firing cycle during which a fresh cartridge is removed from the magazine and loaded into the chamber.

Firing pin: Component which transfers the blow of the hammer to the cartridge primer, to initiate firing.

Flash eliminator: Device fitted to muzzle of a weapon's barrel to prevent or reduce the visible flash or flame produced on firing.

Flechette: Long, narrow, fin-stabilised, dart-like projectile.

Fore-end: The front portion of the stock, located under the barrel, which may be held by the user to support and stabilise the weapon. Also known as the forestock.

Foresight: Front element of a sighting system consisting of foresight and rearsight.

Friendly fire: Fire mistakenly directed towards a soldier or unit by friendly forces.

FIBUA: Fighting in built-up areas (known by US forces as MOUT = military operations on urban terrain).

Frog: Part of bayonet sheath that attaches to a soldier's webbing belt, from which the scabbard part hangs.

Fuller: Longitudinal groove in knife, bayonet or sword blade, sometimes referred to as 'blood groove' or 'blood gutter'.

FWE: Foreign Weapons Evaluation.

Gas cylinder: Housing for the gas piston in gas-operated weapons.

Gas system: Components of a gas-operated weapon which tap propellant gases from the barrel on firing to eject the empty cartridge case, cock the action and load the next round.

Gauge: A system of bore measurement used for shotguns. The system was originally based on the number of lead balls fitting the bore which would weigh exactly one pound.

GPMG: General Purpose Machine Gun (nicknamed 'Gimpy') – the British version of the FN MAG 7.62mm belt-fed machine gun.

GPS: Global Positioning System – an electronic navigation aid that receives signals from satellites orbiting the earth and displays the user's position, and, if moving, speed and direction.

Guard: The cross-piece at the distal end of a knife's handle, which prevents the user's hand from slipping forward on to the blade, and affords a degree of protection from an attacker's blade.

Hammer: A component held under tension by a spring until released by the trigger, which strikes the firing pin to ignite the primer of a cartridge.

Hangfire: The failure of a round of ammunition to fire immediately when the primer is struck by the firing pin.

HE: High explosive.

Hollow ground: Knife blade profile in which the edge is formed by grinding the flat edges of the blade in a concave shape, giving the edge a more acute angle than if the edges were flat (c.f. bevel ground, qv).

IED: Improvised explosive device (such as terrorist bomb or booby trap).

IRUS: Infantry Rifle Unit Study.

IW: Individual weapon.

Lands: Raised portions of barrel's bore between rifling grooves.

LAW: Light Anti-tank Weapon (figures may refer to calibre, as in LAW80, meaning 80mm LAW).

LUP: Lying-up position.

M203: 40mm grenade launcher which may be fitted beneath the barrel of the US-built M16 assault rifle

M79: Single-shot 40mm grenade launcher

Magazine: Removable container for ammunition. When filled and placed in its housing in the weapon, allows rounds to be loaded quickly into the breech.

Magazine follower: Plate in magazine which is pushed up by the magazine spring, on which the cartridges rest.

Magazine spring: The spring which forces the follower against the cartridges.

Mainspring: The primary spring of a trigger and firing mechanism – the spring that provides the power to set off the primer in the cartridge.

Matched ammunition:	Ammunition made to exceptionally close tolerances for use when extreme accuracy is required.
Mk19:	Fully-automatic belt-fed 40mm grenade launcher, normally vehicle-mounted.
Milan:	Wire-guided anti-tank missile system used by British forces.
Misfire:	Failure of a weapon or round of ammunition to fire, despite being operated correctly.
MIWS:	Multi-Purpose Individual Weapon System.
MRTF:	Mean Rounds to Failure.
MoD:	UK Ministry of Defence.
Muzzle:	The distal end of the barrel; the end from which the projectile exits.
NBC:	Nuclear, Biological and Chemical warfare.
OEG:	Occluded Eye Gunsight.
OP:	Observation post.
Open sights:	Simple sighting system comprising rearsight and foresight elements which are aligned with the target.
Optical sight:	Sighting system which makes use of optical lenses to form an image of the target, often magnified, with an aiming mark superimposed.
OSS:	Office of Strategic Services – US organisation responsible for covert operations in German-occupied Europe during the Second World War.
Paracord:	Strong nylon cord used in parachute manufacture, which has many survival uses. It consists of a nylon core contained in an outer nylon sheath.
Pistol grip:	The handle by the trigger mechanism, by which a pistol, rifle, etc., is supported by the firing hand.
Pitch:	The degree of twist in the rifling of the barrel, usually expressed in one turn per X inches or centimetres.
PNGs:	Passive night vision goggles.
Pommel:	Cap on proximal end of a knife or sword handle. May be shaped for use, e.g. as a 'skull crusher' or a hammer, or purely decorative.
Primer:	Container for the detonating compound which is struck by the firing pin to initiate firing by igniting the propellant.
Propellant:	Nitro-cellulose based compound which burns to provide the energy to propel the projectile from the barrel.
Pump-action:	Hand-operated mechanism used in some repeating shotguns, where the fore-end is moved back to eject a spent round, and forward again to chamber the next round from the magazine.
RAW:	Rifleman's Assault Weapon
Ricasso:	Part of knife blade immediately in front of the hilt, which has not been shaped to form the blade and remains rectangular in cross-section.
Rifling:	Spiral grooves cut into the interior of the barrel to impart stabilising spin to the projectile.
Rimless:	cartridge with no projecting rim at its base.

Round:	A unit of ammunition, comprising cartridge case, bullet, propellant and primer.
RPM:	Rounds Per Minute.
RV:	Rendezvous.
Safety (safety catch):	Mechanical device to prevent firing of a weapon.
SAR:	Singapore Assault Rifle.
SAWES:	Small Arms Weapons Effects Simulator.
SAS:	British Special Air Service.
SBS:	British Special Boat Service.
Sear:	Part of the firing mechanism, linked to the trigger, which engages with the hammer, firing pin or striker, and when pulled clear by the action of the trigger allows the weapon to fire.
Selective fire:	A weapon with a selector mechanism which allows it to fire in either semi-automatic or fully-automatic mode.
Selector:	Switch or catch on a weapon by which the user can select either semi-automatic or fully-automatic operation.
SF:	Sustained fire; special forces.
Shot (birdshot):	Pellets, usually of lead, steel or tungsten alloy, fired from a shotgun. May also be used to refer to larger projectiles, as in the phrase 'fall of shot'.
Sight:	Device attached to a weapon to allow precise aiming.
Sitrep:	Situation report.
SLR:	Self-Loading Rifle – name commonly used for the L1A1 7.62mm FN semi-automatic rifle which was the British Army standard issue rifle until replaced by the SA80 in the 1980s.
SOE:	Special Operations Executive – secret unit formed during the Second World War to run agents in German-occupied Europe.
SOPs:	Standing Operating Procedures – standing instructions on how a soldier should behave in a given set of circumstances.
Solid slug:	Single projectile fired from a shotgun, usually with angled ridges to impart spin for stability in flight.
Stgw:	Sturmgewehr (Swiss).
Stun grenade:	Grenade designed to create a powerful flash and loud report, momentarily stunning persons in a room, vehicle, etc. Often used in hostage rescue operations to disorientate terrorists so that the assaulting force can overpower them and recover any hostages unharmed. (Also referred to as 'flashbang')
SUSAT:	Sight Unit Small Arms Trilux.
TA:	Territorial Army – British Army volunteer reserve force, sometimes disparagingly referred to as 'weekend warriors'
Tab:	Parachute Regiment slang for march (from TAB = Tactical Advance to Battle)
Tang:	Part of knife blade that extends into the handle.
Tanto:	A knife blade shape derived from an ancient Chinese sword type, with blade end cut off more or less squarely, like a chisel. This shape was originally designed for

penetrating metal armour, and has excellent penetration.

TI: Thermal imaging.

Trajectory: Curved path followed by a projectile after it leaves the muzzle.

Trigger: Lever by which the firing mechanism of a weapon is actuated.

Trigger guard: A protective guard fitted around the trigger to protect against accidental firing.

Trigger stop: Means of arresting travel of trigger after firing.

Twist: The spiral of the rifling in a barrel. May refer to degree of twist, as in 'a twist of X turns per metre'.

Velocity: Speed of a projectile's travel, usually measured close to the muzzle.

Vertex: Highest point of a bullet's travel.

Windage: Horizontal deviation between line of sight and the bullet's trajectory at a given distance from the muzzle.

Yaw: Horizontal deviation of a bullet's axis from its direction of flight.

Zero: To adjust a weapon's sights so that the aiming point coincides with the point of impact at a given distance from the muzzle.